Woody Herman

Woody Herman

CHRONICLES OF THE HERDS

William D. Clancy

with Audree Coke Kenton

Foreword by Steve Allen

Schirmer Books
An Imprint of Simon & Schuster Macmillan
New York

Prentice Hall International
London   Mexico City   New Delhi   Singapore   Sydney   Toronto

Schirmer Books
Simon & Schuster Macmillan
866 Third Avenue
New York, NY 10022

Library of Congress Catalogue Card Number: 94–42276

Printed in the United States of America

Printing Number

1 2 3 4 5 6 7 8 9 10

Library of Congress Cataloguing-in-Publication Data

Clancy, William D.
    Woody Herman : chronicles of the Herds / William D. Clancy with
  Audree Coke Kenton : foreword by Steve Allen.
        p.   cm
    Includes bibliographical references (p.   ) and index.
    ISBN 0-02-870496-7 (alk. paper)
    1. Herman, Woody, 1913–1987.   2. Jazz musicians—United States—
  Biography.   I. Kenton, Audree Coke.   II. Title.
  ML419.H45C53   1995
  781.65'092—dc20
    [B]   94–42276
                                                              CIP
                                                              MN

The paper used in this publication meets the minimum requirements of American National Standard for Information Sciences—Permanence of Paper for Printed Library Materials. ANSI Z39.48-1984. ∞ ™

To my loving wife, Pauline, who endured the plight of an "author's widow" for the better part of five and one-half years

Contents

Foreword

Bill Clancy has done an incredible job of collecting both factual information and insightful comment on one of the dominant figures in the history of Big Band music.

The number of important players, many of them distinguished jazz artists, who worked in Woody Herman's orchestra since it was originally organized in 1936 is truly impressive. Mr. Clancy has successfully solicited quotations and general reminiscences from most of them, the result being that the reader is given not just an author's observations about one of the major orchestras of the 1940s and 1950s, but a thousand and one separate points of view, which makes for a much more interesting and even somewhat kaleido-scopic summation.

Steve Allen

Preface

As the band started its theme, "Blue Flame," for perhaps the eighteen-thou-sandth-and-one time, the crowd whistled and clapped at the fairgrounds in Hemet, California. The audience was made up of all ages. Jazz knows no gen-eration gap.

About thirty seconds into the melody, a very hip 72-year-old, stooped and balding gentleman, slowly made his way on stage. Dressed in a white suit, wearing light blue European deck shoes, he picked up his clarinet, and blew his familiar blues solo.

With the closing bars of "Flame," Woody picked up the mike and said, "Hi, good evening, how are you? It's lovely to be here! We're pleased to play for you tonight. It's very pleasurable for us. To get things started, I've dug up an old tune from the swing era. I figured that you could find this one some-where in your memory (said with a slight note of Herman satire). It was a good one because it was written by Duke Ellington and his son Mercer, and it's called 'Things Ain't What They Used to Be.'" Woody turned around, faced the band and counted off. "One, two, three, e-e-h-h!"

The five-man trumpet section led by Roger Ingram stated the melody, playing a powerhouse chorus, and the rhythm section laid down the funky, straight-ahead jazz beat in which most Herman Herds excelled.

Baritonist Mike Brignola came in with a humorous but swinging solo. Woody, in a relaxed mood, added his comments here and there. "Blow your horn, my man!" He swung his hips hula-hoop style, picked up the mike again, and encouraged Brignola with "Yeah!"

He called out the name of each soloist as he completed his solo, and the crowd applauded with pleasure. As the tune ended, Woody said "That's the way it was, believe me!"

The old war horse, Woodrow Charles Thomas Herman, in his final years, manifested a stubborn determination and grit that few individuals possess. Beginning in 1977, Woody had had a series of personal and professional set-backs. In March 1977 he was nearly killed in a head-on automobile collision in Kansas. He had been involved in litigation with the Internal Revenue Service since the mid-1960s, and the situation was still getting worse in the early 1980s.

In 1982 the "Woody Herman Room" in the Hyatt Regency Hotel in New Orleans folded. It was a location that the Herman Herd had hoped to use as a semipermanent home for the orchestra. The death of Woody's wife of forty-six years, Charlotte, occurred almost simultaneously with the closing of the club.

Woody's tax problems seemed to reach a climax in 1985 when the IRS seized Woody's home and refuge from the road and auctioned it off to defray back taxes exceeding one-and-a-half million dollars. Woody's stubborn, determined spirit kept him going when others would have given up. Typical of his attitude were some comments he made to me in 1986: "[My problems with the IRS] have never been a serious threat to my mentality or sensibility because I'm involved in music, and as long as I have enough health to push myself around, I'll be doing what I do. And I'm not terribly concerned with how the IRS feels about me. I doubt if I could get too warmed up by them, and I'm a little too old for boxing."

On the afternoon of September 19, 1985, Woody's Young Thundering Herd was booked at the fairgrounds of the high desert town of Hemet, about eighty miles southeast of Los Angeles. I had arrived early to secure front row seats for my family. After waiting almost an hour, I saw the Woody Herman band bus approaching. It stopped near the makeshift outdoor bandstand. The road manager, Bill Byrne, spotted me almost immediately. He knew that I was acquainted with the town, as I maintained a small vacation home there that we called "The Great Escape." Bill asked if I would take Woody to dinner. Of course I was elated, as I would have Woody to myself for almost two hours until concert time.

At the Embers restaurant in Hemet, I asked him if anyone had ever attempted a Woody Herman biography. He replied that the late Ralph J. Gleason had started one back in the 1950s, but that the project was never completed. It was during that dinner with Woody that the notion of writing his biography was born. A year later I began to interview the fiftieth anniversary Herd and a broad selection of Herman alumni and others who had played significant roles in Woody's life.

The concept of the project evolved from a biography to a comprehensive review of Woody's life and career, including an oral history assembled from interviews with key Herman sidemen. Inevitably, there are gaps in the story, as we are dealing with almost seventy-five years of annals. However, it is hoped that any Herman fan or big band jazz enthusiast will be satisfied by the profile of Woody Herman presented in this volume.

Woody died in October 1987. He left a legacy of exciting big band music that spanned fifty years. Today, his Thundering Herd lives on, fronted by twenty-year veteran of the Herman Herd, Frank Tiberi.

W. D. C.

Acknowledgments

I am extremely grateful to every participant in this archival study of Woody Herman's life and music.

Most special thanks go to Woody's daughter Ingrid who encouraged me to write this book and gave me almost unlimited access to her family's personal photos and scrapbook memorabilia.

To Jean Gleason, the widow of the late jazz columnist Ralph J. Gleason, for her graciousness in granting permission to use the 1956 Gleason/Herman interview material. Most quotes from Woody in Chapters 1 through 5 are drawn from the Gleason interviews.

To Audree Coke Kenton for her time, journalistic talents, invaluable guidance, suggestions, and flexibility.

To Ray Sherman and his brothers Irv and Father Dan, Bill Byrne, Nat Pierce, Mark and Cappy Lewis, Shorty Rogers, Tom Linehan, John Fedchock, Chubby Jackson, John Bennett, and Bill "Red" Koster,* who were always available to help fill the gaps in this chronicle.

And to Woody Herman, for giving me his love, friendship, and confidence in this project.

---

*Bill "Red" Koster died the day before Woody on October 28, 1987.

Woody
Herman

1.

Genesis
1913-1936

Woodrow Charles Thomas Herrmann was born May 16, 1913 in Milwaukee, Wisconsin, on Racine Street (later renamed North Humboldt Avenue). Woody's parents were Otto C. Herrmann and Myrtle Herrmann, maiden name Bartoszewicz.

WOODY: Although she was of Polish descent, [my mother] was actually born somewhere in Germany on September 5, 1888. My Dad was born in this country on November 25, 1886, and his father was born in this country and they were of German descent. The two R's and two N's in Herrmann I just threw out when I started to work as a little kid. The editor in me.

My father and mother actually met because they both worked in the shoe industry. And while they were going together and even after they first were married, he did a lot of extracurricular work singing in a quartet. He worked club dates and state fairs and anything that cropped up. This is what he really enjoyed and loved, I guess, because he took it out on me. And when I first started to play theaters and things, if I didn't sing loud enough, I'd get a belt right across the knob! He was a very rough, tough little man, but he was very affectionate, a very warm guy. So it was more or less a bluff, and after a while everyone who knew him got to know that this was just a front.

Otto and Myrtle had been friends for several years with John and Julia Sherman. The Shermans had been married longer and had a son, Erwin (Erv), born a year before Woody. Later, they would have two more sons, Ray and Dan, and a daughter, Joyce.

WOODY: Ray Sherman and I have known each other practically since we were born. He was younger, but we all were pals together. There was Raymond, Erwin, and Dan. Dan eventually became a Maryknoll priest. We were very close all through our childhood.

RAY SHERMAN: My mother and Woody's mother had planned to attend a luncheon at a church nearby. My mother had pushed Erv in the buggy to get there. He was a year old. When they got there she left Erv asleep in the buggy, went upstairs and Woody was just about to be born. My mother began helping the doctor, then Woody was delivered and the doctor handed little Woody to my mother.

WOODY: We grew up together [the Shermans and Woody], and evidently I was a pretty strong screamer. What I liked, they had to like. I was pretty stubborn and horrible.

   Any neighborhood in Milwaukee is a combination of Germans and Poles. In a Polish block where it's all Polish, the kids come out with— instead of an Eskimo pie or whatever—a piece of sour rye bread with lard and salt on it, and I used to steal it from them. I dug it. My mother wouldn't give me this to eat. We were "too high class."

   On my mother's side, I must have had hundreds of cousins and a lot of them are somewhere near my age, and when we were kids they all looked exactly like me! We didn't get together too often, but when we did we would look a little skinnier, and a little more weatherbeaten, because they all worked from the time they could. I was in a neat business where you didn't get your hands dirty, just your brain.

   My mother and father were very kind and loving people. We were a very tight-knit family. We had to be tight-knit. I was an only child. But they were very concerned that I would have every opportunity that was possible for me to have. And they never prevented me from doing anything. As a little boy, I was treated like a grown-up. And from the time I was 12, I was driving the family car. One that I was partner in. Being able to earn money, I bought part of it and was made a partner.

   Living with my family in Milwaukee as a child was like being on the road. My family changed places of residence. They lived in rental properties. My mother always tried to get closer to the lake, but we could never afford to get close enough. I lived mostly in either the extreme north or northeast part of the city.

   My father had great interest in the theater and show biz, and he loved to sing and he played some piano and his sister played piano and his brother sang, so they were always into a musical thing of some kind, semi-pro. But he had a burning desire to have a son do it and that was me. He worked for Nunn Bush Shoe Corporation as a quality control superintendent in later years. In the earlier years, about the time I was born, he worked for United Shoe Machine Company, setting up machinery in the major factories all over the country.

I was encouraged in music from the time that I first arrived on the scene. I was a song and dance kid from the time that I was about 8 or 9, and I went on the road for my first tour when I was nine. And when I got back I took all the monies I had got and bought a saxophone and a clarinet and started with teachers in the Milwaukee area. Fortunately, it was quite a music town back in the old days.

During this period Woody spent some time working the old Orpheum Vaudeville circuit as the "Boy Wonder of the Saxophone."

WOODY: When I did my first road tour and started to travel, I had to have permission and get a child labor law license, which was issued by a judge in Milwaukee. However, I found that the public school teachers didn't like the idea of my working. Then I made a big decision. I decided that I would leave the public school I was attending. They couldn't understand my leaving school for days on end and then returning and trying to make up my work. I heard through a couple of friends of mine that I could do the things that were a little more beneficial for me if I attended a parochial school. So of my own volition and not my parents', I entered St. John's Cathedral Grade School in the fifth grade, and some of the staff were very helpful and would arrange for me to do my required work on the road and bring back the results. I would be tested when I came home and allowed to make up the work that I had missed. They tried to understand that my music was most important to me and to my parents. My mother was a former Catholic so she approved of my decision.

At age 9, Woody went on a tour of the Midwest with a group of kids that traveled the Saxe Theater circuit, performing prologues to films such as *School Days* and *Penrod*, based on the books by Booth Tarkington.

WOODY: The first little revue show that I went out with when I was 9 was a kids' group doing a whole series of Booth Tarkington stories and songs. We were doing a prologue for a movie called *School Days*. Wesley Barry, the star of the movie, was a kid actor in the Jackie Coogan mold. I emulated him to some degree, and I sang and danced and read some lines with the other kids.

FR. DAN SHERMAN: I was "Danny the Wonder Boy" when I was a little kid 4 years old, when I started in vaudeville, and then I lost my "cute" around 8 or 9 and I had to give it up. But in the early days when I was a vaudeville singer, Woody and I played on the same bill.

Woody's first band, circa 1923. Dan Sherman (shown in white pants, 4 years old at the time) would sometimes "direct" the little band. (Courtesy Ray Sherman)

ERV SHERMAN: In the twenties, most of the Milwaukee neighborhood theaters had small-time girlie revues, mainly four girls in the chorus line, and then usually one and sometimes two comedians, a juggler, and then some artist who would come out and play a piano, accordion or sing and dance or imitate a violin or sometimes play the saw. Sometimes four nights a week, and two shows a night, and that was in two different theaters.

FR. DAN SHERMAN: Yeah, we ran from one to another. Sometimes we'd even carry the reels of movies from one theater to another where they had to transfer them back and forth. And we did the suburbs, too, which was quite something in those days, to run around town doing those vaudeville shows. We'd stop in between and have a malted milk for supper, or get hungry at nine, ten o'clock. But those were happy, pleasant memories. Woody's Dad was like our impresario and our dog trainer. He kept us in line, and we were always kind of scared of him, but we loved him because we knew he had a good, warm heart.

ERV SHERMAN: It was sometimes a two-car caravan with our Buick and Woody's Dad's Chevrolet chasing between these theaters. And when Dad couldn't drive them I would be driving, shagging around town. Come to think of it, there were times when you actually played three shows in one night. We'd start a seven o'clock show on the north end of town, go to the south side to the Juneau Theater and play one show there, and then come back to the Fern or the Peerless and play one of those.

FR. DAN SHERMAN: Right, I booked the show, and that was something for a kid in those days.

ERV SHERMAN: In the twenties that was big money. High school tuition in the twenties was only twenty dollars a semester.

WOODY: My first music teacher was a man by the name of Art Buech, and he had been a very good, legitimate saxophonist. Buech was an old German-type fellow who would accept nothing but hard work! Practice until you turn blue, and your lip is numb and your teeth hurt, and you may be accomplishing something. But he was very good, and I was very fortunate in starting with someone like that.

ERV SHERMAN: We [Woody and Erv] took piano lessons together from the same piano teacher, and he even tried violin, believe it or not. His Dad was sort of a stubborn type guy and told Woody, "Well, you're going to have to learn to play some instrument! You're going to have to pick out something!" So Woody picked out the saxophone. He would rather play the saxophone after a while than he would baseball, tennis, or marbles. Music was really his love and his life.

WOODY: For the next few years I practiced and studied and worked some more and took on a couple of other music teachers probably more modern than the original one. One of these teachers had a dance band in a hotel and his name was Arthur Krueger. And he became a very good friend of mine and helped me a great deal, trying to get me involved in playing jazz.

RAY SHERMAN: A couple of things that come to mind are things we did when we were kids and Woody was working the theater circuit. One afternoon, Woody and his folks came over to our house to have dinner and we kids went up into our attic—we lived in a big flat and we had a huge attic—and we had some old carpets up there, some room-sized rugs which we threw over the clothesline and used them as forts, and we chose up sides to have a slingshot fight. We all had slingshots in those days and for ammunition we had a bushel basket full of hickory nuts. If you know what a hickory nut is, it has a lot of sharp points on the shell. Woody was going to be playing at some theater that night and, as it happened, he caught a hickory nut right in the middle of his forehead and it started bleeding.

Well, we were frantic for fear that he wouldn't be able to go on the stage that night, so we sneaked down the backstairs into our flat which was on the first floor and we went into the bathroom very quietly so our parents didn't know what was happening, and we put a little piece of toilet tissue over the wound and got it to stick real good, and it covered up and stopped the bleeding. Then we took face powder and doctored him up so you could hardly tell he had been injured. As it turned out, our folks and Woody's folks never found out about it.

Woody's father had a tremendous interest in show business but never could get beyond the level of semiprofessional. He was a singer in a quartet known as the Cream City Four, sometimes referred to as the White City Four. According to Woody, he played very bad fake piano using only the black keys.

WOODY (talking about his father's group):   They never really got too far because they would become disoriented some way going to the engagement. They'd stop at a few taverns on the way to the state fair that they were supposed to be working. They had the Cream City Four and then they had an earlier group known as the Melpomene Four [after one of the Greek muses]. One of the little bands I had while I was in school, finishing grade school, we called The Melpomene-type Orchestra, because of my Dad's prodding. Nobody knew what the hell it meant, but that was the name of the group!

RAY SHERMAN: When we got a little older we managed to get radios, crystal sets, and we'd listen with earphones. We'd hear Jean Goldkette, and we would hear Freddie Berrins and we'd be able to get KDKA, East Pittsburgh, on the radio or KOA in Denver. We started to pick up a few records here and there.

WOODY: In high school, I first heard some sides which were recorded by the Duke Ellington band. It was an eight-piece band and was called The Washingtonians, and I was very intrigued with some of the weird sounds they got. As a matter of fact, some of their records came out under the name of The Jungle Band, so you can tell what they were into. I have always been interested in Duke down through the years. To this day [1986] he is still my biggest inspiration and most important influence.

I never really liked working in theaters or the vaudeville-type operation. As a matter of fact, when I got to be about 11 or 12 I couldn't stomach it, but I was still being booked. I was in Chicago. I couldn't get a child labor permit to work in the Loop. So we were out on the South Side in the Capitol theater. I was on the side of the stage and they had these two big fountains. These were those deluxe, million dollar theaters they used to build during the depression. I wore some kind of a Navy uniform and I played my saxophone solo and did my song and dance. I was bowing myself into oblivion, when I did a back type header into this fountain on the end. Well, they couldn't get me to go on for the next two shows. I was so embarrassed.

In one of the shows, I was out doing this very hot version of "Oh Gee, Say Gee, You Ought to See My Gee Gee from the Fiji Isles" and the orchestra leader in the pit kept pointing to the button on his shirt or his cuff and I thought he was making a joke, and I was going "Ha, you bet." When I got off all the kids were laughing. It seems that my fly was open. They couldn't get me to go on for two days after that!

My mother became a real fan of the whole thing. We had two vaudeville houses in town, and if it meant my missing a whole day of school, I had to catch both shows on the opening day.

Sometimes my mother traveled with me to the jobs. As a matter of fact, on some of the dates, after I got to be about 12, I drove the car and sat on two pillows. I was always very small. She would accompany me on these dates. She had all the faith in the world in my driving ability.

ERV SHERMAN: Woody was an accomplished dancer. I remember going over to his house after school. I was the guy with the hammer and saw, and I made hurdles eight to ten inches high, and he would do a dance routine over the hurdles, around the basement floor, working out routines. I don't believe that we had a Victrola or a record player down there at that time. He would just hum and sing these songs while he would dance.

WOODY: By the time I got into high school, I announced to my family and to anyone who would care to listen that I was forsaking the theater for music. I was going to become an involved jazz musician. Well, I think that my parents both went into a dead faint because that isn't what they had in mind at all. In 1926 I played with Myron Stewart's band at a local Milwaukee club called the Blue Heaven Roadhouse. I didn't think the group was very good, but it was a place to play.

One of my very closest high school buddies was Red Koster. You know that's the age when you make those undying friendships. He was captain of the football team and for one season I was manager. It was an honorary job. I was supposed to be at all the games but usually I was gone playing music somewhere. Red and I went through some terrible things together. Real daredevil stuff. We tried things at the Marquette football game, it was the big game of the year. We went out this particular night, it was a big night in the city, and in our anxiety to do something or another, we ripped the pay telephone off the wall somewhere and took it home. Red was very powerful. We hid it in his basement, and we died with fear for the next two months . . . "the FBI . . . oh, we're going to go to a Federal pen!"

He married right after high school while I was still around town, still going to school, and this was a very amazing thing to me, very impressive. He was a great dancer, and whenever I got a gig, he would come to the dance and say, "You see that kid up there with the saxophone? He's great! Listen to him, he's the end. Like, this guy is going to be one of the biggest things." Red was a great "press agent."

These are the kind of friendships that you don't have to see somebody for ten or fifteen years. It doesn't mean a thing. You haven't lost one inch.

BILL "RED" KOSTER: Woody and I both attended St. John's Cathedral Grade and High School. We lived in the same neighborhood. I used to go to the Fern, Jackson, Oriental Theaters to see him play, dance, and sing. He was a natural showman. I played football and Woody was at all the games he could attend and still take care of his show dates. Woody was one of the cleanest-cut kids that I ever knew. We pulled a few pranks at times, but none of them bad.

Woody always thought he had a big nose. I never thought so. He used to ask us to hit him in the nose, hoping that we'd break it. He figured he would look better. Honest, tears used to come to his eyes.

Woody's folks were great people. His mother was rather nervous, but if you knew his father, Otto, you would know the reason why. One time Otto told me that he had discovered how to cut down on the electric bill. He would turn off the refrigerator when going to bed and turn it on in the morning when he got up.

Otto had a deep bass voice, lots of volume, and fair quality. His favorite song was "Asleep in the Deep." When Otto cut loose, Woody's mother used to put her fingers in her ears and close all the windows so not to disturb the neighbors on Third Street. It was like going to a show.

WOODY: I joined probably the best band of the area in my sophomore year at High. I played four nights a week and one afternoon at a place called the Eagles Ballroom [later known as the Million Dollar], and I got seventy dollars a week for the four nights and one afternoon, and that was a lot of money back in those days. As soon as I could, I got a driver's license, because I had been driving my father's car without one. I bought my first automobile, which was a convertible Whippet, which was a product of the Willys Corporation. It was like a little miniature car, but it was a convertible and was pretty sporty and it had a body that was built to look like a French car. You could get a driver's license then at 14. I joined the Musician's Union when I was about 12 and was on my way. That's all I wanted to do.

I worked at the Million Dollar Ballroom with Joey Lichter's band most of my high school years. Joey Lichter was a very good musician and he had played in all of the theaters around town. That was a good stepping stone for me. Most of the guys were much older than I, and they were mostly Chicago musicians and they had more experience in the local [union]. They taught me a lot, like how to read music.

Since we were the house band at the Ballroom, we played opposite other bands from all over the country, bands like the Kansas City Night Hawks, Coon Sanders, and Paul Whiteman. It was a pretty heavy scene to be involved with at 14 or 15.

Later, when the Lichter band went to Tulsa on a road trip, I was ostracized completely for about twenty minutes by my parents. But I pleaded and screamed and ranted and raved and Dad gave me a few last-minute instructions about how to take care of the body and mind, and I left in a blaze of dust in my Whippet Four. I never got near Tulsa with that. It busted down so often I was under it more than I was in the seat. On the way we stopped off in Kansas City. I ran into the whole Kansas City group of musicians who were around then. I had already been introduced to some of the wildness of the American musician, the marijuana and so forth. I knew what it was and I wasn't particularly interested. When we got to Kansas City, I went to these guys' apartment, there were about nine living in the pad, and they were now soaking old goldenleaf in Italian red wine and letting it dry, and they had large pipes. They were in beautiful shape! I think some of our guys never got out of Kansas City. It didn't intrigue me, and I can say that truthfully.

We had a trumpet [player] from Kansas City who joined the band somewhere along the line. He was probably about fifteen years older than I was and we became roommates because I dug the way he played. So in Tulsa, we lived together in the Alvin hotel, a beautiful spot. This new, hot, Plains type climate was new to me. Consequently, I was drinking Coca Cola and Dr. Pepper until they were coming out of my ears. We had them lined up along the windowsill. And this trumpet player was quite an addict as far as marijuana was concerned. He kept pretty numb day and night. He used to hit panics when he would go to sleep. All of a sudden he'd leap up—straight up—and this was very unnerving, especially when you had just fallen asleep. This one morning he was unbearable. I had just fallen asleep and probably an hour had passed, and he leaped up and started screaming "Fire" because these bottles were lined up on the window and there was a red neon sign across the street and the reflection on the whole thing. He was getting everybody up, out of the building, calling on the phone, oh, it was miserable!

We were not on the road that much. We went out a couple of summers, mostly in Oklahoma. We played one summer in Tulsa. In my Whippet one day, Al Mack—the pianist, from St. John's Cathedral—and myself were making a long jump somewhere in the Midwest. It was a very bad day for the Whippet. It broke down two or three times. We were both full of grease and dirt. We walked into the ballroom, Joey [Lichter] yelled at us, "Get right up here on the stand," and we leaped up, and immediately he sent me into my song and dance, with the grease on and beat to the socks and no sleep. "Dance, you bastard, dance!" Discipline they called it then.

I really became very clothes conscious about 14 or so and found a tailor. This was the big move. You had to find the right tailor. We were wearing the one-button with the large peak lapel, very large shoulders and pants that were somewhat like Oxford bags, very full from top to bottom with deep pleats. A lot of hand stitching around the edges. We have a band picture someplace of the Lichter group in its finest outfit. It was always logical that all bands must wear morning jackets with black trousers, but these were cut very extreme. We all had black patent-leather shoes and white linen spats! Too much! And oh yes, double-breasted grey vests.

BILL "RED" KOSTER: In my junior year, Woody arranged for most of Lichter's band to play at the prom, with Woody conducting. We went to the prom together—with dates, of course. The same group played in his [Woody's] junior year. I think Woody paid the musicians out of his own pocket.

In my junior year my ankle was broken in a football game. I was on crutches for two months. Woody picked me up every morning and brought me home each night in his new Whippet convertible. Can you imagine a high school sophomore with a convertible in those days? Most people didn't have a dime for the bus in the Great Depression. He would give anyone a ride. He was never anything but a nice guy.

WOODY: At St. John's Cathedral High School at the eight o'clock class in the morning, especially when I got home at four in the morning, I would be falling asleep. So I would constantly be in trouble with the office, and Sister Fabian Riley would come to my rescue and bail me out. She knew that I was only interested in music. Without her defending me all the time and encouraging me in my music, who knows what might have become of me?

Many years later, we did some benefit things together to raise funds to build a gymnasium. She accomplished many things in her lifetime. A very wonderful lady.

Hildegarde, later a noted cafe singer, and her sister attended St. John's Cathedral High in Milwaukee during the same years that I did. They were a year or two ahead of me, but they used to play piano duets whenever we had an affair at school and later I would wail a little on my alto. We never worked together: our styles clashed. I never knew the girls well, other than to say "Hi."

At one point, I worked this club before the Eagles Ballroom until 4:00 A.M., and my first class was at 8:00 A.M. I did that for about a semester and a half. If I overslept I got plenty of hell at home. As a matter of fact, I left during the last semester of my fourth year and got enough credits later to graduate.

But when I was with the Joey Lichter band, the one from the Eagles Ballroom, it was like pulling teeth, reading music. And sometimes I would have ten guys on my back saying "Man, are you kidding?" Joey was a very fine musician, a violinist, not a jazz musician at all. But we had an out and out jazz band. This is what he liked. He had been a theater leader for years and so he had all these large stock arrangements of things like "Three Shades of Blue," and he'd make us wade through this. None of us was a tremendous reader, and I was impossible! He would hit me with the violin bow and sing it to me and kick me! But I always felt that I owed Joe a great deal, because anyone who would have the patience to put up with that . . . you know.

I was always looking for somebody to jam with, and I did practice sensibly to a certain extent. Because we were always told, and I always believed, that your foundation was very important in music. By that I mean your knowledge of your own instrument. That you just couldn't pick up an axe and sit down and make your own ideas and let that be the complete answer. We always felt that there was a lot more to it than that. There were always guys along the way to prove it to you.

I forgot about two bands that impressed me very much in the early stages. One—I had some of his records right before I joined Gerun—[was] Don Redman. And then too, we played some dates with the Lichter Band out in Toledo, on the way to somewhere, and we ran into Andy Kirk and the Twelve Clouds of Joy. It was practically a new band then and it was a very good band.

In my senior year in high school, a band came to town and they had been told by someone about me. So they contacted me. I had a long conversation with Tom Gerun who had this band that was playing at the Schroeder Hotel in Milwaukee. He met my parents and had a long talk with them and told them that he would be responsible for me and that he would be in charge of me, like a guardian. They finally agreed that they would try it, and I joined the band.

Tom Gerun (Gerunovitch) had a national reputation as a society bandleader playing in most of the major hotels across the country. In addition to conventional instrumentation, the band included violins and a tuba.

WOODY: We were playing Chicago at a place called the Grenada Cafe. It was actually a front for the Capone gang, fronted by a Capone man; his name was Al Quadback. The club was very plush and it featured all the stars. We followed Paul Whiteman's band in there. We had in the band people like Harry Richman and later baritone saxist Al Morris, who later became known internationally as singer Tony Martin.

One night, after a gig, I got held up on the South Side of Chicago. With me were a bass player, Steve Bowers, and a comic who was working the Grenada with us, and Fuzzy Knight [who later made many films]. The three of us had been to the Grand Terrace Cafe to hear Earl Hines' new big band. We would go there every morning when we were finished because they would have a breakfast dance. We were stopped at a red light and the three of us were piled in there, and a guy jumped out of a big black sedan, and then four of them were on one side and one on my side and one of them had a gun and one had a blackjack and they wanted us to get from my roadster into the big black sedan. In those days if you got taken for a ride, then that was it. We didn't know who they were, so we wouldn't get out of our car. It was a roadster and it was wintertime. I had a black bearskin fur coat. I was very chic, wearing a homburg hat and driving a roadster! Everybody started flailing away with their arms and they kept hitting me with something and the only thing that saved me was the homburg hat and the black fur coat. In the midst of all this melee, the guy who had the gun, pointed it at our feet and fired to get us to stop. We were causing too much of a scene and people were waiting for street cars on the corner. My foot was on the brake pedal and I was going for the gas pedal and one second later they split! They must have been stoned or something because no one would ever pull this kind of coup sober. They evidently cased us at the Grand Terrace and decided to follow us, so I wound up with a bullet hole in my leg. My mother became hysterical in Milwaukee and was there the next morning and her young budding son was in some kind of state with a bullet hole in his leg at the age of 16.

Woody recounted later that when he showed up for work at the Grenada Cafe, using a cane, Al Quadback had only one comment to make. He said, "Look, punk, put your hands up next time!"

WOODY: Eventually we went to San Francisco and Tom Gerun and his partner, a food man by the name of Frank Martinelli, opened a club in 1931, called the Bal Tabarin. For a while Gerun was the house band there but after a while he brought in people like Kay Kyser and his band. Tom would continue on the road and make money so he could afford the night club.
        It was a very interesting time of my life. I had just heard, maybe a year or two before, the early recordings of people like Coleman Hawkins. I was trying to emulate that kind of playing. So, I was considered very hot in 1931 in San Francisco.

During this time with Tom Gerun, Woody was being featured on tenor sax, and he has been quoted as saying, "I sounded like Bud Freeman with his hands chopped off."[1]

WOODY: In 1931, when I first went to San Francisco with Tom Gerun, I was 16, and I had my 17th birthday while I was playing at the Bal Tabarin. And Charlotte, whose last name was Neste, opened in a revue in San Francisco at the Curran Theater. It was a musical called *Nine O'Clock Revue*. They brought the whole cast over to the club that night to have a celebration, and she was with a friend of mine, Bunny Burson, a bandleader around San Francisco, who had been designated as her escort. I let him know immediately that he was just helping out for the night and she would never be seen again by him, otherwise it was death! He's a guy about six feet three or four and I was a shriveled-up little guy.

   We were both 17 when we met and we waited and had a romance via the telephone, mostly, because she would be in one part of the country and I would be in another. She was born in North Dakota and her family was somewhat like my family, kept moving around. She was very interested in the theater and very taken with it and very serious about it. She acted mostly in theaters and things like that, in the West.

   Eventually she went all the way back East. She was in a show with Barbara Stanwyck and Frank Fay. They did this musical and took it all the way to New York. After it folded, Charlotte went to Boston and became mistress of ceremonies at the Metropolitan Theater, which still stands in Boston. We had a long and exciting young courtship period.

   When I met Charlotte's father, he found out that I was a saxophone player. He loved the saxophone, he played saxophone and fiddle in a country group, and he asked me to try his mouthpiece to see what I thought of it. It was terrible. I didn't want to tell him that I could get him something better than that! But I picked up his horn and got some terrible noise out of it and he said, "Wow, what a sound!" So I knew that I was home free.

Woody hired a female singer named Virginia Simms for the Gerun band. She would eventually gain national renown as Ginny Sims with Kay Kyser's band.

WOODY: When I got to San Francisco with Tom's band, I was a brand new sound to most of the guys, you know, because I could play louder than a steam whistle and growl harder and make some fierce noises with a very staccato approach! Gerun's was an entertaining band basically. Tom Gerun was a business person and he was not a musician, but he knew that it was important to have very good musicians, and so that's what he tried for.

   I got to know Phil Harris, who had a band across town at the St. Francis Hotel with a partner named Carroll Lockner. It was a pretty decent swing band for those days and he offered me a job. But after I listened to the band quite carefully a few times, I decided I'd stay with the Gerun band because I felt we were playing better music. Phil Harris was quite a street brawler in those days. He liked to get a little beef going with taxi drivers, cops, and anybody. He was big then, he was heavy, and quite a dashing man. We became very good friends.

Later Bob Crosby came down from up north and we became roommates. He had one of those bachelor-type rooms over at the old Fairmont. If you were an employee at the Mark you could get an exceptional rate in the basement rooms, so he invited me to stay with him, and I did. And I made my payments to him weekly for the use of the hall. Some weeks later he got mixed up with some people in a little party affair and they flew to LA and no one heard from Bob for a few days, and I was locked out of the room. I went to the desk and tried to get in and they told me that the bill hadn't been paid in several weeks. It seemed that Crosby had been spending the loot. So I slept in the furnace area in the hotel in my tuxedo for a few nights because Gerun, with his "sense of humor," wouldn't give me an advance.

BOB CROSBY: The only recollection I have about Woody at all is I came down as a kid, I was about 16 and a half, to sing with Anson Weeks, at the Mark Hopkins Hotel in San Francisco. That was kind of a Mickey Mouse band, but it had some good people in it. Xavier Cugat was the third violist and Griff Williams was with him for a while. At the same time, Tom Gerun had a band at the Bal Tabarin in San Francisco. In the band Woody would do an act which was tap dancing and then he played tenor sax. Also in that band was Al Morris, who now is known as Tony Martin, who played saxophone and sang.

I knew both Tony and Woody, in fact they used my room frequently at the Fairmont Hotel to change clothes. I don't know why that was except it was close to the Bal Tabarin and Tony was coming over from Oakland and I guess he was living somewhere out in the marina. But it was all right with me to let 'em use my room. And that's about as close as I ever got to Woody.

WOODY: After I was in the Gerun band for some time, we had spent a year in San Francisco, and we were now going on the road for a short spell. Most of the guys were from San Francisco and so they decided to stay at home, and we made a lot of changes in the band, and I did a lot of needling as far as Tom was concerned. Being a very fine and easy-to-get-along-with person, on numerous occasions he took my advice, and by the time we went out on the road the second year, we had a pretty wild band. I don't know if it was any better commercially, I don't think it was as good, but it was a much better band! We went to New Orleans and stayed for several months. It was a great experience for me, because I got to meet a lot of guys and play a little with people that I'd heard of for a long time—people like Louis Prima.

After New Orleans, the Gerun Band traveled up to the East Coast and played dates in New York, Pittsburgh, and other Eastern cities. One thing about that trip to New York with Tom's band, I ran into a couple of guys at Keen's and they said that Pee Wee Russell was in town, and I wanted very much to meet Pee Wee. As a matter of fact, we had picked up a trumpet player down in New Orleans—Red Bowman. He played very good jazz. He was a good friend of Pee Wee's and a couple of the boys, and he heard that they were in town living way up somewhere in the Bronx, in an armory that had been condemned. At this point I was very serious about maybe staying in New York and getting with the right guys, and playing the right things and so forth. So I was very much intrigued with the thought of meeting Pee Wee and these guys. We took a cab for about eight dollars worth and went up and found this armory and beat on the door for about forty minutes and Pee Wee opened the door. He had on a bathrobe with a great big pin holding it together. There was a single light bulb hanging some place in this eerie-looking joint. I'd seen the instruments and not much else—a couple of jackets hanging, and a bottle of gin and a light bulb. This kind of made me reevaluate the whole thing—whether I should go ahead with my plan or not! I was used to living fairly well.

As a matter of fact, it changed my opinions about a lot of things. Just a little happening that lasted probably five minutes.

In Pittsburgh, while on the band stand, Tom received a wire. It was the market crash and he was wiped out, a goodly sum of money. He stood there a minute or two with a blank expression on his face and then broke up completely with his wild, high laughter. "Ha, ha, ha, ha," he says, "how do you like this? I'm wiped out!" So that night he threw a party for the band. He took us all to a club and got more rooms at the hotel and dames and the booze, and this was his way of celebrating. This taught me a great lesson: how important it is to be a good loser.

Woody recorded his first vocals while with the Gerun band on August 1, 1932. The titles were "Lonesome Me" and "My Heart's at Ease." The recording session took place in New York, for the Brunswick Label. On August 19, 1932, the band recorded "Sentimental Gentleman from Georgia," featuring Woody on vocal.

WOODY: Jack Kapp, who later started Decca Records, was then the head at Brunswick. And musical director on the dates—aside from the bandleader whose band was recording—Victor Young had that job. If there was any quick arranging that had to be done on the date, or any changes in back of the vocal, instead of using the usual background, Vic would play a little obbligato on the fiddle.

I'll never forget what a disappointment it was to me in Chicago at Brunswick when we did this first date, because we were recording all these ballads and commercial tunes. I had this great bug and urge to really get hot and get a few guys out of the band to whip it up. I made it my business to talk to Kapp myself. I just moved in like gangbusters. He wondered who this little character was, probably, but he was kind enough to give me a complete explanation how he had Red Nichols and several other people under contract who were really very good and they didn't need any more fellows to play hot.

RAY SHERMAN: According to my personal diary, [Woody] left Gerun in July, 1934, in Denver. Woody's mother, my mother, and my sister, Joyce, and Erv left for Denver on July 10 to pick up Woody and bring him and his horns and baggage home.

After returning home to Milwaukee, Woody made an attempt to form his own band but was unsuccessful. In the fall of 1934, Woody joined the Harry Sosnick Orchestra. He stayed with Sosnick about eight months. The band's chief arranger was David Rose.

WOODY: That was an odd band for me to be in, inasmuch as it was a kind of Mickey Mouse band. We played mostly hotels. But then we had a booking in the old Palomar ballroom in Los Angeles, and I warned Harry. I told him that the music we were playing might not be right, 'cause it was a pretty hip ballroom. But he didn't pay much attention to me until after the night we opened. After it was over, he said, "Let's rehearse tomorrow," and he had a whole mess of Dave Rose arrangements. They were jazz things, standards. We rehearsed like mad the next day, and after that, at least we lasted out the four weeks or six weeks. But that opening night was pretty horrible. We looked like we were idiots, playing this "waterfall" music, you know.

Actually, the guys in the band were good. There was a trumpet player, Fran Baker. I really enjoyed the way he played. He had a kind of Bix Beiderbecke way of playing. Very pretty and had good time.

After his stint with Harry Sosnick, Woody joined the orchestra of Gus Arnheim, in which previously Bing Crosby had been the vocalist and Stan Kenton had been the pianist. Woody joined the Arnheim organization primarily to do a theater tour that lasted about ten weeks.

WOODY: I was with the remains of the band that Stan Kenton had played with. It was a kind of a Benny Goodman-style band, but I was hired because they were going to do a theater tour, and they knew that I was a performer, I could do something besides play the saxophone. That was an important factor in those days. It was good experience playing for him, because a lot of the people that I respected and admired had worked for him, people like Bing Crosby and quite a few instrumentalists who were well known in California then.

I played a couple of tunes, but I was kind of in the show [dancing], you know. I was a right-footed dancer. The left one was always a little late. I used to run into people who really were dancers. They said I was one of the greatest fakers they had ever seen. It looked right from the front, but they knew that what I was doing was all wrong. The dance part had to be the windup. You'd turn blue if you tried to blow after that.

It was while he was with the Arnheim orchestra that Woody had his first big break. It happened that both the Gus Arnheim and Isham Jones Orchestras were playing in Pittsburgh. Isham Jones was well known nationally as the leader of a big-sounding, conventional dance orchestra. Starting in 1912, he had built his band into a sensational attraction. By the middle twenties, he had collected almost $500,000 in royalties for his successes as a song writer. His credits included "There Is No Greater Love" (which featured a Herman vocal), "Swingin' Down the Lane," "I'll See You in My Dreams," "It Had to Be You" and "On the Alamo." The band was a favorite on the college circuit, where there was a steady demand for dance music.

WOODY: We were playing one theater in Pittsburgh and the Isham Jones band was playing the other theater. I got to see some of the guys in the Jones band, particularly Walt Yoder, who had been a friend of mine in Lexington, Kentucky, when I was with Joey Lichter. He was a local banjo player. One night while we were playing in Lexington at Joyland Park, some of the kids from the university came over and they wanted to hear their fight song or something and Yoder hummed it to us, and we blew it.

He was the one who really steamed up Jones into hiring me and when I went over to meet Isham backstage at the other theater, Jones said, "Do you play a tenor?," and I said, "Yes." "Do you play the clarinet?," and I said, "Yeah." He said, "You sing?," and I said "Yeah," and he said, "These guys tell me you dance . . . is that right?," and I said, "Yes." He said, "Well, if you do all those things then I better hire you." And that's the way he hired me.

In the band were Saxie Mansfield, Joe Bishop, Sonny Lee. I joined the band right after Milt Yaner left and I replaced Johnny Sedola. Pee Wee Irwin had just left. Sonny Lee had replaced Jack Jenny. We had a very nice jazz trumpet player named Chelsey Quealey and, all in all, the musicianship was very good.

There were two distinct musical sides to the Jones band. Part of the group favored the sweet, hotel "society" sound; the other side leaned heavily toward blues and jazz. By this time, the idea of "white jazz" had gotten started. Bands like Glen Gray's Casa Loma Orchestra were playing music with a driving beat that stood out from the "ricky-tick" sound of the sweet hotel bands. Benny Goodman was swinging. Of course, Duke Ellington, Jimmy Lunceford, Andy Kirk, and other black bandleaders had long been probing the "swing" sounds unfamiliar to most of the dancing public.

WOODY: It never really was an out and out swing band because Isham was famous for his ballads and the songs he wrote, and that was our best thing. But we played some jazz that was pretty good. At that time the swing bands were Glen Gray and Benny's band, which was just coming up. Even Tommy Dorsey had just started. It was the beginning of a new era, actually.

The time that I spent with Isham, we were at very few locations, for long durations. We were on the road mostly, but we played a few hotel spots. But it was always a big, round sounding, loud band, and so basically it wasn't really a hotel band. In those years, the type that was expected in a hotel room was something quiet. The band was a large one. It was eighteen men.

Musically it was the best band I had ever played in, and everything was very clean. It had to be. I enjoyed the whole thing quite a bit.

Mostly the jazz things were standards. "Blue Room" and stuff like that. We had some very nice arrangements. Jiggs Noble did a lot of those things and also Gordon Jenkins. Then we had a couple things that Fletcher Henderson wrote for us. I don't remember the titles, but they were very good. And Joe Haymes wrote some things.

With Isham, it didn't matter if you had the wrong suit, or brown shoes with a black suit, as long as you showed up in your right mind. And after you got there, don't ever miss a note, even an eighth note, because this was death! He stood in front of the band with a complete score of every tune. We played these tunes night after night, seven nights a week, and he still had the score out there.

If a customer asked, "Mr. Jones, would you play 'Stardust'" or something, he'd say "Get the hell out of here, you don't want to hear that!" Warm personality on the stand, but he kind of hated all audiences. It was a concession if he turned around once or twice at night and looked at them.

It was a band that was respected by most of the musicians around the country, and I made a lot of acquaintances and friends I probably wouldn't have had the opportunity to meet if I hadn't been in that particular group. In other words, it was the kind of band musicians came to hear. Ish had a very good name, and even though it was near the end of his career, we still did very good business.

This is when I first began to sing ballads and not just entertain with specialty numbers. Jones was the guy who really touted me onto it. As a matter of fact, I remember Jenkins, Noble, or somebody came in with a thing on "I'm in the Mood for Love," and Eddie Stone, the regular singer, was doing one of these rhythm and cute tunes, and Jones decided that somebody else would have to do this tune. He just threw it at me and said, "Sing it!" I said, "I can't sing that kind of song." He says, "Sing it!," and that was it. So then I had the great fortune of introducing a song of his the same year or the next year, "No Greater Love."

Because of union policies, Woody wasn't allowed to play an instrument for three months, so he sang. When he wasn't singing, he would crawl under the piano and play his clarinet in the shadows. In 1935, Woody recorded nineteen titles for the Jones big band on the Decca label. "Four or Five Times" and "Every Time I Look at You" featured Woody as vocalist.

WOODY: I did a few things in my day that were pretty weird. We played a place in New England one night with Isham's band, and on the bandstand they had a large kind of a box affair for the conductor to put his music on. Isham liked this very much because, as I said earlier, he used a score for every piece. It was a high stand. It almost came up to his chest. The back of this box affair was open. After I went out and sang a chorus of something and played a little bit, I was supposed to go back. Ish was always very intent on reading the music and not aware of anything else. So I got in the box. I was there for about three tunes. One of the slats on the top that held the music was kind of ripped away, so I put my hand through the slats. It was kind of an eerie blue color on the bandstand, and Isham went straight out of the park! He chased me off the bandstand.

The Isham Jones band was heard via many live, remote radio broadcasts throughout its years. These broadcasts had a significant influence in making the public aware of big bands. Shortly before Jones disbanded, the band was heard live on WOR, New York. A few of these live broadcasts were recorded between January and March of 1936 and later sold on certain illicit record labels.

On a live recording dated March 6, 1936, Woody does a vocal on "Old Man Mose." His phrasing is in the style of the black singers of that period and an indication of the singing style he would eventually incorporate in his own band.

Woody was also featured with small group recording units labeled the Swanee Singers and the Isham Jones Juniors.

WOODY: I was playing tenor, but later played alto again because alto had been an earlier instrument with me. I fooled around with clarinet a lot. I always knew that I would not be the kind of clarinet player I really wanted to be because it would take complete devotion and I wasn't ready to give up the band.

Pee Wee Russell was an early influence on me and so was Barney Bigard. I had the good fortune of doing some early jazz concert things with Eddie Condon and different people, and when Pee Wee and I would be together on these things, we would maybe play against each other. Of course Barney was still with Ellington when I first got to know Duke. Pee Wee and Barney were opposite type players. Technically, Barney was much more proficient. But Pee Wee was a very soulful player, and his ear and his feelings were quite tremendous. He was able to expound in a fashion completely different from any other jazz player.

Isham Jones retired in the middle of 1936 at 40 years of age. Stories circulated in the press for years that Jones' retirement was for health reasons. Woody gave another version.

WOODY: He was a very successful song writer the whole time he had a band. I think he was tired of the whole thing and he was in a financial position where he didn't need much. He was an ASCAP triple-A writer and he wasn't hurting, to put it bluntly. Our last date was in Nashville, in September 1936.

When the Jones orchestra split up, the faction in the orchestra that was of the "sweet school" reorganized with vocalist/violist Eddie Stone as the front man. They continued playing the commercial charts in the Jones library, using his name.

There were others, such as tenor saxophonist Maynard "Saxie" Mansfield, trumpeter Clarence Willard, and bassist Walt Yoder, who were yearning to work in a band more oriented to blues and jazz. This unemployed jazz nucleus of the Jones orchestra persuaded Woody to become leader/front man of a new "hot jazz" outfit.

WOODY: While we were still with Jones, we discussed the possibilities of it [Woody being the leader] after we heard Isham was going to quit. Partly it was the guys' idea because they knew I had ambition. I was constantly talking about "when and if I have my group," just like guys do today.

Meanwhile, Woody hadn't forgotten the stunning redheaded showgirl he had met in San Francisco when they were both 17, five years earlier. Their romance continued by long distance telephone, postcards, letters, and any means of communication that was available. On September 27, 1936, in the midst of hiring musicians, rehearsals, and other preparations for a new band, Woody found time to take a wife.

WOODY: There was never any formal engagement or anything like that. But we'd known each other almost five years before we decided to get married. I talked her into coming to New York to be married. She had been visiting her parents in California and naturally I knew in advance that she was arriving, but I goofed with everything. I didn't get a license or make any attempt to. She got off the train dead tired, hadn't slept for three days, all excited, and then I kept her up for the remainder of that day and that night. I took her to Armonk, New York. We first went to Harrison, which is closer to New York, and the guy slammed the door in our faces because it was too late. We finally wound up in Armonk about two in the morning with a borrowed ring for her and this justice made it a very hurried affair because he was going fishing and he was dragged with our being there. It was pretty funny the way they hustled us through alleys and things. It was like we were doing something real bad. All we wanted to do was get married!

Walt Yoder and his wife and Nick Hupfer [the violinist], who later changed his name to Nick Harper, were with us. The day we got married, Charlotte retired from the theater completely and never looked back and wondered what happened to her career. And for this alone, I'd have to give her many points, because not too many people who are the least bit involved in performing would give it up for someone else. But we had a long, very long, good marriage, and when she passed away in 1982, we had been married forty-six years.

We spent our honeymoon on 52nd Street in New York City, my wife and I. We were married in Armonk and went right to 52nd Street. Beautiful! With no job in sight, I cashed in an insurance policy and we were swinging.

Woody now had a new wife, and he was about ready to launch a new band. The stage was set.

2.

"The Band That Plays the Blues"

1936-1943

Getting established with a band of his own was an uphill climb for Woody in the early days.

WOODY: After Jones broke up his band, most of us went to New York and started to rehearse. We didn't know what we were rehearsing for, but we were rehearsing, trying to organize a band. And we messed around for about eight weeks, before we finally got a nibble. We changed a lot of guys, because as the guys would get a job, they would leave us. During that period, I got so broke that I started to take casual [band] dates and wound up with, I think, the Meyer Davis unit a couple of Saturday nights. They were beautiful jobs because they paid forty bucks.

The only way we could get guys for our band was to offer them a piece of the band, a piece of nothing, you know. Originally there were just the guys who had been with Jones. There were probably five or six of us left who were going to be partners, but then we had to give pieces of the corporation away in order to get guys to stay, to even rehearse.

Members of that first Herman Orchestra were Woody Herman (leader, clarinet, alto sax, vocals); Clarence Willard, Kermit Simmons, Joe Bishop (trumpets—Joe doubled on fluegelhorn); Neal Reid (trombone); Murray Williams, Don Watt (alto saxes); Maynard "Saxie" Mansfield, Bruce Wilkins (tenor saxes); Nick Hupfer (later Harper) (violin); Norman Sherman (piano); Walter Yoder (bass); Chick Reeves (guitar); and Frank Carlson (drums).

FRANK CARLSON: I was playing at the Roseland Ballroom. I was still in high school, and that's where Woody spotted me, and that's when I joined the band. I quit school to go on the road, which I really didn't want to do, but music was much more important to me.

Trumpeter Kermit D. Simmons worked with dance bands in college and recorded for Gennett Records in Richmond, Indiana. He was with the Don Bigelow Band at the Biltmore Hotel in New York, with Charlie Barnet from February to October 1936, and with Benny Goodman in the early forties.

KERMIT SIMMONS: I was with Barnet for eight months, and sax man Bobby Parks knew Walt Yoder, and he was telling me about a new band that was being organized. I was ready for a change, as being with Charlie was an experience. I auditioned with the band at Decca Studios. There were three trumpet players there waiting to audition. I asked Woody if there was an elimination contest and said I didn't care to try out under those conditions. He said he would let the other two go, and try them some other time. I tried out, and I made it. I liked the band, as it was so different from Barnet's band, and all the fellows were really friendly.

The new Herman aggregation was booked at the Brooklyn Roseland Ballroom. According to Woody, "If you made it big at Brooklyn, then they would book you into the New York Roseland Ballroom." The New York location offered greater exposure, prestige, and opportunities to be heard by larger audiences. The band's opening night in Brooklyn was election night, Tuesday, November 3, 1936.

WOODY: In the late thirties and early forties, just like it is today, the one big factor was if you had hit records, you were successful. You would play the best ballrooms, the best theaters, and make some motion pictures. Then the air time and all the radio you did would be advantageous to plug your records. In that respect, we were extremely fortunate for a brand-new band to be able to start recording for Decca. It was a new, young company, and Isham had done some dates for them prior to his leaving the band scene, and they decided they would like us as a house unit. So, we were required to do all sorts of things such as cover tunes that were hits by one person or another on another label.

There were only three major record labels in those days. It was Victor, Columbia, and Decca. There was always the possibility of making some money with records on the basis of royalties. But I think it was really more important to a band of that era to have records that were being played, because it made the band more popular, and that's really where we derived our salaries and our money. It was very important to be on live radio in those days. As a matter of fact, bands used to invest a great deal of money to play hotels and ballrooms where there were air lines for radio broadcasting. If a network had a line in a particular location, the band would accept the engagement for far less money, and they might sustain some heavy losses in order to keep up their salary and payroll, because they knew that when they went back out on the road after a long engagement with air time they would probably do some business.

During the first week of the new band's Brooklyn debut, "The Band That Plays the Blues" recorded "Wintertime Dreams" and "Someone to Care for Me" at Decca's New York studios. Two days later, on November 8, it was heard via a local remote radio broadcast from the Roseland Ballroom. The radio broadcast was preserved.

WOODY: We were going to be a jazz band, you know, and we decided on being a blues band, because we played that best. We had our limitations. We didn't feel we could play anything that would be as good as Benny or whoever was around at that time. So we decided to stick to the blues and be in a class by ourselves, which to a certain degree was a very bad move in the early stages because nobody knew what the blues were. But we stuck with it, we were very stubborn people. In the beginning, we didn't have much of a book. As a matter of fact, when we opened in Brooklyn's Roseland, our first date, we had twenty arrangements. It was on election day afternoon, and when we got through the twenty, we began with our heads [head arrangements], making them up on the spot. We got by all right and stayed there about four weeks, and then they took us to New York's Roseland, and we stayed seven months. It was a great break for us except that we had no place to go when we finally left.

At this point, pianist Thomas Gordon (Tommy) Linehan joined the band. Tommy had arranged and played with various society bands and groups including Paul Tremaine and Charles Boulanger.

TOMMY LINEHAN: The original piano player was Norm Sherman out of Philadelphia, and then Horace Diaz was on the band just before me, so in the space of six weeks the band actually had three different guys. I think it was Bruce Wilkins who called me. Wilkins said, "We need someone to play piano for a couple of nights down here at the Roseland Ballroom." I said, "Okay, I'll help you . . . it's the Roseland Ballroom, great!" So I did the couple of nights and they said, "Well, if you don't have anything else to do, why don't you stick around for a few weeks?" So I just stayed on with Woody until December of '42.

KERMIT SIMMONS: The manager, Joe Belford, liked Woody and the band very much. A couple weeks after we opened, the American Legion had their national convention in New York, and they actually took over Times Square one night. Roseland was packed every night and some of those clowns were in the crowd, and, of course, loaded. And two of them stood in front of the band giving Woody a rough time. Belford employed longshoremen for bouncers. The Roseland was on the second floor, and the two bouncers came over and picked these two hecklers up by the seat of their pants and their necks, carried them across the dance floor and tossed them down the steps.

WOODY: We had been there for a few months when Basie came. By that time we probably had thirty arrangements. I don't think Basie had any. Like we had him thirty to one. And, of course, we knew all the gimmicks of the ballroom, you know. Like there was a set group at Roseland called the Peabody dancers. You know what a Peabody is? You glide around on the floor in a circle, it's kind of a rat race. They would start out and go *hup hup*, and they would make it around like 80 miles an hour, and the faster the tempo the more they dug it. We had by this time found this out and we had quite a few breakneck flag wavers. You know, old "Weary Blues" and all those old good ones. And, of course, Basie had a good old swinging, easy-tempo band, and this was quite a rough go for them until they got this thing figured out.

I was more impressed with Herschel Evans with the Basie band than Prez [Lester Young]. I thought he [Evans] was a fantastic player. Of course, all the deep-throated tenor players, they were the favorites of mine at that point, everyone from Coleman Hawkins to Ben Webster to whomever was on the scene at that moment.

FRANK CARLSON: Basie came, and of course Jo Jones was with him. Up until that point, I was still banging on wood blocks and all that crap! But when I heard Jo play with the hi-hat cymbals, I thought, "That's for me!" That was the biggest influence in my life, because Jo was not a rudimental drummer like some people were at that time. He played so loose and free. I used to sit in with him all the time. Between Jo and Chick Webb, those were the two that did it for me.

TOMMY LINEHAN: We used to have fun with the Count's band! Oh boy, we became great buddies with them. In fact, several years later, they would have mock battles of the bands, and they would ask Basie about different bands and Basie would say, "The only band that ever cut my band was that Woody Herman Band!"

WOODY: Joe Belford had a wild sense of humor. You were supposed to play one tango and one rhumba every set and we didn't have any tangos or rhumbas, and he kept sending me notes and I kept sending him dirty answers back on the back of the notes. And he would talk right over the PA system while I would be singing, and he'd say "Shut up, you bum, and come up to my office." And one day at a matinee, we were playing one of our best arrangements, and from the PA in the sound booth, he put on a record of "Sugar Blues" twice as loud as we were playing and he's loving every minute of it, and the people are going out of their minds. And it got so bad that unless he bought each guy in the band a bottle of beer between each set, we wouldn't go back on the stand.

We had three matinees a week. It was kind of rough and I was kind of skinny and kind of beat in those days, and he would meet me at the back door. We would come up the back way with a hand truck that you carry trunks and luggage with, and he put me on the truck and wheeled me up to the stand and said, "You're too damn weak to make it!"

TOMMY LINEHAN: Our music was almost like big band Dixieland, that's what we were playing. It wound up just like the Bob Crosby band. They were also a cooperative band, but they went to Bob Crosby as their leader. And they were playing pure Dixieland back then.

WOODY: The Glen Gray Casa Loma Band and Crosby band had just started, and we were the third such cooperative group. It always seemed to me that several heads were better than one, and I guess it was true about some things but not the band! We had more meetings than we played notes. Everything was a meeting. I was the one who became a complete gibbering idiot, because I couldn't make a decision, I couldn't do anything! I had to quick call a meeting, and this takes up a lot of time, you know. A guy would say, "Well, my wife doesn't like to travel on Sunday nights." But, of course, there were a lot of laughs with it too. There were weeks on end when we had to pool our resources and live on nothing, and the guys were good about this. And their wives, too! They all played a part in it. It was like a family affair, and some of the weeks were very rough.

TOMMY LINEHAN: Everyone was so interested in what was going on and trying their best to help. And Woody was right in there pitching with everybody. And I'll tell you, they made a wise choice when they voted him as the leader of the band, because he had a real good presence, and he was always at home no matter what the situation was.

WOODY: After the New York Roseland gig was over, they took us up to New England for a little bit, and from New England we jumped down to Mississippi, and then jumped back to New York. Then we went out to Chicago and about the second year after we got working, if GAC [General Artists Corporation] was able to book us at all, they kept booking us into places with two- and four-week contracts, and we'd be closed

Woody and Charlotte visiting Milwaukee. (Courtesy Ray Sherman)

out the second night. It was very embarrassing and very hungry, too, because we never were able to force any of these contracts to mean anything! We even went to my hometown in Milwaukee and opened with a contract at the Schroeder Hotel for two weeks, and when we got there they decided they liked the band they had before and they held them over two more weeks. And some of the guys had to eat at my house with my parents and we were really hung up there, worse than we were before. I was so ashamed of the whole thing because here I was back home making good.

ERV SHERMAN: Those were lean years. Woody got married about the same time that he started the band. They lived in an apartment in New York. They would eat White Tower hamburgers and oatmeal. Charlotte would serve breakfast with oatmeal and graham crackers. And some of the times being a little bit lean because those were Depression-like years in the mid-thirties, he didn't call home too often.

WOODY: Those were frantic days on 52nd Street. A group of musicians bought a place on the street and named it the Famous Door. Lenny Hayton and a bunch of guys who were stockholders in this little club brought Bunny Berigan in. And in the intermission they had Teddy Wilson, and then later he brought in Billie Holiday, this kid he found who sang tunes. It was a wonderful place. And Red McKenzie sang, and handled the room, kept it alive. Red was a great, warm singer. He was his own man and he sang what he felt. I became very friendly with Red and he was kind of our fatherly adviser in our new marriage, you know, and kind of straightened us out about everything. He was a man who was very, very happily married and very much in love. I was so intrigued with this guy's ability as a singer, and then, too, as a person.

We must have had some terrific guardian angels, all of us, because there were people who were exceptionally kind. There was a pizza joint in Jackson Heights, kind of a musicians' hang-out. We would go in with our fifty cents which meant we could have four beers or something, and invariably they would lay a pizza on us as a gift, and a couple more quarts of beer. We spent hours on end, all of us together. We all lived in the same buildings. We were either across the street or nearby, and playing ping-pong all night was the cheapest entertainment, with a couple of quarts of beer, you know. But these people who had this little bar and grill up there were just fantastic on holidays. They would insist we have dinner at the restaurant, or they would give us a turkey. And by the same token, all of us were always behind in our rent and the apartment house manager where we lived in Jackson Heights couldn't face us. He even loaned us some money. He was always in trouble with the owners of the building about us guys. But he just couldn't hurt us! He couldn't throw us out!

I met Jack Siefert after we had the band about a year, at Wildwood, New Jersey. This place on the East Coast kept us eating over a period of time, because Guy Hunt, who was then a very young man, was taking over from his dad, along with his brother. They had all the theaters and the ballrooms and the little pier in Wildwood, which was kind of the poor man's Atlantic City. Guy became a fan of our group after he brought us down there as a favor to someone in the booking office, and then it would seem that every time we would be out of work, we'd just call Guy and he'd say, "All right, come down and we'll work something out." And during that period I met Jack Siefert. He was a young kid and he became so intrigued with the whole thing, he would emulate us in his dress—copy the whole thing right down to the last notch. And, over the years, through his own problems and business and marriages and everything else, he still makes the weekly rounds of every radio station in the Philadelphia area, and pounds at their door and calls them up and needles them. And, consequently, we get more plays in that area yearly than we do anyplace else in the country.

Meanwhile, the fledgling Herman "Band That Plays the Blues" continued to grind out Decca recordings, both on its own and as the Decca "house band" backing the label's roster of singers.

WOODY: In the early days at Decca there were some amusing things. It was really a shoestring operation. They had to buy used equipment, and oh, some of the wax that they put on, it looked like it had been used and reused about eighty times. I mean, some of the other companies were going ahead and developing, particularly RCA and Columbia with all their massive appliances and scientists and people on their staffs working on sound. We were just working on trying to make a record that wasn't warped before it was pressed! In spite of it, Decca became probably the outstanding record on the market, and did more to revive the record sale business than anyone else. And it was always done the cheapest way possible. It had to be, because they put out a thirty-five-cent product when the rest of the world was selling a seventy-five-cent product.

Technically, I have never particularly liked recording. I have never become interested other than the fact that I want to hear what we play, played back once. And if I agree that that is the best we can do, that will be the final product. In the early days you had three minutes or three minutes and five seconds, and that was the limit of anything you might want to do. Plus the fact that it had to be done in one complete take because there were no other possibilities. And so you maybe would do fifty takes or maybe do two, and you had to make momentous decisions about whether you should go any further with a tune and blow your chops for the next four tunes. Today, it's a whole different ball game. But I'm not so sure that I really understand it any better or like it nearly as well. Whenever you have sixteen tracks, and some places now have double that amount, you are at the complete mercy of whoever does the final mix with all these tapes. The whole idea of a big band is to have it balance within itself. And really, this is fruitless when everyone is being miked and you're on a separate channel.

We were there at Decca eight years, and one of the things that helped the band so much was that we did everything, from backing people to doing dates with Bing Crosby and Mary Martin.

The Kapps had great imaginations. They did it the hard way, without any help. Of course, later, they were able to get people to invest money and it became a great venture, but they had to prove the point first, and they did. Jack must be given complete credit for being able to sign the right artists when he started the company. Some people left big important labels to go with them because they felt that he could do a better job for them, which would be a pretty hard thing to do today.

We had a violin in our band, which was a commercial concession. But the guy, Nick Hupfer, wrote a lot of the jazz pieces. He was a very good musician, a very good writer. He did quite a few of the flag wavers we did in the early period. One of the things he did was our pièce de résistance on several occasions. He did "Meditations from 'Thais,'" and he played the melody line, and he had the band wailing in back of him, and it made for a helluva thing.

The full band in late 1937. Front row: Hy White, Saxie Mansfield, Joe Estren, Woody, Pete Johns, Ray Hopfer. Back row: Walt Yoder, Kermit Simmons, Clarence Willard, Frank Carlson, Joe Bishop, Tommy Linehan, Neal Reid. (From the Woody Herman Collection)

TOMMY LINEHAN: The first thing I always see in my mind when I think of Joe Bishop is the way he played fluegelhorn! Out of the right side of his mouth! A right-handed embouchure, we used to call it! It just looked wild, because he was originally a tuba player, and he converted to the fluegelhorn. But Joe was a real talent, and he was a real, real nice, very soft-spoken person and musician. He was the one that composed "Blue Prelude" when he was still with the Isham Jones band. He never came back after he got sick—oh, boy, what a shame. He was a little older than the rest of the boys.

   Until 1939, we were having a lot of fun! I think everybody was borrowing from everybody's father. We were in Cincinnati, playing at one of the hotels, and right across the river is Kentucky, where they had gambling. And I had a roommate, either Carlson or Mansfield, I don't remember. We're sitting there reading and there's a knock at the door, and here comes in Neal Reid, Walt Yoder, and Nick Hupfer. We needed some money, so we have an idea. We're going to take up a collection and anyone who has any extra money can donate a couple of bucks. We're going to send Nick across the river to Kentucky and let him play some poker for us. I had two or three dollars or something, and I think my roommate had about the same amount, so we just donated the money. We didn't see Nick the rest of the night, and woke up the next morning and found out he didn't do so well. I think we were worse off than before. [Laughter.]

WOODY: It didn't matter what agency you were with, or who was trying to help you. They just couldn't help you and they naturally had to make you feel better, and they would say, "We think we have something coming, call me tomorrow." There was a time in New York when I spent most of my life in the outer office trying to get in the inner office, just to get a single date anywhere. And the guy who almost always was sitting next to me was Glenn Miller. Glenn had been through the mill a couple of times already. He started a band and had to break it up and he was now down in the dregs. He borrowed from his parents and his wife's parents, and he was getting frantic. It got so bad for awhile, there were so many bands doing nothing, that they had a back door fixed, on the 22nd or 23rd floor in the RKO Building, where the guys in the band department could sneak out if the heat got too bad in the outer office.

In the fall of 1938, Nick Hupfer, the violinist, had left and the band had added one trumpet. Replacing guitarist Oliver Mathewson was Hy White.

HY WHITE: I remember vividly the first night, sort of an audition, in September 1938, a one-nighter in upstate New York. It was thrilling being in the midst of this big band, hearing those great harmonies and wonderful solos and playing real arrangements. I sat there quietly reading the charts. I do mean quietly, because without amplification, there was very little chance of anybody hearing the guitar. At some point later in the evening, Woody called out "Blues in B Flat." A slight panic came over me since not only had I never played the blues, I don't believe I ever heard the blues! I listened as Tommy Linehan began by playing three or four choruses. I had heard that each chorus consisted of only twelve bars and three basic chords. I listened as each soloist improvised, using rather strange off-the-chord notes, and creating a rather melancholy mood. About ten minutes had elapsed and we were still playing "Blues in B Flat" when Woody held the microphone in front of me and said, "Play one!" By now I had the feel of it. I more or less imitated what the others had played. Moreover, this was my kind of mood. Since I had not worked in about six months, left a young wife at home in Boston and needed this gig, it was not hard for me to make the guitar cry! I completed one chorus and Woody held up a finger as if to say "Go again, and again, and again." When my solos were finally over, my legs were so weak that I actually collapsed into my chair, completely spent. Then the most wonderful thing happened. All the horn players, probably led by Joe Bishop, began to applaud. That was a feeling hard to match. I had the job!

TOMMY LINEHAN: The man who gave us quite a boost when we were just about ready to flip our lids was Charlie Shribman of the Shribman Brothers out of Boston, just before 1939. The Shribmans were personal managers and owned or operated a string of ballrooms in the New England region. Cy Shribman had Glenn Miller. Charlie had done well for Artie Shaw, and so we decided to hire Charlie and he got the band going. He did such a good job getting us work, he eventually was voted in as a member of the corporation along with our lawyer.

WOODY: We did much better in the East in the early stages. New England was very band conscious. They could keep you working for months up there if you built anything. And you could build yourself in New England without records, without anything. Just show up and do a good job. It was the best band audience that the country had in those days.

We went to the Rice Hotel, in Houston, for a four-week contract. And they hurriedly got Cugat to come in and follow, to get us out. I think they flew them in! We opened at a noon session in the hot Houston sun, on the roof, and just played some quiet luncheon music. And I got a little memo from the manager of the hotel saying he was very happy with the band, and he thought our music was lovely. So we played a dinner session and we were all right. Then, that night, we played the late session on the roof for dancing. The night club setup. So now we decided to play a little of *our* music. And I got a memo the first thing in the morning. "You will stop playing those nigger blues or. . . ." Oh! We were out! It lasted, I think, less than a week!

As a matter of fact, we struggled and starved for several years, in spite of the fact that we had a so-called hit record called "Woodchopper's Ball" in '39. But it was well into '41, '42, before we actually started to become remotely successful. "Woodchopper's Ball" happened to be something we had been playing at the Roseland Ballroom. It's a head arrangement. Something that everyone in the band contributes his thoughts to. There wasn't really anything written until after we had been playing it awhile, and then Joe Bishop wrote down the parts. It was thrown in on the record date as a fourth tune. We were not depending on it for anything. I don't think most people, in most cases, ever know when they might have a potential hit in the bag.

TOMMY LINEHAN: "Woodchopper's Ball" is a prime example of what can evolve from jamming some blues. One evening at the Brooklyn Roseland, we decided to play some blues at a slightly up tempo. As usually happened, while Woody or one of the saxophones was taking his solo, the brass section huddled together softly trying some riffs to use in backing a soloist or for an ensemble figure. It just so happened the rhythmic-beat figure they came up with built up into the theme for "Woodchopper's."

Joe Bishop put everything together for us and it became one of our most popular efforts.

Incidentally, by this time we were more than a little bored with doing blues in the usual keys of C, B-flat, or E-flat, so we would take turns selecting the key. This time was my turn so I chose D-flat, and it was always done in that key until a stock arrangement was put on the market.

During the early years, the band's corporate officers and board were:

President	Woody Herman
Vice-President	Joe Bishop
Second Vice-President	Walter Yoder
Secretary/Treasurer	Neal Reid
Attorney/Comptroller	Michael L. Vallon
Board of Directors:	Woody Herman, Frank Carlson, Maynard Mansfield, Joe Bishop, Neal Reid, Walter Yoder, and Tom Linehan.

In April 1939, a 19-year-old girl named Mary Ann McCall joined the band for about seven months. She was discovered by song plugger Lou Levy (not the piano player) in a club called Frank Columbo's in Philadelphia. Mary Ann had been with Tommy Dorsey and with the Charlie Barnet band. She joined the Herman band at the Ritz-Carlton Hotel in Boston.

MARY ANN McCALL: We weren't too terribly successful in Boston, because it's a very Mickey-band town, especially in a hotel. When we got into the Trianon in Chicago, it was the same thing. Woody's was the first jazz band they put in there. We didn't even finish "Woodchopper's Ball," we played like *doot, doot, doot, doot*, and the next thing from the management was "Forget it!" And I think that Woody had to drive in from Milwaukee or Minnesota in freezing cold weather. Very bad!

Woody was trying to organize a kind of jazz band and a lot of the guys who were with the band played more Dixieland style. He was going into an Ellington mode, and trying to get with the Benny Goodman whole kind of thing, only not tight. I loved Glenn Miller's band and Les Brown's band and Tommy Dorsey's band, but they were all tight bands. Tight when they started to play. It wasn't relaxed like Count Basie or Woody Herman's band.

So I stayed with Woody for a time, and then I went back with Charlie Barnet's band in New York. And we went on the road for one and a half years. Any girl singer who has ever been on the road will say it's a very lonesome life for a girl singer who's 19 years old. And nothing but guys in the band, and you don't have any companionships or relationships, and if you don't fall into the things that they do and sit back and play poker and have a couple of drinks, you're not one of the gang, you know. So it was very hard for me, but I handled that.

WOODY: Mary Ann made her first recording with our band, "Bigwig in the Wigwam." She sounded like Betty Boop. Mary didn't really start to sing until she got with Charlie's band and started to develop. But she was a young jitterbug, and that was the type girl we needed. She could sure jitterbug!

Our first New York theater date was the Paramount with Bob Hope. This was when Hope had just scored via radio and made his first picture. In New York, you were as good as the picture that was billed with you, I don't care what theater it was or who you were. They gave him a picture called *The Magnificent Fraud*, and it was! We hit an all-time low in New York, and if you ever want to see a busted-up comic, this was Hope. After we were there a few days, Hope was doing his act and he had Jerry Colonna and his wife working with him, and at one of the matinees all of a sudden he started saying, "And I was standing out in front of the theater" . . . and there would go *phfft*. A sound like that! So he said, "Ah, some smart kid. It's nothing but kids in the theater, that's what it is." And he goes, "And then I went around" or something, and there would go *phfft* again! Right on the punch every time, right on the punch! You know, it was murder. So now they were bringing cops to go through the balconies and they were checking everything. This went on for two days. Every show! And by now, Hope was a very unnerved man, and so was everyone else, and he was to a point where he was accusing the band, and it got to be a very tight, bad situation. The wind-up was when they finally found out what it was. They were leaving the sound on from the picture, the speakers were behind the curtain, and there was a leak in the line. And every few seconds, you couldn't pick the intervals, naturally, it would go *pphhhffftttt*. And beautiful, with good hi-fi quality.

We followed Glenn Miller into the Glen Island Casino, and this was the summer Glenn hit, 1939, and it was probably one of the biggest music things that ever happened in this country. We had been waiting for about three years for our chance at the Casino, and they told us if we closed the season for Glenn—he wanted to go out on the road a little earlier—we would definitely get it the following year. Well, it was like following the world war to follow Glenn. We went in there and one night it was jam-packed with people waiting to get in, and the next night we were there and there was no one, only a couple old friends.

We wound up the season that way for two or three weeks, and we were never asked back. Blew it! Seems funny now, but it was pretty heart-breaking at that time. We closed out of so many places, you know. Sheer, stupid guts kept us going! Even though it was the age of bands happening, it was a really hard struggle for everyone almost without exception. Even Artie Shaw got a little taste of it in the early stages, and there were so many guys who never did survive.

We played some pretty interesting special parties with the first band. The most interesting one was our first big private party. It was a very hoity-toity party in Tuxedo Park in New York. The son had heard us play on a college campus or something, and he conned his parents into hiring us. But the invited guests didn't dig us at all. First of all, they sent us to one of the costumers in New York, and we had to get French sailor uniforms. So now we leap on the stand, and mute everything up as best we can because it's a marble room, but our tempos and everything were wrong. But the kid is all for us! He comes up after every tune and says, "Man, too much. Great!" And the people are hissing us and saying, "Get out, who are these bums?" But he's patting us on the back.

So comes the end of the gig, we were now ostracized completely, but the kid still was fighting this battle for music. I wonder what ever happened to him? I think his father drowned him, right after the dance. So now he gave each guy a bottle of champagne and it seemed that they had squab or something for the guests, and he had one of the flunkies wrap us up a squab apiece. And boy, we went home feeling like kings. You know, now life was beautiful again. We got food to take our old ladies and a bottle of wine. My champagne, incidentally, was flat when we opened it. This is how bad things can get! Didn't bubble at all!

The next morning, bright and early, like eight o'clock, the apartment house manager's beating on the door. "There's a phone call for you, very important. Emergency!" And I staggered down the stairs, got to the phone, and it's "Madame Guzunte." She said, "How many squabs, and how many bottles of champagne did your musicians steal last night?" All right? "And there are two French navy caps missing." This was our entree and our close of our society dates!

In August 1939, George T. Simon, who was then editor of *Metronome* magazine, first labeled Woody's band the Herd. The name stuck, although not immediately. The media began to refer to the band as the Herd in 1941.

GEORGE T. SIMON: The first time I called Woody's band the Herd was in an August 1939 issue of *Metronome* when I headed a short history of the band with "Herman's Herd Plays, Never Sings the Blues." Throughout the article, I kept calling the band the Herd.

For some reason or other, it was thought that I first called the band the Herd around 1944, when I reviewed what has been commonly known as the First Herd. I never quarreled with that, just let it ride, though I knew I had used the word several years earlier.

In September 1939 trumpeter Carroll (Cappy) Lewis was hired, replacing Clarence Willard. Prior to joining Woody, he had worked with the bands of Wally and Heine Beau, Stan Jacobsen, and Nick Harper (also known as Nick Hupfer).

CAPPY LEWIS: I was in Milwaukee with a band and Woody's arranger, Jiggs Noble, lived at that time near Milwaukee, and he came up to see the bandleader I was working for, who was a friend of his, and I guess he heard me, because about a week later I got a phone call from New York City, and boy, that was something! And Woody said, "How would you like to join the band?" And you know, the leader I was working for said, "I used to work for Woody, and I'll let you go, that's fine!" I was around 21, I believe. As soon as I joined the band, Jiggs, God bless him, wrote some nice little things for me. It seems like every other week, we would do a record date, and there would always be something nice for me to play.

I didn't belong to the New York musician's union, and I got called up there. They said, "You can't join the band, you don't have a New York card!" I said, "But my first job is in Boston." So they said, "Oh, well, that gets you off the hook!" So we played a hotel in the Back Bay section about six weeks, and that was a lucky thing, otherwise I would have had to go home to Milwaukee. There was another group alternating with us, The Six Spirits of Rhythm, a black group, and they were great, too!

I was playing cornet with the previous band when we all had cornets. It gets a little nicer, fatter tone than a trumpet, but I couldn't play cornet too long with Woody. I found that on the radio broadcasts and records, the cornet didn't have the penetrating quality that the trumpets had.

There was a little tension in the group. The band started off as a corporation when they left Isham Jones' band. When fellows would join the band, we came in on salary. The corporation would, at the end of a certain period, see how much money they had grossed and split it. So there was a little animosity there between us and the corporation. But from day to day, we were all human beings and it wasn't that bad.

"Woodchopper's Ball" I liked to play. Of course, we got tired playing it so much. We started every gig with that and then again maybe two or three times a night, and then in the theaters, that was our first number. But it was a loosely knit tune, loosely knit enough so it wasn't physically demanding.

Woody was Woody, he had a distinctive sound and style. The Bob Crosby band, in comparison, their music was all charts all the way down the line. It opened up here and there for solos, but it was more rigid in the respect that you were confined to a certain amount of time. But Woody was so gracious with us, he let us do anything we liked to do. If somebody had an idea without any music, we'd just start with a riff and progress from there. So I think, by and large, he got a sound that way, a looseness that was evident from his recordings. When we would record, we would have everything worked out in advance. But some nights, Woody would say, "Ah, men, somebody start something," and something would happen from it.

It would get out of hand once in awhile. For a while, Woody wanted to have a "glee club" in the band singing behind him. When he was singing ballads, we would come down and sing *oooh*s and *aaah*s behind him. So you know, there's always some "Peck's Bad Boys" around, so somebody would start with a little water pistol during the *oooh*s and *aaah*s. And, finally, the water guns weren't enough. We would just get a bucket of water. And Woody couldn't see what we were doing because he's singing to the audience. Well, he finally found out about it and things would tighten up for awhile.

WOODY: Our first road manager came after a couple of years, or maybe even longer. We were having trouble on some of the dates getting our money, so we hired a fellow by the name of Mike Vetrano, an ex-wrestler, and he looked very rough. He had the cauliflower ears and he was I'd say, 270, just as wide as he was tall. He really was a very mild, very religious man. But this you only found out after you knew him a little bit. From the day he started, we had no trouble about getting our money. He would just walk in the office and they'd start counting up old due bills or anything and lay it on him. He did a good job. He had been out with a couple of black bands prior to joining us. After he left, I think we got Jack Archer who had been a friend of mine, a music publisher. He was out of work in Los Angeles, and I hired him. And he lasted until he went into the Army, which was a couple of years. He later married Billie Rogers, the girl trumpet player.

By the end of 1939, the Woody Herman orchestra was beginning to achieve some national prominence via the live radio remote broadcasts and its recordings, especially of "Woodchopper's Ball."

CAPPY LEWIS: On "Blues on Parade," I had quite a bit to play, and it wasn't too long after I had been with the band that we did this [November 20, 1939]. And it was both sides of a 78 [rpm] record. I started out with a little jazz lick from "Rhapsody in Blue," and several months after the record had been released, Charlie Teagarden, a well-known trumpet player, said to someone in our band, "That Cappy Lewis, I really dug that open lick that he did on 'Blues on Parade!'" To me, that was very, very nice.

We opened at the Famous Door after Boston, shortly before Christmas, 1939. That was a marvelous place! We worked from about ten in the evening till four in the morning. And the Ink Spots were there with us. When we were off, they were on. We had a broadcast out of there. This was the original Ink Spots, and they were hot stuff in those days. They had valets, each of them, and one of the valets had his own valet.

TOMMY LINEHAN: Carol Kaye replaced Ella Harris as girl singer in late November 1939. She recorded "Smarty Pants" with the band in December. She was with us at the Famous Door and the Hotel Sherman, Chicago. She was secretly married to Bill Robbins, trumpet player with Tony Pastor's band. She had a good voice.

WOODY: The turning point came about when we went into the new Famous Door on 52nd Street. Basie had been there and a couple of other bands. We followed Charlie Barnet in, I think. This caused a little excitement around New York, and opened the door a little bit for us.

　　Sammy Cahn and Saul Chaplin were a couple of young, budding song writers, and Lou Levy [not the pianist] was their manager, and they all lived in a pad on 7th Avenue, across the street from Decca. And Lou was constantly trying to help us. As a matter of fact, he would borrow money from Sammy and lend it to us so we could get gasoline money to get out of town if we did get a date. And so, later on, when we wound up with a couple of hit tunes, I gave them to Lou [royalties], because we couldn't pay him for his help, you know. So we gave him "Woodchopper's Ball," "Blues on Parade," and some of those things.

On January 5, 1940, the Herman band went into Decca's New York studios and produced four titles. One of these, "It's a Blue World," features Woody in a nice, relaxed forties crooner mode punctuated with Hy White's rich-sounding, amplified guitar solo.

　　On February 5, six more titles were recorded in New York. One of them, "Blue Prelude," was Woody's first theme song. It established a blues mood from the first bar, Woody doing a "moody-blues" vocal with a nice, full-sounding tenor solo by Saxie Mansfield.

　　Later that month, Woody took the band into the Panther Room of the Hotel Sherman, in Chicago, for a successful extended engagement. Personnel during this period included Bob Price, Steady Nelson, Cappy Lewis (trumpets); Toby Tyler, Neal Reid (trombones); Joe Bishop (fluegelhorn); Saxie Mansfield, Nick Ciazza (tenor saxes); Herb Tompkins, Ray Hofner (alto saxes); Tommy Linehan (piano); Walt Yoder (bass); Frank Carlson (drums); Hy White (guitar); Carol Kaye (vocals); and of course Woody (clarinet, alto sax, and vocals).

　　In September 1940 the band played an engagement in the Terrace Room at the Hotel New Yorker in New York City. Woody recorded with a quartet, Linehan, Yoder, and Carlson, billed as "Woody Herman's Four Chips," on September 9, 1940.

CAPPY LEWIS: "Golden Wedding" was recorded in September 1940. On it, I would follow Woody, and I would make a statement, and Woody would make a statement, then I would go into a solo. And we featured this in the movie, *What's Cookin'?* "Golden Wedding" and "Blues on Parade" were both typical head jobs. No manuscripts written. We would just fake them. You know, the jazz trumpet players hardly ever played first trumpet. They would play second or third trumpet, so they could save their chops for the solos. And we did a thing called "Frenesi," and I played lead on that and they wanted me to get a nice, soft sound, so I said, "C'mon guys, everybody take out your handkerchiefs; and trombones, you get out your towels that you use to wipe the spit from the spit valves, and stuff them into your cup mute, and we'll get up to the microphone and see what kind of sound we get." And boy, it was just a beautiful sound, so nice and soft.

Dillagene Plumb joined, replacing Carol Kaye, as the band's female singer in the summer of 1940.

TOMMY LINEHAN: I went with Woody to interview Dillagene at the sorority house at Oklahoma A&M. We were working the prom there. She joined the band shortly after, and her first record was in September 1940. Dillagene married Frank Carlson.

In the fall of 1940, Joe Bishop was diagnosed as having tuberculosis, and was confined to Saranac Lake Sanatorium, in upper New York state. Before Joe left the band, he scored the superb classic twelve-bar blues entitled "Blue Flame," which would replace "Blue Prelude" in early 1941 as the band's theme song. "Blue Flame" remained the band's theme song for more than forty-five years. It was written because "Blue Prelude" and all other music licensed by the American Society of Authors, Composers and Publishers (ASCAP) was banned from the radio networks that year in the course of a struggle over licensing fees.

WOODY: Our first theme was "Blue Prelude." Joe Bishop wrote that. It was already a standard tune, and we used that until the ASCAP fight, and we couldn't use any ASCAP tunes on the air, and Joe—undercover, under wraps, during one intermission in the theater, because we had a broadcast between the shows—wrote out this little sketch on the blues, and we called it "Blue Flame," and that's been going on since about '41. In the case of "Blue Flame," it just happened. It was a necessity. We had to get something fast. We had played another thing we had in the book called "Casbah Blues." We actually used the styling of that for a theme, but a different melody line.

By the end of 1940, the band had added a third trombone, giving the brass section a fuller, fatter ensemble sound. Dillagene was replaced by a new girl singer, Muriel Lane. Her first recording was "Bounce Me Brother with a Solid Four," in January 1941.

In February 1941 a nucleus from within the big band, labeled "Woody Herman and his Woodchoppers," recorded "South" and "Fan It." The small group consisted of Cappy Lewis (trumpet); Neal Reid (trombone); Tommy Linehan (piano); Hy White (guitar); Walt Yoder (bass); Frank Carlson (drums); and Woody (clarinet and vocals). It's interesting to compare the vintage performance of "Fan It" with the later version done by the First Herd in May 1946.

CAPPY LEWIS: The original recording of "Fan It" was done by the small band, just one trumpet, one trombone, et cetera. And it's really Dixieland, I would say. Woody has always updated his musical style, but at that time, it was just plain clambake. We would do that once a night, and the crowd always ate it up.

In July 1941 the band made its first Hollywood movie. Originally entitled *Wake Up and Live*, it was released bearing the title *What's Cookin'?*. On July 18 the Herman crew had its debut at the new Hollywood Palladium. The Palladium engagement was extended for three months as the band gained popularity.

CAPPY LEWIS: In 1941 I came out to the Palladium with him. We were really about the second band to appear at the Palladium. Tommy Dorsey was the first band.

WOODY: It [the film *What's Cookin'*] was an opportunity. The Andrews Sisters were in it, and Donald O'Connor made his teen-age debut in it, after having been a little kid star many years before, so it was interesting. The director, Eddie Cline, who lives in Hollywood, was a very kind and very lovely gentleman. He used to amaze us and amuse us all day long while we were waiting to do something, with tales of what used to be the movies. He was one of the original Keystone Kops. And he also knew how to handle the movie moguls, evidently, because he had girls paid off in the main office, and if there was a producer or anybody from the front office on our set, we would get like a ten-minute warning. So the guys would be out playing touch football or baseball, and when we would get the cue, we would all rush in and play the same music we had been playing for a month. We had already recorded it and what the hell were we supposed to be rehearsing? Then they photographed you, and you sat there and emulated playing, and it was terribly monotonous to a professional musician.

On August 21 the band recorded six titles in Los Angeles. One was a chart entitled "Woodsheddin' with Woody." It moves at a bright tempo and demonstrates excellent clarinet work by Woody in a slightly "Goodmanish" mode. Linehan does nice "Basie-like" piano, and Saxie's big-sounding tenor swings.

Down Beat magazine, in its "New Numbers" column, ran the following caption with a photo of Charlotte Herman and the "new number" in the Herman family: "Here is the first photo of Woody Herman's new girl baby, Ingrid Herman, with her mother, Mrs. Charlotte Herman. She's the Hermans' first child, and was born in Los Angeles, September 3 [1941]."

WOODY: According to our calculations, and the doctor's, Ingie arrived about six weeks late. And most of that time we were in the Palladium ballroom, and it was driving me mad, and just about every customer that came to the place knew that we were expecting, and I spent more time during the course of the night giving them a negative answer, "No, the baby hasn't arrived yet," than I did playing music. So, during this period I went home one night and I fixed myself a drink and sat down and we talked for maybe thirty minutes and then Charlotte said, "Maybe you better call the doctor, I've been having pains now for the last few hours, and they've been arriving fifteen minutes apart or something," and I called the doc and he asked how often they came and so forth, and he said, "For God's sake, go back to bed and call me when they tighten up a bit." So it got down to every few minutes, and he said, "Hurry up and get her down here immediately!" Oh, God, this man was a big help! I nearly stripped the gears in the car, and got to the hospital, and I then sat down in the "sweat room," you know. This lawyer who was handling my affairs had a place a couple of blocks from there, and finally after I had sat up about nine hours, it *seemed* that length of time, he said, "Why don't ya come over to my place and just stretch out for a half hour, and if the phone rings, we'll go right back?" And sure enough, I got there and stretched out. And my mother-in-law called me and said, "Don'tcha want to see your baby?"

  That night, I went to work, and now I'm very happy and excited and completely whipped. And we went on the air. Evidently, the guys had this cleared for weeks unbeknownst to me, and I gave the down beat for the theme, and out came "Daddy." En masse they played this, and I didn't know what the hell was happening, and mentally I fired everybody. You know, like, "Whaddya doin' to me?"

On September 10 the band recorded its next blockbuster hit, "Blues in the Night," with Woody vocalizing Johnny Mercer's lyrics to Harold Arlen's melody.

WOODY: I had always sung since I was a child, and it just seemed logical, you know. To put it bluntly, if we weren't selling records on the old blue label, Decca, I would do a couple of vocals, because we knew they would sell.

Also in 1941, Woody did something virtually unheard of in those days: he hired a female trumpet player.

TOMMY LINEHAN: Of course, when we first heard of Billie Rogers, we didn't know if it was a she, a he, or an it, you know. But the gal came in and started playing trumpet, and we said, "Pretty good!" She played almost like a Louis Armstrong type of trumpet. I really liked Billie, it was great to hear someone who wasn't playing a thousand notes to the bar or continually working for an F above high C.

WOODY: She played very good trumpet. She played a lot like Roy Eldridge. Sammy Cahn heard Billie someplace in Los Angeles, and he became so enthused, he insisted I listen to her. We were on a recording date and he brought her over to play and sing a little. She sounded pretty good, so we added her. She stayed for a long time.

BILLY ROGERS: I joined Woody's band in October 1941. And I was with him over two years. I came from a family of musicians and started playing when I was about ten years old. My mother played piano. My father played violin, and I had an older brother, who died in his early twenties. He was really the genius of the family. He played almost everything and was a great arranger. I had perfect pitch and so did my older brother. I was nine years old before I knew it. I thought everybody heard music the same way I heard it.

I was living in California when Woody hired me. I think Woody, himself, has never been given any kudos at all for being brave enough to hire a female musician at the time he did. No one had done it, and the opportunity that he gave me was really something! Ozzie Nelson, I think, had a girl trumpet player, but she wasn't a featured part of the band at all, and I think that hardly anybody knew she was there. But Woody really stuck his neck out when he hired me. And I went through some very uncomfortable times, because I don't think, at heart, I was ever a trailblazer, but I think that I turned out to be one whether I wanted it or not! And some of the guys really made it uncomfortable for me! One trumpet player even left the band because he was terribly embarrassed even to have a woman in the section. They did accept me after a while, bless their hearts.

I don't think for one minute that Woody would have hired me if I hadn't also been a vocalist. And there were times that I was the only girl vocalist on the band. I know this played an important part in it, but I still think that the man really stuck his neck out to hire me in the first place, and I'm very grateful for all the wonderful experiences that he gave me.

Cappy Lewis was a very underrated trumpet player. I liked Vido Musso, also. He was on the band when I left. I left Woody to form my own band.

Joining the band at the same time as Billie Rogers was featured vocalist Carolyn Grey. Carolyn was a lovely honey blonde who had won first prize in a San Francisco amateur singing contest while still in high school. After graduation, she auditioned with Woody and got the job.

The Herman band at the end of 1941 was no longer an unknown musical entity, but had started capturing enthusiastic media coverage. In January 1942, Frederick C. Othman wrote in the *Chicago Sun*: "Maybe you'd be interested in the young man who now has one of the most popular dance bands in America. Six months ago, nobody much would listen to it. 'And then all of a sudden we got hot,' Herman said. 'It wasn't us, either! It was the customers. We played like we always had, but the customers suddenly began to act like they liked it.'"[1]

FRANK CARLSON: Every place we would play, and all of the different colleges and places like that, people would just scream, you know, and stuff like that. And of course that gave me a hell of a thrill to know that people enjoyed the band that much.

In early 1942 drummer Frank Carlson came down with appendicitis, and Davey Tough was brought in as a substitute. Later, during the first two years of the First Herd, Tough would be an integral part of that band's formidable rhythm section.

From 1937 into 1946, Woody and Charlotte's primary residence was at 7711 35th Ave., Jackson Heights, Long Island, New York. However, soon after Ingrid was born, it was necessary for the family to rent apartments in the Hollywood area, because they would be going back and forth between the East and West Coasts. A reason for that was the fact that the Hollywood film studios had decided to cash in on the popularity of big bands. Consequently, many of the popular big bands found themselves busily playing before the cameras. Benny Goodman, Glenn Miller, Charlie Barnet, Tommy Dorsey, Harry James, and Jimmy Lunceford were all involved in films by the end of 1941. Some films featured several big bands.

During this period, one of the most successful showcases for the vastly popular big bands was movie theaters. Movie houses like the Paramount, Capitol, and Loew's State in New York, the RKO in Boston, and the Orpheum in Los Angeles would feature a name big band, with various other entertainers, and generally a first-run feature film. The theater bookings were grueling for the big band musicians. A band would play up to six shows a day between film showings, starting work at eight or nine in the morning and continuing after midnight. The Paramount in New York had a unique feature. When the movie ended, the band rose up on a hydraulically operated stage originating in the basement, as its theme could be heard playing. It was a novel, dramatic entrance. When Woody played "Blue Flame," the lights would be out and as the band rose, the only visible objects would be Woody's hands and his clarinet painted with phosphorescent paint.

The film *What's Cookin'?* opened in theaters across the country in February 1942. One New York review of the film said, " . . . But since the audience is obviously being lured to the theater by Woody Herman's piping and the crooning of the Andrews trio, the story and supporting cast of the picture are of small importance."

April 1942 appeared to be the time of the Woody Herman Band's "official" acceptance into America's growing coterie of famous big bands. Across the nation, the media carried feature stories about the Herman band's role in *What's Cookin'?*, and reviews recounted the band's impressive performances in theaters, ballrooms, hotels, and other venues.

WOODY: We played theaters sometimes forty weeks out of the year. Miserable existence! At one point, we'd just go from theater to theater, and on our closing night in one theater in one city, we'd get on a train, and get off in the morning and go to the next theater and start again. And there was a big deal among the guys about who had uppers and who had lowers on the Pullman car. We'd draw straws out of the hat and the whole gimmick, and then of course, no one went to bed at all, you just skipped it! Because I used to set up bar either in the drawing room at the end of the car, or in the can. And I had a little portable bar the guys laid on me. A little leather case, a beautiful thing.

CAPPY LEWIS: Woody had a manager, and he also had some lawyers, Mike Vallon and Chubby Goldfarb. Whenever you would ask for a raise, it had to go through them. These lawyers were all right, but they were squares. Black and white, and a figure is a figure. And they knew absolutely nothing about a musician's way of life. They just couldn't fathom it. So when I asked Woody for a raise, he said, "Sure, go ask Mike," and Mike would say, "You want a ten dollar a week raise? My gosh, if my secretary got a two cent an hour raise, she would think she was in heaven!"

Dizzy Gillespie had written some arrangements for Woody and one of the arrangements he hadn't got his money for. So he came over to see us at the New Yorker hotel, and he says, "Woody, I haven't been paid for my arrangement," and Woody says, "Go up and see Mike!" And he goes to Mike's office, and they're kind of disregarding him. So he got a big knife out of his pocket and carefully gets the blade out and starts paring his nails. Now, the secretary runs into Mike's office and says, "That black man out there has a big knife!" And Mike says, "Show him in! Show him in!" So Diz went in, got his check, and left with no problems.

WOODY: Dizzy subbed for us one time, I think it was a week we did at the Apollo Theater. Dizzy had this great urge to blow all the time. He would stick in a note whenever he could. He would go straight through, without stopping. Like "Let the other fellows play the parts, and I'll fill in," you know. Many times, it got out of hand, but he was a funny cat. I enjoyed his company!

He showed up with a couple of arrangements at different times, and then he got to write a few things for us, and that's how I got to know him. And I thought he wrote "the end!" He did a thing for us called "Swing Shift" during the war. We never recorded it, but it was beautiful. There was simplicity, and it swung like mad.

Dizzy also wrote a chart entitled "Down Under," recorded by the Herd in July 1942. Among his other contributions to the Herd was "Woody 'n' You," which for some unknown reason the Herman band didn't record until 1979.

The band began to go through a period of change in style and conception, as the Herd developed more pulsating rhythmic qualities like those of the Jimmie Lunceford band, with harmonies reminiscent of Duke Ellington.

WOODY: I wanted to do something different with the band. I loved the voicings of the Duke Ellington band, and I got Dave Matthews to write for us.

The wartime draft was taking its toll in the ranks of the big bands, and Woody's was no exception. Later, Woody told jazz writer Gene Lees, "As each member was drafted (I don't think anybody enlisted), I bought his stock in the band."[2] By 1944, Woody had purchased the entire band.

In the middle of 1942, James C. Petrillo, president of the American Federation of Musicians, imposed a ban on musicians recording for the commercial companies. The rationale was that if the record companies couldn't devise a method of compensating member musicians for the use of their recordings on radio programs and in jukeboxes, they shouldn't be able to record at all. Had it not been for the efforts of collectors to save the many live radio air checks of the big bands (and these did not surface until decades later), a vital period of jazz history would have been lost.

RAY SHERMAN: From the latter part of June until September 1942, I was the band boy. The band came and played the Riverside here in Milwaukee. And on the way into Milwaukee, somewhere down South, the truck went off the road into a bayou, and all the instruments were damaged. And they had to get a new panel truck, and all the guys had to get new instruments, and Dick Ables, the regular band boy, ended up in the hospital. The band was here in town and they were getting ready to continue the tour with a new panel truck, and there was no band boy available. So Woody asked me if I would do him a favor and go out with the band. Then we got out to California on our way to the Palladium, after about ten or twelve one-nighters on the way. Woody said, "You can come back to Milwaukee once we get out there, or stay if you want to." I stayed. I quit my job. It was wartime, it was uneasy, you didn't know when you

The Herman band at the Hollywood Palladium, 1942. Front row, L to R: Carolyn Grey, Woody, Mickey Folus, Sam Rubinowitch, Pete Mondello, Jimmy Horvath. Second row: Tommy Linehan, Hy White, Neal Reid, Tommy Farr, Wally Nims. Back row: Walt Yoder, Frank Carlson, Cappy Lewis, Chuck Peterson, George Seaburg, Billie Rogers. (Courtesy Ray Sherman)

were going to get drafted. But I joined the band, I think it was in Lacrosse, Wisconsin. I took the train the next day after the band left here. We got out to the Hollywood Palladium, and we stayed there for a long time, all summer, practically. Then the band played some side dates, and then I got my draft notice. And the band was coming back to Minneapolis, so I left the band in Minneapolis and came home. It was quite a thrill!

In November 1942 the Herman band was back in the Paramount Theater in New York helping the house celebrate its sixteenth anniversary. The bill was headlined "The Woody Herman Orchestra, and Hazel Scott."

About this time, Tommy Linehan left the band. He was replaced by James George (Jimmy) Rowles, who came to Woody's band via Benny Goodman's band.

JIMMY ROWLES: I took Tommy Linehan's place, joining Woody in the fall of 1942. And I got there just in time to get my Christmas present, which was a beautiful Gladstone bag. And I stayed with Woody until they drafted me the following June.

The new year, 1943, started for Woody and the Herd at the RKO Boston Theater. In February, the band was back in Hollywood to make its second film, *Wintertime*, starring ice skater Sonja Henie and Cesar Romero.

WOODY: That was a budget picture. We did several musicals for them. There were a lot of cheap musicals made during the war years.

Vido Musso was in the band on and off for a long time, but he never recorded with our band. He'd always be there when there was a recording ban on. He made a couple of movies with us. As a matter of fact, 20th Century Fox must have spent, one morning alone, $40,000 or $50,000. The ice wasn't hard enough, and they decided they would do a couple of little bits with the band, like scenes. No music! We did a snow thing riding in a sleigh. The Austrian actor Cuddles [S. Z.] Sakall was in the film. And they liked Vido because he looked like he might have been an Italian actor or something. So they gave him one stinking line! "Hello, I'll see you later," or something. This took one whole morning and part of the afternoon in ninety-degree temperature outdoors. With all the lights, it must have been 100, and we're in fur coats, ski boots, with a fur robe over us in a sleigh, with the guys making it go up and down, with a montage in the back. And Cuddles, like, was going "straight up." He says, "Vat's the matter wit you, boy?" And Vido's going, "Well, er ah, I goofed!" Then he finally made it, the guy said "Cut!," and all the grips, electricians, everybody applauded . . . "Bravo! Bravo!" And Vido is walking around the set, "Thank you! Thank you!"

And Cesar Romero was in the picture. And Vido decided that he was his type of fellow, like he wanted to be like Romero. Well, poor Cesar didn't have a chance. We were on that picture for eleven weeks, and he had his little dressing room and the minute we had a break of any kind, Vido would be in Cesar's room, like taking charge, making coffee and all that, running him out of his own dressing room. He'd say "How do you get like you? Did you get an agent? How do I look? I look pretty good, right?"

Future bandleader Les Elgart was on the Herman band during the filming of *Wintertime* and is seen in the trumpet section in the film.

LES ELGART: I really became an old man doing one-nighters with Woody. We never stopped. We just kept on and on. Of course, we had it easier then, because we would play theaters that would last for a week, so we had a rest on occasion.

Vido Musso, the tenor player, kept trying reeds. He drove us all nuts. Oh, man! I'll never forget that between shows, when we traveled by train, Vido would be trying out reeds all night. I was ready to kill him or throw him off the train every day.

In addition to Vido Musso, tenor saxophonist Pete Mondello joined the band, replacing Herbie Haymer.

WOODY: We had two or three barbers in the band. Pete Mondello was probably one of the most excellent barbers we ever had, and as a matter

The band tours a brewery in 1943. Front row, L to R: Skippy DeSair, Woody, possibly Dave Matthews (arranger), Jimmy Horvath. Second row: Chuck Peterson, Neal Reid, Cliff Leeman, Jack Archer (manager), unidentified band boy. Third row: unidentified trombonist, Carolyn Grey, Billie Rogers, Pete Mondello. Fourth row: Cappy Lewis, Hy White, Tommy Farr, George Seaburg, Vido Musso, Les Robinson. (From the Woody Herman Collection)

of fact, I went so far with Pete, I got him all the equipment, the thinning shears and all the best steel, and a beautiful kit, and had barber coats, two, one in salmon color and one in white made with "Pete" on top, and on the back, "Woody Herman's Orchestra." You never saw such a clean-cut looking band in your life.

During the summer of 1943 the band returned to the Hollywood Palladium. In July, drummer Frank Carlson quit to remain in California. Woody auditioned a drummer (recommended by Artie Shaw) who played in the house band at San Quentin Prison, and was about to be released. After four nights of tryouts at the Palladium, and after buying him clothing and a new set of drums, Woody decided the man just wasn't working out and called the whole thing off. Eventually, Cliff Leeman from Charlie Barnet's band filled the drum chair.

Anita O'Day joined the band as female singer for a brief time, replacing Carolyn Grey.

BILLY MAY: I played trumpet in Woody's band during May, June and July 1943. We played one-nighters in San Diego, then the Palladium, then the Orpheum Theater in downtown Los Angeles. It was a great, relaxed band, and a pleasure to work in. In 1955, I did some arranging for Woody.

From the spring of 1943 until the end of the year, the draft continued to cause turnover in the band's ranks. Trombonist Eddie Bert, tenorist Allen Eager, altoist Johnny Bothwell, who would gain some fame the following year with the Boyd Raeburn Band, all came through the ranks briefly. Walt Yoder was drafted, replaced by bassist/composer Gene Sargent. Trumpeters Billie Rogers and Chuck Peterson both left; Billie to form her own orchestra, and Chuck for military induction.

Beginning in late summer, a string of replacements came in from the Charlie Barnet aggregation, starting with drummer Cliff Leeman and bassist Greig Stewart "Chubby" Jackson. Also joining from the Barnet band was singer Frances Wayne, who had worked with several name bands and was working as a single when Woody dropped into a Boston nightclub to hear her. Two days later, she was with the band. In December a talented pianist/composer named Ralph Burns replaced Dick Kane in the piano chair. Ralph, like Frances Wayne, was from Boston and had worked with Frances's brother, Nick Jerret, in his band.

WOODY: Ralph was recommended to me by a group of newcomers to the band, people like Jackson and Neal Hefti and Frances Wayne, because they had worked with Charlie Barnet's band and were pretty much impressed with the young man. And he brought in a couple of things, and I, too, was impressed. He was 21 at the time. The very first arrangement he brought in was "I've Got the World on a String," which we recorded several years later. That was his first attempt. A very shy kid, very gentlemanly, less like a jazz musician than most of them.

CHARLIE BARNET: Woody and I bumped heads a few times there, but we were always good friends, at least I always felt that way. Some of those who left the band in '43 to join him, I wasn't too sorry to see go. I won't mention any names.

As far as that "stealing the men" was concerned, that went on all the time in those days, and although outsiders may have thought there was a lot of ill-feeling about it, there really wasn't, because in most cases, if you wanted to keep the person, all you'd have to do is raise his salary. You'll find that the same group of musicians pulsated around from one band to the other.

CAPPY LEWIS: I left Woody in 1943, to go with Tommy Dorsey's band. I asked for a 50-dollar-a-week raise, because I knew that is what I could make in Tommy Dorsey's band. Up to that point, Woody had been very,

The last edition of "The Band That Plays the Blues," about November 1943. Cappy Lewis, Bobby Guyer, Ben Stabler, Nick Travis, Ray Wetzel (trumpets), Eddie Bert, Al Mastren, Ed Kiefer (trombones), Johnny Bothwell, Chuck DiMaggio (alto saxes), Allen Eager, Pete Mondello (tenor saxes), Skippy DeSair (baritone sax), Dick Kane (piano), Chubby Jackson (bass), Cliff Leeman (drums), Hy White (guitar). (From the Woody Herman Collection)

very gracious about giving me raises. But he felt that fifty dollars was just too much. And I said, "That's what Tommy offered me," and so he said, "Join Tommy, then."

I was with Tommy about six months, then he broke up his band and he went back to New York to reorganize. He only took one or two men with him, and I wasn't one of them. So I called Woody and said, "I'm available!" So he gave me the fifty dollars raise that he wouldn't give me before, God bless him!

Joining the Herd in the fall of 1943 was bassist Chubby Jackson. Chubby had been active with dance bands and show business since 1937. With his extroverted personality and ear for talent, he became the catalyst, cheerleader, and chief talent scout for many Herman Herds.

CHUBBY JACKSON: It was a gentle dance band that leaned quite heavily on arranger Dave Matthews, and Duke Ellington's influence was evident. At that time, April 1944, we were recording for Decca Records, using some of Duke's key players as soloists, Ben Webster on tenor sax, Johnny Hodges on alto sax, and trombonist Juan Tizol.

Two new replacements late in the year were powerhouse trumpeters Ray Wetzel and Nick Travis. Both players would come into prominence in big band jazz circles: Wetzel with the Herman First Herd, and later with the Stan Kenton, Barnet, and Dorsey bands. Travis would become widely known as a New York-based jazz trumpeter on numerous jazz recording dates in the fifties and sixties. By October, trombonist Neal Reid was in the Marines.

Trombonist Ed Kiefer joined from the Bob Chester band, and somehow Woody was able to borrow the rich-and-breathy-sounding tenor saxophonist Ben Webster from the Ellington band for some recording dates in late 1943 and early 1944.

In November the band recorded "The Music Stopped (But We Were Still Dancing)." There's a distinctive Miller-ish clarinet lead on top of the saxes introducing Frances Wayne's lovely vocal. This was a preview of shades to come with the loose rhythm section and Chubby's steady, driving beat, and Ben Webster's fervent and distinctive solo. On November 17 the band recorded Gene Sargent's "Basie's Basement" with Chubby soloing on bass, lightly riffing saxes and brass, a Hy White guitar solo, an articulate Ben Webster tenor, and a statement from Woody's ebullient clarinet. Also cut was the more commercially popular "Who Dat Up Dere?," with vocal by Woody and ensemble chorus with some more Webster tenor and Bothwell on alto.

The events occurring in the last months of 1943 were only a sampling of things to occur with the Herman band in the next three years. A developmental pattern had occurred in the seven-year history of the "Band That Plays the Blues." It was about to become Woody's most successful band, in terms of financial worth and public acclaim. This band would be legendary with musicians and fans alike. It would be brilliant and modern in approach, yet never sacrifice the swing beat basic in all the Herman bands.

As Woody told this author in our first interview, "It began to happen already in 1943." The nucleus of musicianship was now available to define the character of the band that would be known as Woody Herman's First Herd.

3.

The First Herd
1944-1946

The numbering of the early Herman bands has caused much confusion among fans and musicians. A few individuals consider Woody's first band, or "The Band That Plays the Blues," the "First Herd," but among the majority of music critics and writers, "The First Herd" refers to the band of 1944–1946. Naturally, the First Herd wasn't labeled as such until years later, after the Second Herd or Four Brothers Band.

WOODY: The First Herd was unique for that period. I think it was the best band in the world at that time.

By 1944 Woody, Charlotte, and Ingie made their West Coast residence at the Garden of Allah, a famous hotel-apartment complex at 8150 Sunset Boulevard in Hollywood, built in 1921 by the noted actress Alla Nazimova. The Garden was a favorite with Hollywood luminaries, including such residents as Robert Benchley, Tallulah Bankhead, John Barrymore, Clara Bow, Marlene Dietrich, W. C. Fields, Errol Flynn, Greta Garbo and Gloria Swanson. The hotel also attracted some of the better-known writers who had come to Hollywood to work at the studios, including F. Scott Fitzgerald and John O'Hara. In 1950 long after its heyday, the 3.5-acre property was sold to Lytton Savings and Loan, which tore down the rambling collection of Spanish-style bungalows and built its home office on the site.

WOODY: It was a group of motley buildings that were practically like huts, for which they received a fabulous amount of money. The location was very good and it was a good address. The pool was the best thing in the place. It was an extremely large, sort of kidney-shaped pool, very beautiful. The buildings were grouped around this pool and there was a main building with a few hotel rooms and a dining room. The place was made up of mostly transients, people who were in Hollywood for a little while to do a picture or two—Louie Calhern was one—and then back to New York.

Bob Benchley and I were neighbors. We got to be quite good friends. In Southern California, it's always been pretty much an early-to-bed town. The bars close at two. If you walked into the Garden, all the lights would be out at 2:30, and everyone asleep at 3:00. And Bob would arrive home about that time. The only villa that would have a light on would be ours, because I would be just beginning to settle down and relax, have a couple of drinks, talk the day over with my wife, and we would hear a little scraping sound on the shutters and it would be Bob. I would open the door and look out and he would say, "How are you? I just wanted to say goodnight!" "Well, Bob, why don't you come in and have a nightcap?" "Oh," he would say, "I couldn't interrupt you people and barge in like this." I would have to go through this same procedure every night, and con him and talk to him, and after about ten minutes he would come in. Then he would proceed to empty me out of what Scotch I had. At seven in the morning, he'd give me a very polite "Thank you," and take his leave and go about ten paces to his place and pick up his little bag where he had his cold martinis to take to the studio and he would leave and go directly to work. I don't know when this man ever slept, except in a chair, for an hour at a time.

He had a butcher's apron made out of black leather. He was very proud of this, and he wore it often. He had two different ways he wore this apron, one with shorts and one without. And he would answer the door and either invite the guest in or send him on his way, and turn around and walk away bald-ass. It was beautiful.

The lamentable Petrillo/AFM recording ban continued until November 1944, but thanks to inspired performances on live remotes and the CBS Old Gold radio show later in the year, the band continued to gain in popularity.

Through some unexplained legal maneuvers, the band was able to record some excellent radio transcriptions that were released later on the Decca Label. In January the band recorded a group of transcriptions at World Studios in New York, still utilizing the big sound of tenorist Ben Webster. "Noah," one of the titles recorded, has some nice Cappy Lewis "plunger" trumpet, good tenor work from Webster, and Woody singing a novelty version of the Biblical account. In "I'll Get By," the popular wartime ballad, Woody, not surprisingly, adds a twelve-bar blues strain to the lyrics.

Some of these recordings hint at the excitement that the band would generate in a few short months. It is unfortunate that the early efforts of the First Herd on the last Decca recordings of December 1944 never received the same kind of recognition as the Columbia years of 1945–1946.

On January 10, the band left New York for Hollywood to make its third film, United Artists' *Sensations of 1945*, starring Dennis O'Keefe and Eleanor Powell. For Cappy Lewis, the first event after the film was receipt of his "Greetings from Uncle Sam." Vido Musso returned to the band briefly during the early months of the year and is seen in the *Sensations* film. Cappy Lewis was replaced by a Dizzy-bebop-influenced trumpeter named Neal Hefti. He had been trumpeter and/or arranger for Earl Hines and Charlie Barnet, prior to a tenure with Horace Heidt.

NEAL HEFTI: Woody was doing a picture called *Sensations of 1944*, but since the picture didn't come out until 1945, they retitled it *Sensations of 1945*. Chubby was there. Ralph Burns was there. Frances was there. I knew them all from the Charlie Barnet days. I replaced Cappy Lewis, and he had this great trumpet solo book. I had been with Horace Heidt, which was a great band, but you know, there were no solos in that band, so I joined Woody.

The author asked Neal how the new bop sounds and harmonies had influenced him at that point in his life.

NEAL HEFTI: I had already been "affiliated." I became a Dizzy Gillespie fan when I saw him in Omaha while I was still in high school and he was with Cab Calloway's band. So when I went to New York in 1941, Dizzy was one of the first people I found, which wasn't very hard because he was always someplace on 52nd Street. I think the first time I saw him, he was working with a little group led by Benny Carter.

The advanced harmonic patterns of bebop were coming rapidly to the music scene. Charlie Parker and Dizzy Gillespie had both spoken, and their echoes influenced Neal Hefti's compositions and began to be reflected in the conceptions of a majority of soloists in the band.

Replacing pianist Dick Kane early in January was a talented 21-year-old pianist/composer from Newton, Massachusetts, Ralph Burns. He had taken piano lessons in the Boston area, then attended the New England Conservatory of Music. Burns had worked in the bands of Charlie Barnet and Nick Jerrett.

Neal Hefti and Ralph Burns became a formidable duo of composer/arrangers for the Herman band. Hefti's use of bop elements combined well with the warm moods of Burns, whose chief influences were Stravinsky, Ravel, Eddie Sauter, and the Ellington/Strayhorn team.

RALPH BURNS: I lived with Frances' family for quite a while. Her brother, Nick Jerrett, was the leader of the band. I was the piano player and arranger for him right after high school. We played around Boston. This was during the first part of World War II, '42 maybe. Frances was a wonderful lady and I worked 52nd Street with her. We worked Kelly's Stables and the Famous Door. Then she went on to Charlie Barnet, and I think she told Charlie about me.

I joined Woody right after Frances and Chubby Jackson, because they recommended me. I was with Charlie Barnet's band with them.

It seems to me that my first arrangement for Woody was "Happiness Is Just a Thing Called Joe." I had done it for Charlie, and when I came to Woody, he asked me to do it for him because Frances wanted to sing it. So I really did the same arrangement. Originally, I did the same arrangement for Mary Ann McCall with Charlie's band. There was a whole bunch of them that I did at the beginning, "World on a String" and "Happiness."

Burns remained chief arranger, and a major contributor to the Herd's library, well into the mid-sixties, and became a counterpart to Ellington's Strayhorn or Kenton's Rugolo in relation to Woody.

In March the band was back in New York at World Studios, recording eight more titles for radio transcription. "Irresistible You" is another sentimental and sensitive Frances Wayne ballad with the distinctive sound of the First Herd's rhythm section. Chubby's bass is prominent, and there is a rich clarinet solo by Woody. "It Must Be Jelly" features a humorous vocal by Frances, Woody, and the band and an early example of some bop figures in the brass section. The effect of Woody's and Frances' vocals is reminiscent of some of the Roy Eldridge/Anita O'Day recordings with Gene Krupa. This latter chart was played innumerable times during this period and was popular with the fans.

A few days later, four more titles were recorded. Apparently, two-and-a-half-year-old Ingie Herman was developing some vocabulary, as the lightly swinging Dave Matthews chart recorded at that March 29 session was entitled "Ingie Speaks." It features a tight saxophone riff chorus, Woody's Goodman-like lower-register clarinet, with the brass riffing behind an unidentified trombone, some Georgie Auld tenor (he was briefly with the band), and Hy White going out in style with a nicely constructed solo, his last recorded effort with the band. In March, he was the oldest member of "The Band That Plays the Blues" in seniority. When he left, he was replaced by guitarist Billy Bauer.

HY WHITE: By 1944, I had really had enough of the road. The glamour had worn off, "Detroit looked like Cleveland," I missed my family, and the band was going through a drastic style change. So I departed to try my luck at freelancing in New York. I did enjoy a successful career as a studio player, teacher, and author, but it is very possible that I may never have enjoyed that success, had it not been for my association with Woody.

BILLY BAUER: Woody called and asked me to come and play with the band. They were leaving the next night. I told him I couldn't, as it was my daughter's birthday. He asked me how old she was, then said, "Look, tomorrow, go to Mr. Goldfarb's [Woody's New York manager's] office, and sign a contract, and meet us in Detroit." When I arrived, the only one I knew was Flip Phillips. The rhythm section was Ralph Burns, Davey Tough, and Chubby Jackson. I guess they all said, "Okay!"

In early April the band was back at World Studios in New York, recording with added Ellington players: alto saxophonist Johnny Hodges, valve trombonist Juan Tizol, and trumpeter Ray Nance. Among the titles recorded was the Ellington/Juan Tizol classic "Perdido," featuring solos by Woody on clarinet, Tizol, Hodges, Nance, and tenorist Pete Mondello.

WOODY (on the use of the Ellington players):   It was a transition period for us. I had become quite ambitious about trying to create a better band, and I wanted to have better players. The war had come along and pretty much threw our band to the wind, and consequently, if I was going to be around, I was going to try to improve the standard of what we were doing. Working with our band gave them a little independence, which they sought. And as long as I had record dates they could have them as far as I was concerned, because they were the epitome.

By midsummer of 1944 the First Herd would be galvanized into a potent swing machine. Before this could happen, some additional personnel changes came about in each of the orchestra's four sections. In April, drummer Cliff Leeman gave his notice.

WOODY: What we were really looking for was a drummer who could help to swing the band, and at that point we weren't looking for a soloist or anything else. If he could do it, well swell. But the main thing was to get someone who could fit into the group. The only thing that bugs me with drummers is when the guy's time is bad. And there are plenty of those. You know, moving tempos! Each chorus is at a different speed. Frankie Carlson stayed about six or seven years, and after him we got Cliff Leeman. And there were times when Cliff reached some great heights. After Cliff, we made the luckiest move that I can ever remember when we got Davey Tough. By this time, the band went through the turnover change, where we were coming out of "The Band That Plays the Blues" into the First Herd.

   It seems that Cliff Leeman had recommended Chubby [Jackson] very highly, because I had been getting wires for months, in 1943, from my New York lawyer, Goldfarb. Every time I'd write him or call him that I needed a trombone player or a saxophone player or a trumpet player, I'd get a wire in return: "Can't find any of those, but Chubby Jackson's available!" And this was bugging me because I didn't know who in the hell

Chubby Jackson was. What kind of a name was that, and what does he play? And finally, when Leeman joined the band he said, "Oh, man, he's crazy! Like he can get laughs. He does a lot of stuff!" So that's how come we hired Chubby! We were playing theaters, and the first show was, I think, in Youngstown, Ohio. It was a split week with Akron. And the first show that Chubby played with the band, man he was dancing up a storm! Not too many bass notes, but there was plenty of action on that stand! So after the show, I said to Leeman, "What the hell is with this guy?"

So Leeman gave him a big pep talk and said, "Hey, in this band, like, you don't have to do any of that stuff, just swing, man! Wail! That's all that counts!" So the next show, he still danced it up. It took about four days before he came down from dancing, like where you could find the bass line. But when he did, it started a whole new beef, because he and Leeman now started to argue, and after a couple of weeks it was a battle of nerves up there on the stand. Leeman was cussing him and he was cussing Leeman, and Leeman was the guy who recommended him. So finally, by now, Chubby had made his worth felt, he was valuable to us, so we decided to get a different drummer. And I decided that Davey Tough would be the guy for our band and, of course, all these guys put me down and said, "Well, man, he's a Dixieland drummer!" I said, "I don't know what kind of a drummer he is. The only thing I know is that he'll keep better time than anybody in the whole world, and this thing will swing like you've never felt it or heard it." So we sent for Davey, and these guys immediately were "embalmed"! They never heard anything like this in their lives. I don't think I've heard anything since like it either!

CHUBBY JACKSON: Davey came in and he was like the "grandfather" of the band. I had a strange feeling about that because he was so much older than all of us kids and I was saying to myself, "He plays great!" I ended up learning so much from this man. We would be on the bus and discuss the concepts of adventures in rhythm, and how to try certain new things. And he was an advocate of nonmetronomical time. He didn't feel that a band should finish precisely where it started.

It was just starting with the bop sounds, and there was a lot of fire with these younger players and in the writing of Ralph and Neal and Bill Harris, and we felt like if we brought somebody in that's close to 40, it might suffer, because it would go back a generation. And I was totally wrong because Dave ended up teaching us all what to do. If we were lagging behind, he would hit five straight notes on the cymbals to let us know where the time was. And he also had different cymbals for different instruments, and one for an ensemble sound that had the nuts and bolts in it. He took out all the nuts and bolts but one, and gave it a gentler, "sizzle" sound, instead of a heavy Chinese gong sound. He always wanted to play on a certain ride cymbal when a tenor was playing, or if a trumpet was playing up in the treble. And as I mentioned, he had that nonmetronomic philosophy of playing with the soloists. Then when the ensemble came in, it was his turn to take over. And if a bass and a drum cooked together, the entire band would really make it. This was his philosophy.

WOODY: He had probably the greatest collection of cymbals. I know guys have been looking for them for years. I don't think anybody ever wound up with them. The way he played them made the big difference. He would never be caught with what the kids are trying today with the rivet-type cymbal. Back in those days, they used the Chinese-type cymbal with the rivet around loose, and it made a terrific roar, but it was great. Davey used to get a thing going where it actually sounded like a shuffle and yet it wasn't at all. It's just that it was swinging so hard that it came out a shuffle. You heard eight beats to the bar and he was only playing four. We'd get into a final shout and the band was screaming, and you could hear him right even or above, with this thing, and it was really pulsating.

Overnight, the guys in the band became number one fans and then they would go on bended knees, like to say hello, and Dave didn't dig this at all. He was a very sensitive man and he didn't like any of that adoration shit. But he got a boot out of them. He enjoyed them.

NEAL HEFTI: I used to sit next to Davey Tough, and I used to be mesmerized by his cymbal sound. He just had a very good sound on the drums, the first one that I ever played with that I became conscious of his sound more than the time or tempo. The drums became a very melodic instrument to me for the first time.

CHUBBY JACKSON: He was a little, bitty guy with a little, bitty foot. And he couldn't play with his straight street shoes on. He had little black, laceless rubber-soled shoes that he would wear. He tuned his instruments to C, E, G, in scale. The key of C, a lot of times, would leap ahead because he wasn't playing a "thud," he was actually hitting like a C. If I hit my top C string, it sounded like four basses. And one time at the Paramount, he slowed the tempo down while I was doing a bass number and it frightened me, but it also thrilled me, because the band sounded twice as heavy. It sounded like there were nineteen trumpets. He did so many things, he knew just when to play with brushes, he had some pretty accents, he couldn't play a dishonest two-bar break. But he could propel a band better than anybody who ever lived.

By the beginning of the summer of 1944, the rhythm section consisted of Ralph Burns, piano, Chubby Jackson, bass, Billy Bauer, guitar, and now Davey Tough on drums. Sometimes Ralph's arranging and composing abilities seemed to overshadow his talents as a first-rate jazz pianist. Bauer had a steady rhythm beat, coupled with a modern and unusual amplified sound on solos. Chubby's strong beat was always evident and distinctive.

Between April and June, the turnover of personnel continued, but it began to wane by the end of the summer, as several brilliant and original artists joined and settled into their positions in the brass and reed sections. One of these was a 28-year-old tenorist, Joseph Edward Phillips, better known as Flip. He had played around 52nd Street and had worked for trumpeter Frankie Newton at Kelly's Stables. He started his career on clarinet and switched to tenor in 1942. At the time he received his call from Woody, Flip was playing for Russ Morgan, a name band, albeit a commercial, society unit.

Flip's style was manifestly influenced by the deep, breathy styles of the Coleman Hawkins/Ben Webster school. He could swing incredibly on the up-tempo flag wavers, and then evoke a sensitive and haunting sound on ballads, as on his own composition "With Someone New" (recorded in 1946).

Sam Marowitz took over the lead alto chair in April. Sam came from the Harry James band. His powerful, assured lead saxophone voice would be a part of every Woody Herman saxophone section until mid-1950. His personality represented stability in the band, particularly during the turbulent period of the Second Herd.

In midsummer, trumpeter Pete Candoli joined the Herd at the Circle Theater in Indianapolis. Before the Herman band, he had stints with Ray McKinley, Sonny Dunham, Benny Goodman, Freddy Slack, Charlie Barnet and Tommy Dorsey—an impressive resume for a 21-year-old. Pete was a superb and powerful section man, capable of creating trumpet fireworks in the upper register, in addition to being an exciting soloist. Pete had a younger brother, Conte, also a trumpeter, who would soon emerge as a remarkable artist in his own right.

CHUBBY JACKSON: Pete is one of my closest friends, and has remained so all these years. To me, he was the epitome of lead trumpeters. We used to call Pete "Walter Camden," a name thrust on him by trumpeter Ray Linn, also from the Herd. It was his acting name, Hollywood style. On the road, Pete would get in the front part of the bus and do impressions of movie stars.

PETE CANDOLI: "Camden" . . . that was when I did my "stage" routine. I was the Shakespearean ham, I guess.

WOODY: We were in the Indianapolis theater, and I saw Chubby backstage in a little hallway with a pay telephone, and he's chuckling and laughing and scratching and I stopped by and I said "Who are you talking to?" And he said, "Mom!" So right at the end of the conversation, she said, "Chub!" He said, "Yeah, Mom!" She said, "Are you high, Chub?" He said, "Yeah, Mom!" She said, "That's good! Have a good time, Chub! Bye!"

In mid-June, the band began a four-week engagement in the Panther Room of the Hotel Sherman, in Chicago. During this engagement, the band signed a contract to broadcast each Wednesday evening on the Old Gold (cigarette) summer replacement show aired nationally on CBS and affiliate radio stations.

Sportscaster Red Barber was signed as emcee, and pop/light classic singer Allan Jones (father of singer Jack Jones) was brought in to share the vocal spotlight with Woody and other members of the Herman orchestra. The Herman band replaced one of the more commercial bands of that period, the Frankie Carle orchestra, originally scheduled for eleven weekly broadcasts running from July 26 to October 4.

WOODY: We were more or less a fill-in. We were on the show about ten or eleven weeks and it was a pretty incongruous meeting because the star of the show really was Allan Jones of "Donkey Serenade" fame, and he sang a lot of ballads and semiclassical pieces, and when we started, we first put together more head things, you know. But it did cause a lot of excitement, at least it got us to the front where other agencies and people were listening and wanting to find out what made this thing go, and that's how come a few months later we got the Wildroot show.

Joining the Herman team in July, at the Eastwood Gardens in Detroit, was trombonist Willard Palmer (Bill) Harris. Looking more like a college professor than a musician, Bill was 27 and originally from Philadelphia. He had studied tenor sax, trumpet, drums, and guitar, in addition to his major instrument, the trombone. He had briefly been with Gene Krupa, Ray McKinley and the Buddy Williams bands. Later he had been with Bob Chester and finally, a year with Benny Goodman. His trombone style was unique and original; it blended easily with bop, swing, or Dixieland, using vastly different moods. He could be wild and carousing, which fully utilized his instrument's powerhouse properties, yet on ballads he could play with tender and poignant emotion. He could make the trombone "cry" and "laugh" as on "I Wonder," recorded live on a radio remote from the Hotel Sherman, March 27, 1945.

RALPH BURNS: Bill was one of those natural musicians and one of the nicer human beings that I knew. You could take his remarks two ways, you know. You could think that he was making fun of you, but he really wasn't. I can remember getting stoned and playing cowboys and Indians with him. They were a lot of wonderful days.

WOODY: Bill had one of the wildest senses of humor of anyone I've ever met. What was so good about it is that he didn't look like that kind of person, and he didn't act that way. He just did little mean things, wonderful things! Bill was talking to a couple of musicians in front of the Croydon Hotel one night, and for no reason at all, he just dropped his trousers!

LARRY ELGART: I was pretty young, just in my early 20s. I was with the band that was called the First Herd, and I was there as that transition was happening. Woody, to me, was an extremely nice guy. A very affable and wonderful guy, and the band sort of took shape right about that short period of time that I was playing with it, and the thrill for me was really learning right down to my toes what swing was all about. And I think that probably the rhythm section, basically Davey Tough, took the lead in that department and we stopped playing certain arrangements, because guys like Flip Phillips weren't that good at reading, but they had a lot to say musically. So we started playing riffs and it was a very interesting learning process for me to know the difference between bands, when the band played head things, as opposed to reading arrangements. And so it was probably the closest that I ever came to jazz.

Like his older brother, Pete, Secondo (Conte) Candoli was from Misawaka, Indiana. Ultimately, Conte would become a major force as a first-class modern trumpet soloist whose playing displayed definite roots in the Dizzy Gillespie trumpet school.

CONTE CANDOLI: I was 16 when I first joined the band, on my summer vacation from high school. I could just barely read music, but when I told Woody, he said not to worry. He let me play a couple of choruses on "Woodchopper's Ball" and he said, "You're playing good enough, you can learn to read later on." I hated to go back to high school that fall, but my folks and Woody felt it was best for me. He said a chair was open for me any time.

WOODY: We had a lot of young guys in the band. Pete was young, Conte came in at 16 during the summer vacation from high school. Pete was beautiful! He made him carry his case, his horn and like pistol-whipped him twenty-four hours a day. "Get up, Conte! Up, boy; down, boy!"

During the summer of 1944, George T. Simon, jazz editor and writer for *Metronome* magazine, was an Army GI, recently transferred to New York to supervise the formation and distribution of the U.S. military V-Disc program. The Captain told George, "You know a lot of people in the business and you ought to know what the men want, so go ahead and record anybody and anything you want."[1] Under the terms of the AFM recording ban, musicians were restricted from recording for the commercial labels, but were not restrained from recording for the Armed Forces. These were twelve-inch discs produced without any payment to the band, with the agreement that they would never be marketed or sold commercially. In recent years, many have appeared commercially nevertheless on various bootleg record labels.

During the war, the V-Disc program provided the U.S. Armed Forces personnel ample exposure to the latest in American bands and vocal music.

On August 21 the band began a six-week engagement at the popular Cafe Rouge, at the Hotel Pennsylvania. Some live broadcasts during this period have been preserved and marketed on various labels.

RALPH BURNS: We had a powerful rhythm section in the band. Davey was like the master. He had an unusual cymbal sound and when the cymbals started to get a strange sound, then we knew that he was going to "go off" again. Davey was the first alcoholic that I ever knew. He also had epilepsy. Now they know more about alcoholism, but in those days, we were never quite sure if it was epilepsy or those fits that they get from withdrawal, the DTs. His cymbals would start sounding strange and the time would start going a little bit strange and that was the danger signal.

WOODY: As close as Dave and I were, we never discussed his past much. One time we were playing the Oriental Theater and a gal showed up, a beautiful girl, and it turned out that it was one of his ex-wives or something. And I was flabbergasted because this was a beautiful dame, and so charming, and I said, "Dave, where does this fit into your life?" And he said, "Oh, I was married to her once!" You know, little shocks he liked to give you.

Something that we never knew until he was too ill to help really, was that he was a victim of seizures [epilepsy]. He was subject to that for a period of years and he tried to keep it very cool and very quiet. And before he left the band, he had a couple of spasms and we knew that something was definitely wrong with him. But he died on the street. He could not drink, but he would drink sometimes to fend off the fear of having an attack, and to him it was definitely embarrassing.

The author asked Woody if Davey had a problem with drugs.

WOODY: Not really, he couldn't handle any kind of potency, whether it be liquor, marijuana, or anything. Any of it was too much for him. He would just become a rag doll when he messed with it. But I think now, as I look back, that it was mostly in fear of having another attack, he would try anything to keep from it.

It seemed that whenever we had something important to do like when we had an opening at some important spot in New York or California, he couldn't take it and he would "go off." And then it was pretty drastic because Dave, being a very bright and intelligent man, knew all the gimmicks. For instance, one opening at the Pennsylvania Hotel, he arrived with both feet bandaged. He said he had very sore feet. And here was a little ladder to get up to the last tier on the bandstand, and I knew his condition, and I knew that this was a "bit" again. So I chased him up the ladder, and with each movement of the leg, he screamed with pain. And he got up on the stand, and we did the first dinner set and he's moaning through every tune.

We came to the end of the first set and he's started to get away from the drums and started for the ladder, and I said, "Oh, no!" I parked myself with a chair right at the ladder, and I said, "You try to come down and I'll kick the shit out of you!" He had to stay up there. But finally after two or three sets, one of the captains or headwaiters called over to tell me something and he sneaked out. That was the last time we saw him for the next week.

After that, we were going to the Palladium, our first "big time" out there, and our band had become fairly important, and I wanted to make a big scene. So I hired another drummer, a spare, an "in case" drummer, Lou Fromme. He had worked with Barnet and Georgie Auld. And we opened the Palladium. Dave was pretty good. You weren't quite sure about tonight or the first couple of hours, or the last couple of hours, but he came through part of the time. But it got to be a contest after about a week whether to put in the sub or put in the regular guy, because Dave's condition got very bad. Both performers, it was a toss-up, you know. You'd throw a coin in the air and see if heads or tails was going to make it. This was a very nerve-racking experience. And it was to the guys, too. Because every time you got up there, you didn't know who was going to play and whether he was going to make it or not.

There's something that should be mentioned about Davey before we get off the track. He was really a brilliant guy besides being a swinging drummer. He used to write a request to Abe Turchen, who was the road manager, to draw out twenty dollars, and when you read this piece, you knew that you were reading something written by a genius. Sometimes he wrote amusing, short pieces for *Down Beat* magazine about situations in life. A very talented guy, besides music. Very well read!

CHUBBY JACKSON: Davey was an excellent writer. One thing I recall was "Black Narcissus," which was his view on being married to Casey, who was black.

He always had an insecure feeling of being in his 40s, when the majority of the band were in their 20s, so he constantly apologized.

On September 5 Woody brought his potent new band into RCA's studios in New York City for its initial V-Disc recording session. Later that month, the band recorded additional V-Disc material in the acoustically superior old Liederkranz Hall Studios. It was now possible for the U.S. Armed Forces, scattered all over the world, to hear samples of this exciting band.

The First Herd in October 1944. Front row: Ralph Burns (piano), Margie Hyams (vibes), Billy Bauer (guitar), Flip Phillips, John LaPorta, Sam Marowitz, Mickey Folus, Skippy DeSair (saxes). Second row: Chubby Jackson (bass), Davey Tough (drums), Ralph Pfeffner, Bill Harris, Ed Kiefer (trombones). Back row: Neal Hefti, Charlie Frankhauser, Ray Wetzel, Pete Candoli, Carl Warwick (trumpets). (Courtesy The Hugh Turner Collection, Hollywood)

In September Woody augmented the already hearty rhythm section by hiring a female vibraphone player, Margie Hyams.

WOODY: Every time I would hire a girl, it was a big hassle with the guys. They said, "Oh, man, what are you doing?" Until after they got to know them, of course.

MARGIE HYAMS: I met Woody in the summer of 1944, while I was playing with my quartet on the boardwalk at Renault's [in Atlantic City, New Jersey]. He liked my playing and thought I could fit in with the band. We met several times in New York and I joined the band toward the end of the year.

On October 10 the Herman Herd stampeded into the Hollywood Palladium for a five-week engagement ending November 26. During this period, the band continued to gain exposure via live CBS network remotes and Armed Forces Radio Service broadcasts, a few of which have been preserved and made available on commercial record labels. During November the AFM recording ban officially ended and Columbia Records was quick to jockey the Herman crew into a recording contract.

In November the band was before the Hollywood cameras at Republic for its fourth feature film, *Earl Carroll Vanities*. The film also starred comic Pinky Lee.

On December 11 and 12 Woody fulfilled his commitment to Decca by recording seven titles in Decca's Los Angeles studios. "As Long As I Live," a Frances Wayne vocal, is a beautiful ballad of that time. There is a solo from Woody's lush, full-sounding alto, Margie Hyams' vibraphone recording debut with the band and Frances' usual romantic and melodic vocal mood. Another title recorded was "Saturday Night," a successful pop tune again featuring Frances Wayne. It's unfortunate that perhaps the greatest jazz contribution in the final Decca session, Ralph Burns's head arrangement of "Flying Home," was never issued.

WOODY: Our very last stuff for Decca was made with approximately the same musicians who later did the things on Columbia. That was the great big turning point; it was the time we spent together getting unified that contributed.

When we did the last Decca recordings, Ralph had just barely started to write for the band, and he was experimenting as to the band's possibilities and what to compose for them, and we were still shooting for some fairly solid commercial things, too, trying to keep it musical. But by the time we went to Columbia, we felt that we had arrived at what we really wanted to do and we didn't give a damn if it sold two copies or what, but let's make it!

And one of the big reasons that we went with Columbia is the fact that during the V-Discs, we were not recording commercially. We did sessions very often and we had carte blanche to any of the studios around New York, and we tried Victor, Decca, and Columbia, and we found that Liederkranz Hall was a real gasser for us. That was one of the big reasons that we went with Columbia, that plus the fact that we had a deal that I still think was a beauty. There was a shortage of shellac, it was wartime, they couldn't guarantee the amount of records pressed, or guarantee too much about money. But we found a loophole! We made them guarantee us an equal amount of exploitation and advertising with their two biggest artists, who at that time were Sinatra and Dinah Shore. People thought we were selling records no matter what. Full-page ads every week. It was beautiful! They sold as many as they could press. In other words, each record sold on an average of somewhere between 250,000 and 350,000.

On January 24 the small group within the big band, now designated The Woodchoppers, recorded several titles at a V-Disc recording session in New York. During the First Herd years of 1944–1946, The Woodchoppers may have been the best band within a band that ever existed, including the Goodman sextet of 1941 and 1942.

Two new faces appeared in the band in early February. Altoist John LaPorta replaced Bill Shine on third alto. LaPorta, from Philadelphia, was an accomplished musician who would later demonstrate considerable depth and conception as a composer, on the chart "Non-Alcoholic." The brilliant trumpeter Saul "Sonny" Berman, from New Haven, Connecticut, also joined. Sonny, at 21, was already a veteran, having been with Louie Prima, Sonny Dunham, Tommy Dorsey, Georgie Auld, Harry James, and Benny Goodman. Sonny had his roots in the Roy Eldridge school, but was evolving rapidly into a creative and sometimes quite radical style for that period.

In early February additional titles were recorded at a V-Disc session again at Liederkranz Hall, New York City. The band was also booked into the famous roadhouse venue for big bands, Frank Dailey's Meadowbrook at Cedar Grove, New Jersey, February 15 to 30.

On the evening of February 18, on the eve of its initial recording session at Columbia Studios, the band was heard on a live CBS broadcast, which has been preserved and marketed on an album. The method used to record this and three other broadcasts between February and July 1945 was called "direct line transcription." The original sound quality has been preserved, producing extraordinary results. The band cooks and sizzles in these live recordings. The recording ban had partially kept the band under wraps, but now the First Herd would soon be a national phenomenon.

One of the titles performed that night was a humorous thing called "Chubby's Blues," featuring bassist Chubby Jackson. Woody's lyrics were: "Woke up this morning with the blues 'round my head, had the blues so bad, I had to go right back to bed . . . I got fourteen cousins, all of them are dead, they all had the blues so bad, they was dead in the head . . . poor cousins! Chubby, you look so sad and so weird, with your big fat bass and your funny little beard." When asked if he remembered this number, Chubby responded, "Yeah, of course, 'cause that was my 'theater number.' On one-nighters, I would play it once in a while. I would come out with my bass and Woody would sing. It was cute, just a blues."

Another head arrangement performed on the same broadcast was "Red Top," a tune Woody did not record commercially. The rhythm section shines, with Davey propelling the band, and Ralph, Chubby, Billy, and Margie. Woody's buoyant clarinet is heard; other sounds include Flip's earthy tenor with the brass coming in at intervals with wild bop punctuations, Bill Harris's relentlessly driving trombone and Margie Hyams proving that she was a proficient swinger on the vibraphone. Everything culminates in an exciting full-band ensemble with Pete Candoli's trumpet in the upper register.

February 19, 1945, was a significant day in the history of the Woody Herman band. The First Herd entered Liederkranz Hall in New York and cut a group of titles for Columbia, some for commercial use, and others to bolster the V-Disc program. Virtually all the titles cut became blockbusters in terms of musical substance and public acceptance.

CHUBBY JACKSON: I should say that at our first recording date for Columbia, Woody insisted to Mitch Miller, who was in the booth representing Columbia, that we had to have a special mike for the bass!

This was the band as it went into the Columbia recording session: Woody (clarinet, alto sax, vocals, and leader), Sonny Berman, Chuck Frankhouser, Ray Wetzel, Pete Candoli, Carl Warwick (trumpets), Ralph Pfeffner, Bill Harris, Ed Kiefer (trombones), Sam Marowitz, John LaPorta (clarinets/alto saxes), Flip Phillips, Pete Mondello (tenor saxes), Skippy DeSair (baritone sax), Marjorie Hyams (vibes), Ralph Burns (piano), Billy Bauer (guitar), Chubby Jackson (bass), Dave Tough (drums), and Frances Wayne (vocals).

David Raksin's "Laura," the theme music from the film, has since become a cult classic. Woody's recording eventually sold a million copies. Woody's alto is featured and his sensitive 1940s crooner stylings touched the ballad realm of Sinatra, Haymes, or Torme. Margie Hyams gives a brief vibes introduction to a warm Bill Harris trombone solo. (Years later, the original Ralph Burns chart of "Laura" was lost and the band continued to perform the song as a "head thing." But it was still in the band's library in July 1951, when the Herd used it as a backdrop for Charlie Parker sitting in with the 1951 Herd.) "Apple Honey," named after an alleged ingredient of Old Gold tobacco, featured another exciting head arrangement, based on the chords of "I Got Rhythm."

On February 26, back in the New York studios, additional titles were cut. "Out of This World," a Johnny Mercer-Harold Arlen pop tune from the film of the same name, was recorded. Ralph Burns's titillating dual Latin-swing score features a bold use of dynamics. Frances Wayne's vocal is sultry and effective.

Recorded at the same session was Woody's novelty blues hit "Caldonia." Woody gave background information on the score to George T. Simon: "Ralph caught Louie Jordan doing it in an act and wrote the opening twelve bars and the eight-bar tag. The rest is strictly a 'head' thing, except for that unison trumpet part. That was Neal's, and we used to play it in some other arrangement, but Neal thought it would fit here too."[2]

"Caldonia" has Woody's outrageous vocal and Flip's humorous and catchy tenor, followed by the typical choppy and swinging Bill Harris solo, Ralph's piano and key change, the soaring trumpet section passage, and Davey's famous carry-over tag. Successive Herds continued to inch up the tempo a little each year.

The flip side of the original 78 record, from the same session, was "Happiness Is Just a Thing Called Joe." The tune was another Harold Arlen composition, from the movie version of Cabin in the Sky, with a fine Ralph Burns arrangement (a carry-over from the Charlie Barnet band). Frances projects a profound emotional quality and beautiful intonation.

On March 1, 1945, the band was back in Liederkranz Hall recording another combination of commercial and V-Discs.

"Goosey Gander" was a head arrangement based loosely on the old tune "Shortnin' Bread." "Northwest Passage" was another head arrangement. Both Ralph Burns and Neal Hefti contributed, beginning with the trombones, with Harris' horn powerfully evident, and a catchy riff played by a trio of Woody's clarinet, Flip's tenor, and Sonny's trumpet. Ralph, Margie, Woody, Flip, and Bill Harris all get a chance to play. The ensemble "shout" was Neal's, according to Woody. Pete's stratospheric trumpet takes the band out in wild abandon. This chart was refitted by Nat Pierce in the sixties for the three-tenor, one-baritone voicing, and remains in the Herman book in the nineties. Woody derived the title from the slogan used by Northwest Airlines after it received approval to extend its route to the East from Milwaukee.

The band also cut the Ralph Burns chart of "I've Got the World on a String," which featured Woody's vocal, as well as some nice tenor from Flip, Woody's clarinet, and Davey's steady metronomelike brushes.

NEAL HEFTI: It was the first band that I played solos with, and it was during that band that I started making almost every issue of *Down Beat* or *Metronome* and the top ten as trumpet soloist. It was the first chance I ever had to have a tune of mine recorded, because if you recall, all during the forties, there were a couple of strikes against the record companies, so there wasn't a lot of recording business. And the first time I ever got a royalty check was for "Apple Honey." I got married in that band.

   That was the top band. You might say Glenn Miller was or Tommy Dorsey was, but it was a toss of the coin. Woody's band made pop records. They played hot places! "Apple Honey" was every fifteenth tune. The majority of the things that they did were "Saturday Night Is the Loneliest Night of the Week," "Laura," "It Must Be Jelly (Because Jam Don't Shake Like That)"—sort of novelty. They were the pop tunes of the day. We would do movie tunes. The song writers and the song publishers would be around all the time to get some new material played. It was later on that it became sort of an underground jazz band.

WOODY: The '45 and '46 band used to reach heights on some nights that were unbelievable. This was only because of the unity of the group. We all played above our heads many times. There's no way to describe it. You can sit down, "woodshed" or practice, or rehearse, like forever, and you couldn't get what you found on the spur of the moment.

RALPH BURNS: Woody was like a godfather to a lot of us. He was such a great organizer. He'd say, "Ralph, go home and write a first chorus for this, and Neal, go home and write a last chorus for this." And Woody would put everything together. We would collaborate, and that was a lot of fun. There was one thing, I think it was "Blue Moon," Neal would do one chorus and I would do one chorus, and on things like "Apple Honey,"

I would write an introduction and Flip Phillips would write the first chorus melody and then Woody would turn around to the trumpets and say, "Play something here!" Like on "Caldonia," the same thing.

NEAL HEFTI: We had a very good trumpet section. We were all Dizzy Gillespie lovers. I think we had our own club. No one else in the whole band could even penetrate unless we were going to let them in. We were all about 19 or 20 years old and real brats.

MARGIE HYAMS: There were a lot of extremely talented musicians in the band when I was there. One of the sweetest and funniest was Dave Tough. Neither of us could sleep on the bus, so we read and talked the nights through.

Neal Hefti also had a terrific sense of humor. I remember once when we got to a ballroom, there weren't many people there yet, so we did what we usually did and opened with something like the blues. Woody would wait to appear and the guys would take choruses and we would try to get something going to get the audience involved. This particular night the song really took on a life of its own and developed into a fantastic head arrangement. Instead of a nice, subtle, quiet tune so that Woody could make his unassuming appearance, it evolved into a loud, wailing, cooking arrangement. Woody came on the stand and stood looking at us with his "What is going on?" look, and we finally, reluctantly, ended it. When everything was quiet once again, from the back row Neal Hefti said, "Guess what we did?"

WOODY: Chubby was probably the most visual "spark plug" that any band ever had! He had it going in all directions.

The author asked Woody, in one of our interviews, if Chubby's cheerleading ever got too exuberant for him. His reply was in typical, wry one-liner form: "Oh, sure, at least once a day, but it's all part of it!"

CHUBBY JACKSON: Being rather flamboyant, I felt the urge to encourage a huge measure of show business for the band. To this day, I still get the blame for some of the absolute eccentricities that occurred on and off the bandstand. However, I'd like to set the record straight. All of these far-out situations were well planned by Woody and myself. During that period, it strains me to admit to being terribly obese and at the weight of 263 pounds, I got away with murder. In California, we had a week off before flying home to New York City and the engagement at the Paramount Theater. So I raised a Vandyke beard and showed up at rehearsal. I used Frances Wayne's eyebrow pencil to shape the beard perfectly. Woody stared for a quick moment, then asked me if I actually had nerve enough to wear this adornment. "Of course," I replied, and our public relations department had a picnic with the thought of having a bassist with a beard. While I'm at it, Woody also instructed me to wear a gray suit with knickers and a bebop bow tie, while the rest of the band wore standard blue suits with blue ties.

So all these things we had planned. Nobody knew that but the guys in the band, Woody and myself, of course. I ended up finding out that I stuck out in a crowd, on account of wanting to be an individual. And bass players, as a rule, always complained that the public would always look at everybody but the damned fool bass player and I figured that I couldn't allow that . . . so I got the attention.

It was at this time that I decided to change my string bass. As you probably know, for centuries the string bass had four strings. My never-asleep mind decided to add a C string on top of the G string, which made it easier to play notes in the higher range. The Kay Bass Company in Chicago made one as a gift to me and then proceeded to put "The Chubby Jackson Bass" on the market.

Woody was also the most gentlemanly bandleader of that era, this era or any era, for that matter. He never made us feel uncomfortable nor did he ever tell us how to play our instruments. I actually learned how to play bass in that early Herd. I learned time from Davey Tough, and the harmonic written structures from Ralph Burns and Neal Hefti.

WOODY: Chicks have followed bands since the beginning of time. I guess it's just the fact that you're offbeat, and you're a little different, and your appearance is a little different, and your life is very upset and shook up. During the war years, there used to be little girls who would follow the band around, little teenagers, scare you to death. I used to have heart-to-heart talks with them, try to send them home, and little girls would say to me, "Look, with the shortage of fellas, why couldn't I be a band girl?" There was one that followed us clear out to California from Chicago. A very beautiful girl. She wouldn't give up, her family had to move to California so she could be there. She fell in love with Ralph, and then one night, Ralph got picked up on a bum rap, and wound up in jail, and that was the end of that romance.

MARGIE HYAMS: Once, at the Paramount, when the stage was about to rise, we noticed that Ralph Burns wasn't at the piano and the opening song was "Apple Honey" with a four- or eight-bar piano introduction. Since I also play piano, the guys told me to play the intro. As we rose out of the darkness, Woody did a double-take when he saw me at the piano and announced to the audience that I was Mary Lou Schwartz.

There was no such musician as Mary Lou Schwartz, but Woody may have been thinking of Mary Lou Williams, the noted jazz pianist. In subsequent years he would often jokingly call attention to his pianists by saying "Let's have a nice round of applause for Mary Lou Williams."

WOODY: One time, we were at the Paramount for a long stay, and you get bored in a place like that, and Bill Harris and Sonny Berman went out and bought a monkey! And they named her Hazel. And, of course, the newness of having a very funny monkey lasted about twenty minutes, and by the third day you couldn't go on the fifth floor because of the odor, because no one cleaned up after Hazel. She was now running wild in this room, she was out of the cage and leaping from window to mirror to whatever she could latch onto, and Ralph Pfeffner, the trombonist, who was quite an old mother in the band, finally took it upon himself. He bought a pair of long rubber gloves that went over his elbows, and cleaned up after Hazel, and felt very bad for the treatment Hazel was receiving.

After a couple of weeks, we decided we'd have to make a little better use of Hazel. So when the song pluggers would come in to show me songs or to discuss plugs, we'd say, "Well, we just hired a new girl secretary, and if you'll leave the tunes with her, I'll look them over on Monday. Go up on the fifth floor and ask for Hazel." So they'd get 'em in the room and lock 'em in with Hazel.

On March 16 the band started a month-long engagement in the Panther Room of the Hotel Sherman in Chicago.

WOODY: Duke showed up right after we had started to sound pretty good, and he came in several mornings to the Sherman Hotel and actually tried to figure out what the hell we were doing. He was the only one that had that much interest. As far as the other bandleaders, I can't remember one of them that paid that much attention. However, the musicians did. We were loaded with them no matter where we went. But Duke actually said, "I'd like to hear what these young boys are putting down." He sat there and he ate three quarts of ice cream, and he listened to all our noises.

I forgot just what month, but maybe it was March or April of '45, this thing took off like gangbusters! And we had some theatrical lawyers who were handling our affairs and they and Milt Deutsch, our manager, and I, sat down and decided we could make this into one of America's really important attractions by planning an attack. This would mean spending perhaps six weeks in Chicago at the Sherman Hotel and immediately going into New York or vice versa, to the Hotel Pennsylvania for six to eight weeks for the summer period and then, immediately, going right into the Palladium in Hollywood for another long period to keep this thing on the air. And because we saw the tremendous reaction this thing had in person, we wanted to exploit it to the whole country. We thought this was the thing to do, and we had a very uphill battle to sell it to my

June, 1945. Front row: Flip Phillips, John LaPorta, Sam Marowitz, Pete Mondello, Skippy DeSair, unidentified guest vocalist, Woody, Margie Hyams. Second row: Ed Kiefer, Bill Harris, Ralph Pfeffner, Chubby Jackson, Davey Tough, Ralph Burns. Back row: Conte Candoli, Pete Candoli, Ray Wetzel, Billy Robbins, Sonny Berman. Billy Bauer (guitar) is behind Woody. (From the Woody Herman Collection)

guiding lights, these legal eagles, because we were now a nice little act who got $6,500 a week in theaters and worked every week and had no trouble, no problems, not an important band, but a "nice" band. I don't think they wanted an important band that bad, and second was the thought of throwing away thousands of dollars. It meant an investment every time you played these important locations. It cost us anywhere from around a few hundred dollars a week to sometimes $2,000 a week. But we finally put it through, and that's what made the band happen in 1945.

MARGIE HYAMS: I left the band in June, 1945. I left mostly because I didn't want to go out on the road again and I had several offers to stay in New York. Woody was a lovely man to work for. There was some talk at the time that I left with bad feelings. Not so! Every time I opened any place, if Woody was in town he would bring a large group in to celebrate. Woody and Charlotte loved to party and I don't think I ever missed a chance to be gracious.

My greatest disappointment was that I left just before Woody connected with Stravinsky. I had been studying theory and composition and traveled on the road with a well-worn copy of *The Rite of Spring*. Stravinsky was my hero and it took a long time for me to listen to *Ebony Concerto* without getting a lump in my throat.

On July 16 the band went into the Cafe Rouge of the Hotel Pennsylvania in New York for a month-long engagement. During this time, the band was heard live via Armed Forces Radio Service transcriptions and live broadcasts. Two titles that have been preserved are worthy of mention. "Katusha," a Neal Hefti chart, has Woody doing some hilarious vocal antics. Flip, Ralph, Bill Harris and Sonny Berman all contributed with fervor.

CHUBBY JACKSON: "Katusha" was a take-off on "Caldonia." In many ways, it was a swinging throwaway.

"Good, Good, Good," originally written as a samba, was a pop tune of the day. Xavier Cugat had the hit record of it on the Columbia label. Woody's rendition is completely in another mode from his Columbia stablemate's version. It swings like mad. Woody sings the lyrics, but the excitement begins when the ensemble ignites. Davey's bass drum beat helps drive the band to an explosive climax with the newly developing bop figures manifested in a dazzling trumpet and brass display, Bill Harris in a particularly electrifying mood, and Chubby encouraging the band with his gleeful shouts. Both "Katusha" and "Good, Good, Good," were recorded off the air, utilizing the "direct line transcription" process.

WOODY: The idea of *Summer Sequence* came about when Ralph stayed out at Long Island at Chubby's place in the summer of 1945. I think someday it will be used a lot more than it has. We came close one time in the mid-50s when Johnny Green wanted to use it for a Gene Kelly picture. Kelly was all for doing it. But the producer and someone else decided it was too modern and the piece was then like nine years old! And it's not a frantic piece at all!

RALPH BURNS: I stayed out at Chubby Jackson's house at Freeport, Long Island, during a summer. I had been writing for Woody and I stayed with Chubby's mom, who was a great person. I think Chubby was on the road with Woody. I had a wonderful time writing at Jones Beach all summer. Woody had asked me to write a semisymphonic piece. I wrote it for myself with Woody's band.

Mom Jackson was a crazy, wonderful woman. She was like Chubby. If you knew the mother, you knew the son! She was an old vaudevillian. She used to play the piano and sing. I mean the thing was to keep her away from the piano. She was terrible, but she was a wonderful woman!

WOODY: One time, we were in Bridgeport, Connecticut, playing a one-nighter, it was our last date after a long road tour. We were coming into New York, and sixty miles from New York, and oh, boy, "The Apple," tonight! And we were on the job, and I get an emergency phone call from Mom Jackson. I ran to the phone. She had a very low voice, kind of an Ethel Barrymore type. And she said, "Wood?" I said, "Yes." She said, "The heat's on in New York, tell the boys to dump all the shit!"

It seemed they picked up a bass of Chubby's. Some Army kid had been using it. Already Chubby had basses in every town. He was just leaving them for firewood. And this cat had the bass down in some military installation, and a bag of "shit" [marijuana] fell out of it.

On August 14, 1945, World War II ended. In America, whistles blew, church bells rang, strangers embraced, workers walked off their jobs, crowds filled the streets, and bars overflowed. There was jubilation everywhere. People were excited about a bright future. The steady stream of Columbia recordings being ground out by the Herman band, coupled with the band's exuberance, seemed to meet emotional needs and fit the mood of the hour. Returning servicemen, who had been exposed to the band on V-Discs, wanted more.

FRANKIE LAINE: Woody got me my first Paramount theater date in New York, in 1947. He was the greatest, and was always nice to me. I was staying with Al Jarvis, who was a disc jockey in Hollywood. At that time, Al was the top deejay in town. And I was struggling and scuffling hand to mouth. So I used to go out with him on Sundays to do those shows for the service guys, at all the different military forts and complexes, and the rest of the time I was working in a war plant down in South Gate. And Woody was staying at the Garden of Allah as was Perry Como, and we were all across from each other. So we used to meet at the pool and Woody didn't know anything about me. He just knew I was living there with Al Jarvis. Then, later, after I hit, he came in to see me at Morocco on Vine Street and realized I was the same guy.

After he saw the show one night, he says, "How would you like to play the Paramount?" And I almost fell down. I said, "Really? You think I'm ready?" He says, "Oh, yeah, let me speak to Bob Weitman." And you know, I thought it was just night club talk. But he did. And he got me my first date based on his say-so.

In the late 1930s, Woody met Abe Turchen for the first time. He had been an early fan of the band. Before the war, Abe owned and serviced a string of jukeboxes in South Dakota and Iowa. Abe was a promoter with an entrepreneurial spirit. He was also a heavy gambler. He was a stocky five feet eleven inches and looked tough. He could be caustic when the situation called for it, but was adept in making friends as well as enemies. In World War II, he was in the famous First Marine Division at Guadalcanal, and was severely wounded in his lower legs. To compound his health problems, he was suffering from malaria. He was medically discharged in 1944.

WOODY: Abe spent eighteen months in the hospitals; he was all shot up. They went all out as far as seeing that this boy was happy, now that he was home. So he got a special dispensation to get this car, and they gave him gas coupons like they were nothing. He told them that he was too nervous to sit. He had to drive. He got tires! He was loaded! Things were pretty rough transportationwise during the war, and some office in Washington took our bus one morning, so Abe found out our predicament and an hour later, he had a bus. I don't know how he got it. A hot bus! And he said, "You'll drive with me. We'll use my car. I'll go out with you for a week." So three months later, he was still with me and still on the same premise, like for laughs.

     And then we broke up to go to California on a business switch. I broke up the band and made everyone swear that they wouldn't tell anyone that it was merely a vacation. This raised our salary from $1,750 a night to $3,500 and $4,000 a night. We laid off, I think, for ten days. These were the little "bits" sometimes you had to do. I told them I wasn't going to work until they got me the proper money. So during this period I went home. As a matter of fact, I left Abe somewhere in the Midwest and took a train home, and I was home at least one day, when there's a knock on the door at the Garden of Allah. I opened the door, and here's Abe. He said, "I didn't have nothing to do, so I thought I'd drive out." Milt Deutsch was just leaving the band as road manager. So a couple of nights later, in the bar at the Garden of Allah, I said, "Abe, Milt is leaving the band. It seems that you like to travel. You've been with me now for months for no reason and we may as well make this some kind of a sensible business proposition. You'll travel with me. You'll be the road manager." "Oh," he said, "I'd love that, it really would gas me, but I can't make it. I can't do it." I asked him why and he said, "I don't know anything about music." You want to know about switches in people? Later, he would tell me how the piece should go.

In mid-August, the band was back in Columbia's New York studios recording. Some more Herman classics were born from these sessions: "Love Me," another Frances Wayne sentimental ballad was recorded. It has all the ingredients of a lush Ralph Burns chart, and a nice Flip Phillips tenor taking the band out with a novel rhythmic ending. "The Good Earth" was originally titled "Helen of Troy." This chart was also reworked by Nat Pierce in the 1960s for the Four Brothers saxophone voicing and was still a staple in the Herman book in the late eighties.

Regarding "Bijou," Woody gave George T. Simon some background information: "Ralph wrote this for Bill. . . . I gave it the 'Rhumba a la Jazz' subtitle because I was trying to explain why we were abusing the Latin rhythm."[3] Bill was always creative, but here he achieves a mood in his classic solo that most big band fans cherish.

In early September, Davey Tough apparently had one of his dreaded epileptic seizures. Buddy Rich subbed for him on the September 5 New York recording session that produced the classic "Your Father's Mustache" and "Gee, It's Good to Hold You."

WOODY: Buddy walked in for the date and he was very busy. He was then working with Tommy Dorsey, and he had this date in Bridgeport, or somewhere, that night and he said, "I can only stay for a little while." But like Dave was sick, we were doing some little pop tune, and it was nothing, you know. He didn't dig this scene too much, and the guys took one look at him and they all knew him and his reputation and the "draft" went on immediately. Like eighteen "drafts" came up *strong*. And as brash as Buddy is, he dug this draft. It was "high gale," so he sweated out this piece and we finally got onto this head. In "Father's Mustache," there are a lot of little noises and things in it he had to catch, and we had to go through it two or three times and the guys are looking at him like, "What's the matter, kid, can't you make it?" Like "You don't swing," you know, like they gave him some terrible heat, and the old Rich steam came up and he says to himself like, "I'll swing these mothers off the groove," and he did! And it turned out real good. We went overtime and he couldn't possibly get to Bridgeport in time, and he says, "Let's do another take, we can do that better, can't we?" He became like a member!

"Gee, It's Good to Hold You," recorded on the same date, has Woody's rich alto serving up an introduction for Frances Wayne's vocalizing of a World War II ballad. Flip solos and Red Norvo, in his Herman record debut, plays rich chords in the background. Although Red was present on the record date, he did not join the Herd until January.

Trumpeter Shorty Rogers was a new face in the band in late September, replacing Conte Candoli. He studied classical music in New York and played with Will Bradley and Red Norvo in 1942 before going in the Army.

WOODY: Shorty was always a pretty serious guy, but with a good sense of humor and a happy soul. I'll never forget when Red Norvo first brought him around. He was in Army uniform and he was only about 20. This little grinning puss never said a word. He wanted the gig so badly, but he wouldn't say anything. He just waited for Red to handle everything.

Another brewery tour in late 1945. First row: Ed Kiefer, Woody, Frances Wayne. Second row: John LaPorta, Shorty Rogers, Irv Lewis, Tony Aless, Bill Harris, Billy Bauer, Flip Phillips. Third row: Ralph Pfeffner, Pete Candoli, Don Lamond, band boy Nat Wexler, Chubby Jackson. Back row: Skippy DeSair, Neal Hefti, Sam Marowitz, Steve Condos (dancer who worked with the band), Mickey Folus. (From the Woody Herman Collection)

SHORTY ROGERS: I was in the Army in 1945, and I had a few months to go. But I was told that I was going to get discharged early. After all that time in the Army, wanting to get out, I was faced all of a sudden with a fear: "Hey, if I'm going to get out, cast out into the world, what am I going to do?"

Red Norvo, whom I had worked for previous to coming in the Army, was a very close friend of mine. I think it was even before he and my sister got married. And he knew Woody from having worked with Woody on a few recording sessions. So Woody started talking to Red about joining the band. Well, as I was ready to get out of the Army, I saw Red when I was on furlough and also Chubby Jackson, who was a good friend of mine. I came into town on furlough and told Red I was going to be getting out of the Army pretty soon and let it go at that. Red talked to Woody and Chubby did also, and of all things, Conte was getting drafted, and he actually was sent to the same camp that I was getting discharged from.

Davey Tough had left, just a matter of days before I joined, and then Don Lamond joined the band just a few days after I did. Don and I were the newcomers on the band. For the first few days they put us together, roommates for a short while. Then ten days after joining, I got married.

It was an unbelievable thrill for me to get out of the Army into what at that time was *the* band. I was just a little kid, I was just 21. And to be honest with you, scared to death. And that's when Pete Candoli adopted me. I sat next to him in the chair that his brother, Conte, vacated. He treated me like Conte was still there. He took me in like a brother and just watched over me, made me feel comfortable, spoke to me, taught me things that helped me get through that whole new experience.

Woody represented someone of very high stature to me. I was just in complete awe of this man. And I have to be honest with you, I'm *still* that way [March 1987]. I love him. When we spend time together, we hug, and I feel closer today than back then.

I did my first arrangement for Woody's band. He was very encouraging to me, and started to give me arrangement assignments, you know, "Let's do this tune and feature so and so." I was a real quiet kid who never said anything except "The E7 goes to 3 and the F7 goes to B-flat."

You could talk about Bill Harris, a giant, a pioneer on his instrument, a guy that at that time changed the whole direction of trombone jazz playing. Just to be there and hear him every night was an experience. Flip Phillips was another phenomenon. The energy, and kind of second in command, so to speak, was Chubby Jackson. For me, sitting in the trumpet section with Neal Hefti, his talent was something that I was in such awe of that I just listened to everything he did and tried to analyze it. I was just beginning as an arranger at that time, and Neal didn't realize it, but he was one of my teachers. I never took a formal lesson from him, but he was gracious enough to speak to me, and anything that I would ask him, he would take time to answer, and make sure that I understood it. And he was also a great player.

A whole other study that was going on at that time in Woody's band was the head arrangements. One guy could write the last chorus, another guy the first chorus. I wrote some things in the middle. Other bands have done it, I'm sure. You know Basie's band. But it became a fine art in Woody's First Herd. A definite part of the band, not subliminal, but up front, and everyone was aware of it, waiting for it, and appreciating it. The feeling of fellowship was great, we were on a winning team.

Drummer Davey Tough briefly reappeared in the band after his early-September illness. However, by late September, weighing 95 pounds and overtaken by ill health and personal problems, he left the band for good. Within a few days after Davey departed, he was replaced by Don Lamond, a brilliant drummer in the Tough tradition, yet more modern in conception. Don would eventually achieve a certain fame on the basis of his unique style with Woody's Second Herd. He had worked for Sonny Dunham and Boyd Raeburn and, just prior to joining Woody, had his own group in Washington,

D.C., with future Hermanites Fred Otis (piano), Mert Oliver (bass), Marky Markowitz (trumpet), and Earl Swope (trombone).

DON LAMOND: I was pretty scared, because back in those days, Davey was the first white drummer that really swung for a band without taking a lot of solos and all that. Well, he was a legend, let's face it! It was pretty creepy for me coming in there. And I had to play on his drum set for about a month.

It's a long story. The band was on a Southern tour and there was a big flood all the way down the Eastern seaboard, from Washington to Florida. They called me in Washington to join. I was supposed to join the band in Norfolk, Virginia. I went to the airport and I sat for about an hour. All the flights were canceled because of the flood. So I went over to Union Station and got a train. They were creeping along like about 10 miles an hour, because they were using old, different-gauge tracks that they hadn't used in years, and this train is going through country that looked like jungle. You could reach out and touch the leaves. It was an old steam engine pulling it. So it took me almost a week to catch the band.

Davey got sick first, I think, in Birmingham, and then someplace in Virginia. And I got down to Norfolk, Virginia, and the band had left for Raleigh, North Carolina. When I got to Raleigh, they had left for Charleston, South Carolina. I got to Charleston, and I finally caught up with them in Augusta, Georgia. Davey was in the hospital somewhere down south. John Hammond found him and kept him from going into some other miserable hospital. During the interval between Davey getting sick and leaving, and me joining, Woody was using substitute Army drummers. Wherever there was an Army base near the band, they would use the local Army drummer. He would use Davey's drums, then I used them too, because I wasn't able to ship mine down on account of the flood.

When I finally caught up with the band in Augusta, Woody said, "C'mon up to my room!" So I was black from the train soot, and he said, "Where the hell you been?" I said, "I've been trying to catch this band, that's where I've been!" And he said, "Well, go in there and take a bath!"

RED NORVO: I liked Don Lamond better than Davey. It was just a different style. His [Tough's] bass drum was very heavy. He was wonderful on the up choruses, but he was a little stiff for some people. Bill Harris and those guys loved him, but guys like Flip, I think, liked Don better. Davey could just do one thing.

From mid-October 1945 until July 1946, the Herman Herd was featured weekly on "The Wildroot Show," a live radio program. Wildroot was a popular hair cream of that period. Many of the tapes from those classic broadcasts have been preserved and a few of them have been made available on bootleg record labels.

WOODY: We usually tried to do the shows from New York, but then, when the band would move, the show would move. And we played it from some pretty weird places at times, armories and anywhere.

The real reason for us getting the show was the fact that there were two young fellows in the promotion and ad department of the Wildroot Company in Buffalo who were real jazz fans from way back, real wonderful people, and of course I got to know the man who was the head of the company, and he was a fantastically wonderful guy. He'd sit in the sponsor's booth, come down from Buffalo every week, and bob his head, he was a man in his sixties, like he really enjoyed it. We really were selling hair oil and I guess this was important.

They never gave us any limitations or told us what to do. It wasn't that way sometimes with the network and the advertising agency. At one point, they didn't like the tunes I was playing, but they were evidently afraid of us, so instead of just coming to the point and saying "We'd like you, particularly on an opening tune, to play one that everyone knows like 'Digga Digga Do' or something," they sent out a spy! It took me about three weeks to find out what this man's job was. He was supposed to be coaching me with my lines! Except we never got around to that. We'd have a few drinks, but no rehearsal of lines. But if I plied him with gin on a long jump, I could get a little more out of him, so I finally found that he had stashed a whole suitcase of old music, tired standards, that we were to play. The way I first even began to think about it, was Ralph would come in with these tunes, and they would be wonderful arrangements, but why play "Nagasaki," you know? And Ralph was afraid to tell me where he was getting these tunes. But the guy they sent out really turned out to be a wonderful person, and after a while we forgot about the tunes and just had gin instead.

RALPH BURNS: Woody had the Wildroot show, and that's when I stopped playing piano for the band. I would just stay in one town and write, and meet them once a week and bring the stuff [arrangements] for the radio show. There was so much writing to do. I can't remember all the tunes that I wrote for him. Tony Aless came on the band and replaced me permanently. At the Carnegie Hall concert in '46, I just came out and played one piece.

WOODY: In Newark, the Adams Theater was probably the wildest audience at any theater in the country, at least during the war years. In the early part of the day, the audience was made up of kids, but they were a special breed of Jerseyites who came out of the rocks or something! I remember this one little guy who used to hang over the side boxes and he'd come in maybe two or three days out of the week, and at any point where there wasn't too much noise or melee happening in the audience, he would, in his little, terrible voice, say *"Eeeeeeehh, Woooooody!"* This would go on maybe a hundred times in one show. Bug you right to death! And I finally used to look forward to playing this date because we did what we called the "Segue" show. There were no announcements, not a thing, and very rarely did a talking act ever get through their performance at all, they'd just come out and if they had a dance or a song for them to finish up with, they went right into it, because no jokes with this audience!

There was more action in the audience most days than there was on the stage. No matter what a three-ring circus you might think you were doing, it was complete pandemonium down in the audience. They had police who went up and down the aisles and never stopped. Way before rock 'n' roll! So one afternoon, my daughter came over with her mother, I think Ingie was about four at the time, and she was standing backstage listening to the band. She got away from her mother and walked on stage in her little slacks and sweater, and I was just in the middle of a song and she stood next to me for a while and gazed up at me, completely enraptured at the whole thing. When I finished, I said, "What can I do for you?" And she said, "I would like to sing!" So I dropped the mike and said, "Have you anything in mind you would like to sing?" And she said, "Jesus Loves Me." Now with these characters and this audience, I didn't know if we should make a "direct cut" right away, but it was a funny thing, she got into the thing and did about four complete verses and it was so quiet you could have heard a pin drop. It was probably the first time in the history of the Adams Theater that there was any real peace and quiet.

PETE CANDOLI: Most of the guys were strung out all the time, but I was a health nut and never took any stimulants. I used to work out all the time at Sid Klein's gym in New York. Weight lifting was my thing. They used to ask me to move heavy things around and so they called me Superman, because I used to flex my biceps.

CHUBBY JACKSON: On a train in Iowa during a real hot summer, we were sweltering and were trying vainly to open a window. No! No! None of 'em would budge. However, along came Pete, and he opened a window with his fingertips.

PETE CANDOLI: They said, "Wouldn't it be funny if you would really have a costume and the whole thing?" Well, as it wound up, we used to close the show with "Apple Honey," and I wrote an in-between segment after the solos, and went into some dramatic, elaborate writing with symphony sounds. And I had the Superman suit made with "S" on the front. And at

"Superman" Pete Candoli. (Courtesy Pete Candoli)

that time, the actor George Reeves was doing Superman—he did him later on TV. The act got so hot that I posed for some shots for photo postcards. The office would send cards out when the fan mail would come in—"Sincerely, Superman" or whatever.

The Bradford Theater in Boston had the idea of me jumping on the stage during the first half of "Apple Honey." Then we came into the Paramount Theater in New York. I think we were in there for six or eight weeks. The band used to stay there quite a bit at that time. I dressed like with the band uniform on top of my costume, and as the band was playing, I'd sneak back of the bandstand, go around on the side, and we had it worked up that I would jump on stage during an overture as they would go into the dramatic music. And I'd throw everything off but my Superman outfit, and Don Lamond had a couple of timpani on the sides making *b-o-o-o-m*, and some low chords from the trombones, and the lights would go on and off and the sound-effects people in the sound booth were making thunder sounds coming through the loudspeaker. And Chubby would yell . . . "It's *Super-r-r-m-a-a-n-n-n!!*"

I had a belt with a hook on it, and a cable flexed out, and it went clear across the stage. At that point, I would jump off a big, six-foot carpenter's horse, and I would slide down the cable a bit, and go back to the middle, and unhook myself. Meanwhile, the band is playing and I would flex my muscles and hit my chest several times with each hand, and as I did it, Don Lamond on the timpani would go *boom-ba-boom-ba-boom*. The audience was screaming, it was such a hilarious thing. And then Mickey Folus in the saxophone section would stand up and hand me my horn like a bellboy, wearing a bellman's hat, and I'd play a big cadenza, and we would take "Apple Honey" out with me screaming above the band.

Well, one time the cable didn't sag back to the middle of the stage, and I went straight across to the other side of the wall as I was flexing and looking out at the audience. Right through the air! And I went *smack* with my head into the wall where the cable was hooked, and saw stars. And finally I came to a bit and I went through the rest of the routine while half of the band was playing and half of the band was laughing!

WOODY: The Superman thing was Pete's idea. And his wife made him the first suit by hand. It was red, long underwear, made to look like tights. We did the routine in Newark and a couple of places, and the managing director of the New York Paramount came over to catch the thing. He said he was just as stunned as the audience was because in the last chorus of one of the tunes, this flying madman would come out of the wing and start screaming some high notes and would just leap off stage again, like for no reason at all! And the audience would just look in complete amazement at this whole thing.

PETE CANDOLI: The regular comic that used to do the theaters with us a lot of the time was Buddy Lester. And he had a bit that he would do with a trumpet. It looked like he was playing like crazy, and he'd turn around and say, "Okay, trumpets up!" And I would do a trumpet bit with him, I would imitate him back and forth. As a rule he would play the lines fast, but, like, no tone! But the payoff was, half the time he'd play *omm pa pa, omm pa pa* on "Carnival of Venice," and either he would pull one of his valve slides off, or stick one valve in the wrong place! And he already played bad enough without that! And he'd turn around and the whole band would be breaking up!

WOODY: Bob Weitman, head of Paramount Theaters, said, "Woody, that thing is pretty far out. If we could make a 'bit' out of it, or get some humor out of it, maybe it would be all right." So I said, "Do anything you want, it'll be all right." So Pete's wife made him a second suit because he had to have a fresh suit for the opening at the Paramount. Buddy Lester was opening at the Paramount with us and Weitman told him the problem and Buddy said, "Don't worry about a thing, just get me Pete's old suit," which was about forty sizes too big. First Pete would leap out from one side of the stage and go *ya ta ta ta ta ta* and out from the other side, Buddy would leap out in his overly big Superman suit with his trumpet or cornet, and the wind-up was Pete would pick him up and carry him off, because he blew himself out, and this went on and was a big hit for a couple of days. Then Pete came to me and said, "I don't t'ink I wanna do Superman anymore." And I said, "Why?" And he says, "I think Buddy's putting me on." So I told Pete to forget it! His trumpet playing meant more to me than Superman!

In an interview with Neal Hefti, the author asked him what he could recall about Woody's home life at that time or about Charlotte Herman.

NEAL HEFTI: We all thought that Charlotte was one of the most beautiful women we ever saw. Striking, porcelain-like skin. Very charming! Frances Wayne was beautiful too. Very well-dressed! Very well-groomed! Also a real fan of Charlotte Herman.

WOODY: I think one of the cutest things that happened was when Neal Hefti became engaged to Frances Wayne. We were out in the Midwest someplace, and it was right before their wedding date. Probably a week before, or ten days before. And Neal came to me very out of breath and screaming at the top of his lungs, which was his natural tone of voice, and said, "It's 400 miles to Omaha and I should see my mother and tell her what's happening, and you don't mind if I miss one night?" I said, "No, we still have four trumpets without you. Go ahead, tell your mother!" Eight days later, Frances is crying on the stage, she's crying in her dressing room, she's crying in the toilet, this girl's crying everywhere! She hadn't heard a word from her future husband. Nothing! One night, about eight days later, he just showed up like nothing happened and leaped on the stand. Nobody, to this day, knows what happened to this cat, for like eight days! His mother never saw him. This we checked on! I thought maybe he got a bum rap or something, but nothing. No explanation!

Woody said that years later, both Neal and Frances apologized for "the way they acted" when they worked for him.

NEAL HEFTI: I'd say the most humorous thing in a way was when I borrowed Woody's suit to get married in, because Frances and I were to have been married two weeks later. The band was on the road. We were just finishing up its tour, then it had maybe a few days off, then we were going to go into the 400 Club in New York and then to the Paramount. So we were going to be in New York for awhile. And Boston was our last engagement on the road for a week before we were to go to New York. And then Francie's family said this was their only chance that they could see their daughter getting married, she must get married here in the church and do the big wedding. So I didn't have anything to wear except a real scroungy band uniform which I was going to burn as soon as I got to New York. I borrowed one of Woody's suits to get married in. He's short-er than I am, but we were both about the same weight. I was only about 130 pounds when we got married.

The wedding was attended by Woody, a few intimate friends, and the entire band.

On November 16 the band was back in Columbia's New York studios. One of the charts recorded was a First Herd flag waver by Neal Hefti appropriate-ly titled "Wildroot," after the radio show, based on the chords of "Flying Home." The recording featured Flip Phillips, a driving Bill Harris solo, Woody's clarinet, and the whole band climaxing into a breathtaking finish with Pete Candoli's trumpet blowing the roof off.

On December 10 in New York, the band was back for another recording session for Columbia. One of the titles recorded was a head arrangement called "Blowin' Up a Storm." Most of the ensemble work was written by Neal Hefti, with Pete Candoli collaborating. According to Woody, the title origi-nated as a gimmick on the radio show when people were asked to submit titles. This is the one that won. It's a blues beginning with a Basie-ish-sound-ing rhythm section and developing with Woody's buoyant clarinet, a trumpet cadenza highlighting some brilliant bop figures, slurs from Billy Bauer's gui-tar, and a rapid build-up with the whole band interacting in a roaring finale and Pete's trumpet once more on top. Also recorded on December 10 was a brilliant Hefti arrangement of a simple pop tune of the day, "Let It Snow, Let It Snow, Let It Snow."

WOODY: This was a tune that was destined to be a big hit, Vaughn Monroe wound up with the hit record, but we had the jump on everybody. I assigned the tune to Neal Hefti and he came in with the arrangement, a gorgeous chart, but it had an extra-long twenty-four-bar introduction. It could have been cut; I usually never went for this bit. I usually started lop-ping off bars immediately to get into the piece, but this was so pretty. The chords were so rich and the way he voiced the whole thing, it was so love-ly, that we just felt we couldn't cut this, it would be ridiculous. This record sold like four copies!

NAT PIERCE: After Woody decided that the reason "Let It Snow" wasn't the number-one-selling record was the long intro, from that time on, hardly any intros, or two-bar intros, or four-bar intros . . . no more "symphonies" on the front of the tune [laughter].

Stravinsky conducting the Herd on the top floor of the Paramount Theater. L to R: Woody, Stravinsky, Billy Bauer, Don Lamond, Chubby Jackson, Flip Phillips, John LaPorta, Sam Marowitz. (Courtesy The Hugh Turner Collection, Hollywood)

Woody always considered that the high point and greatest thrill of his musical career was when classical composer Igor Stravinsky approached him to "write a piece" for the band.

WOODY: The first that I knew about it was when I received a wire from him out of the clear blue sky one day, that said, "I have listened to your orchestra and I wish to write a piece for you as a Christmas gift. It will be delivered on . . . ," and he named a day. When that date arrived, so did the music! Pretty wild! And Stravinsky arrived a day later to rehearse with us.

I wasn't completely aware, at the time, of the events that led up to this occasion. But it seems that we had a mutual friend by the name of Goldie Goldmark, who used to be a bass player with the Mitchell Ayres band. And at this time he was working for a song publisher, Lou Levy, and evidently in the process of getting copyrights for some foreign music, he became friendly with Stravinsky. Well, he wound up spending a lot of hours with him and I guess drinking vodka, and Goldie would come on with some of our records and then some more vodka, and he must have prodded Stravinsky pretty good and kept bringing different records over, and shortly before Christmas, this would be 1945, I received this wire from Stravinsky.

We were playing the Paramount Theater in New York at the time and were just winding up an eight-week engagement when *Ebony Concerto* and Stravinsky arrived. He rehearsed us for three days and would have rehearsed us longer and even conducted at Carnegie Hall if he hadn't had commitments elsewhere. But as it was, it was a great experience and a tremendous thrill, not only for me but for all of the guys in the band. Remember, this was the First Herd and we were really "shouting." And we had some avid, mad, Stravinsky fans on the band like Pete Candoli, and this was like "The Master" to them.

The whole rehearsal thing started off in what now seems an amusing fashion, but wasn't so funny at the time. We were playing like six shows a day at the Paramount and for the first day and a half or so of rehearsals, Stravinsky wasn't aware of this. Of course, the very first rehearsal, after whatever show it was, you can imagine the scene, the boys in the band are all dressed in their best suits, clean shirts and neckties; you never saw such a bunch of clean-cut guys on any band. Then in comes Stravinsky with a turtleneck sweater and a pair of beat-up slacks and sneakers.

We would rehearse after every show and after a while, Stravinsky would call a halt and go next door to Sardi's and have a couple of vodkas and we would go back to the theater and do the next show. We were walking around numb after a while. We didn't even eat! Who had time?

I should say something about the composition itself, the *Ebony Concerto*. What we were doing then, the First Herd, that sold Stravinsky on us through our records, were heavy, strong, jazz things, with lots of open brass and so forth, but that was the great switch; when he wrote something especially for us to play, it was a very subtle, quiet piece. The brass were never out of mutes for more than a moment or two. It's a very delicate and a very sad piece; a lot of emotion, and a great deal of sadness. Here we were, a wild, happy-sounding group, and this was the piece he wrote for us.

Here we were, this bunch of wild men, who didn't seem a bit wild to Stravinsky at this point, I feel sure, because they were acting so unlike themselves! They were like a bunch of kids going to class for the first time, and I know Stravinsky loved every minute of it. He made no bones about expressing his feeling that that was the greatest musical family he had ever come in contact with. He was intrigued with our group because we were just a bunch of travelers who wanted so much to play his piece well, and were so limited in our musical ability!

This man had the patience of Job, which was an education in itself. None of us was a really great reader and Stravinsky would hum parts to us and count out loud, always with lots of hand clapping to keep us going and wheedle our parts out of us. You know, he wrote the whole damn thing out in four. He said it took him hours! Usually he would change every bar or two. But he felt that jazz musicians would have difficulty with different tempos. And he was correct. We had plenty of trouble even with four!

Pete Candoli had the trumpet solo on it, and it was a hard thing. Conrad Gozzo would probably have played that particular solo better, but

Pete was such a wild Stravinsky fan, you know, incorporating phrases from *Firebird* into head arrangements and things like that, and he insisted he *had* to play the solo. He's a hard trumpet player and this could have been played a lot more delicately, I'll tell you that!

FLIP PHILLIPS: During the rehearsal of *Ebony Concerto*, there was a passage I had to play there and I was playing it soft, and Stravinsky said, "Play it, here I am!" And I blew it louder, and he threw me a kiss!

WOODY: And Chubby Jackson, he provided some fun at the very first rehearsal. When the parts came in and Chubby looked at his, well, there wasn't very much activity in the bass part, just a bass line to fit the piece. When Stravinsky showed up for the first rehearsal, Chubby immediately jumped up, probably out of his nut, and said, "Mr. Stravinsky, you must have made a mistake here. You want more things to happen on my part, don'tcha?" Stravinsky said, "No, son, you just play this. It'll be nice!"

CHUBBY JACKSON: Woody gave us all our parts. And if you can visualize this, the first bar had a quarter note on the first beat of the bar, then the next bar, like maybe on the third beat, there was a quarter note. Then on the next bar, et cetera. It went down like that for about twelve bars. "Jeez, I'm playing 90,000 notes all over the place and here I get a part written by Igor Stravinsky, and this looks like amateur hour to me," I'm telling the guys. Well, to make a long story short, Stravinsky himself beat the band off and started to conduct. I didn't realize that he didn't have the rhythm section leaning on one another. I was all by myself and into about the third bar I got so lost, I didn't know who I was, and I almost burst out in tears because here was Stravinsky conducting, and this is supposed to be *bup, bup, bup, bup*. And to read it is easy, but I thought maybe the drum would be playing the same accents and the guitar and the piano. No! They were written into some other things, and I took it as another one of my amiable defeats! But I learned something.

WOODY: As for the way he worked with me, I can't say enough about that! He showed me where to breathe, wrote in breath marks and tried to give me confidence in the whole thing. Once he said to me, "You know, the French clarinetists, they get very small sound, but technique, beautiful! The German clarinetists, big sound, not too much technique. But you, you're different" . . . miserable! No, he didn't say the word; in fact, what he said, he meant as a compliment! But I broke up, fell right on the floor laughing!

SHORTY ROGERS: The music of Stravinsky, the name of Stravinsky, the whole image was something that everyone sort of bowed down to. And it was mind-boggling that the composer was writing something for us and that he would come to our rehearsal. We kept waiting and waiting and finally Stravinsky comes to the rehearsal and we were at the Paramount Theater, and they had a little elevator backstage and you got into the elevator and there was a little schedule posted on the wall that everyone would read as they were going up to the next floor: "The first show is at 11:20 A.M., the second show is at 1 P.M., et cetera." And at the bottom, there was a blank space that had room to write in any extra statements that had to be made. So the day of the rehearsal, the guy that ran the elevator backstage took that space at the bottom and wrote with his kind of Brooklyn accent, "Notice: Woody Herman's band, *youse guys* will be rehearsed by Professor Stravinsky this afternoon between the first and second shows."

WOODY: We were rehearsing upstairs at the Paramount. It was supposed to be a recreation room in the theater, for the various acts to go and play ping-pong and stuff. And that's where we used to rehearse, up on the top floor of the building. This was also the place where we used to have parties. Christmas parties, New Year's parties, we were always there for the holiday season. But we were always so beat, we didn't know whether there was a party going on or not.

INGRID HERMAN REESE: That Christmas [1945] would be the most vivid early recollection of my dad. It would have been about my fifth Christmas. It was really the first year that he had considerable money or something, because he brought both sets of parents to New York to the Jackson Heights apartment for Christmas. He transported my mother's parents from California and his parents from Milwaukee. And that is when he got my mother three fur coats. Those were the only fur coats she ever got, but he got them all at the same time. His father, Otto, brought this special little "church" that was a music box that went under the tree. I mean both sets of grandparents brought very special stuff. It was incredibly elaborate.

The December 31 edition of *Newsweek* magazine gave the band almost a full page entitled "Woody's Blue Heaven," making mention of Woody's current hit record of "Caldonia" and likening it to the former success stories of Tommy Dorsey's "Marie" and Artie Shaw's "Begin the Beguine." As 1946 began, Woody Herman and his Herd were doing top box office business. The Columbia records were selling, and the current Wildroot radio shows were receiving fervent public response. To top it all off, the band won the *Down Beat*, *Metronome* and *Billboard* musician polls. It also won in *Esquire* magazine in two categories, the Silver and New Star Awards. In addition, several sidemen won in their respective categories, including Bill Harris,

Dave Tough, Chubby Jackson, Pete Candoli, Ralph Burns, Red Norvo and Frances Wayne.

CHUBBY JACKSON: All of a sudden, certain musicians in the band began to win all of the music polls held in the nation. The managers saw a good thing and naturally worked us beyond any human capacity.

Joining the band at the Paramount Theater engagement in December was Red Norvo on vibraphone. He was a contemporary of Woody, having worked as a single in vaudeville and later with the orchestras of Victor Young and Paul Whiteman. In the early forties, he led his own small group on New York's 52nd Street with people like Eddie Bert, Specs Powell, and Shorty Rogers. Just previous to Woody, Red had been featured with the Benny Goodman sextet and big band.

Early in January, when the band was still at the Paramount Theater, trumpeter Irving Markowitz replaced Neal Hefti and Conrad Gozzo replaced trumpeter Irv Lewis. Powerhouse trumpeter Gozzo achieved recognition in the ensuing years as a member of an elite group of respected big-band first trumpeters.

RED NORVO: Gozzo got out of the service, and he didn't know where I was living. But he knew I was playing with Benny. So the only thing he knew to do was call Benny Goodman's office. And Benny answered and said, "Who is this?" and he says "Conrad Gozzo." And he was supposed to go with Woody, instead of Benny. And Benny talked him into going with him right away, that night. He met the band in Hartford, which is his hometown. He was on the bandstand that night. When I came on, I looked up and saw Gozzo up there and nearly died! Gozzo was so nice in his way, he was so kind, he just couldn't turn Benny down when Benny asked him to join.

But Woody kept asking me to come into his band and so finally I told Benny I was going to leave. I told him I just had to get away, it's too much work and everything. And he said, "I understand." So about two weeks later Woody called me and I said, "Okay!"

Benny made Gozzo give a month's notice, which forced him to go to the Coast with the band. But as soon as his notice was up, he flew back and joined us at the Paramount. I told him to be there early. Shorty and I met him in our dressing room, and Shorty had written out all those head things that we were doing, and Gozzo read them right off! Pete Candoli was a pretty strong trumpet player himself, and he was ruining a lot of first trumpet players by playing the second part loud, because the lead man is supposed to have the force. He has the top part and he has to play above the second part. We had a guy named Irv Lewis, from Detroit. He ruined his lip playing so loud. He had to leave on account of his lip.

So Gozzo came in and he took his place and played the first show, and we played "Bijou," which was basically a solo for Bill Harris who is featured all through it. So Gozzo is playing lead, he's reading it, and there's a part in it, like a big crescendo—it breaks off and then Bill Harris plays again, right? And Candoli kept getting louder and louder and louder, and so Gozzo kind of looked in the direction of Pete, not realizing what was going on, maybe Pete was trying to help him, I don't know . . . but anyway, Gozzo started to play loud, and it's the first time that I ever heard the brass section "splatter." I've only heard three brass sections in my whole life that had that attack.

WOODY: During some of that band's splash of success, we won a poll in *Esquire* magazine, and Duke was the natural winner and we were the new band on the scene. And so we did a radio broadcast together promoted by the magazine. Besides Duke's band and our band, the Nat Cole Trio won an award that year.

That was a very thrilling experience. We were the unknown quantity, we were just coming up and the band played "above its boots" most days, and Duke's band was in its usual state. He had all the right guys with him, but they were at a very independent stage. I remember in the afternoon, we had a rehearsal for the sound balance, and about four guys from Duke's band showed up. Of course we were there *en masse*. Chafing at the bit and ready. And evidently someone carried back the message because when we came back at five or six o'clock in the evening, before the broadcast, all their fellas had showed up! It was pretty fantastic. We would play a tune and they would play a tune, and it was a great comparison of what the kids were thinking up and what the older fellas were doing. It was a very exciting broadcast. Orson Welles did the commentary.

PETE CANDOLI: Duke's band did their thing and we did our thing. And I think we did "C Jam Blues" or something together with both bands, and that's when the Ellington band had Johnny Hodges and Cat Anderson— bless him! And we did our things, "Apple Honey" and "Caldonia" and all that type of thing. And they were introducing the award winners . . . Bill Harris, Chubby, Flip, and I all won that year. And we each individually did a solo, and it went live throughout the country.

It was so amazing to have my name being introduced and stepping out in front of the orchestra. Funny about it, a few years later, I came to the West Coast and joined the staff at ABC, and we were doing one of those mystery radio shows. A small studio staff orchestra playing background. Jack Webb was doing a show called "Pat Novac for Hire." He was a radio actor to start with, and he started talking to me one day and he said that he had been a disc jockey for a San Francisco radio station. And he had taken the concert off the air on his affiliate station, on transcription, so he could play it later. And he still had the transcription. He said, "I'll never forget when both bands played together, it was the thrill of my life!"

WOODY: Leonard Feather was very important to *Esquire* at that point, and the whole jazz program, the way the magazine was involved. So when we got our last radio show, the Wildroot Show, I hired Leonard as a writer on our show because I just figured he would be a good influence to have on our side.

Back in those days, the *Esquire* magazine had this thing, and they would give you gold "Esquies" and silver "Esquies" and bronze "Esquies," depending on how you finished in the "Olympics," you know. And our guys were loaded! They had "Esquies" comin' out of their joints. And I tried to remind them that this and a nickel would get you a cup of coffee anywhere, you know. But it was a whole cult and band of people who moved around the country to listen to you. They were fanatics. It was the excitement, the pulsation, whatever they felt, whatever they derived from it.

On February 6 and 7, the Herman Herd was back in Columbia's New York studios, recording. By now, the Columbia 78 rpm waxings of "Caldonia," "Apple Honey," "Laura," "Bijou," "Out of This World," and others were top sellers, and disc jockeys were plugging them nationally on the airwaves.

On February 17 in New York, the band recorded "Panacea," with Leonard Feather's earthy, humorous lyrics: "Mama, you are my tonic, the best pick-me-up in town. . . ." The recording features a bristling Bill Harris solo, and Pete's trumpet takes the band out.

In mid-February, vocalist Lynne Stevens joined the band, replacing Frances Wayne. Frances returned briefly in March as a substitute for Lynne.

WOODY: Sonny Berman emulated Chubby in everything he did. Anything Chubby did was good and correct. Chubby would leap into the air at the end of a tune and wave his arms and do "takes" and milk the audience. So Sonny was feeling very effervescent this particular day in Chicago and when he finished whatever this piece was, he leaped from the top tier, down to the tier where my stand was, and he went through the wood up to his knees. It was beautiful! A complete lost expression, like "Wha . . . What?"

On March 25, 1946, the Herd performed Stravinsky's *Ebony Concerto* at the historic Carnegie Hall concert. The orchestra's conventional instrumentation was augmented with a harp and a French horn for the debut of the Stravinsky composition. This was the band as it performed at Carnegie Hall: Woody (clarinet, alto sax, vocals, leader); Conrad Gozzo, Pete Candoli, Sonny

Berman, Marky Markowitz, Shorty Rogers (trumpets), Ralph Pfeffner, Bill Harris, Ed Kiefer (trombones), Sam Marowitz, John La Porta (clarinets/alto saxes), Flip Phillips, Mickey Folus (tenor saxes), Sam Rubinowitch (baritone sax), Tony Aless (piano), Billy Bauer (guitar), Chubby Jackson (bass), and Red Norvo (vibes). John Barrows (French horn) and Abe Rosen (harp) were added for *Ebony Concerto*. Ralph Burns played piano on *Summer Sequence*.

WOODY: When we finally performed *Ebony Concerto* at Carnegie Hall, the assistant conductor of the Philharmonic, Walter Hendl, conducted. Stravinsky wasn't available to do it, though I know he would have loved to. He conducted twice when we performed it. But on our first night at Carnegie, he couldn't make it. It was a pretty hectic backstage scene. Typically, the new jackets we had ordered were there, but nobody could find the box with the pants in it until two minutes before bell time. I had ordered a new dinner jacket and it turned out to have been made for a guy who weighed about 180. At the time, I was about 130! So I stuffed all the inside pockets with handkerchiefs and took on some quick weight!

Of course, there were a lot of people there that night who wouldn't ordinarily have gone to hear a jazz band and we all knew this would be the case. This added importance to the concert from our point of view and also, of course, increased our nervousness and excitement.

PETE CANDOLI: I guess the highlight for me was the Carnegie Hall concert. I wrote an original at the time called "Superman with a Horn," which I performed. I ended "Superman with a Horn" that night on another key, 'cause that was the way I felt. And like in woodwinds, I used cascade effects and strange harmonies, as a brush painting of harmonies right through the composition, as a color in itself, and as background for the solo that I was playing.

The concert was recorded sans *Ebony Concerto* and *Summer Sequence*, and with only one microphone. Consequently, the recording is of poor quality. There is, however, enough fire in the band's performance to make it a worthwhile record in any jazz collection. The concert tapes were put aside and forgotten until 1951, when MGM released them in an album. One of the titles recorded was "Sweet and Lovely," an elegant Ralph Burns score for Flip Phillips. Flip was in a soulful mood, and the recording captured his ability to convey emotion, with the band weaving gentle harmonic patterns that complemented his big tenor sound.

WOODY: We ended the first half of the concert with the *Ebony Concerto*. Considering that it's not really an exciting piece—it's pure Stravinsky, it ends as subtly as it begins—considering all that, the reaction was very gratifying to us.

Also worthy of mention is Ralph Burns's chart of "Mean to Me," recorded from the concert, which showcases Bill Harris in a warm, delicately phrased solo performance, the band once again providing a panorama of background tonal colors and concluding with a full, rich ensemble chord.

WOODY: We also introduced *Summer Sequence* at Carnegie the night we did the Stravinsky piece. As a matter of fact, it received even more critical acclaim than the Stravinsky piece did, because it was much more easy to understand, and it was in the style of the band.

RALPH BURNS: One of my most exciting moments with Woody was that concert in Carnegie Hall when we played *Summer Sequence*. That was something I wish I could remember more. It was a thrilling night. The band was at its absolute peak. We thought nothing of it at the time, like a baseball team that went on to the World Series.

WOODY: Of course, the music critics were all there and they reviewed it and, as I recall, they didn't really know exactly how to treat it. It *was* Stravinsky and we *did* play it and it was clean and the intonation was all right and so forth, but I remember they were pretty mixed up on just what it was supposed to be!

After the concert, though, I ran into quite a few people who thought it was wonderful. For example, Charlie Barnet, who can be a pretty wild guy and is not one to get up on a soapbox and shout anyone's praise unless he means it.

The *New York Post*, on March 26, printed Harriet Johnson's review, "Rhythm and Reason—Woody Herman's Concert Up on 'Long Hair' 57th Street."

Woody Herman and his orchestra sold out Carnegie Hall last night for his first concert venture there and went partly 'long hair' in the bargain, too. *Ebony Concerto*, by Igor Stravinsky, written especially for the Herman ensemble, had its World Premiere with Walter Hendl conducting. . . . Stravinsky's piece, although filled with syncopated rhythms, was pretty tough stuff to take on first hearing, but the enthusiastic audience swallowed it nobly. He utilized, however, all of the virtuosity of the band and its possibilities of instrumentation. There were, for instance, some stunning effects with muted trombones and trumpets. . . . I hope Woody gets inspired to break down the bars again on 57th Street.

The *New York World Telegram* headlined in its music section: "Stravinsky Wows the Hep-Cats—Joins Woody Herman at Carnegie Hall." The *New York Daily News* featured the story as "Igor's Back and Woody's Got Him, At

Carnegie Hall" (a takeoff on the advertising slogan for the film *Adventure*: "Gable's Back and [Greer] Garson's Got Him").

The composition by Stravinsky drew a mixed response from the critics. Barry Ulanov commented in *Metronome* that it was "more like a French imitation of Igor than the great man himself. . . . Rhythmically, tonally, and melodically it is as dry as dehydrated eggs and far less palatable."

During this period, the Herman band had offices in the RKO Building in New York with the management counsel team of Goldfarb, Mirenburg, and Vallon. General Artists Corporation handled the bookings for the band.

WOODY: My business advisers decided, after the Carnegie Hall concert, that we should go out on a forty-day tour, our first actual straight concert tour. *Ebony Concerto* was to be a part of each performance, and to conduct it Stravinsky got for us Alex Haieff, sort of a protege of his, who had come to rehearsals with Stravinsky before the Carnegie performance. This was a great thrill to Alex to conduct Stravinsky's composition with a jazz orchestra. Well, he really had an opportunity to live the part, too, on that tour.

In a lot of the big cities we did okay, but when we didn't, Alex was in his glory. We were hissed! We were booed! The guys were all nervous and perspiring and shook up. Not Alex! "This is what you have to go through for music, you know!" It was beautiful!

We hurt ourselves somewhat in our billing. In great big letters it said IGOR STRAVINSKY and EBONY CONCERTO. And this not only kept a lot of the kids away, but the ones that came, well, I don't know what they expected, but this piece, after all, was only nine minutes out of a two-and-a-half-hour concert. But two minutes into it and the hissing and booing would start. These were the evenings we dreaded, but for Alex, I'm sure, they made the whole thing worthwhile. He was, like, reliving Stravinsky's life.

Here was a very young, handsome man, a European or a Russian, who became a protege of Stravinsky's as a young kid. He wore an ill-fitting tuxedo that he'd borrowed from someone and he conducted with a pencil. Well, the cats on the band dug him quietly for two or three days and then, like they figured, "We better take this kid in hand, he ain't goin' no place like this!" About a week later, I have never seen such a complete change in a person. "I never knew such living existed!" he said. And like, Mary Ann McCall was leading him around by the nose. Everything was *wunderbar* from then on with Alex.

In March and April, two former members of the "Band That Plays the Blues" returned to the Herd after fulfilling their military tours of duty. Pianist Jimmy Rowles replaced Tony Aless, and trumpeter Cappy Lewis returned replacing Irving Markowitz.

CAPPY LEWIS: I was in the Army from '44 to '46. And when I got out of the Army, I called Woody once again, and he said, "C'mon back!" So I came back. But now there was a change. Bebop had started to come in. I came back but I didn't feel as at ease as I did when I joined Woody the first time. But it worked out all right. I was with him for about six months in 1946. When he broke up the band in December, that was the end of my time with Woody Herman. I guess salaries were just getting so huge it was starting to weigh him down.

WOODY: We carried about eighteen or nineteen musicians on our payroll, twenty or more than that when I had the vocal group, Blue Flames. And there was always a band boy, a road manager, an assistant to the band boy, and usually a valet or something. I had three lawyers. It was a combine, but you had to like pay each one's tariff. And we paid for the light and the heat in their building too, even though they did much legal business aside from ours. We had an accountant, publicity people, we usually carried one for advance on the road and one permanent guy in New York. I'm sure I'm leaving some out. Arrangers, copyists! It became a hassle dealing with forty or more people, and everyone had to be paid every week. Like fifty-two weeks a year. Our overhead became fabulous, but it didn't seem to make a difference at the time, because of our intake. I don't remember exact figures, but everyone was being paid very well. There was no reason not to pay them very well. And there were bonuses and gifts and stuff, you know.

SHORTY ROGERS: The first writing that I did for the band was while we were in Chicago. Woody told Red Norvo that Columbia wanted us to do a Woodchoppers album with the small group. We were just in town for a few days, and we didn't have any arrangements to record. And Red said to me, "Do you have any ideas how we can put this together?" Actually, before I went in the Army I was with Red's small group in New York, so we worked over some of those tunes and wrote new arrangements of them. Some were "Igor" and "Steps," and I don't remember all of the titles, but I definitely remember that those were the first things where I took a pencil and wrote something down.

On May 16 and 20 the Woodchoppers small group cut a set of titles for Columbia in Chicago. On the tune "Steps," Woody commented: "I gave it its title in honor of Barney Bigard, whose nickname is Steps. I tried to play like him as a tribute." Beginning with a simple introduction, a bass solo, Woody's low register clarinet and Red's vibes, the small ensemble plays in the Ellington mode. A second title recorded was the propulsive head arrangement of "Fan It." Originally recorded by the early Woodchoppers in February 1941, it had undergone a dramatic transformation by 1946.

Taken at a bright tempo with Woody's whimsical vocal ("Fan It Red"), it swings, and it's fun to listen to. Featured on solo work were Red Norvo, Flip, Sonny Berman and Bill Harris. The band riffs its way home with a wind-down out chorus.

According to Woody, "Shorty, like just about everyone in the band, was a Stravinsky fan"—consequently the title "Igor." The chart features Woody's clarinet and a bop-tinged riff, Red's vibes, Bill Harris moaning and chopping his way through the score, Flip in a lightly swinging mood, Sonny's trumpet, more of Woody's clarinet, and some Billy Bauer guitar.

In May two more personnel changes occurred in the rhythm section. The stalwart cheerleader and lieutenant of the First Herd gave his notice. Chubby Jackson would return, however, in the next two Herds. He was replaced by Joe Mondragon.

CHUBBY JACKSON: Woody's First Herd had the greatest expression of excitement and spirit on a bandstand. Of course, Duke had his own spectacular untouched approach, and Count Basie was the perfect example of the laid-back sound combined with great soloists and amazing ensemble shouts, but Woody's band had that well-known "huge grin on its face" along with some of the greatest musical sounds yet heard anywhere.

The other change in the rhythm section was guitarist Billy Bauer's departure, and his replacement by Chuck Wayne. Chuck Wayne (actually Charles Jagelka) started with mandolin and switched to guitar. Prior to Woody, Chuck worked with Clarence Profit, the Nat Jaffe Trio, Joe Marsala at the Hickory House, and Phil Moore at Cafe Society.

JIMMY ROWLES: There was a club called The Pour-A-Drink-On-Your-Head Club. I don't know if Woody still has the habit, I doubt it, but he used to in 1946, when I became a member. After the job, if you were on a train, you'd have time off and everybody would be having a ball. I can remember, I was standing there talking to Woody and I think we were on a train on the way to Texas and we each had a drink in our hands. All of a sudden, he just reached up and poured a drink on my head, and then he backed off and said, "Don't hit me!" And he's laughing, saying, "I couldn't help it! Now you're a member of the club!" I said, "I wouldn't hit you, Woody, if you kicked me in the balls! Do you have a comb?" He would only do that if he was just really bombed!

After thirty-six weeks of consecutive weekly broadcasts, the Wildroot radio show concluded in Fort Worth, Texas, on July 5.

WOODY: Giveaway shows were getting very big then, and we were trying to think of a gimmick, and so to have a good blow-off for this show, we

The First Herd, mid-1946. Front row: Flip Phillips, Woody, John LaPorta, Sam Marowitz, Mickey Folus, Sam Rubinowitch. Second row: Red Norvo, Ralph Pfeffner, Bill Harris, Ed Kiefer, Neal Reid. Back row: Joe Mondragon, Chuck Wayne, Don Lamond, Sonny Berman, Cappy Lewis, Conrad Gozzo, Pete Candoli, Shorty Rogers. (From the Woody Herman Collection)

decided the only thing we could do was "give the band away." And some young sailor in upper New York won it, and it was lots of fun, because he had the band from that morning right through the night and could do any-thing he wanted with the band. And one of the things was that we sere-naded a girlfriend of his in her back yard, and played a few riffs, and she was the daughter of a Greek Orthodox priest, and he was pretty upset about the whole thing, because their backyard was the courtyard of this church.

In mid-August, the band journeyed to Southern California for an extended engagement at Tommy Dorsey's Casino Gardens Ballroom at Ocean Park, a beach town adjacent to Santa Monica. The Herd had contracts for three more films in the next two months.

WOODY: Cappy Lewis had been in the first band and then he went in the Army and when he got out, we brought him back, and he and Flip Phillips traveled together. To say that these two young men were conservative was putting it mildly. They would buy a nickel newspaper and then sell it to one another for two cents after one read it! For a short period we used cars and they had their own little car, and they found that by driving 42.5

miles an hour, they got better mileage than at any other speed, and they had to leave four hours in front of everybody, because they were paid so much a mile for driving and using the car, and so this made a bigger profit, you see. And the other guys were putting them on something terrible.

For quite some time Bill Harris carried this life-sized dummy with him in the car. Three had to sit in the front seat because the dummy had to sit next to him at all times. And the dummy looked pretty real, his suit was something like Bill's. And by the time we got to California on this one tour, we opened at the Casino Gardens, Tommy Dorsey's place, and the first night I came up on the bandstand and looked, and we were now using "four" trombones. The dummy is next to Harris and Harris is talking to him: "You have eight bars there," and he wants to know why he didn't play it right.

So on this tour, on the way out to the Coast, they decided to do a little episode on film, and they decided to make Cappy and Flip the victims of this plot. We're making a jump to Texas somewhere and Pete Candoli and Bill and Goz were in Bill's car and they left early and got ahead. There was a big turn on the highway with a shoulder on one side and they put Pete out as the lookout and waited until Flip and Cappy were seen chugging up the road at 42.5 miles per hour. Just as they rounded the bend, they threw out the dummy on the highway, and Cappy and Flip went straight up. They nearly turned over the car. Meanwhile, the camera was grinding away!

SHORTY ROGERS: Bill Harris would do things like go out on the street, and a car would be coming, and he'd throw it under the wheels and start screaming, "You killed this guy!" I heard the story about him up in one of the upper stories of the hotel, and he's got the dummy out on the window sill, and he starts yelling, "Don't jump! Don't jump!" And he got a crowd of people gathered, and then threw the dummy over.

On August 18, CBS held a radio workshop. Igor Stravinsky was present to conduct *Ebony Concerto*. Stravinsky was interviewed briefly by radio announcer Chet Huntley. A portion of that interview follows:

C.H.   Mr. Stravinsky, what first interested you in Woody and the boys?

I.S.   The sounds the orchestra makes, Mr. Huntley. It is rare to find any group of musicians capable of such precise ensemble effects.

C.H.   This is the first time you have conducted *Ebony Concerto*, isn't it?

I.S.   Yes, it is!

C.H.   Would you tell us something about the composition?

I.S. Well, it is a concerto in three parts. First, an allegro, second an andante—a kind of blues—and the third, theme and variations.

C.H. And why did you name it *Ebony Concerto*?

I.S. Vell, it features Voody's clarinet, and the clarinets are black. I called it Ebony Concerto, but the title is only for identification. It's the music that counts.

WOODY: Stravinsky conducted twice when we performed *Ebony Concerto*. Once was on the Columbia workshop program when they did a whole program built around the band, a kind of a tribute thing. It really gave us a chance to show some of our wares. The other time was when we recorded it for Columbia [August 19, 1946]. This was in California. At least out there Stravinsky and I were neighbors!

We rehearsed a couple of days before the recording date. It was mostly reviewing because the personnel of the band was almost the same. We rehearsed out in Santa Monica in Tommy Dorsey's ballroom and I would pick up Stravinsky in my car because it was, like, "If you pick me up, I come." And besides, he said he would never own a car in this country. "In Paris, I still own three automobiles, because in Paris, they don't embarrass you by asking for a driver's license or making you take tests!" On the drives to and from the rehearsal, we'd discuss everything under the sun, except music! One day, a group of dogs was crossing the street in front of us and he said, "Ah, look, Voody, they have da life! No vorries on their backs, no taxes, no nothing! *You* have to do better than you did the last time, top yourself, but they, they are happy. Eat, sleep, and make love!"

Another thing we had to do, or rather Stravinsky had to do, for the recording, was to chop away at the composition. This was before LPs, and it had to be cut to go on a 78 record. One of Stravinsky's big beefs with the movie companies and other people who would call on him to write something was that he wouldn't allow cuts on his music. He would write a piece and that was that! You play it *all*! And correctly! But this was something *he* wanted to do, and he lopped and chopped away like it was nothing!

On August 21, 1946, Woody and Charlotte bought, from Humphrey Bogart and Lauren Bacall, their first and only home. The Bogarts had used it as their "honeymoon" home for a year. The home would remain Woody's permanent home and refuge from the road for forty-one years.

The house is located high above Sunset Boulevard in a residential section, at 8620 Hollywood Boulevard, west of the primary Hollywood business district. Originally built in 1939, it was constructed on three levels on the side of a hill, with the garage, dining room, and kitchen on the top level, where one entered. The house had four bedrooms and three bathrooms. One bathroom, on the second level down, had an oblong bathtub at least five feet deep, resembling a miniature swimming pool. Eventually, the staircase leading from the second to the third level would serve as a gallery for Woody's numerous awards, plaques, and various honors. From the patio, one had a magnificent view of the city below. Woody, Charlotte, and Ingrid were animal lovers and there were always at least two dogs or cats, and at one time a duck, roaming the premises.

During this period, Woody made a film entitled *Rhapsody in Wood*, a George Pal "Puppetoon." The film was mostly animated, utilizing puppets. Woody was seen, but the band played only on the soundtrack. Pal had won a special Academy Award in 1943 for his work using puppets in films. Later, he was an innovator in other areas of special effects and made some films with a science fiction twist, including *Destination Moon* (1950) and *War of the Worlds* (1953). Just before his involvement with Woody, he had made an eight-minute Puppetoon with Duke Ellington entitled *Date with Duke*.

WOODY: George Pal used to use a lot of jazz people. He did things with Peggy Lee and Nat Cole. He evidently liked our band. I think it was one of the best things we ever tried to do. Ralph wrote the music. George Pal always had a little story line with these things. This was the story of "Grandpappy Herman," supposedly how I got my first clarinet. It seemed that Grandpappy Herman was an old woodchopper and he used to go through the forest, and with one clean sweep, hundreds of these tremendous oaks would just like lie down. And then with just a few whacks of his axe, he carved out this clarinet, and I did a little opening "alive," sitting at a fireplace with a clarinet saying, "You may think this is just an ordinary clarinet, but it really isn't, it is a kind of Stradivarius of its type, because my Grandpappy was such a great woodchopper and he carved this clarinet out of a giant tree." Then at the end, I come back and say, "That's how it really happened, and that is the story of Grandpappy Herman and the old woodchopper." And out comes the little puppet in the doorway and he says, "Who are you trying to kid with this story? You know damn well you bought that in a hock shop for twenty bucks!" So we get into this terrible beef and that's the end of the short. But it all has musical value. Visually, he caught everything in the music, and of course vice versa. Ralph worked with him and just did some fantastic things and we took one little bit of it and recorded it [July 20, 1949] and called it "Rhapsody in Wood."

The Republic feature film *Hit Parade of 1947* was also filmed during Woody's extended Southern California stay.

RED NORVO: The First Herd was something. When we came out to the Coast, we followed Kenton's band back here to California. We used to hear these things the Kenton band would say about us like, "Woody's band doesn't kill me," because they thought they were so modern. So we were out here at Tommy's Ballroom, and I looked up and saw these guys from the Kenton band. And I said to our guys, "Hey, look out there!" And they did! And man, I mean, those guys in our band *played*! I'm telling you, the brass section was hittin' like *boom*! I only heard three bands in my whole life that ever hit with that force—I heard Duke Ellington once do that and Whiteman do it once at a concert. The Kenton band couldn't swing like we did, that's one thing.

We moved out of New York and came out here to the Coast. I married Shorty's sister. We were out here with Woody for most of the summer. We just stayed here in Southern California and worked around here most of the time. I got a little apartment over there on Ocean Avenue in Santa Monica. We liked it so well out here, the beach was so nice and everything. Finally, we went back to New York with Woody. When he broke up the band, I went back to New York and got on the plane and came back out here.

In September, vocalist Lynne Stevens left the band. Replacing her was Mary Ann McCall, who had been in the 1939 group. Mary Ann had been working in the San Diego area and Juggy Gayle, a song plugger and friend of Woody's, called him and advised him that he had heard her singing in a club and she "was singing better than ever."

Between September 17 and 20, the Herd recorded thirteen titles for Columbia Studios in Los Angeles. Among them was "Sidewalks of Cuba," a Ralph Burns score, which begins with a catchy riff, Woody's clarinet, and Sonny Berman's most famous solo on record. He begins with a quote from "Flight of the Bumblebee," then rips through the ensembles with savage intensity, leaving an indelible impression on the listener's memory. Also featured is guitarist Chuck Wayne's first recorded solo with the big band. Don Lamond gives a technical sample of the approach he would use in propelling the next Herd.

"Lady McGowan's Dream" definitely reflects Ralph Burns's classical leanings, yet is more than palatable to the connoisseur of mainstream jazz. Woody's rhapsodic alto is superb, playing the haunting melody against various background ensemble moods ranging from Ellington to almost Oriental sounds. The record includes Shorty Rogers's first recorded solo with the Herd. Unfortunately, his solo is underbalanced; the low fidelity is also aggravated by the use of a mute. The score is garnished with Red's vibes playing some light chords and finally Woody's alto taking the ensemble out.

WOODY: We were playing the Hotel Sherman and there was a character
who came through Chicago who presented herself as a writer or novelist.
She checked into the Ambassador East Hotel, one of the better hotels in
Chicago, with el mucho baggage. She looked pretty classy and like she
might make some sense, and her pen name or the name she used to register was "Lady McGowan." Shortly after her arrival, she came to the Hotel
Sherman and was evidently a jazz fan of some sort, and this gal was probably in her late thirties, fairly attractive, and evidently a great con mer-
chant. And she talked to the boys in the band. They were invited to a gala
party at the Ambassador after the gig. And the guys were ready for any
kind of action, so they all leaped up to the Ambassador East, and when
they arrived, she had a lovely suite, they knocked on the door and when
she opened the door, she was wearing a leopard skin leotard or something. Very scantily clad! It was more like a bikini-type operation, and it
proceeded immediately to go on from there to a real orgy and a fantastic
kind of affair, and she had the hotel catering department prepare hors
d'oeuvres and tidbits of foreign food. And the windup of this whole affair
was that caviar was spread all over the walls and nobody knew where the
smorgasbord was, you know.

About two days later, somebody caught up with this gal. She had an
unpaid five-dollar tab in the Panther Room of the Hotel Sherman and
was booked on this charge! She was caught, like with the $3,000 bill at the
Ambassador. It was for a lousy fin for two drinks. She sent 'em to the
bandstand. And she was madly in love, momentarily at least, with Billy
Bauer. He kept running all over the Hotel Sherman, trying to evade her,
and he got hung for the five-dollar tab so the cops wouldn't take her. So
later, when Ralph brought in an original, we thought it only fair that we
make some sort of tribute to "Lady McGowan." And my original title was
"Lady McGowan's Triumph." But Ralph said, "It's not that kind of
piece," so we changed it to "Dream."

"Romance in the Dark" was Mary Ann McCall's first recording with the band
after returning. The chart was also used for Mary Ann in the Second Herd,
and her roots in the jazz/blues idiom are evident.

Summer Sequence, by far the Herman orchestra's greatest contribution to
concert jazz, was originally composed by Burns as a three-part work for piano
and orchestra. The first part is slow and rhapsodic, featuring the entire band,
but the accent is on piano, guitar, and bass, with composer Ralph Burns sitting in at the piano. Woody's clarinet, Ralph's piano in legitimate form, laced
with Chuck Wayne's warm guitar, and some interplay between the rhythm
and brass sections produce an impressive overall effect, and finally Bill's
trombone bursts in with his characteristic emotion. The second part goes into
a swing beat change of mood, some more piano, and Sam Rubinowitch's baritone sounding like Harry Carney and initiating a chorus with the saxophone

section, brass section, and Woody's clarinet. The third part returns to the original rhapsodic mood with the rhythm section weaving some intricate figures, Flip's soulful tenor, Woody's alto, and finally the rhythm section again. The entire ensemble brings the third movement to a shouting finish. The epilogue, or fourth part, was recorded fifteen months later by the Second Herd. It bridged the First and Second Herds and introduced the "cool era" by highlighting a tenor solo by 20-year-old Stanley Getz. An adaptation of this piece was recorded in December, 1948, under the title "Early Autumn." With considerable justification, critics have compared *Summer Sequence* to the transcendent longer works of Ellington and not found it wanting.

"They Went That-a-Way," a Sonny Berman original, was recorded, but never released. The 1950 band recorded it on the Capitol label with the title of "Sonny Speaks." "Uncle Remus Said" was a pop tune of the day from a Disney film, *Song of the South*. This is another outstanding example of how the energy and creativity of the First Herd could transform a dull pop tune into a timeless and creative piece. Woody vocalizes, assisted by the Blue Flames vocal group. There is some aggressive drumming from Lamond, Red's vibes, and nice trumpet from Sonny.

"Everywhere" was composed by Bill Harris and arranged by Neal Hefti, and showcases Bill's remarkable trombone style. It is a slow and sultry score based on variations on a three-note phrase, with a background that introduces some nice scoring for reeds, followed by an abrupt contrast in the brass section's entry after sixteen bars. The tension increases with a series of glissandi near the end, then the original serene mood returns briefly.

"With Someone New" was written by Flip and scored by Ralph Burns. Featuring Flip's tenor, it's an emotional and stirring recording. Red plays some tasty vibes behind Flip. The recording underscores Woody's comment: "What an emotional player Flip was!"

"Wrap Your Troubles in Dreams" demonstrates what a great jazz singer Mary Ann McCall is. This record became a hit with musicians and fans alike. Mary Ann performed this song again at Woody's 1976 40th Anniversary Concert.

"Back Talk" was Shorty Rogers's first recorded big band chart for Woody. Based on the chords of "I Found a New Baby," the composition features a riff by the rhythm section, Red's vibes, Woody's clarinet, some exciting Bill Harris trombone, Flip's tenor, and the ensemble shouting as it takes the band out with Woody's Barney Bigard-style clarinet on top. This is a precursor of the scores Shorty would do later for the Second Herd, Stan Kenton, and his own exciting big bands in the fifties.

During late September and early October 1946, the Woody Herman orchestra was featured in the United Artists movie *New Orleans*. Woody performed well in a small acting part. The band performed only incidental background music and was seen in the film's finale with Louis Armstrong, Billie Holiday, and other artists.

WOODY: One of the funniest films that we ever did was the one where we worked with Louis Armstrong. It was a good deal. We went in to record one morning and we finally had the stuff cleaned up, ready and done about three in the afternoon. And they said, "Now you go over to Hal Roach Studios," or someplace. I said, "That is impossible, we were through at three o'clock." "No," he said, "the director wants you over there." So we got there and they said, "Have the boys on the set in ten minutes." I said, "Well, they haven't eaten." He said, "Have them go eat and have them make it thirty minutes," and I said, "Well, they have to go to makeup. What's the sense?" He said, "What makeup?" We were all done the same day. We worked no more than a day and a half on this and got paid for three.

After the lengthy stay in the Los Angeles area, the Herd traveled to the East Coast for a series of one-nighters.

In November trumpeters Sonny Berman, Pete Candoli, and Shorty Rogers left the band, replaced by Al Porcino, Chuck Peterson (who was a veteran of "The Band That Plays the Blues"), and trumpeter Bob Peck. Tragically, Sonny Berman died two months later at the age of 21, reportedly from a heart attack.

DON LAMOND: It was something that was very ridiculous. The guys were waiting around to get some "shit" [marijuana], and they injected themselves with sleeping pills. And it stopped his heart! They would melt it down like they do with dope. They would put the dope in a spoon with some water and boil it, and put it in a syringe and inject it in their arm. I've heard a lot of versions on how Sonny died, but I think that's the true version.

Al Porcino rapidly developed a reputation as an exceptional lead trumpeter. He began his big band resume with Louis Prima. After Louis came Georgie Auld, Tommy Dorsey, Jerry Wald, and Ina Ray Hutton. Al came to Woody via Gene Krupa. After a brief stint in the First Herd, he later played the lead trumpet book for the Second and Third Herds. Intermittently with the Herd, he also played the lead book for various Kenton bands, Basie, Dorsey, and the brief but exciting 1949 Chubby Jackson big band.

AL PORCINO: While I was playing with Gene Krupa at the Hotel Sherman in Chicago, I got a telegram from Woody. This of course was a big thrill for me, because Woody's band was really hot then. It was on Sonny Berman's recommendation that I got the job.

I joined the band in Fort Worth/Dallas. They were on a tour. Chuck Peterson and I joined the same day. We actually replaced Shorty Rogers and Pete Candoli, who had both elected to get off the band and get out to

Hollywood, which was a good move for them because they became quite well established out there.

This was really a kick for me to be working with these great players. I was only 21 years old at the time.

MARY ANN McCALL: We stopped in Trenton, New Jersey, and this is when I got so mad at Red Norvo. I hadn't been home for two years, and we were opening at the Fox Theater in Philadelphia and I wanted to go home. My folks lived in West Philadelphia at the time, and I wanted to go visit them before I had to go to the theater in the morning, because we were leaving in two nights, and I wouldn't get a chance to see them.

We all went in and had breakfast. This was like three o'clock in the morning, and Red was the last one out of the bus. So he walks in and I said, "C'mon, hurry up. What are you going to have for breakfast?" He said, "I'm going to have some pork chops!" I said, "Oh, no, you're not!" He said, "Whaddya mean? I'm going to have some pork chops!" I said, "Oh, no, you're not!" And Woody was on the other side of me, laughing, and I picked up this metal napkin container and knocked Red cold! I was so mad at him!

On December 10 and 11, 1946, the pile-driving Woody Herman First Herd entered a Columbia recording studio in Chicago and waxed its last sides. The band recorded six titles. Two of them, "Woodchopper's Ball" and "Blue Flame," were remade scores from the "Band That Plays the Blues" period.

About "Woodchopper's Ball," Woody once said, "The chart was great for the first 1,000 times!" Nevertheless, most notable on this updated version is Bill Harris' stirring but humorous solo. Also recorded and worthy of mention was John LaPorta's "Non-Alcoholic," named for the "non-alcoholic" ingredients of Wildroot Cream Oil. The recording features a solo from Flip, a biting solo from Bill Harris, a statement from Woody's clarinet, and some stratospheric trumpet by Al Porcino.

During the first week of December, Woody gathered the band together for a meeting and gave them the startling news that he was calling it quits. The First Herd played its final performance two weeks later, on December 24, at Castle Farms, just outside Cincinnati, Ohio. The decision was not based on financial reasons. The band had just completed a two-year peak of popularity, unrivaled by any modern big jazz unit. In 1946 the band grossed a million dollars. Never before and never again would there be such a correlation between big band jazz and mass public taste.

AL PORCINO: It was kind of a shock in a way. I was very unhappy about it because I really wanted to stay on the band, and I'd only been there a few months. Our last engagement was Cincinnati, and I drove all the way non-stop back to New York. I only had about twenty-five dollars in my pocket. It was a very sad Christmas for me.

WOODY: That was kind of a sad thing. Because the guys would have liked to have continued, and I would have, too. But, of course, there were a lot of stories about the reason for the break-up, and most of them didn't make much sense because I wasn't in a position to really give out a story. It was a personal situation, and something that I thought wasn't anyone else's business. And, consequently, most of the stories said it was a financial situation, and the band was too expensive, but that wasn't true. At the point when we quit, the thing was grossing a lot of money and showing a very big profit.

There were many explanations over the years as to the rationale behind the First Herd break-up. The most common one was "illness in the family." This was close, but the real reason was never printed until years later. Woody's absence and the constant touring on the road threatened to destroy his marriage. Charlotte, alone at home with a young daughter, had developed an addiction to pills and alcohol.

WOODY (1987): She was "paying the dues" for my not spending time with her. . . . I felt I should spend more time right there in the house. I was still on the road, and I didn't really know my little daughter. That is reason enough to break up the band. But another reason was, I felt I had probably run the gamut of what the band had to say.

Ironically, the music and entertainment magazines added their stamp to the Herd's public acclaim as the band won the 1946 Best Band award in *Billboard* and *Metronome*, the Silver Award in *Esquire*, and the Best Swing Band title in a *Down Beat* poll.

Some date the end of the Big Band Era to that fateful December of 1946. As George T. Simon noted, "Even though seven other bands—those of Benny Goodman, Tommy Dorsey, Harry James, Les Brown, Jack Teagarden, Benny Carter, and Ina Ray Hutton—had all given up during the same month, it was Herman's disbanding that was felt most acutely."[5] All those bands, including Woody Herman's, eventually reorganized, but the superb band that was the First Herd was no more.

4.

The Second Herd
(The Four Brothers Band)
1947-1949

The year 1947 promised to be one of rest and relaxation for Woody, but resting didn't come easily for a man who had been on the road for the greater part of seventeen years.

WOODY: After I was home about two weeks I got a call from the accountants that someone had miscalculated, and now I owed the government $30,000 more than they had said. This was the money I was going to live on like a king. So I went down and borrowed what I could on future things, and I took care of the debt, but now I had nothing to live on. So I was pretty sick. Abe said, "Whaddya worryin' about? I'll handle it." He decided to bet West Coast baseball. This was hard to do even if you're a winner, but that's how we lived for a good six months. He averaged between $750 and $1,500 a week and we split it. He had some bookmaker, and he'd meet him in front of the ball park every night and finally I couldn't go to the games any more, I couldn't take it, 'cause the bookmaker was always handing him an envelope at the end of each game, and that was about the time Bugsy Siegel got bumped off. Nobody knew how we were making it, 'cause I was still coming around in style, and I had this lovely home and everything was cool. But "Schwartz" or whoever the bookmaker was, was taking a lopping, boy, and that's big stakes on the West Coast.

Woody continued to work low-key by making some relaxed records of current pop tunes. From February 4 through the end of March, he was backed on several sessions with a rhythm section made up of Ralph Burns, Don Lamond,

Gene Sargent (bass), Chuck Wayne on guitar, and even drummer Tiny Kahn, who before his death at age 29 in 1953 would gain a reputation as an arranger and composer of splendid ability. Early in April, Mike Vallon, of Woody's management team of Goldfarb, Mirenburg and Vallon, scheduled a recording date for Woody and Dinah Shore to do a "boy-girl" record on both sides of a 78 single. Woody always hated the boy-girl gimmick but went along with the idea. The result was "Tallahassee" and "Natch," recorded on April 22, 1947. In April and May, Woody recorded an album of vocals entitled *Twelve Shades of Blue*.

Making records wasn't enough for Woody, however. Soon boredom set in.

WOODY: A friend of mine, Al Jarvis, was on radio station KLAC in Los Angeles. He asked me to help him out because he had too many hours. So I used to go in on Saturdays and do kind of an ad-lib show, playing music that I thought should be listened to. The show was called Make Believe Ballroom.

When word got out, many of his music cronies such as Johnny Mercer began to show up at the studio to appear with Woody. This caused a stir among the local Southern California deejays. They found the bandleader a difficult act to follow and ultimately a few stations refused to air Herman recordings. After this, Woody politely bowed out of his association with radio station KLAC. This incident reportedly contributed to the formation of the disk jockey's union.

FATHER DAN SHERMAN: I was ordained on June 15, 1947, and I was assigned to China. On my way, I stopped off on the West Coast to visit relatives. My uncle drove me out to say hello to Woody and visit with him and Charlotte. We spent the afternoon chatting. As we were getting ready to go, Woody said, "Say, you know, Father Dan, Charlotte and I were kind of waiting for you to get ordained so you could fix up our marriage for us. We've always wanted to have our marriage blessed by the Church." Well, they were married eleven years before and already had Ingrid. She was about five and a half years old. I said, "Holy mackerel, Woody, I've never performed a marriage in my life! I was just ordained about three weeks ago."

So we went down to see the pastor at St. Victor's Church in Hollywood, right down the hill from where Woody lived. The pastor was Monsignor Devlin, and he was very friendly and cooperative, and he told me all the rigmarole to get everything set.

WOODY: There was a lot of red tape because at the time Charlotte was a non-Catholic, and you have to see people and get releases and statements, and normally it would take maybe a matter of weeks, and he got it all done in one day! This is what a ball of fire this guy Dan is. I went with them to talk to the Monsignor, and he was very gruff and said "Sit down." I was shaking in my boots, and Father Dan looked worse than I did. Finally the Monsignor stared at me for a split second or two and said, "I read in *Variety* where you broke up the band."

FATHER DAN SHERMAN: The Monsignor took care of getting a dispensation for me to perform the ceremony, because Woody was marrying a woman who at that time was a non-Catholic. Later on Charlotte did take instruction and became a Roman Catholic too. The dispensation came through the next day, but that night Woody, Charlotte, and I sat up most of the night talking about marriage. I gave them some instructions in "marriage preparation." After eleven years, I had to tell them what marriage was all about.

   That evening, we went down to the little church of St. Victor's, and the Monsignor met us and told us what to do, and they had a little walk down the aisle. We had a simple marriage ceremony where they repeated the vows they had made earlier, and then I pronounced them man and wife according to the rite of the Holy Roman Catholic Church.

WOODY: Father Dan didn't know what page you started this thing on, and here was Ingrid, and Judy, the girl who worked for us, our witness. I think they locked the doors, and when we walked out of the church, Ingie and the maid threw rice on us. What a horrible experience! We felt like criminals at that hour.

   So then we went back to our house and Father Dan, Charlotte, and I were sitting around and we had a drink in celebration of our "new" marriage, and I suggested that we go somewhere for a little while. I said, "Is there anything you would like to hear around town, Dan?" He said, "I don't know whether this would be all right with the clerical collar and all, but I noticed that Duke is working at Ciro's." So we went to Ciro's. Now [Herman] Hover is a real brain trust, you know, like he greets us and he says, "Good evening Reverend," and Dan is like holding his throat, and before I can even grab Herman Hover and say, "Just a nice table, like off to the left a little bit," he's got us right in front of the band, ringside, and Duke spots us and says, "Woody, how are you and the lovely Mrs. Herman, and Reverend, good evening," and does a low bow, and now Dan is under the table.

During his nine-month vacation from active bandleading, Woody got interested in hockey through song plugger Juggy Gayle.

WOODY: After hockey, I got interested once again in football. I used to catch the pro games in New York, and then in later years, baseball, because of my family. My wife was an ardent fan, and my daughter was, too. Later I became quite a ball fan and became interested in most sports. Of course, auto racing. That I never lost interest in. Ever since I was a little kid, I used to go for miles to see it. At one time in Hollywood when I was home for some months without working, there were about five nights a week and Sunday afternoons when there was midget-auto racing in the Southern California area. Do you know that I was there every night, and on Sunday? My wife thought I was, you know . . . you hear about golf widows? This was worse.

Driving the cars didn't particularly interest me. I've been invited on a half dozen occasions by drivers who said, "If you want to take the car around the track or something . . ." and I've always bowed out. So evidently my guts are not where my mouth is.

On a summer night in 1947, Woody went over to a Hollywood club to hear the Phil Moore Group, consisting of a four-piece rhythm section with two horns, reed man Marshall Royal and his brother, Ernie, playing trumpet. When Woody heard Ernie, he said, "I've just got to get that guy in a band!" The only problem was that Woody didn't have a band.

MARSHALL ROYAL: Ernie and I were in Lionel Hampton's first big band in October 1940. In fact, I was the one that helped Lionel form his first band and the one that rehearsed it and sent it out on the road in 1940. It was Ernie doing the high-note work on the original record of "Flying Home." During the war, from 1942 to the end of 1945, Ernie and I were in the St. Mary's Pre-Flight Navy Band. I was the bandleader. Ernie played lead trumpet.

After Ernie got discharged from the Navy, he went with Duke Ellington for an overseas tour. Then he came back to his hometown, Los Angeles, and he started working with the Phil Moore group and that's when Woody heard him. We had Irving Ashby, guitar, possibly Lee Young on drums, Joe Comfort on bass, and Phil on piano. Woody came in and went nuts when he heard Ernie play.

By the second half of 1947, the band business was deteriorating fast. Operating costs had soared, and there was a gradual shifting of mass musical tastes from big bands to singers, who were tightening their grip on box office revenues while the ballrooms were gradually going out of business. In spite of these circumstances, the restless and determined Woody made plans to front another band. Woody's home life was restored to a degree of stability. During his time off, he had taken Charlotte to some Alcoholics Anonymous meetings, and she had been successful in bringing her drinking under control. In later years, she would meet Woody in some of the major cities when the band would be at one location for an extended period. She also traveled with him on many of his overseas tours.

The Second Herd was doubtless Woody's most innovative orchestra, in terms of musical values. Unfortunately, it never exerted the mass public appeal of the First Herd and was a financial disaster. Big band music was no longer the nation's pop music, and Woody's Second Herd deliberately veered off the comfortable and contrived road of commercialism that pop music was taking by the late 1940s. Woody said once that "Lemon Drop" alone cost him at least $75,000.

The new band would be conceived around the bebop conceptions of Charlie Parker and Dizzy Gillespie. It would utilize revolutionary sax voicings that changed the sound of all future Herman Herds.

First Herd veteran and strong lead alto saxophonist Sam Marowitz returned to lead the section, along with four other First Herd members: trumpeters Shorty Rogers and Marky Markowitz, drummer Don Lamond, and chief arranger Ralph Burns. Two veterans from "The Band That Plays the Blues" also returned: Walt Yoder on bass and Gene Sargent on guitar.

Stanley (Stan) Getz was with Jack Teagarden's band at the tender age of 16. In 1944 he was with Stan Kenton, and later with Jimmy Dorsey and Benny Goodman. Stan would come to international prominence through his solo on the December 1948 Herman recording of "Early Autumn." His beautiful, languid, lyrical quality officially established the "cool school" of elegant saxophone stylists and gave him the nickname "The Sound" with fans everywhere.

Tenor saxophonist John Haley (Zoot) Sims had played with Bobby Sherwood, Sonny Dunham, Teddy Powell, Bob Astor, and the Buddy Rich big bands in addition to working with various small groups. After Woody, in the 1950s he toured with Stan Kenton and various Benny Goodman units. Although he was greatly influenced by the style of Lester Young, Sims developed a distinctive sound that critic Ira Gitler described as "marked by a natural sense of swing, perfect structural concepts and melodic creativity that seemed equally intense in up-tempo and ballad performances."[1]

Another member of the original "Four Brothers" sax section was Herbert "Herbie" Steward, who doubled on alto and tenor sax. By the time he joined Woody, Herbie had played with Artie Shaw, Alvino Rey, Bob Chester, and Freddie Slack. After Herman, he had stints with Elliot Lawrence and Tommy Dorsey.

HERBIE STEWARD: It started out with Zoot, Stan, Jim Giuffre and myself. We were around LA about 1946. Gene Roland was on the scene too. So one day Gene says, "With all these tenor players around . . . I've got it! We'll have a band with four tenors, and I'll play trumpet." Gene was something else. He could sit down and write arrangements fast. So we had a book real quick, a library. This was early in 1947. We had a couple of rehearsals with it. A trumpet player named Tommy DeCarlo got a job down at Pontrelli's Figueroa Ballroom and he didn't have a band, so he took over our band. Anyway, that finally folded up. Woody was just re-organizing about that time. I don't know how he heard about us, I guess he knew Stan or something. So anyway, he hired all of us except Giuffre.

WOODY: Gene Roland was probably the first guy who experimented with the idea, but he was using four tenors, and the guys were all out of work on the beach. So it didn't make much difference. But the guy that really put it together was Jimmy Giuffre. Up until then, it was just a lovely idea.

James Peter (Jimmy) Giuffre received a music education degree from North Texas State University (now University of North Texas). Later, he attended the University of Southern California for one semester, then studied privately with Wesley La Violette. Before his association with Woody, he played and wrote for Boyd Raeburn's band.

JIMMY GIUFFRE: Gene Roland discovered a four-tenor sound by experi-menting at Nola Studios in New York. Everybody used to hang out there. In fact, he had a band one time with twenty-five people, including Bird and Dizzy. He would get them all together and he would write some music and they would play it. So he tried this idea using four tenors. Then he came out to Los Angeles, where I was, and we got to know each other out there, Stan Getz, Zoot Sims, Shorty and myself. We got a band together at Pete Pontrelli's. Then, I got a job with Jimmy Dorsey. Afterwards, the Second Herd started up. The three other guys, Herbie, Zoot, and Stan, all got jobs with Woody.

In keeping with Woody's shrewd ability for finding and exploiting new talent, he brought in Serge Chaloff on baritone sax. Chaloff has been recognized as one of the most important and inventive voices on the baritone saxophone. His father played piano with the Boston Symphony; his mother had taught at the Boston Conservatory. In his earlier years, he studied piano and clarinet, but for the most part taught himself the baritone sax. His early mentors on that instrument were Jack Washington of Basie's band and Harry Carney, but his exposure to Charlie Parker completely changed his ideas. Serge became the first big-band bop baritonist.

Until Chaloff, the baritone saxophone had never been a featured instru-ment in any of Woody's bands. With the Second Herd, Serge became one of the most featured soloists. His full use of dynamics has rarely been equaled by any other baritone saxophonist, and he achieved a subtle, yet intense lyricism.

Unfortunately, his influences on the band were not always positive. Serge was a heroin addict and was instrumental in "turning on" some of the other sidemen to his habit. He became known in time as the band's "druggist" as well as its number-one "junkie." He was known to drape a blanket in front of the rear seats of the band bus in an attempt to hide his dispensing activities.

WOODY (1956):   I think Stanley [Getz] was and probably is the finest saxophonist around as far as actually being a saxophonist. He certainly has had his share of wealth of ideas and used them in the very best taste. Musicianwise he was far above the rest of the guys, although each one had some talent, and quite a bit in a couple of cases. Zoot was a very rhythmic type player, always has been. Serge was probably the freshest, newest-sounding baritone that had come along in years. He did what Leo Parker did on occasion. He twisted it around so it became musical, instead of just being a chain of thoughts. Probably one of the finest musicians in the band was the other tenor man, Herbie Steward. Actually, we hired him to double on alto and tenor. We still were using a five-man section and Sam Marowitz was playing lead and Herbie played third alto.

    We kept the same saxophone voicings as we had in the First Herd on most things for a while. I didn't know whether the Four Brothers sound would hold up as a section for everything. But when Herbie left, we decided to use a tenor next to the alto. So we used one alto, three tenors, and a baritone, and actually there was no difference in the sound. But eventually, I decided that if we were ever able to make it identifiable, we should cut out the alto, and if we wanted it, I could play lead alto on top of the section.

Joining the trumpet section was the superb black player Ernie Royal. Woody had gotten his wish: "to get that guy into a band." Although Woody had used certain Ellington sidemen at times in recording sessions, Ernie was the first black musician to go out on the road with a Herman band. Ernie was a powerful section man and an exciting soloist, known for his tasteful high-note work.

    It was risky business for a white band to have black musicians as sidemen in the late 1940s. This caused Ernie and the band some ill treatment on jobs and many times prevented them from getting desirable hotel accommodations. Undaunted, Woody would hire Shadow Wilson, Oscar Pettiford, and Gene Ammons in the 1949 edition of the Second Herd.

    Another notable newcomer to the brass section was trombonist Earl Swope. He had worked in D.C. with Don Lamond's small group and also with the big bands of Sonny Dunham, Boyd Raeburn and Buddy Rich just prior to joining the Second Herd. Swope was one of the first bop trombonists. He had a fine wide-open sound and would later provide an intriguing contrast with Bill Harris when the latter rejoined the Herd.

DON LAMOND: Earl Swope was the one who first got me in the big bands. We grew up together in Washington, D.C. He had a tremendous jazz feeling, like he played a lot of notes with his lips. He kept the slide up close to his face, so he didn't have to be slipping it all around. It's too bad that he wasn't more well-known.

Don Lamond's return to the drum chair proved to be a crucial element in this first edition of the Second Herd. When the First Herd broke up, Don had remained in the Los Angeles area, freelancing, doing club and record dates. Most notable was his participation in the Charlie Parker recording of "Relaxin' at Camarillo."

James A. Treichel wrote in the excellent and exhaustive *Woody Herman and His Second Herd*:

> . . . with all due respect to Tough, who was a magnificent musician, it was Lamond who established the style and standard for Woody Herman's drummers. Buddy Rich said of him recently, "Don Lamond was one of the greatest jazz drummers that I have ever heard, in every respect. He knew exactly what to do for Woody's band . . . he gave it a sound totally different from any other band Woody ever had. It became truly a hit band. Lamond was responsible for that change." His was a relatively simple, direct approach, similar in some respects to two other big band drummers of the 1940s who perhaps did not receive all the recognition which they deserved, namely Kenny Clarke and Tiny Kahn. The styles of these men did not rely on flash but rather were based on the understanding that as a unit, the rhythm section was felt as much as heard. Lamond mixed together a light, yet swinging top cymbal beat, plenty of snare accents to goose the soloists along, and some wonderful rim and bass drum combinations. He got such a strong, hard sound, that even the most ordinary bomb took on an element of added drama. Herman's arrangers took full advantage of his sharp ear and quick reflexes, leaving openings in their scores for him, so that his one, two, and four-bar fills became as much a part of the Second Herd's distinctive sound as the "Brothers" or Woody's clarinet.[2]

WOODY: In the First Herd, Don tried to follow, or to a certain degree, emulate what Dave had been doing. But in the Second Herd, I said, "Don, we're going to have a different type of rhythm section. We'll have three cats just blow time and I want your operation to be loose. Like whenever you feel like experimenting, I want you to have that freedom. The guitar, piano and bass will make the rhythm pattern and you will be the loose part of the operation." I felt that this was a new thing . . . the way music was going. Like the music that I had been hearing in New York and other places, in small groups. I thought if we applied it to a big band, it would be exciting and different. I think, musically, sometimes it came off very beautifully. Of course, we immediately lost what dance audience we had! They left in droves after the second set.

DON LAMOND: It was a very relaxed situation, like Woody used to give me a real free hand once I got established with the band. As a matter of fact, one time he told me, "Listen, I've got other things on my mind. If I beat off the wrong tempo, then you take it. You know where the tempo should be." So he never pulled any of that crap like Benny or some of the other leaders did. In other words, if they would beat off the wrong tempo, they would continue playing. Woody always said, "You're the drummer, if you don't know the tempos, you don't belong here."

This author asked Don Lamond, "What was different about your drumming in those days?"

DON LAMOND: I don't know, that's the only way I knew how to play. I didn't try to play any different. I was lucky, because I came in at the tail end of the really great drum stars. All the black drummers and Buddy, too, and Gene [Krupa], they were very kind to me. Sid Catlett was one of my favorite people of all time. He gave me a lot of encouragement, and so did Jimmy Crawford and Cozy Cole. I've listened to all of the different guys and just tried to apply whatever I could to my own playing. I've never tried to copy anybody.

The Herd's three young tenor saxophonists were all ardent admirers of the sound and technique of former Basie tenor virtuoso Lester Young, known as "The President" of tenor saxophonists, or simply "Prez." By 1947, Getz, Sims, and Steward had already absorbed the bop idioms of Parker and Gillespie and incorporated them into their "Lestorian" sound. This sound became the pattern for the "cool school" of tenor playing that began about 1947 and continued until the Coltrane period of the early sixties. Contemporary with Herman's "Brothers," and also exponents of the "cool school," were men like Allen Eager, Brew Moore, Al Cohn (who replaced Herbie Steward), and Buddy Wise. These were followed by such players as Dick Hafer, Bill Perkins, Jerry Coker and Bill Trujillo, to list a few who were influenced by what they heard from Getz, Sims, and Steward.

Whether for better or for worse, the avant-garde improvisational style associated with John Coltrane, featuring a hard tone with admirable but clamorous technical displays, would overshadow the influence of the coolly elegant Parker/Young manner as well as the deep breathy styles of Hawkins and Webster. In 1987 the author asked Stan Getz why he was one of a few left who still used the "cool" sound. His reply was: "Other tenor players keep changing styles because they want to be the most modern. They change as the times change. I believe that you should always be yourself."

In late September, the new band went into rehearsals with the following personnel: Ernie Royal, Stan Fishelson, Bernie Glow, Irving "Marky" Markowitz, Shorty Rogers, trumpets; Earl Swope, Ollie Wilson, Bob Swift, trombones; Sam Marowitz, alto sax; Herbie Steward, alto and tenor sax; Stan Getz, Zoot Sims, tenor sax; Serge Chaloff, baritone sax; Fred Otis, piano; Gene Sargent, guitar; Walt Yoder, bass; Don Lamond, drums; Jerri Ney, vocals; vibes. The Second Herd played its debut performance on October 16, at the San Bernardino, California, Municipal Auditorium.

On October 19, the new band went into Columbia Studios in Hollywood and produced its first recordings. One of the titles was a facetious pop tune of the day, "I Told Ya I Love Ya, Now Get Out." The arrangement features a vocal by Woody and tenor work from Stan and Zoot; Herbie sounds like he may be playing alto. Ernie's recorded solo debut with the band arrests the listener's attention.

The new band launched a short shakedown series of one-nighters in Central and Northern California, settling in the San Francisco Bay Area for two nights.

WOODY: It was a pretty exciting band, but we did have our dull moments. It was immaturity in the group that stymied it on occasion. We weren't prepared to play to larger audiences. The band looked like a confused group of young men, where the other band was just the other extreme, just loaded with confidence. This had a lot to do with not getting as broad an acceptance as the band should have at that time. Since then, it has received a great amount of [historical] acceptance. This has been my problem for many years! By the time they catch up with me, I am off on another tack.

On December 9 the band went into Tune Town Ballroom in St. Louis for nine days. On December 18 and 19, the band played one-nighters in Chicago and Milwaukee, respectively.

HERBIE STEWARD: It was a good band. Serge was something. I know a lot of people who recognize him as a soloist, but he was something else in the section.

I was only in the band for the first three months and I quit, because I was switching to alto [full time], and I was just going in a different direction. We only had two arrangements for the three tenors and a baritone. We had "Four Brothers" and something else. So I was playing second alto most of the night.

In early December, James Petrillo of the American Federation of Musicians imposed another recording ban. It was scheduled to go into effect at midnight on December 31, and would continue until November 15, 1948. (As with the

First Herd during the recording ban of 1944, however, many live broadcasts of the Second Herd during this time were preserved.) The Herd went back into Columbia's Hollywood studios on December 22. They had less than ten days to record, and they made the most of their time. Mary Ann McCall rejoined the band during the December sessions. During her time with the Second Herd, she produced some of her best work.

The first title recorded was a Ralph Burns score of Khachaturian's light classical piece "Sabre Dance." It has been speculated that Woody chose this piece of more serious music as a kind of continuation in the vein of *Ebony Concerto*. Actually, the pop music sensibility of early 1948 accepted "Sabre Dance" as a novelty, and it was a popular jukebox tune recorded by other artists as well. The Burns score contributes nothing meaningful to the jazz idiom.

"I've Got News For You" features Woody's nutty vocal and Ernie Royal demonstrating a mature conception and a full clear tone in the upper register. The most unusual thing about the piece is Shorty Rogers' orchestration of Charlie Parker's solo on "Dark Shadows" for the saxophone section. Med Flory, the founder of the group Supersax in 1972, has acknowledged that Herman's recording of this chart inspired him to build a library of arrangements based on Parker solos from various sources, voicing them for a five-man saxophone section.

"Keen and Peachy" is a Burns-Rogers reworking of "Fine and Dandy." It opens with a line from Rogers's trumpet and the four saxes. There is some fine Earl Swope trombone, Serge Chaloff's first recorded solo with the Herd, tenor work from both Zoot and Stan, and Royal's high trumpet concluding the performance.

"The Goof and I" was a chart submitted by Al Cohn during the early rehearsal period of the Second Herd. Mary Ann McCall, who later married Al Cohn, had introduced him to Woody. She knew Al's ability as a writer and composer and told Woody, "I want you to hire him to write a couple of songs for me, I want you to listen to him."

MARY ANN MCCALL: Al wrote a song called "It's You or No One for Me." That's the tune he wrote and brought to an audition with Woody, and Woody said, "Fine, we'll do it." Of course he wrote "The Goof and I." He wrote so many great songs for Woody, even when he wasn't in the band.

He was the only musician I ever knew who could sit down and take blank music sheets and write the whole score. He would write the whole arrangement, and take it into rehearsal the next day. They would have to copy all the parts, but he would write every part the way he wanted it. He would write it all *that* night, he would be up all night until 6 A.M., it was amazing!

The "Goof and I" title was a play on a movie title of the time, *The Egg and I*. Woody said once, "Students of word origins might like to note that the record was one of the first uses of that musicians' expression, 'to goof,' which since became part of the 'hip' language. If your musical sense is warped enough, you might agree with me that the opening line is reminiscent of 'We Were Sailing Along on Moonlight Bay.'"[3]

The score is a strong, blues-based number with Woody's clarinet followed by the saxes playing a simple boppish head, while Lamond kicks the band with well-timed bombs. Following a magnificent drum break, Serge comes in with a swinging, tumbling solo employing his own particular version of Charlie Parker's style. A typically effortless and relaxed Swope is heard, then Woody's clarinet finishes the solos.

"Lazy Lullaby" was recorded the same day, but not released until the 1960s. Woody co-wrote it with Don George, who did the lyrics of "I'm Beginning To See the Light." The tune has a melody that lingers, with a pretty chorus from the tight-voiced saxes. Woody does the easygoing vocal.

On December 27 the brilliant Jimmy Giuffre composition "Four Brothers" was put on wax at a recording session at Columbia Studios in Hollywood. The score not only became a Herd classic, but the definitive grouping of three tenors and one baritone saxophone changed the sound of all future Herman bands.

WOODY: I don't think that we knew it was going to be important, but I felt it was a good composition, and that it had an unusual approach, and a different sound. To this day, we still use three tenors and a baritone, because it's a sound that's unique.

JIMMY GIUFFRE: I came to a rehearsal and they introduced me to Woody. He said he'd heard about this sound and why didn't I write something using it? So I wrote the piece "Four Brothers."

SHORTY ROGERS: Jimmy Giuffre had been a friend of mine. We were studying from the same composition teacher. Jimmy lived just down the street from me in Burbank. He had spoken to Woody about doing some arranging for the band, and Woody said, "Fine." Jimmy came to me one day. We were having a great struggle, just doing a few jobs, trying to realize a little income before Woody re-formed the band. Giuffre asked me, "Would you do me a favor and carry this arrangement to the rehearsal and pass out the parts?" I said "I'd be glad to." The arrangement was "Four Brothers," and I had the joy of transporting it to the rehearsal!

JIMMY GIUFFRE: After eighteen takes, we got the right one. They got that sequence at the end with the two-bar breaks perfect on the last take and that did it. As I understand it from Shorty, Woody said that Columbia Records believed that "Four Brothers" was going to be a good seller. He had a little chuckle, because he hadn't thought it was that attractive. He was used to the "Caldonia" and "Apple Honey" kind of stuff, and it was a cooler piece. We'd play it cool. They have now got it up to where it's hot. The stage bands around the country usually play it real fast, but I think the key to the piece is to play it at a relaxed tempo. But the record happened to hit.

Once you get a break that big, where you have that many people say they like it, you start feeling, well, maybe I didn't make a mistake. Everybody had a contribution to make, but make sure that Gene Roland gets credit for finding the sound.

The "Four Brothers" chart is based on the chord changes of "Jeepers Creepers," and features the three-tenor, one-baritone saxophone section with a light airy Lester Young sound in both ensemble and solo performances. Woody said about this one, "For those who want to get their hip cards punched by knowing the order of the solos on the record, they go like this: Zoot Sims, Herbie Steward, Serge Chaloff, Stan Getz. At the end, they take breaks in this order: Stan, Zoot, Herbie, and Serge."[4] Woody's clarinet solo is of a different idiom, but he always seemed to blend with any period.

Part Four of *Summer Sequence* was literally added as an afterthought. When the time came for the release of the original first three parts recorded by the First Herd in Los Angeles in September 1946, Columbia suddenly realized that they had run to three ten-inch 78 rpm sides, and having nothing suitable for the fourth side, they induced Woody and Burns to do something about it.

The fourth part, recorded on December 27, effectively bridged the First and Second Herd, with a crystalline beauty enhanced by masterful solos. It is a sort of recapitulation of the rhapsodic first and third parts. Burns plays piano, and it features trombonist Ollie Wilson's only commercially recorded solo with the Second Herd, Woody's Hodges-like alto, and Stan Getz's gorgeous "cool school" interpretations of Lester Young's stylings. Most significant are the three-tenor, one-baritone saxophone voicing on the end, and the descant from which the Burns chart of "Early Autumn" originated.

Heard as a complete composition, *Summer Sequence* reveals traces of Beethoven and Mozart as well as Ellington. There are many pieces that testify to Burns's gifts as an orchestrator, but on the occasion of *Summer Sequence*, he surpassed himself.

On December 30 the band recorded additional material. "Swing Low, Sweet Clarinet" was arranged by Burns and features Mary Ann McCall and, of course, Woody's clarinet, both in a very warm style. Mary Ann's voice had a unique flexibility of mood and tone. She was probably the most jazz-oriented female singer the band had until Polly Podewell's brief stint with the Herd in 1986.

MARY ANN McCALL: Woody had been talking to an old black man whom
someone had met on the beach, and he had a copy of this tune. It was
similar in mood to "Nature Boy." Anyway, Woody brought the song in
and said to me, "I don't know if the tune is good for you or not," but we
were searching for something to start the new band with, and "Swing
Low, Sweet Clarinet" came up. I'm sure that this man was inspired by
"Swing Low, Sweet Chariot," and that's the feeling he wanted to get out
of it.

"My Pal Gonzales" opens with a quote from Dizzy's "Emanon." It's another
Shorty Rogers chart with lyrics by Don George, a typical humorous Herman
vocal, and Lamond's tasty drum fills propelling the band. The saxes execute
rapid and intriguing bop figures, followed by solos from Chaloff and Sims. So
went the first major recording session of the Second Herd.

WOODY: We got off to a bad start. Those first sides for Columbia were all
made in Hollywood in a studio where something was wrong with the
board. All the things made there were muffled. They had to run them
through an echo chamber to use them at all.

Nevertheless, the recordings produced between December 22 and 30, 1947,
were prophetic of the music the band would be turning out in the next year
and a half. With the recordings of "I've Got News for You," "Keen and
Peachy," "The Goof and I," and "Four Brothers," the new band had given
birth to its own personality. Burns continued to write charts for the band, but
it was now the bop era, and the new music permeated the band with its
unusual intervals, sweeping phrases, flatted fifths and major seventh chords.
The bop charts were primarily contributed by Rogers, Cohn, Tiny Kahn, and
Jimmy Giuffre. There was a special chemistry between Getz, Sims, and Al
Cohn (who replaced Herbie Steward). The sound and blend they achieved
together made possible the brilliant solo careers of Getz and Sims.

In a band seemingly dominated by saxophone virtuosos, trumpeter Ernie
Royal established himself as a solo voice. Then came another awe-inspiring
Herman rhythm section in the fall of 1948: Lou Levy, Chubby Jackson, Don
Lamond, and Terry Gibbs.

The year 1948 began with the Second Herd returning to the Edgewater
Beach Ballroom in San Francisco for a four-day stay. There were three
changes in the band's personnel. Guitarist Jimmy Raney replaced Gene
Sargent. Singer Terry Swope (no relation to Earl Swope; later married to
Don Lamond) temporarily replaced Mary Ann McCall until she was able to
rejoin the band on the road. Also joining was Alvin Gilbert (Al) Cohn, com-
poser and tenor sax (later he played baritone and clarinet), who had sent
Woody the score for "The Goof and I." Al came to the Herd from the Buddy
Rich band.

AL COHN: I'll always be grateful for the opportunity to have played in Woody's band. It was the first chance I had to be a part of something fine and successful, and the first chance I had to be noticed by the public. Woody didn't hang out much with the guys and it wasn't until much later that we became friends. But then and now, I have a lot of respect and good feelings for him.

On February 2, the Second Herd was headlined with the Modernaires vocal group in the Universal-International film short *Woody Herman and His Orchestra*. The Herd is seen on "Blue Flame," "Sabre Dance," and "Caldonia" with Woody's vocal and a brief solo by Zoot Sims. The best jazz contribution is the band closing with "Northwest Passage," and brief but excitingly visible solos by Getz, Cohn, Sims, Chaloff, Swope, and Woody. Ernie Royal plays on the soundtrack, but is not seen because of an unfortunate ruling that prohibited the appearance of black musicians in certain films.

On February 3 the Second Herd opened at the Hollywood Palladium. The Palladium had a radio wire and the band was heard live on numerous occasions during the five-week engagement. These were Armed Forces Radio Service-sponsored air shots. Many have been preserved and made available on various pirate record labels.

The uncut broadcasts recorded during the Palladium engagement provide the listener with a mixed menu of live performance, in contrast to the professional image of the Second Herd preserved in studio recordings. Woody was aware that the band had to make certain concessions to the pop music of the day and placate the dancers and the nonjazz-oriented listeners. Consequently, the band intermingled "Ballerina," "Sabre Dance," "Nature Boy," and "Golden Earrings" with material from "The Band that Plays the Blues" and the First Herd and new bop charts from Giuffre, Rogers, Cohn, Burns, and Kahn.

During the Palladium engagement, "Four Brothers," "The Goof and I" and "Keen and Peachy" were all heard regularly. On February 12 the band closed with an electrifying performance of "Apple Honey." Woody liked to use it as a closing number throughout his career. In this Second Herd version, all the "Brothers" have space to blow and the listener can detect the beginning of the brass fireworks finale that concluded the chart in the fifties.

"Lullaby in Rhythm" was a bop-laced score that Woody used to start at least two broadcasts. It featured a Jimmy Raney guitar intro and solos by Getz, Chaloff, Swope, Woody, and Lamond. "You Turned the Tables on Me" featured Mary Ann McCall in a swinging arrangement with solos by Woody, Swope, Royal and Getz. "I Cover the Waterfront" is a lovely treatment of the song that became a jazz ballad standard. It features solos by Woody doing typically warm alto work, with Royal and Cohn. "Just for Laughs" is a pretty Ralph Burns score featuring an exceptionally tender vocal by Mary Ann with Woody playing a delicate clarinet solo.

WOODY: We were working the Palladium for five weeks when Mary Ann
    was in the band. Doris Day was there six nights a week. She was like "The
    Number One Fan." She had just started to do pretty well in pictures and
    she wanted to do something for Mary Ann. So she kept giving her old
    clothes. You know, Doris Day is six foot, or something like that, and Mary
    Ann is five feet one. You want to see some creations? Mary Ann looked
    like a midget singer going into a hole. She'd say, "Do you like this,
    Wood?" Oh God!

On March 15 the band closed at the Palladium. Bassist Walt Yoder became
the band's road manager, and was replaced on bass by Harry Babasin. Harry
achieved some fame in the 1950s on the West Coast jazz scene, playing jazz
cello in addition to bass. He was also a principal in the Pacific Jazz record
label during this period.

    The band opened on April 20 in the Century Room of the Hotel Commo-
dore in New York City (later the New York Statler). During the 1940s, the
Century Room was a constant venue for big bands. During the Herd's month-
long stay many more AFRS broadcasts were made and preserved.

    On the broadcast of April 20, three charts were performed that are worthy
of mention. The Tiny Kahn chart of "Tiny's Blues" is a medium tempo blues
done in an easy groove. The line is typical Kahn, and is stated by unison saxes
and trombones. The solos are by Swope in his usual boppish form, Zoot,
Woody, Lamond with some well-placed fills, and finally Otis.

    "The Happy Song," an eloquent score by Ralph Burns, was finally record-
ed by the Herd in 1958 for the Everest label under the title "Fire Island."
Solos are by Woody, Chaloff, Raney, Getz, Swope, and Royal.

    "This Is New" is a melodic jazz ballad, characteristically Burns, with solos
by Ollie Wilson, possibly Irving Markowitz, Zoot, and Al Cohn.

HARRY BABASIN: There were moments when you never heard a band sound
    better, but there were many, many disappointments in it, being what
    looked like a perfect band, only we couldn't be our own band. This band
    didn't have any records of its own yet. So we were pretty much wrapped
    into playing "Apple Honey," "Northwest Passage," "Bijou," and those
    things from the previous band. It was a source of quite a bit of frustration
    for us because we had all of those Al Cohn and Tiny Kahn charts and
    even the Neal Hefti charts that were in the book. But Woody, somehow,
    wasn't playing much of them. We also had some good Giuffre things; the
    only one that we played much was "Four Brothers," which the band did
    get to record—therefore we were able to play that with some recognition.
    We would try to play some of the stuff, but the people only wanted to
    hear what they wanted to hear. Woody could justify playing "Keen and
    Peachy" and the other new records, because they had been recorded, but

The Second Herd at the Century Room of the Hotel Commodore, New York City, May 1948. Front row: Fred Otis (piano), Mary Ann McCall (singer), Jimmy Raney (guitar), Stan Getz, Al Cohn, Woody, Sam Marowitz (hidden), Zoot Sims, Serge Chaloff (saxes). Second row: Harry Babasin (bass), Don Lamond (drums), Ollie Wilson (hidden), Earl Swope (hidden), Bob Swift (trombones). Back row: Ernie Royal, Bernie Glow (behind mike), Marky Markowitz (hidden), Stan Fishelson (partially hidden), Shorty Rogers (trumpets). (Courtesy Frank Driggs)

the people didn't even particularly like those in the beginning. They just wanted "Northwest Passage," "Caledonia," and stuff from the other Herd.

The Second Herd was nonpareil in terms of innovation and musical substance, yet it was a band with serious problems. Some of the men were sullen and withdrawn, trying to cope with heroin and other addictions.

WOODY: The Second Herd was sometimes a great band, and at other times, it was probably the most unwieldy group of people I ever worked with. But I think I kept my cool. They didn't keep theirs. But I didn't have their disease, which was drugs. That was one of the most heartbreaking things—trying to get the most and the best out of players who were not at all at their best on too many occasions.

   We had no preparation for it. Nobody in the music business had any preparation for it. It was something that just happened as part of the human process, and I was concerned very often, but I also knew that I didn't have the intelligence to cope with the whole thing on a huge scale. Consequently, I did the best I could and tried to keep their noses clean.

MARY ANN MCCALL: Woody couldn't even turn around and look at the guys. One or two would be falling asleep on the stand. It was terrible. The

FBI was following the band for months . . . marijuana trees were growing in the aisle of the bus.

HARRY BABASIN: Serge was the leading "doctor," and he was always trying to convert everybody to his way of thinking. Serge was one of those people like Bird. He had such an amazing tolerance for doing whatever he did to himself that he hardly ever knew it was a problem. The whole scene is another part of what eventually ran me away.

SHORTY ROGERS: To be honest with you, I don't like to talk about it. I think a lot more has been made of it than actually happened. There've been horror stories circulated that "this guy was falling over on the bandstand, they had to bring in a stretcher," et cetera. I never saw any of that kind of stuff going on. It's true, the guys were messing around with it, but whoever was doing it was making every effort to keep it a secret. A lot of guys who were doing it were just wonderful guys, who were nice to me and my family. The real tragedy of it is a lot of those guys aren't here any longer.

NEAL HEFTI: I think that if Woody ever had a fault, it was that he was too easy. After Frances and I left, I would go out to see the subsequent band. Musicians in the back, behind Woody, sort of making fun of him. He was being humiliated up there and I thought, "Why don't they shoot those guys?"

During Woody's engagement at the Commodore Hotel, the band played the Gerry Mulligan chart "Elevation" live on the AFRS "One Night Stand" broadcasts at least twice. Still virtually unknown, the baritone saxist, composer, and arranger Mulligan had been with the Gene Krupa band in 1946 and at the time he sent the chart to Woody was playing baritone and writing for the Claude Thornhill band. Woody never recorded Mulligan's "Elevation," although it was recorded by Elliot Lawrence's band in 1949. There is no evidence that Gerry Mulligan contributed additional material to the Herd's library.

The chart manifests a swinging arrangement, done in a medium tempo. It opens with a fanfare, followed by the trumpets playing the melody and the saxophones reestablishing it. Soloists are Otis and Getz, demonstrating the improvising techniques of the new Cool School. A rolling, ascending trumpet section chorus prepares the way for Ernie Royal's Gillespie-ish solo, followed by Swope and some well-placed drum fills by Lamond. The performance concludes with some screaming brass. Finally the saxes, playing the melody with the brass ensemble, take it out.

The Second Herd was a band that generally featured the saxophone section (the "Four Brothers"). Notwithstanding, other players contributed greatly to the spirit of the Second Herd, among them trumpeter Ernie Royal. The author asked trumpeter/composer Shorty Rogers what he remembered about working with Ernie Royal.

SHORTY ROGERS: Just a sweet, wonderful person. An incredible trumpet player. He was not only a nice guy as a person, but a team player. To sit next to him in the trumpet section was a great privilege and a great opportunity. He had a beautiful gift-of-the-art of playing the trumpet with no mouthpiece pressure. It was just effortless! The curse of all brass players is that you can't use pressure and botch up your lip. But with Ernie, I think it just came to him naturally. It was just a trip to sit next to him, 'cause his mouth would be open on the side. You could see his teeth when he was playing. We found out all about it later through Mel Broiles, a friend of mine, who is a great student of brass playing. Mel has written articles about it, relating that Ernie curled his tongue and just manipulated the air between his tongue and the roof of his mouth, and this method enabled him to play with absolutely no pressure. I tried it. It doesn't work for me!

On May 17 the Herd closed at the Century Room of the Commodore Hotel, and on May 20 the band opened at the Capitol Theater in New York City. Ralph Burns was back at the piano chair, replacing Otis. Woody had always played the New York Paramount when working the theater circuit; the shift to the Capitol was apparently due to a change of agencies.

During the Capitol Theater engagement, Bill Harris did some subbing in the band and made a firm commitment to rejoin the Herd once some outstanding obligations were satisfied. Meanwhile trombonist Alex Esposito filled Harris's chair. When Harris joined, the Second Herd's trombone section expanded to a quartet.

HARRY BABASIN: I remember one night in Burlington, Vermont, where some drunk customer decided that we weren't Woody's "real band," and decided he was going to fight Woody, and of course they got Woody the hell out of there, quick. So the customer found Ralph Burns, who was the next smallest guy in sight, and he took out after him. We jumped in our cars, and we had one of the wildest chase scenes you'd ever see. We drove around town until we finally tricked him into chasing us in front of the police station and the police locked him up.

The little interplay between the saxophones was probably one of the remarkable things about the band. Stan Getz was always rather perturbed that he was being singled out as the star, because he had so much respect for the other players. He thought they should be getting more exposure. But there just wasn't room for that many players. Of course Serge, the gigantic egotist, never got enough of anything.

On June 28 the Herd opened at the Click Club in Philadelphia for seven nights. In mid-July, the band went into the Eastwood Gardens at Detroit. There Chubby Jackson rejoined the Herd and resumed his roles as cheer-leader, first lieutenant, and talent scout.

HARRY BABASIN: Bill Harris rejoined just as I was leaving. Bill and Chubby, who replaced me, came back about the same time. Bill was a marvelous trombone player, but the public didn't accept him. I had some trouble with the public, too. Most of my trouble was that I was a little bit older than the rest of those guys. I had been on the road a couple more years, I had already begun to break into the studios a little bit. Actually, I hung around until I got fired, because I was making such a poor salary, I couldn't afford to pay my own way back to the Coast. The pressure was on Woody, because of the old theme, you know, to get back Bill Harris, Chubby, and others. Chubby fit into that picture, so he let me go and paid my transportation back.

WOODY: It was a completely different kind of band. I had brought in some different players and after I changed management, and Carlos Gastel took over, he begged me to bring back some of the guys who were in the First Herd. I did and certainly not reluctantly, because they were great players and would fit in anything.

DON LAMOND: I'll tell you, Chubby had a lot to do with the fire in the band. He was kind of a clown, but if he had really put his mind to playing the bass, nobody would have touched him. The way he can scat-sing bebop, if he could have put that on the bass, nobody could have ever come close to him.

The return of Jackson and Harris added voltage to the band. Chubby was adventurous, and through his energy and influence the conception of the band became more involved with the inflections of bebop. Earlier, in late 1947, Chubby had taken to Sweden an all-star small group consisting of Conte Candoli, Frank Socolow, Lou Levy, Terry Gibbs, Denzil Best, and him-self as bassist-leader. It was the first bebop group to tour Europe. With Bill Harris, the band regained additional power and emotion.

WOODY: With the Second Herd, we were having a piano problem one time. After a few drinks, Bill Harris and I got into a long discussion about what we could or couldn't do, and we got to talking about Erroll [Garner], and decided maybe this would be a great switch. Erroll was just beginning to do pretty well; he was working at the Deuces, in New York, and getting fair money, but I was even willing to try to cope with that to get him, so we called him and first of all, we had a terrible time getting him because the manager of the joint, the minute he heard a bandleader's name, he wouldn't call Erroll to the phone. He had just latched onto him, and Erroll was doing a little business for him and the owner wasn't about to lose him. After the joint folded, we finally reached Erroll. By then, we were in pretty good shape and Erroll was in the same condition. We now started this mumble-type conversation. We made all the arrangements and everything, and in the middle of this whole conversation, Erroll said, "But man, I don't read . . . what about them charts and all that?" We explained to him that "nobody reads in our band" . . . that it was all a big fallacy. He was all set to join in two or three days. Of course, the next day we woke up and forgot all about it, and so did Erroll, but we laughed about it millions of times since.

On August 7 the band began a one-week stand at the Marine Ballroom on the Steel Pier at Atlantic City, New Jersey. On August 8 they were heard on another live AFRS "One Night Stand" broadcast. Two noteworthy titles were performed that night: Shorty Rogers' "Berled in Earl" and Ralph Burns' First Herd classic "Northwest Passage." "Berled in Earl" opens with a voicing of two trumpets, two trombones, tenor, and baritone. Chubby has obviously returned with his vocal antics and his distinctive five-string bass. The performance wails with solos by Swope, Zoot, Royal, Chaloff, and Burns. The broadcast closed with "Northwest Passage," taken at an up tempo with no restraints. Burns solos (trying hard with some bop conceptions) and all the "Brothers" have a share of solo space, Getz, Cohn, Sims, and Chaloff charging in like a raging bull. The Second Herd version features rollicking bop punctuations from the trumpet section with Chubby's audible cheering, climaxing with Ernie Royal blowing in the upper register. The performance demonstrates a significant evolution from the First Herd version.

AL COHN: "It's all sort of blurry. The band worked all the time. We did something like two months of one-nighters one time, but it was great almost every day. It was all very exciting being with a band so popular. The level of musicianship was probably the best I ever played with.

Actually, that was sort of a frustrating time for me 'cause I really didn't get very much to play, and I felt that Woody didn't care for my playing too much. He had Zoot and Stan there, of course, so I never felt comfortable with that situation. Woody was right, I really wasn't ready. I was doing a lot of writing and not concentrating on playing enough. Since then, Woody and I have become a lot friendlier. I've worked with his band several times as a guest and we get along fine now.

DON LAMOND: The real unsung hero of all these guys with the band was Marky Markowitz, the trumpet player. Dizzy used to always come around and see him. Marky played great jazz solos. He played like Sweets Edison, without even trying.

In September vibraphonist Terry Gibbs replaced guitarist Jimmy Raney. In 1936, when he was 12, Terry had appeared on the "Major Bowes Amateur Hour" radio show and was the winner, playing the xylophone. Terry was briefly with Tommy Dorsey. He toured Sweden in late 1947 with Chubby Jackson's sextet and was with Buddy Rich's big band just prior to joining Woody.

TERRY GIBBS: I left the Buddy Rich band in San Francisco. Johnny Mandel, Frank La Pinto, Jackie Carmen, and I all left together, and we made the trip home in a car. Johnny went to LA, and the three of us drove in Jackie Carmen's car. We stopped in Elko, Nevada. We thought we would gamble whatever we had to make the trip. We had about fifty dollars for gas money to get home, and no food money. So we gambled and lost it all. Frank borrowed $400 from his mother to get us home. We bought salami and cheese, that's all we could afford. We got into the Lincoln Tunnel and the car blew up. It was the radiator. This is in New York and they're honkin' their horns and screamin' at us, and we had to push the car through. We hadn't slept on the trip. I swore that I would never go out on the road again, ever in my life! I got back to my house about one in the afternoon. I got a call from Woody about two o'clock. Now *that* band was a band that we all knew about. I left about four o'clock that night for Chicago. That may be one of my greatest moments . . . knowing who was on that band . . . Al Cohn, Zoot Sims, Stan Getz, Shorty, Don Lamond, Earl Swope, Serge Chaloff, you name it! It just knocked me straight up in the air!

I joined the band at the Blue Note in Chicago. I'll tell you, it's a night I won't forget because I was so scared. The whole band was so great, and they had already been together and I felt that I had to prove myself, and playing a bastard instrument, which vibes really is, it's something that doesn't easily blend with a whole lot of instruments. It does now, because they have found ways to do it. But it was really a spot for me to be put in.

I made an enemy of Zoot Sims on the second day I joined the band. They had a baseball team and I happened to be a very good baseball player. I had played high school baseball, and around Brooklyn I was a very good shortstop. So Zoot and I had to go out for the same position and they gave it to me because I was better. Zoot never forgot that till he died! Every time we met, he would say, "I don't know why you got the job, I was better on shortstop, anyhow."

Joining the band in late September, replacing Ralph Burns (who had been subbing on piano since Fred Otis left), was Louis A. (Lou) Levy. Lou had played with Boyd Raeburn and was the pianist on the sextet that Chubby Jackson took to Sweden. Chubby's influence over the band's personnel roster was rapidly coming into focus.

LOU LEVY: After returning from Sweden, we worked a couple of gigs like in Washington, D.C., with that same band, and I remember Conte Candoli and I stayed out at Chubby's house in Freeport, Long Island, and had a real nice couple of months. We went out and played football and baseball. We just goofed around on Long Island. Then at the Town Hall concert, I remember being opposite Charlie Parker and Miles Davis. Thelonious Monk also had a group in it. That was an important, wonderful concert. Then somewhere within those months, Chubby went back with Woody and he got Terry Gibbs on the band, replacing Jimmy Raney. Before I went on the band, I went back to Chicago and worked in one of the little bands. For a while, I worked with a group that included Shelly Manne, Bill Harris, Georgie Auld, and Howard McGhee. Then I joined Woody at Aberdeen, South Dakota, during a festival.

The most memorable experiences with Woody were actually the music itself, the guys I was introduced to and the music of Al Cohn, whom I had heard so much about. I had met him before, but I never had really got to play with him. Of course Stan Getz and Zoot were marvelous. Playing with Don Lamond was also a memorable experience. He wasn't predictable, yet he was very dependable, and he was very exciting. There would be a space in the arrangement where most drummers would jump at the opportunity to fill in, and Don would leave you in suspense, and play nothing at all. Then there would be a sudden explosion, and then it would be back to the band again.

My original piano influence was Bud Powell, then listening to Al Cohn and Charlie Parker. Al was a big influence on me because he was such a totally melodic player. He made me realize that music was not just running a bunch of notes and arpeggiating on chord changes and playing predictable patterns. He just composed as he went along, which is the epitome of a really great jazz player. He was like Zoot. Zoot was a real natural. He didn't play by chord changes, or anything like that. It just came out, whatever you heard. Al was even more melodic than Zoot was. Stan Getz once told me, jokingly, but maybe it was true, "The perfect tenor player would be Zoot Sims' time, Al Cohn's ideas, and my technique."

On October 7 the Second Herd opened at the Riverside Theater in Milwaukee for a seven-night appearance.

WOODY: My first real delving into Terry's inner self had to do with doing a show in Milwaukee, my hometown. He had a thing on "What's New?," a lovely ballad, and he used mallets that in appearance and in sound were something like tongs that you would use on an anvil. So one day, casually, after a couple of shows, I said, "Terry, did you ever think about using soft-ies, you know, mallets, for a thing like 'What's New?'" He says, "Man, you can't do that! I can't make it, man, like it's going to ruin the clank, you know?" So I said, "Forget it." P.S. That was it for the next year . . . tongs and anvils!

TERRY GIBBS: In those days, I was in my early 20s, and I played a lot more notes then. Probably senseless notes that I didn't need. I had a feature solo on "What's New?," an arrangement that Johnny Mandel wrote for me. From the intro on, I would go right into the solo and because I had so much to say, I would burst out like in 4,000 notes, and Woody came over to me one time after about my third week of doing that. He was really very nice, but in those days, we were all so cocky, nobody could tell us how to do anything about anything. Woody says, "Terry, I want to suggest something to you. Instead of just one bar, why don't you play about eight bars of the melody?" I didn't even give him a chance to finish, I said, "Who are you telling me about playin' on something you can't play at all?" I told him off, and I really yelled at him. He walked away like a little kid. Anyhow, about two years ago, I played in Toronto at the Royal York Hotel, and Woody came in to see me. I told that whole story to the audience. I said, "Woody, this is for you!" I played two whole choruses of "What's New?" and I just played the melody, straight through!

The band closed at the Riverside Theater and headed east on a string of one-nighters. On October 24 the Herd commenced a month-long engagement at New York's famous jazz club the Royal Roost. Jazz critics and historians agree that at this time the Second Herd was at its zenith in terms of musical excellence. The potent, select rhythm section of Levy, Jackson, Lamond, and Gibbs added spirit and cohesiveness to the unit.

The bop influence was increasingly manifested in the band's repertoire, and at times the Second Herd resembled Dizzy Gillespie's contemporary big band. At the Royal Roost, the band even performed Walter (Gil) Fuller's bop opus "Oh, Henry," probably scored by either Shorty Rogers or Tiny Kahn for the Herd's book.

The Roost had a radio wire, and during the Herd's month-long stay, live broadcasts were produced with bebop deejay Symphony Sid Torin as the emcee. Again, some of these live broadcasts have been preserved and marketed on various record labels.

LOU LEVY: The funny thing was in the midst of all these unusual characters and wonderful players was altoist Sam Marowitz, who was this clean-living, smiling little Jewish face . . .

Chubby used to do these stupid things. Like he'd put on ballet shoes with his tuxedo, and go out front and do his "Chubby act," and Sam would play the clarinet to "Spring Song" or something. Chubby would dance around like a little elf and Woody would stand there with this look on his face, but let him go ahead and do it. The band thought it was so funny, because it was so stupid. The audience probably wondered what it was all about. I think the humor fit into the First Herd better than the Second Herd.

MARY ANN MCCALL: We were at the Royal Roost. On opening night Mike Wallace and Dorothy Kilgallen and Dizzy were all there. It was just a little nightclub. I couldn't even sit on the bandstand, I had to sit up on the end of the bar. Then when they played my set, I would come down and do it.

There was a comedian, I don't know if he's still alive, a very crude and arrogant man, he had been around a long time. I started singing "I Got It Bad and That Ain't Good," and he was like mimicking me, and Woody stopped the band, right then, and he said, "I'm very sorry, but you're going to have to leave that seat right now. We're not going to play another note while Mary Ann sings until you leave" . . . It was just wonderful.

TERRY GIBBS: Guys like Stan Getz had the book memorized. Stan had a genius memory. He would play it two or three times and never take the chart out of his book again. Stan Getz is a giant musician . . . All the saxes were!

Among the titles played on the CBS live broadcast of November 11 from the Royal Roost were "Yucca" and "I Can't Get Started." "Yucca" was written by Zoot Sims and named after a street in Hollywood. The conception is similar to one of the early Gerry Mulligan linear scores done for the big bands of Thornhill, Elliot Lawrence, Chubby Jackson and Kenton. It swings with a nice, tight interplay between the brass and sax sections. In the solos, Zoot has his turn, with contributions from Earl Swope, a delightfully melodic Al Cohn, Lamond booting the band, Bill Harris, Woody's clarinet, Gibbs, and Levy. One of the great features of most Herman bands was a variety of soloists and plenty of allotted solo space.

"I Can't Get Started" was another ballad feature for Gibbs. The eloquent five-man saxophone section is heard behind Terry's lovely chords. Serge's excellence as a section anchor man is evident here. Gibbs displays his finesse and technical artistry along with his sometimes "too many notes."

During the band's engagement at the Roost, an excellent trumpeter joined the band, replacing Marky Markowitz. Robert (Red) Rodney went on the road at age 15 and worked for the bands of Jerry Wald, Jimmy Dorsey, Tony Pastor, Les Brown, Georgie Auld, Claude Thornhill, and Gene Krupa before joining the Herman Herd. Rodney was a potent soloist and one of the leading voices in the new bebop movement. He had jammed with people like Charlie Parker, Dizzy, and Tadd Dameron on 52nd Street. Although his tenure with the band was only five months, Rodney left a memorable imprint on the legacy of the Second Herd, particularly his solo on the recording of "Lemon Drop."

On the final WMCA broadcast from the Royal Roost, the band was in particularly good form. After Symphony Sid's exuberant announcement—"And so once again, ladies and gentlemen, right down here at the Royal Roost, 'The Metropolitan Bopera House,' the house that bop built on Broadway, between 47th and 48th Streets, for the last time on a remote broadcast from WMCA, will you dig the great Woody Herman Herd"—the band went into "Oh, Henry." The saxes play the boppish riff laced with fortissimo brass, and Swope has a loose solo with Levy comping effectively in the background. A brass ensemble interlude serves as an introduction to Royal's solo.

"We the People Bop" is performed by the Second Herd edition of the Woodchoppers, with the Herman rhythm section plus Woody, Royal, Getz, Chaloff, and Gibbs. Woody and Ernie Royal do the bop vocal riff "Eel-Ya-Ah," with solos by Chaloff, Royal, Getz, and Woody on clarinet. Lamond does some tasty drumming.

"Tiny's Blues" seems complete with the addition of Gibbs, who assists on the intro. Solos by Swope, Getz, Woody (clarinet), and Gibbs, with the bone section blowing background riffs and Chubby's encouragement, contribute to an exciting performance.

"Boomsie" is a frantic up-tempo chart with solos from Gibbs, rapid, machine-gun-like brass punctuations, Getz, Levy, Chaloff, Royal, and Rodney in a thrilling trumpet chase, and finally more contributions from Chaloff and Gibbs.

On Sunday, November 28, the Herd closed at the Roost and headed west to the Coast for a month-long stay at Gene Norman's Empire Room Theater-Restaurant in Hollywood. The room seated 600 and on opening night another 500 were turned away. It was advantageous for Woody personally to have the band working close to home during the Christmas holiday.

In the late 1940s Gene Norman was a disc jockey on radio station KLAC in Hollywood. He was one of the original jazz concert impresarios and formed his own "Gene Norman Presents" record label in the early 1950s. In 1948 he was instrumental in booking the Dizzy Gillespie big band on its first trip to the West Coast and the Stan Kenton band into the Hollywood Bowl the same year.

GENE NORMAN: One of the interesting things that we had at the Empire was, since I was a dee jay and a fan and wanted to cater to the kids, as well as have a normal nightclub operation, I had a gallery there. The kids could come in for a buck and sit there and watch the band. It was a small balcony, with no booze served. You didn't have to buy anything. There was no cover charge.

Another thing I remember about that era was Woody bought a new house. He had started to make big money. It had been Humphrey Bogart's house. It was a three-level house and he had a big party and the band was all there.

TERRY GIBBS: Ava Gardner was running after Stan Getz. He sloughed her off all the time at the Empire Room. She would come in every night to get Stan. He'd walk over to her and say hello, and out of the corner of his eye, he'd see a friend and run over to his friend and leave Ava.

During the band's engagement at the Empire Room, AFRS produced numerous live broadcasts. Later, these were rebroadcast in combination with recorded material from other artists. Most of the broadcasts have been preserved, but unfortunately, the broadcast discs in most cases were not kept.

During December, "Godchild," one of the noted bop compositions of pianist George Wallington, was performed by the Herd on an AFRS "Just Jazz" broadcast. "Godchild" was a Tiny Kahn arrangement featuring the saxes playing the riff in an ebullient manner. Royal, Gibbs, Chaloff, and Levy all contribute solos. Lamond's controlled "explosions" are emblematic of his style.

In December, the AFM recording ban ended. Capitol Records in Hollywood signed the new AFM contract. Woody signed a new contract with the aggressive six-year-old record firm and recorded some of the Second Herd's most memorable material. On December 29, the Herd stampeded into Capitol Studios at Sunset and Vine and recorded two classic Second Herd pieces, "That's Right" and "Lemon Drop."

"That's Right" was originally based on a line by Conte Candoli, Frank Socolow, and Chubby Jackson. It is the earlier "Boomsie" with a new head. The score verifies Shorty Rogers's genius for arranging. He had evolved considerably from his First Herd initial big band score of "Back Talk." "That's Right" starts with a line played by trumpet, tenor, and vibes. Gibbs plays a wildly swinging solo in front of the same brass punctuation as in the earlier Boomsie. Other solos are by Getz, Chaloff, Levy, Harris, and Rodney and Royal doing a trumpet chase.

TERRY GIBBS: We recorded it at one tempo, which was kind of fast. But by the time we were into the third week of playing it, it got about twenty times faster. I had the whole ending. At the ending, there's just a lot of notes. We'd be doing those one-nighters and sleeping on the bus, on your arms, legs curled up. You couldn't get comfortable on those bus seats. It would be 400 or 500 miles between jobs, and I'd be sleeping on my hands. We'd get to the job and he'd open up the night with that tune! I'd have to jump in and play that thing, and you'd have to play it clean. I made up that ending myself. It was an F scale going down, and it's hard to play, because there's only one note to aim for, which is a B-flat. On most of the scales, besides the C scale, you have sharps and flats to aim for, but here it's just straight down. It had to be good, especially with *that* band, because they were good!

George Wallington's "Lemon Drop" became another bop classic with versions also recorded by the Barnet and Krupa bands in 1949. The Herd's arrangement was penned by Shorty Rogers, with the vocal trio of Rogers, Jackson, and Gibbs doing the line. Terry's low voice and Chubby's high voice add humor to the performance. When Jackson left the band, Woody took his place with Rogers and Gibbs. Solo contributions are by Chaloff, Swope, Rodney, Gibbs, and Woody.

TERRY GIBBS: Actually, "Lemon Drop" was done before we ever joined the Woody Herman band. It was recorded with Chubby's group in Sweden. The original thing had Conte, Frank Socolow and myself. "The Three Nudnicks." "Nudnick" is a Jewish expression for "a pain in the ass."

How we thought of the singing thing is, when we went to Sweden in 1947, Chubby flew over, and the rest of us went by boat about a week later. Just before we left, we heard George Wallington's new tune called "Lemon Drop." We learned it on our horns, because we wanted to get to Chubby and play him the thing. So when we were on the boat, on the way to Sweden, the instruments were down in storage below deck somewhere. We were like little kids, so anxious to tell Chubby, "Hey, you got to hear this." Conte, Frank Socolow, and I went over to Chubby and said, "You got to hear this tune by George Wallington," and then he said, "How's it go?" We started singing it. Anyhow, Chubby knew show business a lot better than we did. He says, "You guys are going to sing on the stage like that!" And we say, "Are you kidding? We're not singing, forget it!" But we got our nerve up and so we were on stage. Conte, Frank Socolow, and myself all have big noses. We kept our noses together like idiots, and we sang the thing, and then I sang the low part, so Chubby says, "You gotta do that!" And I did it!

On December 30 the band recorded four additional titles, which were exceptional contributions to the Herd's developing reputation. Ralph Burns had contributed an eloquent score of "I Got It Bad and That Ain't Good," a feature for Mary Ann McCall, with Woody's romantic Hodges-like alto. The entire arrangement is reminiscent of Duke.

MARY ANN McCALL: I've got to say it's been done many times before I did it. But I loved Duke's band, and I loved Ben Webster who played "I Got It Bad." Woody and I talked it over, and I said, "Let's do it, it can't hurt." There hadn't been too many vocals on "I Got It Bad." I was really more of an instrumentalist-type singer.

Burns's exquisite score "Early Autumn," adapted from Part Four of the suite *Summer Sequence*, was also recorded at the same session. The recording featured Woody's romantic alto, Gibbs' tasty vibes, and Getz's lyrical tenor, and established Getz as a household word and set a pattern for an entire generation of tenor stylists.

TERRY GIBBS: We recorded a bunch of takes on "Early Autumn," and Stan and I both thought that we played better on another take. But Woody took the overall performance, band and everything else into consideration, and chose that take. We were kind of disappointed. But he picked the best one. The ensemble was so clean on the thing.

Stan and I won the *Down Beat* award the next year because of that record. Funny, where would my career have gone in five years, if Woody hadn't picked that take? I wouldn't have won the *Down Beat* award, and in those days, *Down Beat* awards were more important than they are now.

The last title recorded during the December 30 session at Capitol was Rogers' wailing score of "Keeper of the Flame," based on the chords of "I Found a New Baby." It's taken at a breakneck tempo with some catchy up-front voicing for Rogers and "The Brothers." Solos are by Chaloff, Levy, Woody, Getz, Sims, Harris, Getz (bridge), and finally Royal (bridge).

LOU LEVY: The few records that I made with the band don't have that many solos. There's "Keeper of the Flame," and a few like that. As I listen to them, I think I'd like to take another shot at the solos, but the records are good. When I hear them, I cringe a little and I laugh a lot.

TERRY GIBBS: We had a good baseball team. Lemme tell you about the time we played Harry James' band. It was a "rubber" game: we won one and he won one. Harry was really a baseball nut. He took Don Lamond out of Woody's band because he needed a center fielder, and he needed a drummer at the same time. So he filled both positions. Harry's band would show up and they would have actual baseball uniforms! We would go out in our dirty clothes and play. So Harry said if we beat them, he would have a party for us at the Empire Room. He and Betty Grable made a party for us that night, because we won the game.

WOODY: We used to have ball teams. That was a big thing years ago in all the bands. One of our best games, where we drew the biggest crowd, was when we played the Spade Cooley band in Hollywood. Like our guys, including myself, put on our cowboy boots and our jeans . . . the coolest, you know, and here was Spade's band, and Spade was dressed in nice, casual dress . . . none of this cowboy shit at all, you know. I might add that the best ball club we ever had was the band of junkies. They were the most relaxed ball club. They could catch flies, and they "weren't even there!"

The Second Herd remained at the Empire Room through the New Year's holiday, closing on January 3, 1949. During the early morning hours of the New Year, the band was heard live via two CBS radio broadcasts.

GENE NORMAN: It was very exciting for me because on New Year's Eve, the band went on the air coast-to-coast, and I announced it. That was a thrilling thing for me to do in my own club. I was 26 years old. I can name every man in the band, even today.

Woody chose "Lemon Drop" as the closer for one of the CBS broadcasts on New Year's Eve. Live broadcasts enjoyed a spontaneity rarely heard in the recording studio, and this live version surpasses the recording for straight-ahead jazz and bop vocal fun. Chubby, Terry Gibbs, and Shorty Rogers are introduced by the announcer (not Gene Norman) as the "Three Nudnicks." The boys get an opportunity to do some ad lib scat singing after the bop line is introduced. Chubby is heard during Terry's growl portion asking, "What kind of voice is that?" Chaloff charges in amid Chubby's exuberant cheerleading. Swope also has his say, with Rodney, Gibbs, and Woody's clarinet following.

Worthy of note, and also performed on the live CBS New Year's Eve broadcast was "I Only Have Eyes for You," a Burns arrangement and ballad showcase for Bill Harris' trombone.

In early January, the Herd boarded a train and headed east for Chicago. They were interrupted by a blinding snowstorm in the Rockies.

WOODY: We were snowbound on a train outside Cheyenne for three days. Finally the train got near Salt Lake, and the food was running low. We finally walked into the town of Salt Lake, and I went to see Jazzbo Collins, who was working there. He said, "Man, what's gonna happen? Diz is supposed to play a date at the Coconut Grove Ballroom here tonight and he flew in, but his band is stranded on another train somewhere in Nebraska." So I said, "We're all here, why don't we make the job for Dizzy, you know, it'll be HIS band!" So we had a ball! We went to the ballroom and played the dance that night. Dizzy was leaping all over the stand.

On January 10 the Herd opened at Frank Holzfeind's Blue Note in Chicago. Chubby Jackson had left the band and was temporarily replaced by Jimmy Stutz.

CHUBBY JACKSON: I left to assemble my own band, which turned out to be a great musical band, but I personally lost every penny I had ever saved. I called Woody later, and he said, "When are you coming home?"

On January 23 the band closed at the Blue Note. On the 27th, they opened at the Paramount Theater in Toledo, Ohio, for four nights. This was when the Second Herd began to change in terms of the internal chemistry that had prevailed since just before the Royal Roost engagement the year before. The Second Herd would continue as a great jazz band, but the cohesive quality that contributed to its eminence slowly diminished.

JIMMY GIUFFRE: I took Zoot's place with Woody. They got into some argument. He was playing backstage at the Paramount Theater. Zoot was playing on the upper floor with the door open, and it made a lot of noise, and Woody yelled up "Stop that blowing!" Zoot said, "Screw you," or something, and then Woody fired him.

LOU LEVY: I remember Zoot and Woody getting into it, when Zoot finally left. They had a big argument, yelling at each other from different floors backstage in the theater we were working somewhere in Ohio. Zoot was upstairs, and Woody was downstairs, and they were screaming at each other through the stairwell. Zoot left after that.

TERRY GIBBS: He didn't want to fire him, but I think there were people around, and it was one of those things where he *had* to fire him. He waited for Zoot to apologize, because he didn't want to let him go. That incident started the whole Four Brothers leaving. We also wanted to see Zoot apologize, but I suppose his ego and pride got in the way. He left the band. Then Stan left the band, then Al. Then it went down a little bit. The replacements were all good players, every player that came in was a giant. Jimmy Giuffre was a giant, Gene Ammons was a giant, and Buddy Savitt. But there was a chemistry between Zoot, Al, Stan and Serge Chaloff that was something else.

The rift was not permanent; later, both Zoot and Stan would appear with the band at numerous reunions, concerts, and jazz festivals. But meanwhile, more personnel changes were occurring in the Herd, as trumpeter Ed Badgley replaced Stan Fishelson; ex-Kenton bass trombonist Bart Varsalona replaced Bob Swift; and the inventive bassist Oscar Pettiford replaced Jimmy Stutz.

WOODY: Oscar was with me a few months. It was another one of those personality clashes, or whatever you want to call it. I had wanted to hire Shadow [Wilson] for years. After Oscar got on the band, I suggested that we get Shadow [when Don Lamond was leaving] and he said, "Yeah, let's get him," and they fought from that day on, to the finish.

As early as 1947, Woody had begun to have unfortunate experiences with business and personal managers. He had allowed his zeal for music to overshadow financial and legal affairs; he was naive and trusting in his choice of business associates. In the fall of 1947, when the Second Herd was getting started, Woody's contract with General Artists Corporation expired. The booking of the band was taken over by Continental Artists, run by Jack Archer, Milt Deutsch, and Abe Turchen. Woody's association with Continental was brief, and then he returned to GAC, but Abe Turchen remained with Woody as personal manager and confidante. Eventually, Abe took over the band's financial affairs and booking responsibilities. It was a costly mistake.

Since the "Band That Played the Blues" period, Woody had had a contract with the law firm and managing staff of Goldfarb, Mirenburg, and Vallon. It was apparently Woody's understanding that his contract with them had expired and he made a decision to do without them. This resulted in a series of breach of contract suits against the Woody Herman Orchestra. At one point, the orchestra's music library was impounded. According to the media, Woody had breached a contract dated March 21, 1947, which stipulated that ten percent of his income as an entertainer and five percent as a bandleader be paid to Chubby Goldfarb and Company. The agents were claiming $18,637. In 1949 a judicial decision obliged Woody to pay a commission to Goldfarb and his associates for one year. This created additional burdens for Woody in a climate characterized by rising costs and changing musical tastes. During this period, when his attorneys were haggling over the lawsuits with Goldfarb, Mirenburg, and Vallon, Woody hired the agency of Carlos Gastel and Associates.

Gastel was a colorful and flamboyant character who lived extravagantly. His clients had included Stan Kenton, Peggy Lee, Mel Torme, and Nat Cole. Gastel possessed an astute business sense and was a proficient producer. He assembled a series of concerts aimed at the colleges, combining the Herman Herd with Nat King Cole. The first series of Herman–Cole concerts began in Illinois on February 14 and continued for almost a month. A second series of Herman–Cole concerts began that summer and terminated in early December.

On February 20 the Herd and Cole performed together at New York's Carnegie Hall. February 26 marked the Second Herd's only exposure to the new medium of television when the band appeared on the Eddie Condon show. It was an unlikely combination of the avant-garde Herdsmen with Condon, whose roots were in Chicago jazz and Dixieland. Reportedly Condon disliked not only modern jazz and bop but big-band jazz as well. At one point during the show, Condon commented, "We're boppin' ourselves silly tonight."

About February 27 trumpeter Bernie Glow was replaced by Al Porcino and Red Rodney was replaced by Charlie Walp at Boston's Symphony Hall. On March 4 the band was recorded live at the Blue Note in Chicago. The Blue Note was primarily a jazz spot, and the Herd took advantage of the environment by pulling out all stops. It was Don Lamond's last night with the band. He was replaced in the Herd by the former Basie drummer Shadow Wilson.

The Second Herd about February 1949: Ernie Royal, Ed Badgley, Bernie Glow, Shorty Rogers (trumpets), Earl Swope, Bill Harris, Ollie Wilson, Bob Swift (trombones), Al Cohn, Stan Getz, Sam Marowitz, Jimmy Giuffre, Serge Chaloff (saxes), Oscar Pettiford (bass), Don Lamond (drums), Terry Gibbs (seated; vibes), Woody in front. Lou Levy (piano) not in picture. (Courtesy The Hugh Turner Collection, Hollywood)

Shorty Rogers had written a chart for Don, appropriately entitled "Don Delves In," and it was performed on his final night. An additional title performed at the Blue Note was the first showcase for Serge Chaloff, entitled "Man, Don't Be Ridiculous," another Shorty Rogers composition. The band plays it way up tempo with exciting brass punctuations. In the late 1940s Woody would often identify a chart from the band's music library with the title of a fictitious movie. He would soberly declare, "We would like to play for you 'Man Don't Be Ridiculous,' from the picture 'Framed.'" This vaudevillian flourish remained a part of his routine well into the 1980s.

TERRY GIBBS: There were a lot of sick guys in the band at that time. It was no secret that there were some guys who were strung out. But the funniest thing about the guys were, they were sharp. One time, my ex-wife had a cat on the road with the band. We were told, "You can't bring animals into the hotel." It was wintertime, so she put this cat under her coat. We were sneaking it into the hotel, and about nine guys got into the elevator, and the elevator operator didn't pay any attention, the guys' heads were down, and everybody's half asleep, and all of a sudden, the cat went, "Meow-w-w." Nine guys started going "meow-w, meow-w, woof, woof," and the elevator man couldn't believe what was goin' on. We get out of the elevator with the cat, and I look at the guys, and they're all asleep again . . . until they got to their floor!

Serge, unfortunately, was hooked on all kinds of junk, and if you checked into a hotel, if Serge was on the tenth floor, we'd be on the sixth floor, because he would fall asleep with a cigarette in his hand, and make a hole in the mattress, and every hotel manager would come to him and say, "Mr. Chaloff, you burned a hole in your mattress, and it's going to cost you $18.00!" Serge would say, "How dare you sir! I'm the winner of the *Down Beat* and *Metronome polls!*" Serge had a way of speaking, and his hair was always nice and neat, and his suit was pressed. He may not have taken a bath in a week, but he always looked so nice and neat on the outside. Everywhere he went, he'd say, "How dare you, I'm the winner of the *Down Beat* and *Metronome* polls," and everyone would wind up apologizing to him!

LOU LEVY: Serge was a great musician. He was a great character. The problem he had became a problem he couldn't cope with after a while. When he died [1957], he was in a wheelchair, with cancer. Had he not been into all that other thing, drinking and whatever else went along with it, he would have been an amazing, respectable character. But it was hard to take him seriously, other than his playing.

During the 1940s and 1950s, Woody's father, Otto, who was in charge of quality control for Nunn-Bush Shoes in Milwaukee, would custom-make Woody's shoes, often white moccasins or various two-tone combinations.

WOODY: I've lost so many of my shoes that I valued very much. One of the more amusing times that I was wiped out was we were doing some theater dates with Mel Tormé, and we were closing Baltimore, and we had a day to get to Hartford for a theater date. I had a big station wagon, and Mel asked me if he and his new wife could use the car, like stop in New York, and then go on to Hartford. He had heard that I was going to fly, and I said "Sure you can." Mel is a great moviegoer. He catches about four pictures a day, otherwise he's not happy. So they stopped, way uptown, around 90th Street in New York, because there was something playing there he had only seen eight times, so he figured he should see this one more time. They just parked the car on the street, and went in and caught the picture, and when they came out, the windows had been broken. Station wagons are very bad for bands, because everything is in view. Everything was taken out of the car, consisting of all my personal belongings and Mel's wife's personal belongings. He had shipped his stuff ahead. So his wife was hysterical, and he was pretty shaken, and they got in the car, and he was now going to try to find a police station, or a policeman who could tell him how to get to a police station. In their excitement, Candy yelled, "There's a policeman across the street," and he turned his head and rammed into a row of parked

BILL HARRIS AND HIS CONN 6-H TROMBONE

Consistent Poll Winners With The
Great Woody Herman Band

Woody, wearing a pair of his unique slip-on moccasin shoes, with Bill Harris in 1949. (Reprinted by permission, C. G. Conn, Elkhart, Indiana)

cars and smashed the whole car, like into an accordion. They had just gotten married and all this tumult. . . .

During this period tenor saxist Gene Ammons replaced Al Cohn. Ammons was the son of boogie-woogie pianist Albert Ammons. His sound was somewhat coarser than the previous "Brothers'," although he was a real swinger and an accomplished musician. Like Charlie Barnet, Woody was color-blind when it came to hiring musicians. With the hiring of Ammons, the band now had four black musicians, including Royal, Pettiford, and drummer Shadow Wilson.

WOODY: We were booked into Loews Theater in Washington, D.C., and ten days before the date, I received a call from Carlos, and he had received a call from Loews, and they said they heard we had black people in the band. In order for us to play the theater in Washington, D.C., "The

Seat of Democracy," we would have to dump these guys, and have an all-white band or we would not only be canceled in Washington, [but also for] any other weeks of the year that Loews controls. We wouldn't be able to play in any MGM pictures [i.e., the band would be barred from theaters where MGM films were showing, through MGM's relationship with Loews].

Finally we decided we needed the week's work, because the band wasn't doing very well, and we also needed the rest of the weeks of work and so forth. One guy had been with me for a year and the others for shorter periods, and so I called them in the room and I told them what my problem was. I said, "In order to make it bearable for you, I will pay you your week's salary and buy your ticket to New York on the plane. So go have a ball for a week and come back. Treat this like it never happened, 'cause there's no other way out that I can see. We could cut off our nose to spite our face, but it won't do any good."

So they agreed, and everything was fine until the next day. We had opened with some substitutes, and some black organization grabbed our guys in New York, and before I knew it, I had attorneys calling me every few minutes, night and day, and they flew the guys back to Washington, and kept them "bagged" and threatened and cajoled them, and a terrible tumult was going on until about the fourth day. The third day, I went "straight up," and I called them all into the theater, and I said, "If you people persist in doing this, tomorrow morning, I'll be on my hill in California. This is the only thing I've got going for me, and as far as I'm concerned, I'm out of business. If you want it that way, okay." They were now suing Loews, MGM, everyone. It would be a long legal hassle. Well, it turned out where everyone came back and the thing was forgotten. But those poor guys took a horrible beating. They were accused of not standing up for their rights and their people, and made out to be real bums.

Stan Getz was replaced in late March by Buddy Savitt, who was proficient, but did not measure up to Getz's technique or lyricism.

AL PORCINO: It was around April that I got a call from Woody to replace Bernie Glow. The trumpets were Ernie Royal, myself, Stan Fishelson, Shorty Rogers, and Charlie Walp—Charlie and I joined at the same time. We had just finished working Chubby's band together. I loved Charlie. He was such an original jazz player and so great in the section.

In late April the band was at the Apollo Theater in New York. It was probably during the Apollo Theater date that drummer Shadow Wilson was replaced by Shelly Manne.

WOODY: He stayed for about eight months. He was completely the musician. As a matter of fact, he told me that this was the first time in his life he had ever played with a swing band, and he did an excellent job.

On May 26 the Second Herd recorded one of its classic blockbuster titles, "More Moon." It was scored by Shorty Rogers, based on the chords of "How High the Moon," and featured solos by Gene Ammons, Bill Harris, Terry Gibbs, Woody (clarinet), and Shelly Manne. During the bop era, musicians loved to jam on "How High," and the tune became known as the "bop national anthem." The Herd continued to perform "More Moon" intermittently until about 1953, when it was rumored that one of the trumpeters got into a feud with Woody and in anger destroyed the trumpet parts.

SHORTY ROGERS: I originally wrote the composition for the first concert tour with Nat Cole. He would do his own thing with the trio, but we needed something for the finale, where he would combine with the band. Nat would scat sing the first chorus, then he would play a piano solo, and then on a cue, the band would take it away from him. Woody and Nat had written the first chorus, and it had the same out chorus as the recording. So when the tour ended with Nat, Woody says, "It has a nice out chorus, write a new first chorus and we'll call it 'More Moon.'"

TERRY GIBBS: One time the band got on an air pistol kick. We bought air pistols and we'd shoot out the windows in the band bus. Serge one time put a telephone book against the hotel room door and never hit the telephone book at all. He made a hole in the door instead. I'm carrying my suitcases out, and I'm going by Serge's room and he says, "Wait a second, Terry!" And I hear him say, "How dare you sir! I'm the winner of the *Down Beat* and *Metronome* polls!" The manager says, "I don't care who the hell you are, you made a hole in that door, and it's going to cost you sixteen dollars!" So Serge says, "If I'm going to pay for that door, I want that door!" So he had the guy unhinge the door, and Serge and I walked out of the hotel with my suitcases and a door.

From May 27 to June 2, the Herd played the Howard Theatre in Washington, D.C. During that period, Woody's tolerance for Serge's lifestyle wore thin, culminating in his acting on impulse and taking revenge in a bizarre and unconventionally humorous manner.

In his "Portrait of Woody," writer Gene Lees recounts an interview where Woody told the story.

WOODY: He [Serge] was getting farther and farther out there . . . He kept saying, "Hey, Woody baby, I'm straight, man, I'm clean." And I shouted, "Just play your [expletive] part and shut up!" I was so depressed after one gig. There was this after-hours joint in Washington called the Turf and Grid. It was owned by a couple of guys with connections, bookmakers. Numbers guys. Everybody used to go there. That night President Truman had a party at the White House, and afterwards all his guests went over to the Turf and Grid. They were seven deep at the bar, and I had to fight my way through to get a drink. Man, all I wanted was to have a drink and forget it. Finally I get a couple of drinks, and it's hot in there, and I hear, "Hey, Woody, baby, whadya want to talk to me like that for? I'm straight, baby, I'm straight." And it's Mr. Chaloff. Then I remember an old Joe Venuti bit. We were jammed in there, packed in, and . . . I peed down Serge's leg.

You know, man, when you do that to someone, it takes a while before it sinks in what's happened to him. And when Serge realized, he let out a howl like a banshee. He pushed out through the crowd and went to the telephone booth. And I'm banging on the door and trying to get at him, and one of the owners comes up and says, "Hey, Woody, you know, we love you, and we love the band, but we can't have you doing things like that in here." And he asked me to cool it.

Well, not long after that, I was back here on the Coast, working at some club on the beach. Joe Venuti was playing just down the street, and I was walking on the beach with him after the gig one night, and I told him I had a confession to make, I'd stolen one of his bits. Joe just about went into shock. He was horrified. He said, "Woody, you can't do things like that! I can do things like that, but *you* can't. You're a gentleman. It's all right for me, but not you!"

LOU LEVY: In the couple of years I worked with Woody, I don't know if I knew him that well. He was a great guy, and he was a terrific bandleader, because he let the guys do what they wanted, yet they did what he wanted, without forcing the issue—even with that rebellious band that I worked with. But they respected Woody, and they played real well together, and you don't do that unless you have some kind of a force out there that gets it going for you.

Bill Harris was magnificent, and just playing with him was an outstanding experience. He circumvented style. I don't even know what kind of style you call it he played. It wasn't bebop, it wasn't Dixieland. It was his own. When I talk to guys like Ray Brown and Oscar Peterson, or whoever they are, they loved to play with him. That shows you, it doesn't matter what the style was, everybody felt it.

Jimmy Giuffre, now on the band, was finally able to play his own composition "Four Brothers."

JIMMY GIUFFRE: Woody had all these pieces that he played. ["Four Brothers"] never got played that much, because he just wasn't sure of the performance of it. But every night he would go and table-hop the last set. The guys in the band would request "Four Brothers" from the assistant leader [Sam Marowitz], and they got to play it that way. Finally, after several months, they started really learning it, so that the sax section could stand up and play the first chorus and really make it happen.

In late June 1949, the Second Herd traveled to the West Coast for a July 1 opening at the Rendezvous Ballroom, Balboa, California. The Rendezvous had been a haven for name big bands and jazz music since the early thirties. During the summers, Balboa Peninsula, Balboa Island and Newport Beach would be inundated with high school and college students who jammed the beach to soak in the warm sun. The band was booked at the Rendezvous for weekends during the entire month of July. During the week the band would be on vacation except for record dates in Hollywood, fifty miles up the coast. In the summer of 1949, the Rendezvous was the site of a series of live Saturday afternoon radio broadcasts heard on the Mutual Network, entitled "Excursions in Modern Music."

On July 6 the band went before the cameras of Universal International to film another short, entitled *Jazz Cocktail*, with the Herman Herd and a vocal group called "The Mellow-Larks."

TERRY GIBBS: In those days, they wouldn't allow black musicians to be on camera. Ernie Royal and Gene Ammons were both on the band. There was a guy sitting there in the sax section whom I didn't even know. At least I knew Al Porcino. He stood up and lipped Ernie's solos. Al could never play jazz, he just was one of the best lead trumpet players in the business. It was really Ernie on the soundtrack. In fact, another terrible thing that happened is that whoever produced that thing didn't think Mary Ann McCall was pretty enough to be on the film. There was a girl lip synching, and I don't know who she was, but it was Mary's voice, and Mary sang good!

On July 14 the band recorded "Detour Ahead," a vocal feature for Mary Ann. It is one of her best efforts, a Second Herd classic that has never been reissued on an LP album. Recorded at the same session was another vocal feature for Mary Ann called "Jamaica Rhumba." It was a light-hearted pseudo-Latin score with such daffy lyrics as "Do the rhumba when you go to win him, it will bring out all the *lobo* in him . . ." There are some bright solo offerings from Gibbs, Savitt, and Woody on alto. The recording is an excellent sample of Serge Chaloff's capability as a section man.

The durable Herman flag waver "Not Really the Blues" was also recorded on July 14. It was written by the brilliant composer and former jazz bass trumpeter Johnny Mandel, widely acclaimed in the sixties for his film song credits on "Emily," from *The Americanization of Emily*, and the Academy-Award-winning song "The Shadow of Your Smile," for the movie *The Sandpiper*.

JOHNNY MANDEL: During the days I wrote for him, I was very shy. I never hung out much with leaders at that time. I didn't know Woody. I always hung with the guys in the band. I knew Woody later, but not nearly as much as I would have liked to. I have the same feeling about Ellington. I played with Basie, and I never even hung out with "Base" too much, but I did some, because he hung with us.

Bands in those days were still doing stage shows. We always opened with a very fast thing, usually something very flashy, before any of the other acts came on. The band would open the show. ["Not Really the Blues"] was supposed to be as fast as, say, "The Champ," by Diz, or "Salt Peanuts." It would have played very well that way. But they didn't get around to playing it until at least six months after they got it. Mainly because Bill Harris was a very poor reader, but he made up for it by what he did. You know, Bill Harris hadn't been playing the trombone very long by the time he was with Woody, and Gene Krupa and Benny before that. In fact, he lost those jobs because he couldn't read. Neither am I a good reader. I'm a lousy reader.

I heard the story from Sam Marowitz and people like that, that Bill couldn't hack that part at first, and he was playing the top part. They just put it aside, because there was a lot of other stuff in the book. Woody used to take off sometimes toward the end of the evening, and Sam Marowitz would like be the conductor. They pulled it out one night, and they kicked it off at the tempo they recorded it at, which is really too slow. Much too slow, in fact, because it goes in four, where it should have gone in two.

It was written at a time when Mezz Mezzrow's book *Really the Blues* came out. It was a very self-serving book, and everybody knew what Mezzrow was, sort of the clown of the music business. He hung around and fastened on everybody's coattails. I happened to read it, and it was interesting reading, but a lot of it wasn't true. So I just happened to call this "Not Really the Blues," because it starts off like it's going to be a blues, and then it turns out not to be a blues.

The Capitol recording of "Not Really the Blues" has a rousing solo by Ammons. Swope, Woody, Savitt and Royal also have brief solos.

One other number recorded on July 14 was the easy-groove Neal Hefti score of "The Great Lie," composed by Andy Gibson and Cab Calloway, with solos by Gibbs, Woody, Swope, and Savitt. The recording was held in Capitol's vaults until released in the seventies on Capitol Jazz Classics, Volume Nine.

On or about July 18, the band was engaged in a softball game in Costa Mesa, California, a short distance from Balboa beach. During the game bassist Oscar Pettiford broke his arm in a freak accident. Replacing Pettiford was bassist Joe Mondragon, who had replaced Chubby Jackson in the First Herd.

On July 20 the Herd was back in Capitol's recording studios for what would be its last commercial recordings. The standard "Tenderly," in a lovely 3/4 ballad arrangement by Neal Hefti, was recorded with warm solos by Woody on alto, Harris, and Savitt on tenor. Also recorded was the Rogers-Gibbs score of "Lollypop," done as a sequel to "Lemon Drop," complete with a bop vocal line from Rogers, Gibbs, and Woody. Solos are from Gibbs and Chaloff, with

Harris and Swope doing a trombone interchange and some searing brass. It's effective, although it lacks some of the punch of its predecessor.

TERRY GIBBS: Shorty and I wrote a bunch of things on the band. We wrote "Lollypop" together. It's funny, you can get ideas any time—three o'clock in the morning, four o'clock in the morning. You're about ready to go to bed, and your mind is so active. On "Lollypop," I wrote the first sixteen bars, and I couldn't think of a release, I couldn't think of where to go with it. I would call Shorty, wake him up, and Shorty would usually sing a release to me, and so we would have it.

The Rogers score of "I'll Be Glad When You're Dead, You Rascal You" has a vocal by Woody. The outstanding feature is the performance of the five-man trumpet section. The recording also features standout solos by Chaloff and Levy.

On the July 23 "Excursions in Modern Music" broadcast from the Rendezvous, Nat Cole is present and sits in with the Herd on "Yes Sir, That's My Baby," with a vibes solo by Gibbs. Apparently Cole's presence was designed to plug the upcoming concert tour package of the Herd with the Nat Cole Trio.

Bassist Joe Mondragon left the band and was replaced by Washingtonian Mert Oliver. Mert was an underrated bassist who had worked with Don Lamond's small Washington, D.C. group before Don joined the Herman organization in 1945.

On Friday, July 29, the Herd closed at the Rendezvous in Balboa. The band was originally booked through the weekend, but due to an error in booking by the Rendezvous promoters, a historic event took place on Saturday afternoon, July 30. The promoters had mistakenly booked both the Herman Herd and the Charlie Barnet Orchestra on the same night. The 1949 edition of the Barnet band was a potent big-band bop unit, loaded with talent and including two relatively unknown trumpeters, Doc Severinsen and Maynard Ferguson, who had come over from the Jimmy Dorsey Orchestra. Barnet's band was booked for the entire month of August as Woody's had been in July. Woody's booker was able to get the Herd a Saturday night date in Oceanside down the California coast, but meanwhile Bob Murphy, the Rendezvous owner, with some ingenuity advertised the afternoon performance as a Battle of the Bands.

The concert was performed live on the "Excursions in Modern Music" radio broadcast. Stan Kenton was present, as he didn't have a band in 1949. Kenton had "retired" from the business and had announced to the press his intention to study psychiatry. He was persuaded to "referee" the event between the Herman and Barnet bands.

As the broadcast began, strains of Charlie Barnet's theme, "Redskin Rhumba," could be heard in the background. Announcer Tom Reddy, in his opening comments, drew a deft analogy: "Supposing you had Diego Rivera, Pablo Picasso, and Salvador Dali all in the same room, two of them working on canvas and the third member of the trio looking over the shoulders of the other two with a critical eye. It would be quite a sight, wouldn't it? Well, we have a counterpart of that scene this afternoon here at the Rendezvous in Balboa, California. . . ."

The "first round" had Charlie Barnet squaring off with four titles in twenty minutes. After an intermission, the Herd played five tunes. For a wrap-up session, both bands were gathered on the bandstand with Kenton joining the assemblage on piano to perform "How High the Moon." Thirty-eight musicians crowded together and performed Charlie Parker's "Ornithology" (a reworking of "How High") as the introduction. For the out-chorus, the combined ensembles performed Rogers's chart of "More Moon." The radio station did a fade-out before the completion of the performance. Ernie Edwards, the late band discographer, reported that trumpeters Ernie Royal, Maynard Ferguson, and Al Porcino had a free-for-all contest of their own over who would reach higher into the stratosphere on the final blasting chord.

AL PORCINO: There must have been over thirty musicians on the stand because Woody was using nine brass, and I believe Charlie was too. Tiny Kahn, my all-time favorite drummer, was with Charlie's band at the time.

TERRY GIBBS: The consensus was that Woody Herman's band out-swung Charlie Barnet's band, but that Tiny Kahn out-swung everybody!

DICK HAFER: Woody's balance was better than the Barnet band, because we [Barnet] went on first, and they didn't have the balance right yet. Those engineers that did radio shows in those days didn't know what they were doing half the time, and they tuned everything down and the gain was too strong. Those bands were so powerful, I mean big bands today don't sound like that.

On August 2 the Herd kicked off a new concert tour package with Nat Cole in San Diego. In the next few days, Herman and Cole were featured together for a short series of Gene Norman's "Just Jazz" concerts at the Shrine Auditorium in Los Angeles. These radio broadcasts have been preserved and portions made available on various record labels.

The band's performances during the "Just Jazz" concerts were standouts. "Pennies from Heaven" is a ballad feature for Gene Ammons, who interprets "Pennies" with warm improvisations that feature his trademark husky tone, with the restrained ensemble carefully maneuvering through Rogers's score. "Terry and the Pirates" was composed and arranged by Rogers, who must have spent considerable time on the band bus writing. It's a fast-paced feature for Gibbs. The Woodchoppers' small group intro-

The Second Herd at the Shrine Auditorium, Los Angeles, August 1949. Gene Ammons solos. Also in view are Earl Swope, Bill Harris, Ollie Wilson, Bart Varsalona (partially hidden) (trombones); Terry Gibbs (seated in foreground), Buddy Savitt, Sam Marowitz (saxes). (Courtesy Frank Driggs)

duces the line, with Gibbs ripping through the score and rolling punctuations from the brass ensemble.

Apparently, toward the end of the Second Herd period, Abe Turchen, who had been Woody's personal manager, became more aggressive in cutting costs.

JIMMY GIUFFRE: I knew that guy. He used to try to get out of paying us for writing arrangements. He said that arranging money was "found money."

One Second Herd member had some anonymous comments about Abe Turchen: "I could never convince Woody what a rotten man he was. He took our income tax money. He paid us in cash. He had first paid us by check, and then he would take out unemployment money, but it was never turned in. He would get on the bus and his arms were covered with wristwatches. He would sell these watches to the guys in the band. He would go to El Paso, and those places where you could get the foreign jewelry, and he would sell it to the band for thirty dollars to fifty dollars a watch, and he bought them for something like three bucks. And when we went to play a dry town, he would have four or five cases of Dewar's Scotch, Cutty Sark, VO. He used to buy the booze, and then turn around and sell it to us for sixteen dollars a bottle. The IRS and Woody's lawyers told Woody what he was doing . . . that he wasn't reporting the money. For a long time Woody blamed Carlos [Gastel]. But Carlos had so much money, he didn't need any more."

TERRY GIBBS: When Abe Turchen came in, a bunch of us left over wages. He tried to cut me down from $200 to $150 a week. By that time, the band was still good, but it wasn't the original band. Some nights we would start out with just the rhythm section playing, and just a few guys on the stand. Guys would come in little by little. I would wonder how Woody put up with it. Also, how he put up with not doing as many one-nighters as other bands would do. We played a lot of clubs for up to a month. He never could have got as much money as he would have from one-nighters. But Woody wanted to show the band off. He was very proud of that band! Because that First Herd was hard to follow.

In late August the band went through some significant personnel changes. Milt "Bags" Jackson replaced Terry Gibbs on vibes. Buddy Childers, Kenton's former first trumpeter, replaced Ernie Royal. Billy Mitchell replaced tenorist Gene Ammons, and Bart Varsalona, the bass trombonist, left the band. Mitchell would gain considerable recognition in the late fifties with the Dizzy Gillespie big band and later with Count Basie.

AL PORCINO: It was a known fact that Woody had one of the biggest pay-rolls in the business at that time. Everybody was making pretty good money. Abe Turchen, the manager, decided they just couldn't go on meeting this huge payroll, so we were called into the room, one at a time. Each of us got a pay cut. Of course, everybody flipped out. Some people gave their notice immediately: Ernie Royal, Terry Gibbs, and maybe a few other guys.

　　　　Most of us who hadn't quit on the spot were making plans to leave when it was convenient. In my case, I had to wait until we got closer to the East Coast.

According to James Treichel, "In May (1949), Woody commissioned Leonard Bernstein to write a piece which the band would premiere at its next Carnegie Hall concert in November, with the composer conducting."[5]

　　A cover picture in a *Down Beat* magazine of that period showed Woody and Bernstein gazing at a sheet of manuscript paper. It was speculated that Woody's rationale for enlisting Bernstein was a logical extension of his association with Igor Stravinsky—which produced *Ebony Concerto*. (Later the fusion of jazz with classical music became known as "third stream" music.) According to the report, Bernstein completed the work he entitled *Prelude, Fugue and Riffs*, but was unsuccessful in locating Woody, probably due to the Second Herd's stringent itinerary. The work was shelved until it was performed by Benny Goodman on Bernstein's "What is Jazz?" television program in 1955.

WOODY: Leonard Bernstein thought he was interested in writing something that had to do with bebop. So I suggested that he listen to certain players like Charlie Parker and Dizzy, and certain people in New York, in the little clubs. He saw a big sign on Broadway, and it said "Bop City." So he figured, "Well, they must be playing bebop music there." He told me this story. He went into the club, and here was Artie Shaw with quite a large orchestra with strings and the whole thing. He described it as "playing some of the more morbid works of some of our contemporary composers" and that "Artie was trying to be something that he was not." So, unfortunately, I don't think that Leonard ever found out what bebop was about, because you know, you can't explain something like that.

In late October there were two more personnel changes in the final edition of the Second Herd. Trumpeter Ed Badgley replaced Al Porcino; tenor saxophonist Don Lanphere replaced Billy Mitchell. Lanphere had come to New York from Evanston, Illinois, with the Johnny Bothwell Septet. While in New York, Ross Russell of Dial Records invited him to participate in a historic recording session with Fats Navarro and Max Roach, which produced the original jazz classic recording of Denzil Best's "Move."

DON LANPHERE: Abe Turchen called me from Indianapolis and said, "The band is going south, and Ernie Royal, Gene Ammons, and Terry Gibbs are all quitting the band." Gene and Ernie, being black, didn't want to go south. I don't know what Terry's thing was. They called me and they called Milt Jackson to join the band. Ernie Royal and Ammons told Milt, "You don't want to go south," and Milt said, "Oh, it can't be that bad," so he came on the band the same time I did.

In most places we were playing they didn't get to hear a name band that often. When a band would come in, it would be exciting for them. It wasn't always exciting to the guys in the band, but there would be some nights, maybe once a week, when the thing would just catch fire, and everybody in the place would know it, 'cause the band would just be smoking.

In late October the Herd opened at the Paramount Theater in New York for a two-week engagement, and on November 4, the band played a concert at Carnegie Hall with Nat Cole.

In its last weeks, the Second Herd continued on the road in the concert series with Nat Cole. At the end of 1949, Woody decided to call it quits. The band business was at an all-time low. Television was rapidly becoming a dreadnought that would lure away potential patrons of big band entertainment. Into the sixties, television did little to encourage any interest in jazz or big bands, using the music primarily as a background for singers, drama, and other material. Singers were continuing to achieve fame independent of big bands. Many who had previously been band singers carved hugely successful solo careers: Frank Sinatra, Peggy Lee, Jo Stafford, Doris Day, Mel Tormé

The last edition of the Second Herd in concert at Carnegie Hall, New York City, November 4, 1949. Front row: Don Lanphere, Buddy Savitt, Sam Marowitz, Jimmy Giuffre, Serge Chaloff. Second row: Shelly Manne, Earl Swope, Bill Harris, Ollie Wilson. Back row: Buddy Childers, Ed Badgley, Stan Fishelson, Shorty Rogers, Charlie Walp. (Photo by "Popsie" Randolph, courtesy Frank Driggs)

and Perry Como, for instance. These factors, along with the two lengthy AFM-imposed recording bans of the 1940s, meant the end of the big band era as it had been in the 1930s and early 1940s.

WOODY: I think that the taste in American music was particularly good in the late forties and shortly after . . . that was the end of it. I think some of the influences that created all of this havoc were people like Mitch Miller, who took music back maybe forty years. He would do anything to sell records. There are still millions of guys just like him. . . .

There was always a scuffle and a constant battle to make both ends meet. I had two great years in my entire musical career: 1945 and 1946, financially, were fantastic and before that, and ever since, it's been all downhill.

SHORTY ROGERS: I was there at the first rehearsal of the Second Herd and then at Wichita Falls, Texas, the last gig we played. Everyone went home from there and Woody took a small group to Cuba. They were sad, but it wasn't like the NBA when you take a picture of the losing team on the bench, like the world just came to an end, you know. If there was a feeling of being upset, I think it was primarily, like, "Hey, I don't have a job now," that kind of thing, along with some feelings of "this great band, it's a shame to see it break up."

WOODY: Those of us who remained together, about four, I guess, left to form a group to go to Cuba. We left that same night, before the last tune was over. We just split, and I got into some vehicle, and got out of there. It wasn't too warm a feeling.

The author asked Woody in 1986, "Is it true that you lost $180,000 on the Second Herd?" His answer was brief: "At least!"

The end of Woody Herman's Second Herd was bittersweet. In late fall, 1949, *Down Beat*'s readers voted it the nation's number one big band, with 1,042 votes to 301 for Duke Ellington in second place, and 249 for Charlie Barnet in third place. Though it was a financial failure, artistically the Second Herd was nonpareil. It was a remarkable, blowing band that had successfully incorporated the bebop patterns of Charlie Parker and Dizzy Gillespie into big band patois. The Herman Herd had totally cut its ties with the swing era.

The year 1949 concluded with Woody organizing a small, all-star "Wood-choppers" group for the Cuba engagement. Carlos Gastel had booked them into the Tropicana in Havana. The group feverishly rehearsed in Dallas December 6, then flew to Havana for its debut on December 7.

The "Woodchoppers" group consisted of Woody; Conte Candoli, trumpet; Bill Harris, trombone; Ralph Burns, piano; Keith "Red" Mitchell, bass; Shelly Manne, drums; Milt Jackson, vibes; and Dave Barbour, guitar. Dave Barbour was a noted guitarist and husband of singer Peggy Lee. Red Mitchell was a converted pianist who had played bass with Charlie Ventura. In the fifties, he became a major figure in the West Coast jazz movement.

WOODY: We worked there four weeks. It was a show composed of about 175 people, and we were in the midst of them with our little group. All the musicians in Cuba were there every night, but the general audience didn't know what we were into. So I had to delegate poor Bags, the vibraphonist, to do a medley by himself of some old tunes, and boy, he could really dig them up and play them all correctly, with every change. He had a great influence on the tunes he played.

CONTE CANDOLI: It was strange, the first show started about 11:30 [P.M.]. Of course, being in Cuba was great. It was really free at that time. We stayed at the Biltmore Hotel, it was a wide-open city. After Cuba, Woody kept that little band together for a bit.

MILT JACKSON: I had an instrument that had collapsible legs on it. One night, the legs collapsed on it during the performance, and I never quit playing, I just sort of bent over as the legs gradually went down. That was something that Woody talked about for a long time.

RALPH BURNS: I remember it was so great because all we had to do is play one or two sets a night in the middle of a night club show. I've never seen anything like it. All of a sudden they would open up something, and all these white doves would fly up into the air. It was one of those kinds of shows, money unlimited. I think the bandstand would come out, and we would perform some American jazz for them, and play for about a half hour. Then we would go off into the night.

WOODY: In Cuba one morning, Ralph came into this little bar where Charlotte and I were sitting, just hanging around. They had a little ledge, way up near the ceiling, and up there they had an old box piano, and Ralph climbed up there, he shimmied his way up, and was playing cocktail music. Everything was lovely, and in the midst of the whole thing he became unhappy and cried a little bit. So I went out on the street and found the first girl I could find and said, "Look, there's a fella . . ." and I'm talking English which she doesn't understand, but I conned her into coming in and put a couple drinks in front of her, and Ralph climbs down from the balcony and everything's groovy, and Charlotte and I leave, because Ralph's straight, and everything's gonna be nice. Next thing I know we get a call from the police station at nine o'clock in the morning, and Ralph's in the can again, and this dame had gone down and accused him of stealing her fur wrap, which was like an old tire inner tube. He was apparently trying to hold it for her, and she didn't know what it meant. Oh, was he in for a bum rap that time! I thought they weren't gonna let him out.

It was a terribly depressing thing. They didn't understand our music. We received a whole lot of money, and it was embarrassing to take it. It got so bad by the end of the engagement, I was singing pieces like "White Christmas," anything that they might know. There is a bigger language barrier in Cuba than there is in Europe. We were playing an open-air club, and one of the amusing things about it was the fact that Dave Barbour joined us just to go down there. He was a great artist. We already had seven great artists, and Dave went down for the kicks of the whole thing. We had bad weather the month we were there and when it would rain, if there was any water on the cement or rock floor, Dave would cop a plea and say, "You better excuse me for this show because I don't want to get electrocuted." He would be at the bar, feeling no pain and throwing us little waves of encouragement, while we are proceeding to fight this rain storm. That was most amusing, but kind of sad, too. Their two big holiday nights are the big thing there, Christmas and New Year's. Both those nights it just poured forever, and people were dancing in mud up to their knees, in lovely gowns, and guys dressed to the teeth, real Spanish-nobility types.

Not knowing about the language barrier, we were pretty shaken up. We weren't too prepared for the whole situation. The guy that got us off the hook more than anyone was Milt Jackson. Milt knows more songs than anybody in captivity, and they date back to his grandparents' years.

NEAL HEFTI: Woody had me do a few things for a small group. I think that's the small group he took to Cuba. I always thought he would be dynamite with a small band in places like Vegas. I was surprised when he returned to the big band. I thought he could do like Louis Armstrong, Louis Jordan, and Louis Prima; they all went to small groups from big bands.

Woody did return with another big band, one that would be tagged "The Third Herd." About that exquisite, swinging band, Woody would later comment, "It took me about 200 musicians to find the band I was looking for, but now I'm happy at last. . . . The days of closed musical minds are over. This is a brand new era, and I'm thrilled to be part of it."[5]

5.

The Third Herd
1950-1955

The Woodchoppers small group completed the engagement at the Tropicana in Havana, Cuba, on January 3, 1950.

CONTE CANDOLI: From Cuba, we went to Philadelphia and worked the Click Club for a week. It was about ten to eighteen degrees. From there, we went to Saskatchewan. It was about twenty or thirty below zero. Sonny Igoe joined us on that tour. Shelly left after Cuba.

Owen Joseph (Sonny) Igoe had done stints with the big bands of Les Elgart and Ina Ray Hutton. In 1949 he was with the Benny Goodman "Bop" band that recorded for Capitol. Benny's record of "Undercurrent Blues" captured Sonny's stirring and spontaneous technique.

SONNY IGOE: I actually took Charlie Perry's place. Woody hired me without an audition on Red Mitchell's say-so. The night they closed at the Click, I met them there to go to Duluth, Minnesota. We spent three days on a train from Philadelphia to Duluth before I even played a set with him. I was dying to find out if he was going to like me or not.

    It was a great group with Bill Harris, Conte Candoli, Milt Jackson, Woody up front, Red Mitchell, Ralph Burns, and myself. The group never recorded, so nobody really got to hear how good it was.

WOODY: We had to play saloons, and I don't mind playing saloons, except that we played some pretty bad ones. Places like the Silhouette, on the north side of Chicago. We hurried into the little band thing and hurried out of it pretty much the same way. We had very good musicians, but we never got organized.

After Chicago, the Woodchoppers group continued on the road, touring through the Midwest, Arkansas, Texas, and finally playing at Ciro's in San Francisco. While in San Francisco, Woody broke the news to *Down Beat*'s Ralph J. Gleason that he would be re-forming a big band. The story appeared in the May 5 issue: "Woody Reorganizes: To Go After Dance Crowd."

"Woody Herman is out to capture the college kid dance crowd. . . . Woody's dance book will look toward the sound of his disc of 'Early Autumn,' and will make a strong effort not to confuse the youngsters who Woody thinks are confused enough as it is by the world in general. . . . This is the most sensible bid for broad popularity Woody has made in recent years, the value of his last two bands notwithstanding."

Woody did want to please the dancers, but he also had a commitment he couldn't be extricated from.

WOODY: I had to go back to the big band because I owed a date to Bop City in New York, and the union upheld the commitment and wouldn't give me an out. I went to New York to try to get out of it because I didn't feel I could, in a quick, hurried sort of way, organize a band good enough to take into a spot which was a big jazz room, fairly new, and we might harm ourselves. However, it was a question of doing it or else. So I went back and I was able to capture a few guys who had worked for me at one time or another, along with three or four out of the small group. As long as we were around the New York area, it wasn't so bad as far as men were concerned, but when we had to go on further, then we started a real shuffle routine.

The following is the line-up of personnel for the Herd's April 1950 performance at Bop City in New York: Bernie Glow, Paul Cohen, Conte Candoli, Don Ferrara, Neal Hefti (trumpets); Bill Harris, Eddie Bert, Jerry Dorn (trombones); Sam Marowitz (alto sax); Bob Graf, Al Cohn, Buddy Wise (tenor saxes); Marty Flax (baritone sax); Dave McKenna (piano); Sonny Igoe (drums); Red Mitchell (bass); Milt Jackson (vibes); and Woody Herman (leader, clarinet, alto sax, and vocals).

Candoli, Glow, Hefti, Bert, Harris, Marowitz, Cohn, and Jackson were veterans of earlier Herman bands. New at the piano bench was Dave McKenna. Ralph Burns was writing and appeared with the orchestra at Bop City playing selected compositions of his own. Tenorist Buddy Wise was an excellent addition from Gene Krupa's bop band of that period. A new face in the trombone section was Israel (Jerry) Dorn, who had worked in the bands of Bobby Byrne, Georgie Auld, Johnny Long, Henry Jerome, Jean Goldkette, Les Elgart, and Randy Brooks.

NEAL HEFTI: We left Los Angeles, went back to New York, and then I started working at CBS, so I played just that one [Bop City] engagement. The only thing I can recall about that engagement is that it was the first time I ever conducted for somebody else, outside of Frances. Sarah Vaughn was sharing the bill. About the second night Woody asked me if I would conduct for Sarah, because he had been doing it, and he wanted to take some time offstage. A lot of leaders did not want to stay on the stage during the other acts' performance.

SONNY IGOE: I was thrilled, because I got to play with a bunch of guys who had played with him before: Bill Harris, Sam Marowitz, Bernie Glow. Bill Harris and I became close friends. We were roommates on the road. And in spite of his sometimes dour or studious appearance on the stand, he also had a wild sense of humor . . . I was a perfect foil for him. I would double over laughing.

    Woody was such a nice man. He made feel completely at ease. No tension whatsoever, on or off the stand. He also had a marvelous sense of humor, and loved a good laugh.

After the Bop City engagement, the new Herd made its first recordings at Capitol studios in New York on May 5. Notable was the Ralph Burns score of "Spain," with rich, thick voicings in the orchestration of the saxes and trombones, and nice solid work from Jackson's pungent vibes, Harris, and Woody's alto.

The commercial, but tasty, Neal Hefti score of "Pennies from Heaven" features Woody's lead vocal with background vocalizing from the Alyce King Vokettes and a brief statement from Harris.

"I Want a Little Girl" features another Herman vocal with the Vokettes group again. This was a blues that originated with the old McKinney's Cotton Pickers, a favorite early band of Woody's. It was recorded again in 1956 in a more bluesy mood and arrangement. This one features a nice sax chorus. These first recordings by the new band feature the "altoless" blend of the three-tenor, one-baritone sax voicing.

On June 2 *Down Beat*'s Mike Levin gave an excellent description of the new band, reviewed presumably at Bop City in April or early May:

The new and revamped Herd put on quite an astonishing opening here. Having rehearsed for only five days, considerable raggedness was expected. It did show up occasionally in the trumpets, but all in all, the band showed a great deal of power, zest, and good jazz feeling. . . . Harris, by the way, is playing with some bop inflections these days. Every so often a burst of notes will come out of his horn at distinct variance to his usual "preaching" feeling.

    Standout solo of the evening was played by tenor man Bob Graf on five choruses of "Apple Honey." A young reed man in from St. Louis, previously best known for his jobbing with Basie, this taffy-haired kid put on an astonishing demonstration of truly fluent Lester Young-styled horn. . . . Woody's handlers told the beat that the new dance book, in addition to the Herd jazz, was in preparation, with Neal Hefti and Ralph Burns doing a great deal of the writing.[1]

After the Bop City date, the Herd went on a road tour of theaters, returning to New York City for a May 25 opening at the Capitol Theater. Sam Marowitz left the band and returned only briefly for the Capitol Theater engagement. From this period on, the sax section utilized the lead tenor sound. On occasion, the arrangers would write in a part for Woody's alto on top of the section.

The June 16 edition of *Down Beat* reported: "Woody Herman and his personal manager, Carlos Gastel, parted company early in May by mutual consent. . . . 'I have personal obligations that prevent me from spending anything except for my payroll, current expenses of the band, and my own living costs,' explained Woody on the phone from Washington, D.C. 'Carlos is a charming gent, I am very fond of him personally, but I'm going to try to get along without a personal manager. GAC will continue to book the band.'

"Woody was referring, in part, to the terms of his release from his previous managers, Mike Vallon and Chubby Goldfarb, by which they collect a commission on the band's income for at least another year. . . ."[2]

WOODY: We were trying desperately to get an audience, and that was also probably the lowest time as far as big bands were concerned. Most of them had disappeared, as early as 1949, and it was just a slow trek . . . as a matter of fact, the only survivors were all involved in jazz, one kind or another . . . people like Ellington and Basie and our band.

CONTE CANDOLI: I remember the Capitol Theater gig. I remember all theaters because it's really tough on your lip! One time in 1950, Bill Harris was with the band. And we had just hired a new singer, Pat Easton. She didn't last very long. During one of her numbers, there were about ten feet behind us between the back curtain and the bandstand. Bill Harris had a break in a tune and, unbeknownst to us, went backstage and put on some painter's overalls, and with a stepladder and paint brush proceeded to walk across the stage while the chick was singing right there. It was unreal.

WOODY: We were having a farewell party and a few drinks and Sam Marowitz and I were in Bill's room. It was getting late, and we were just about winding up, but we ran out of something to drink, so we decided to go down to my room. There was more there. So Bill was in his shorts, and people were getting up, and it was in the morning, and he walked right through the hallway and into the elevator, and he was waiting for the

The band at the Capitol theater, New York City, June 1950. L to R: Al Porcino, Conte Candoli, Don Ferrara, Eddie Bert, Rolf Ericson, Bill Harris, Jerry Dorn. (Courtesy Jerry Dorn)

grandioso "take" by the elevator operator, and the guy just looked at him and said, "What floor, sir?" Bill was very brought down by this.

On June 25 the band recorded three titles in Nashville, Tennessee. "Music to Dance To," an Al Cohn score, was probably the 1950 Herd's best contribution to jazz. Newcomer Bob Graf offers a buoyant tenor solo and Woody's ebullient clarinet and Harris's trombone round out the solos. It's an effective performance with good section and anchor work from baritonist Marty Flax. The brass section also manifests nice figures with effective drumming from Igoe.

"The Nearness of You," a Ralph Burns ballad scoring, is tasty and typical of this period. It showcases Woody's creamy alto and Bill Harris in a sensitive mood.

"Sonny Speaks" revives Sonny Berman's First Herd score of "They Went That-a-Way." There's a catchy riff and solo contributions from Harris, Graf, and Woody on clarinet. The tune closes with the old forties Super Suds radio commercial, an obvious throwback to the First Herd.

In July, Harris left the band, replaced by Vern Friley. Friley was a very capable trombonist with a big sound. His appearance with the Herd was all too brief. Harris would return again during the middle to late fifties to bolster both big and small Herman bands of that period.

Also joining the Herd, replacing Bernie Glow, was a superb and under-rated trumpeter, Doug Mettome. Doug had worked in Billy Eckstine's 1944 big band, with Herbie Fields, and in Benny Goodman's 1949 bop band.

On August 9 the Herd went into Capitol's Chicago sound studios to record four titles. The Ralph Burns score of "Starlight Souvenirs" is a lovely ballad, in the "Early Autumn" mode, featuring Woody's alto in the Hodges tradition and Vern Friley's only recorded solo with the Herd. The performance closes with Candoli's muted trumpet out front.

"When It Rains It Pours" is another one of those Herman tongue-in-cheek vocals: "When your baby's bad it rains . . . but when she goes out the door, it pours. . . ." Woody hams it up on alto, Earl Bostic-style. Red Mitchell's walking bass is effective, as is plunger trumpet from Mettome, and "dirty" tenor probably from Phil Urso. McKenna contributes, then the score ends with everyone getting into the act, Woody's treble clarinet on top, à la Barney Bigard. These recordings hold up forty years later.

On "Johannesburg," the band stoops to commercialism with a novelty/pop tune of the day, complete with a banal echo effect. The recording is worthy of mention only because of Woody's vocal versatility.

On September 7 the Herd went into the dance-oriented Meadowbrook in New Jersey for two weeks and was heard live on a series of radio remotes. Singer Pat Easton's only known recordings with the band were captured live during this period.

CONTE CANDOLI: Doug Mettome was on the band. He was great. As a mat-
    ter of fact, Doug and I split the lead book. For a while, J.J. Johnson was in
    the band. Vern Friley, who had replaced Bill Harris on lead, got sick. J.J.
    was real good on the lead book.

Replacing Buddy Wise on lead tenor saxophone during this period was Jack E. DuLong. After graduation from high school in 1939, Jack worked in terri-tory bands throughout the south. Before going into the service in 1942, he was with Muggsy Spanier. Later, Jack played with the bands of Claude Thornhill and Skitch Henderson before joining the Herman Herd.

JACK DULONG: I joined the band in Allentown, Pennsylvania, a one-nighter.
    It was very early in the fall of 1950. Conte was on the band and Normie
    Faye. Urbie [Green] had joined the band, and he played a little bit, and
    then he had to finish out with Krupa or somebody.
        From there, we jumped to that infamous job that all bands hated, that
    all-day thing at the Holyoke Arena in Holyoke, Massachusetts. It was
    Sunday, and you'd get in early in the morning, and rehearse perhaps a dozen
    acts and play three shows; one in the afternoon and two in the evening. You

would start rehearsing in the morning without even an hour's sleep. It was a theater-in-the-round type thing, an "institution" for big bands. After there, we went into Brooklyn, New York, for a theater engagement.

When the band left the New York area in the late fall, it experienced numerous personnel changes. Some of the men Woody had been using had secure and comfortable opportunities in the New York area and balked at the unrelenting grind of the road.

CONTE CANDOLI: I left the band during the winter of 1950. I remember Nick Travis took my place. I went back to Indiana and stayed around South Bend for a few months, and then I went with the Kenton band.

Filling the lead trombone chair at this time was Urban Clifford (Urbie) Green. Before Woody, Urbie had worked in the bands of Jan Savitt, Frankie Carle, and Gene Krupa. Urbie's strong point was his versatility. He could play Dixieland or modern, and effectively emulated Bill Harris's solo on "Bijou." After his tenure with the Herd, Urbie was a favorite choice of Benny Goodman and toured with the B.G. band.

URBIE GREEN: Being offered the job was kind of my ambition at that point in my life, playing that particular trombone chair with Woody's band. On "Bijou," well, I guess I had such respect for Bill, and that particular solo, that at that point in time I didn't want to do it differently. He created that. Woody never said anything to me about doing it that way, it was my own love for Bill on that particular piece.

Replacing Pat Easton as the band's singer in the fall of 1950 was Dolly Houston. Prior to Woody, she sang with the bands of Larry Clinton and Benny Goodman, both in 1949.

Dolly was not a jazz singer. But then again, during this period Woody was majoring in versatility and pleasing the dancers. Dolly's voice was more in the Doris Day–Margaret Whiting category, and in looks she faintly resembled actress Laraine Day. She made a comely impression on the bandstand.

DOLLY HOUSTON: I was singing with Benny Goodman at the time, which is, I believe, how Woody heard about me. When he contacted me, I think it was when we came back to New York, and Benny broke up the band. Anyway, I ended up singing with Woody for about three and a half years.

Woody was a very colorful, down-to-earth guy. We had a lot of laughs together. Woody was a taskmaster, much like Benny and Tommy and Jimmy Dorsey, but he also had a heart.

JACK DULONG: Woody was a very patient and forgiving man, and it is a good thing, or he would have had a heart attack years ago. With his ever-changing personnel, particularly in later years, he had new young men who weren't particularly disciplined coming on the band, but no matter how wild they were, it didn't faze Woody. He'd seen it all years ago. Once, after an argument between Woody and Bob Graf that started on the stand and continued into the locker room where we were changing after a college concert, Bob threw a bottle of beer at Woody from across the room. Fortunately, it missed and Woody didn't fire Bob. I think that Woody had stood in front of a band for so many evenings that one night was pretty much the same as any other, and he welcomed any little diversion, even if it was a bit violent.

SONNY IGOE: We worked in some "toilets" with that band, trying to pay back thousands of back commissions to GAC. It really didn't make any difference how it sounded. We actually worked in a barn where there were live cattle. It was some place down South. The people were trying to dance on this barn floor and underneath us was the livestock.

The following is the December 1950 band as it appeared in New York just prior to Christmas vacation: Doug Mettome, Normie Faye, Don Ferrara, Nick Travis (trumpets); Urbie Green, Jerry Dorn, Herb Randel (trombones); Jack DuLong, Bob Graf, Phil Urso (tenor saxes); Sam Staff (bass); Dave McKenna (piano); Red Mitchell (bass); Sonny Igoe (drums); and Dolly Houston (vocalist).

In December, Woody's two-year contract with Capitol Records expired. Apparently dissatisfied with Capitol's marketing of the Herd's recordings, Woody signed with the MGM label. Woody's first MGM record date was on January 4, 1951, with a pickup band and Billy Eckstine.

WOODY: We did a date and Billy did three or four tunes. We organized a band of guys who had worked for me at one time or another. Shorty did one of the arrangements and Pete [Rugolo] did a couple of them, and it was "B" and our band supposedly, but we couldn't get together in the same town and that's the reason I flew to the Coast and hustled the band together in a hurry.

In January 1951 Woody was back with his regular band recording at MGM Studios in New York. Dolly Houston recorded for the first time with the Herd.

"Lonesome Gal" was recorded on January 9. It was the theme song of the "Lonesome Gal" radio program of that period, featuring a female dee jay with a sexy voice aimed at a male audience. The tune demonstrated what Dolly could do with a lovely Burns score.

DOLLY HOUSTON: Actually, there weren't too many things I recorded that I really enjoyed doing. The band singers in those days were not pushed ahead. They were more or less in the background. If they needed a side on a record, they used the girl singer. That kind of thing. But anyway, "Lonesome Gal" was pretty good and "I Can See You" was okay.

Recorded also on January 9 was "Ninety-Nine Guys," another tune by the "Softwinds" (Carter, Ellis, and Frigo). It featured one of those frivolous Herman vocals and the band ensemble: "Ninety-nine guys have eyes for Liza but Liza has eyes for me." The recording featured tenor solos from Phil Urso and Bob Graf, Woody's clarinet, an interesting unison trumpet section chorus, a muted trumpet solo, and Mettome breaking out with a brief high note solo to round out the score.

In January Sonny Igoe left the band to get married.

SONNY IGOE: It was funny. Woody didn't want to let me go for two weeks to get married, but he would let the guys who were having problems with drugs, or something like that, have time off for rehabilitation. I'll never forget I came back and rejoined the band in Falls City, Nebraska. We're walking across the stage and Woody's there, and he sees me and my wife Clair, and looks at me and said, "You're back, welcome to the Sucker Club!" Oh, my wife didn't like that at all!

In February three replacements occurred. Trumpeter Roy Caton replaced Nick Travis. Tenor saxist Kenny Pinson, another import from Gene Krupa's band, replaced Bob Graf, and bassist Red Wootten replaced Red Mitchell.

Lawrence B. (Red) Wootten went with the Gene Austin "Whippoorwills" in 1940, the Dean Hudson Orchestra in 1945, and the Tony Pastor, Jan Savitt, and Tommy Dorsey Orchestras in 1946, rejoining Dorsey in 1949. Red used a Kay, five-string model "Chubby Jackson" bass, and at times sounded like Jackson, whom he admired.

RED WOOTTEN: I joined the Woody Herman band in Cincinnati, Ohio, in February 1951. Red Mitchell had become ill with tuberculosis. A few days before, I had jammed with some of the players in a session. Had a ball! Abe Turchen met me at the train station. We fast-cabbed it to the job. I was an hour late and walked on the stage with my bass. The band was just beginning "Four Brothers," and luckily I remembered the whole chart from the recording. It was the last tune of that set. Woody waved hello to me with a big smile. Later we chatted. The band had a few other new recruits, but it was still pretty damn good. A loose feeling, and soulful.

What I was going to do was just stay a week or two with the band until they could get somebody else. Woody came to me one night in my hotel room not too long after I came with the band. We had a taste of Scotch and he told me, "If you leave this band I will kick your ass!" I took it he liked me and my playing. So I called my boss where I had been work-ing in Atlanta and it was okay with him.

Some nights the band would just be worn out. We played in jam ses-sions after the gig and we did this no matter what time the bus left the next day. I rode with Abe, Woody and Dolly Houston on some overnight jobs. But when the band was rested and ready, it was a chill a minute on that stage.

Early in March [March 14 and 15] we recorded. The band was roar-ing pretty good. Chubby Jackson came by the studios and cheered us on.

"I Can See You" was a simple but engaging Burns arrangement of a Sammy Cahn tune from the MGM film *Rich, Young and Pretty*. It featured a vocal by Dolly Houston. Woody's warm alto was heard effectively on top of the section.

Woody changed the title of George Shearing's "By George" to "Bop, Look and Listen." It featured a line played by muted trumpets, followed by a figure from the Four-Brothers-voiced saxes, a tenor solo (probably Urso), and Woody's clarinet. After the excitement generated by the First and Second Herds, most of these MGM recordings were lusterless by comparison.

At the March 15 recording session, the band recorded perhaps its most moving offering from the MGM period. Nat Pierce related to the author later, "The original title of 'Leo the Lion' was 'Chicken Fat, Moonbeams and You'!" Obviously renamed as a dedication to Woody's new record label, "Leo" was a fast-moving blues with a piano intro from McKenna, tenor solos from Urso and Graf, Igoe accenting the performance with some effective fills to bolster punctuations from the brass ensemble, and brief offerings from Urbie Green, Woody's clarinet, and Nick Travis.

In April the Herd played a month at the Edgewater Beach Hotel in Chicago. There were several new faces in the band. Ex-Krupa and Artie Shaw trumpeter Don Fagerquist, Roy Caton, and Charles Caudle were Doug Mettome's new mates in the trumpet section. While it was billed as "Woody Herman's Greatest Band Ever," the slogan and many of the reviews were deceiving, as this was Woody's least-inspired period in years.

There were moments of excitement as when the band blew "Leo the Lion" and "Sonny Speaks" or performed a pretty ballad using Burns's modern voic-ings. Mettome and Igoe were also effective sparkplugs. But it was a Herd that remained too unadventurous. And the drug problems of band members that confronted Woody during the Second Herd era did not disappear with the demise of that group.

JACK DULONG: The guys were kind of despondent, in spite of the fact that they were good players. Doug Mettome really went through the motions,

I felt. But he could go through the motions and play better than anybody else. Of course, Dave McKenna was so marvelous, too. . . .

In early May the band worked its way to the Coast for a month-long engagement at the Hollywood Palladium. During the engagement, numerous live broadcasts of the band were aired nationally via the CBS radio network with local Los Angeles KNX announcer Bill Baldwin doing the emcee duties, often trading quips with Woody on the air. The better part of the Palladium broadcasts were preserved by collectors. Few, however, have been made available commercially.

On the trip to the Coast, trumpeter Charles Caudle left the band. Shorty Rogers subbed during most of the Palladium engagement until a replacement was found.

WOODY (in 1956): Shorty wrote for all three Herds one way or another. He subbed with the Third Herd at the Palladium, in the trumpet section. Between sets, he would whip out a little sixteen-bar thing that would help a head we were putting together ["Businessman's Bounce"]. Then he wrote a couple of things we did over at MGM . . . To this day, when I am hung for a trumpet player or whatever it might be, I tell them, "Pick up the phone and get hold of Shorty. See who's available." I don't think Shorty ever sent me a guy that didn't have something on the ball.

SHORTY ROGERS: It was a real good band, I remember Doug Mettome. That was the thing that made it really memorable to me. It was the only time I worked with Doug Mettome. He was just an unbelievably great player.

The other thing I remember about it is during the gig, one of the tenor players [Phil Urso] left the band. Woody kind of happily surprised me and asked me to recommend someone to fill the tenor chair, and I recommended Bill Perkins, and that was the beginning of Bill Perkins' association with Woody.

WOODY (in 1956): The only time I remember doing anything on a bandstand, as far as straightening out a guy, was in the Palladium in Hollywood. I had a saxophone player in the band at the time who was pretty far out. I think we were playing "Early Autumn," or something like that, some pretty tune, and he had the solo on it, and he didn't dig the tempo, so he made his own, did some grimaces, and beat a little time with his foot. We were on the air at the time. I got the next tune started, and I walked over to him very casually and quietly and said, "You know that softie-type bag that you carry, that you put your saxophone in?" I said, "Take this axe and go to the dressing room and put this axe in the soft bag, the one you carry on the bus." And I said, "Then get the *hell* out of here!" And we wound up the broadcast with three saxophones. And you know, this guy still asks me for a gig every time we see him, and he can't understand yet why he left.

JACK DULONG: I was the lead tenor, but on "Early Autumn," the soloist was Phil Urso who played the lead part. Phil almost invariably objected to the tempo Woody would kick off, and he would often say, "No, Woody, no," as he was beating off the tune. On this particular night on the broadcast, he again objected to the tempo and he didn't play the first two or three notes of the tune even though he had the lead. A casual listener probably wouldn't detect the lack of the lead on the broadcast, since it is only two beats, but it seemed much longer when it happened. Phil had actually started to play when Woody leaned in close to his ear and said, "Play, you little son of a bitch, or I'll kill you." The broadcast bears it out that Woody didn't actually fire him on the spot. You hear Phil Urso and Kenny Pinson both solo on "Leo the Lion" after "Early Autumn," so he wasn't fired until after the broadcast. Woody was furious, and as soon as the broadcast was over, he told Phil he was through, and Phil packed up and left.

SONNY IGOE: Phil got belligerent in the dressing room, Abe Turchen backed him up against the wall and was about to take his head off. So Shorty Rogers gave Abe Bill Perkins' number, and Bill Perkins came in and finished the night. That's how Bill Perkins joined the band. . . .

It was on May 21, 1951, that Woody fired Phil Urso. But Woody manifested a forgiving spirit. He rehired Urso in 1958.

William Reese (Bill) Perkins had worked with the bands of Jerry Wald, Desi Arnaz, "and many local Los Angeles gigs." After Herman, Bill went with Stan Kenton. Later he became a central figure in the West Coast jazz movement, working with such small groups as Shorty Rogers and His Giants.

BILL PERKINS: Woody launched my career as a musician. I believe both Shorty Rogers and Jerry Wald had a part in recommending me. Our relationship was always the best. He gave me countless opportunities to solo, yet he never told me *how* to play a solo.

Woody and Stan [Kenton] were very different personalities, but they had one thing in common: Stan and Woody were always looking forward. They just went about it in different ways.

When I was with Woody, he was still one of the best lyrical alto sax soloists around, and he might well have been a clarinet player in a class with Shaw and Goodman. Yes! I have heard early records that prove it. Instead, he chose mostly to make *the band* his instrument, and nobody could have done it any better.

"Woody Herman's Greatest Band Ever" at the Casino Ballroom, Catalina Island, California, July 1951. Don Fagerquist, Doug Mettome, Roy Caton, John McComb (trumpets), Fred Lewis, Urbie Green, Jerry Dorn (trombones), Bill Perkins, Jack DuLong, Kenny Pinson (tenor saxes), Sam Staff (baritone sax), Dave McKenna (piano), Red Wootten (b), Sonny Igoe (d), Dolly Houston (vo), Woody. (Courtesy Frank Driggs)

SONNY IGOE: When we were out on the Coast at the Palladium, my wife was with me. Woody invited us up to his house one night after the gig. We were sitting in his den, and he had all these records and air checks. I said, "What is all this stuff?" and he said, "I don't know, there's a couple of concerts in there." I said, "Do you mind if I listen to it?" He said, "No, you can take them and see what's in there." So I took them and I found that Carnegie Hall concert [March 1946] that they later released on a record.

　　I told him, "Hey, Benny Goodman put out his 1938 concert, and this is better than that! Why the hell don't you release it?" He didn't even know he had it! So that's when they put it out.

The Palladium date closed on Sunday, June 10. From June 29 to July 1, the Herd played at the Casino Ballroom on the California resort island of Catalina. This band did shine on occasion. On the closing night, the Herd's final number aired on the CBS radio network was a rousing performance of Shorty Rogers's "More Moon." The performance included stunning solos from Bill Perkins, Kenny Pinson, Urbie Green, Doug Mettome, Dave McKenna, and Woody on clarinet, all backed by the rhythm section, and

Igoe's exciting snare accents with rim and bass drum bombs. The announcer interrupted: "CBS, with the greatest of pleasure, has presented Woody Herman and His Greatest Band Ever, from the romantic setting of the Catalina Island Casino Ballroom, overlooking beautiful Avalon Bay, just twenty-two miles off the coast of Southern California. . . . Tomorrow night it's Stan Kenton and his fine band, beginning a full week's engagement, followed in turn by Jimmy Dorsey . . . " The big band era was far from over in July 1951.

JACK DULONG: We left Catalina the last night after the gig and went by chartered speedboat to Wilmington and drove to Las Vegas for a gig that night. We were in Vegas for two days, then we went on to Salt Lake City.

In July the Herd worked its way through the Midwest on a typical grueling schedule of one-nighters, climaxing in Kansas City on July 22 for a memorable concert with Charlie Parker.

JACK DULONG: I left Woody in Kansas City. It coincided with the night they played a concert with Charlie Parker. It was one of Bird's first public appearances after he got out of Camarillo [Hospital].

Replacing Jack DuLong on lead tenor was John Richard (Dick) Hafer. Prior to Herman, he was with Charlie Barnet (1949), Claude Thornhill (1949–50), and Charlie Barnet again (1950–51).

DICK HAFER: I remember checking into the hotel, and I didn't know anybody in that band, they were just names to me. I had never worked with anybody that was in the band prior to that night. So I called Woody's room, around 11 A.M. He said, "Oh yeah, you're going to join the band today. Bird is playing with us tonight." I couldn't believe it!
  Jack DuLong was leaving the band. He was going to stay that night, play the gig, and I was going to sit alongside as he showed me the book. So I went down to the lobby about one o'clock to go to the rehearsal, and I saw Jack in the lobby. I had seen him on the Thornhill band one time. So I went up and introduced myself as he was checking out. I said, "Aren't you coming to the rehearsal?" He said, "No, I've got a plane out, something came up and I gotta leave. Woody doesn't know this, but I'm not going to stay. But you'll be okay." And he left.
  I went to the rehearsal. I was sightreading the book and playing with Bird standing right next to me. I'm not really boasting, but I can read pretty well, and I was sort of familiar with a lot of their music, because I had heard the band on some of their recordings.
  Urbie Green had a tape machine, one of the earliest portable, reel-to-reel recorders ever made. He recorded the concert. I have a copy of it.

I had loaned it to a guy and someone got ahold of it and made a bootleg record out of it. I'm quite put out about it because I told the guy when I loaned it to him that he had no right to ever put that out.

Later, I was with Woody one night, and I told him that I had the tape. This is after I had left the band. I told him, "You ought to put it out yourself." But at that time, there was a legal battle going on with two women who were both claiming to be Bird's wife. They were fighting over his estate. Woody said he didn't want to get in the middle of that. And then these bootleggers got ahold of it.

Bird was in great shape that night. He was visiting his mother. He always stayed sober when he was around her because she wouldn't allow it.

We played in a huge auditorium. I think it was a convention center. It's funny, Bird knew what he wanted to play. He was so amazing, it seemed like he knew Woody's whole book. He'd call tunes that he wanted to play.

We played "Four Brothers." The changes on "Four Brothers" are not the kind of changes you can hear right off, you know, especially the bridge. So Bird got to the bridge the first time, and he sort of stopped, if you listen to the tape closely. Then he growled a little the second time around, and then he started to get it. I think one more time around he would have tore it apart! He was so amazing. In fact, on one of the ensembles, he weaves lines in and out that arrangers would have to spend months to figure out, and he was playing off the top of his head!

He wasn't that familiar with the arrangements, so he kept blowing through some of the ensembles. We played "Leo the Lion" twice. But the second time around, he even played it greater. When he really heard what was going on, he was just unbelievable! We took a break and he came back and played it again. We were short of what to do, and he wanted to do it again, anyway.

I was walking down Broadway months later and I had only met Bird that one night, and only casually. My wife and I were walking, and Bird's coming toward us, and he walked up to me and said, "Hey, Dick, how you doin'?" He had total recall about everybody he had ever met. I was flabbergasted, I couldn't believe that he could remember me, just from that one experience.

The event in Kansas City came together at the last minute. Bird wasn't advertised. I think the promoters found out that he was there and somebody asked him to play. They must have paid him, but it wasn't advertised out front.

Later in that evening, when the concert was over, we went to a club in Kansas City someplace, and Mettome and Fagerquist played with him. Mettome, particularly, was very friendly with Bird. Bird knew Doug when he played on the Billy Eckstine band. There was a session there that night. I wish I had a tape of that!

After Kansas City, the Herd continued on the road to Illinois, Kentucky, and Ohio. On August 17 they opened at the Marine Ballroom on the Steel Pier, Atlantic City, New Jersey. During its week-long stay at the Steel Pier, the band was aired on live AFRS broadcasts. On August 20 the band was heard playing Al Cohn's lovely arrangement of "Stardust," which featured a spirited bass solo from Wootten.

DICK HAFER: Actually, the band wasn't that good. Woody was revamping it; he was trying to get some stronger trumpet players, 'cause Doug, as great as he was, was juicing so hard that he couldn't play. After two hours, he'd start to give out.

About two weeks after I joined the band, Woody made a deal with Doug, 'cause he loved him. He said, "If you stay sober for me, Doug, I'll give you a $200-a-week raise!" That would have put him in the $400-a-week bracket, which in 1951 was very good money. Doug stayed sober, he didn't touch a thing. I'll never forget, he started playing so great that it was unbelievable. He had so many good things going that when he stayed sober, it was just scary. He played all of the high-note parts that Ernie Royal had played in the other band, and played all of the lead, and most of the jazz solos.

Fagerquist was playing, too. Fagerquist was really a great player, but there were times when he just couldn't contend with Doug. Woody would turn them loose and they would play like eights and fours. It was frightening. They called Doug "the white Dizzy" for a while. He was so great. He wasn't a pure bebop player. He had a knack of playing almost like a bebop version of Dixieland. He played some little phrases that weren't just bop.

We played Atlantic City, and Doug's downfall was when we came off the pier. It was sort of raining that night, and Bird was there. He was working in Atlantic City, and he called Doug over and I saw them walk off together, and we were concerned about him hanging out with Bird. They had a habit, you know. The next night we got on the bandstand at the Steel Pier, and we played the first set and Woody looked back at Doug and said, "You just blew the raise, Mettome!"

So even though Doug hadn't played any mistakes, Woody knew. Woody was phenomenal, he could hear something. Doug had gone out and gotten stoned, and from then on it was downhill for Doug, he kept gettin' worse and worse, and finally Woody had to let him go. That's when I got John Howell on the band. The Third Herd started a little bit later, when Carl Fontana joined the band.

In 1951 the United States was at war in Korea. As in World War II, the draft began to affect the personnel of the big bands. Pianist Dave McKenna was sent to Korea as a cook. Nat Pierce took over the piano chair, forming a long and durable association with Woody. Before Herman, he worked with Herb Pomeroy and had his own reputable big band in the Boston and New York areas. Pierce was an arranger and composer of exceptional talent and also an ardent admirer of Count Basie. His charts for the Herman band injected a Basie flavor without taking away from the distinctive Herman sound.

Nat stayed with the Third Herd until 1955, rejoining in June 1961 and remaining until mid-1966. In the sixties, he became chief arranger, road manager, and the Herd's straw boss. He was a confidante of Woody's and was instrumental in organizing countless reunion bands comprised of Herman alumni and pick-up units for recording sessions. During his tenure with the orchestra, he brought many new soloists into the band.

NAT PIERCE: I replaced Dave McKenna in September 1951. I had my own band previously in the Boston area and some of the people had gone with Woody so they recommended me. I had just turned down Ray Anthony who was doing a Glenn Miller reject band and I didn't want to be trading on someone else's name. When you're a kid, you're a little feisty sometimes. So Woody called up and I said, "Sure, why not?" In those days, when you joined that band, you automatically got two weeks' [trial] notice. If it didn't work out, they wouldn't have to start your termination later. I'll never forget, on that first night, he called up a tune. . . . He called "102," but I only heard the "2." 102 was like "Bijou" and number 2 was "Sweet Sue." The band was playing "Bijou" and I'm playing "Sweet Sue." It didn't work out at all. They're all looking at me . . . "What's he doing over there?"

RED WOOTTEN: In the late summer, Jim Chapin replaced Sonny [Igoe] for a period. Jim and I had worked the saloons of Atlanta, along with the late Sam Staff, in 1949 and '50 with Freddie DeLand. A ball every night. Sam Staff was my mentor for Woody's band.

Baritonist Sam Staff was an excellent anchor man in the sax team of Kenny Pinson, Bill Perkins, and Dick Hafer. He played a well-controlled baritone and was also a fine flutist. His baritone sound was surprisingly similar to Serge Chaloff's, minus Serge's inventive ideas.

On October 1 the city of Milwaukee and St. John's Cathedral High School welcomed Woody when he came to help the high school raise money for a new gymnasium. Woody posed for pictures with his former chemistry teacher, Sister Mary Fabian Riley.

From October 18 to November 14, the Herd was on location in the Blue Room of the Roosevelt Hotel in New Orleans. During the date, the band was heard live on AFRS broadcasts. Some of the broadcast material from those dates has been available on the Giants of Jazz record label. The sound quality

October 1, 1951. Woody returns home to Milwaukee and St. John's Cathedral High School to perform a fund-raiser concert for the school's new gymnasium. Woody is standing with his former teacher, Sister Fabian Riley. (From the Woody Herman Collection)

is excellent and near studio quality in balance. The band wails on the up-tempo numbers and closely parallels the Second Herd's recording of Johnny Mandel's "Not Really the Blues." Dolly Houston's vocalizing is warm and sensitive on "I Won't Cry Anymore."

Joining the band before it left New Orleans was the exceptional trombonist Carl Charles Fontana. Prior to the Herman Herd, Carl worked in the Al Belletto band. Carl's solo style was characterized by a brusque and choppy swinging pattern with inventive conception.

CARL FONTANA: I subbed for Urbie Green for two weeks at the Roosevelt Hotel, and then I stayed on the band for a while. Then Urbie came back and that was the beginning of the Third Herd.

There were really some excellent musicians on that band. It didn't have the reputation of the Second Herd, the Four Brothers band, but I enjoyed every minute of it and Woody was like my father. I can't say enough about him, I loved the man.

The addition of Carl Fontana gave Woody an exciting trombone choir. Urbie Green's strong lead and versatility coupled with Fontana's modern approach caused sparks to fly in the brass section.

NAT PIERCE: Carl Fontana was completely insane. I don't mean that in a derogatory sense. We first heard him at the Roosevelt Hotel as a substitute in the band. Urbie Green's wife was having a baby, so he went home. Somebody recommended Carl Fontana and we didn't know him from a hole in the ground. But in those days, you would travel up and down the road near Biloxi, Mississippi, and one of the roadhouses had a band called Al Belletto's Band. Al played alto in those days, clarinet, and everything else. Carl was in that band. There weren't supposed to be any Italians or Catholics in that area, because the Ku Klux Klan would come after them, you know. But Carl came in there and just took over the scene. After we went home for a while, we needed a trombone player, so Woody says, "Get Carl!" So we called Carl and he came. Now we had two "monsters." We had Urbie and we had Carl, together.

Two replacements occurred in December and January. Red Wootten was replaced by a third "Red" bassist, Red Kelly. Tenorist Ken Pinson was replaced by Arno Marsh. The Third Herd was taking form.

Thomas Raymond (Red) Kelly no doubt has the distinction of working for more name big bands than any other bassist. At 16, he went on the road with Tiny Hill; after Hill came Ted Fio Rito, Randy Brooks, Sam Donahue, Chubby Jackson, Herbie Fields, Charlie Barnet, Red Norvo, Claude Thornhill, and then Woody in January 1952. After Woody came Stan Kenton, Jimmy Dorsey, Les Brown, and Harry James. He worked alongside Buddy Rich longer than any other bassist, when both were sidemen with Harry James in the sixties.

Tenorist Arno L. Marsh had worked with the bands of Joe Saunders and Johnny Long. After Woody, he had stints with Stan Kenton, Charlie Barnet, Maynard Ferguson, Harry James, Lionel Hampton, and Buddy Rich.

At this juncture, lead trumpeter Doug Mettome left the Herd to go with the Herbie Fields combo. Mettome was replaced by Johnny Howell, a veteran of the Barnet and Kenton bands. Although not known much as a soloist, Howell was a powerful lead trumpeter who bolstered the section.

The saxophone section of Hafer, Perkins, Marsh, and Staff offered a superb blend. Hafer was occupied playing the lead book and thus rarely soloed. This was unfortunate, because his solo work with the Barnet band of 1949 was exceptional. Perkins was Getz-like, with a languid and lyrical quality, and Marsh's sound was huskier, more in the Hawkins tradition, with modern ideas. They contrasted with and complemented each other.

Early in February, the changing Herd went into the Oasis Club in Los Angeles for approximately two weeks. By now, the band was roaring. Drummer Sonny Igoe had returned. The sections were tight and were achieving an excellent blend. The Basie influence through the new pianist Nat Pierce was evident. Once a night Woody featured Nat alone with the rhythm section on an up-tempo version of "I'll Remember April." Ralph Burns was contributing new charts such as "Original Ralph" and "Amazon" (later renamed "Hermosa Beach" and "Aruba").

NAT PIERCE: We did a tune called "Woody's Whistle," but it all started about fifteen years earlier as far as I can remember. In those days, we were young, and so it didn't matter if we were traveling 400 miles in a day. After the job, we would go to some jam session somewhere. Everybody wanted to get up on the stage at the same time, and it sounded like the most horrible mess you would ever hear in your life! So Woody would come around, and we were all having a few drinks and the whole thing. Woody would always blow the whistle . . . "Everybody out!" Any time that anything went wrong, he would blow the whistle, so everybody would know that he was there, and you know, cool it or whatever!

There was this one night, we were playing in Texas in this ballroom, where the owner of the ballroom also had his own band. His house was nearby, so he invited everybody over to the house. So we're all in this house, and he's got the pipes out and we're smokin' this thing. Here comes Woody knocking on the door. So everybody says, "Oh no, what are we gonna do now?" So he comes in and immediately grabs one of the pipes and takes a couple blows on it, and we were wide-eyed, we had never seen him do that before. So he says in his casual way, "I just wanted to see if it was good enough for you guys." He was checking that shit out, too! Woody would do things like that and get away with it.

WOODY: The whistle was a throwback. I guess a lot of the comics used to use a whistle, but this was actually given to me as a gift supposedly from my daughter when she was about 2 years old. It was a little gold whistle to call cabs, because in New York, during the war years, you'd be stuck for hours on the curb. I never could whistle very good, and I wasn't much of a waver. So she laid this whistle on me. It's come in mighty handy since.

We were in Detroit one time and George Shearing was there. We got together after the gig. George and I went into this place and pretty soon our guys started to tromp in, and so did some of the guys from his group. I don't know just what was happening earlier in the evening, but by now they were all on the stand. It seemed they were all out of their heads, loaded and everything. It was one of the worst conglomerations of sounds that I ever heard in my life, and George and I were trying to talk above this noise, and they weren't swinging, it was nothing! So I stood it as long as I could, and there was a kind of quiet part going on, and I let out a blast on my whistle, and yelled, "Cut! You miserable . . ." And they did, they cut, like they were shot! So George went right on the floor. He rolled, and he said, "I must have one of those!"

If you have a drunk in the audience who's making too much noise, go up to the microphone, and with a good PA, it's beautiful! You let him have a blast and say, "All right, get the hell out!" The guy usually will get up and leave.

In late February the band was in the Pacific Northwest. Chubby Jackson met the Herd in Seattle and rejoined for the third time.

CHUBBY JACKSON: Woody eventually called me "the ten-year substitute," because every time I got a little ahead with the dollar, I'd quit him and form my own band, lose the bankroll and rejoin Woody. Eventually I did move on to other things.

The Herd came into Southern California briefly in late February and early March, long enough to play a dance at the Rainbow Gardens ballroom in Pomona and for Woody to record two titles with David Rose's Orchestra.

The April 4, 1952, issue of *Down Beat* featured a rave review of the band from Ralph J. Gleason:

"Sparked by swinging Sonny Igoe and the old master, Chubby Jackson, Woody's band has caught fire again and is going to kick up a storm like the music business hasn't seen since the First Herd. . . . This is exactly what the music business needs: healthy enthusiasm. It can't help winning. . . . Don't worry about the dancers—they dance to this band. And they'll dance everywhere else once the musicians start liking music again. . . . To give you some idea of the enthusiasm this bunch has, they actually petitioned Woody to rehearse during their five-day layoff in Los Angeles in March. When did that last happen in a band? . . . The band plays many of the old Herd standards and it is amazing the way these kids swing that book."

NAT PIERCE: In those days, many years ago, guys were smoking pot. It wasn't an addiction routine. Now they make it like you're an addict. But Woody had already gone through that before with the Second Herd.

We played the Statler Hotel in New York (which was formerly the Hotel Pennsylvania), in 1952. So Chubby Jackson went up on the roof of the hotel and he smelled the smoke and he said to the guys, "I've got these eye drops, put them in your eyes and nobody will ever know." So a couple of us who were up there went back down to the bandstand, there was an hour's break between the dinner session and the dancing at night. And Woody looked up and he pointed at Chubby, and he says, "You've been doing that *thing* again!" And Chubby says, "Who, me?" And he was putting drops in his eyes and we were all stoned and breakin' up and Woody says, "The piano player, too!"

The spring of 1952 was the inauguration period for the Third Herd. The band had gone through two years of evolution before it became the swinging jazz unit that opened at the Statler on April 7. This band had elements of the First and Second Herds, without being a stale rehash of either.

On May 20 the Herd played a variety show/concert at Carnegie Hall. This was part of a tour package with the Herd, singers Tommy Edwards and Dinah Washington, the Mills Brothers and comedian Herkie Styles. Dee jay Al ("Jazzbo") Collins emceed the event at Carnegie Hall, dressed in swim trunks, towel, and sneakers.

One vital element was missing at this juncture. The band required a competent recording firm that excelled in marketing and public relations. Woody was unhappy with MGM. The record firm had not been aggressive in merchandising and distribution programs, nor would they allow Woody to record what he wanted to play. With the help of Howie Richmond, a friend and press agent, Woody formed Mars, his own record label.

WOODY: Howie heard the band and wanted to know what we were doing recordingwise, and I said nothing. We were between contracts and he said, "I would like to do a date with the band and maybe we can talk to Mitch Miller at Columbia and have him put them out." So Columbia gave us their studio and engineers and we did the first session. Mitch wasn't interested, and so we started Mars. There was no forethought or anything, but it was an interesting experience, because on a shoestring, we did a lot of things we wanted to do. I believe that it helped the band a great deal. But I don't think I would really want to be in the record business as a livelihood. We never knew if it was profitable because we kept investing money in the thing, but in the final analysis, we came out with a few dollars, which was pretty good. We just became discouraged because of the lack of interest by the major labels at the time. It was really the only thing we could do.

Ralph Burns's lovely Latin composition "Terressita" was recorded May 25, 1952. The arrangement has obvious classical overtones, with Nat Pierce's piano, a beautiful melody done by the saxes, and Woody's alto on top of the section and soloing. The brass plays some intriguing figures.

Ralph Burns's arrangement of "Stompin' at the Savoy" had the earmarks for the Third Herd's keynote record. An explosive intro leaps into rhythmic

Debut of the "Third Herd" at the Statler Hotel in New York City, April 1952. Front row L to R: Bill Perkins, Dick Hafer, Arno Marsh, Sam Staff (saxes). Second row: Sonny Igoe (drums), Carl Fontana, Urbie Green, Jack Green (trombones). Back row: Jack Scarda, Johnny Howell, Roy Caton, Don Fagerquist (trumpets). (Courtesy The Hugh Turner Collection, Hollywood)

figures from Chubby's bass, Sam Staff's baritone, and one of the trombones. The other two state the theme in octaves, answered by the muted trumpets. Tenorist Arno Marsh swings on the beat and there is some clarinet by Woody before the brass ensemble enters. All this is effectively underpinned by the wonderful rhythm section of Pierce, Jackson, and Igoe.

Jazzwise, the second best of the first four Mars titles is a pseudo-Mexican mambo called "Jump in the Line." It features a vocal by Woody: "Jump in the line, rock your body in time," with the band members shouting back, "No, thanks, I believe you." Carl Fontana solos and opens with a quote from "Small Hotel."

On July 7 the Herd recorded another batch of titles for the new Mars label. "Early Autumn," with lyrics by Johnny Mercer, was redone as a vocal sung by Woody. Bill Perkins does a tasty, Getz-like solo, but somehow, the vocal version never made it as the timeless instrumental did.

"Celestial Blues" was originally called "Eeph"; the title was changed when Nat Pierce played celesta on the recording.

NAT PIERCE: It was a riff that Woody made up and then they used some class chorus left over from the Shorty Rogers days. They put it together in what is known as a head arrangement. Basically, they take parts of this and parts of that and maybe five years later, "Well, let's take this part out and put it in this arrangement." That was Woody's big forte.

In the early days, it was actually very hard to write an arrangement from the beginning to the ending, because you knew he was going to do something to change it. So you just wrote enough material in the arrangement so you could move it around, because rarely would he go from left to right.

"Celestial Blues" is done in the Basie mode. Arno Marsh contributes, sounding like a modern Flip Phillips. Don Fagerquist plays a muted trumpet solo, noticeably behind the beat, and then, in complete contrast, come two superb choruses of beautifully relaxed, full-swinging ensemble work.

"Perdido" features Fontana's choppy and swinging solo style, followed by Arno Marsh in a solo reminiscent of Gene Ammons's work with the Second Herd. It's obvious that Chubby has returned, as he can be heard shouting above the band.

"Moten Stomp" is "Moten Swing" with solos from Fontana, a muted Fagerquist, and Marsh. The rhythm section is exceptional as it carries the band to a wailing finish.

URBIE GREEN: Woody was a great leader in the fact that he left the band alone and let it develop itself. I guess an example of that would have been that old "Moten Swing" arrangement which was something that everybody in the band contributed bits and pieces to. . . .

"Singing in the Rain" is a rousing head arrangement with offerings from Fagerquist and Marsh, the latter opening with a quote from "Rain on the Roof," and Woody closes on alto with a portion from "Stormy Weather."

WOODY (on life on the road): You wind up a combination of Mother Superior and Father Confessor and a bum psychiatrist, and you try to help people with their problems on occasion. Ninety percent of the time the kids will listen very intently and then turn around and do what they planned to do anyway. But that's the way it has to be. That's the way youth is, and you learn to accept this, and you still go through the same bits.

Maybe I am more extreme about this than other people, but I can't stand bus traveling. This, to me, is like being in stir, to have to live together on a bus. Musicians spend too much time together as it is, and then to travel together with those bad moods. Like stopping for a sandwich, it takes three hours because there are twenty-some-odd people. Spending six added hours to make any jump, that isn't necessary. In the fifties, we found that individual car travel kept a happier group of musicians, and it was a better way then. At least they had a few hours to themselves. They came and went as they pleased and all they had to do was show up, make it, and leave. If they wanted to eat in Pottstown they could, and if they wanted to eat in Cicero, they could. The risk, of course, is much worse in private cars, accidentwise.

CARL FONTANA: Every time we hit Louie's 29 Club in Oklahoma City, Woody would get drunk and start ripping the mirrors off the cars and kicking the cars. Every time I'd see him, I would say, "Woody, have you been to Louie's 29 Club lately?" He'd scowl at me and say "No!" He would get a few drinks in him and come out and kick the cars and tear the mirrors off. He would get very mean there. Something about the longitude and latitude there that didn't agree with him. Every time we'd hit there, we'd go out and jam and everybody would get bombed. I remember one night, we tried to leave and Woody wouldn't let Bill Perkins go, and there were four of us in the car, and Woody was ripping the side mirrors off and kicking the front end of the car, and he was just having a good time.

WOODY: Fontana used to make trips home too often for comfort. You know, I had two very wonderful trombone players for about two years, and yet I never had them together. When Fontana was home having his nerves fixed, Urbie would be there, and when Fontana got back, Urbie had to go and paint the house. So when people say, "Wasn't that a wonderful trombone section?" I say, "Yeah, I would like to have heard it sometime, must have been a gas!"

All these people individually were very good players. But we never had the same kind of ensemble that we had earlier. In other words, I have had literally thousands of great players go through the band, but very often they were there with a lot of people who were not very important.

In September and October, the Third Herd stampeded into the Hollywood Palladium. During the Palladium engagement, possibly to fulfill a previous commitment to MGM, the band cut ten titles of dance material for the label. Eight titles were released on a ten-inch album entitled *The Third Herd*. Woody was still trying for some versatility, and the music manifests a tight, well-rehearsed band, somewhat in the Les Brown mode, but unmistakably Herman.

CARL FONTANA: When we were at the Palladium, Woody had reminded the band not to be late and to be on the stand. The band was on the stand, but Roy Caton, a trumpet player, was at the bar having a drink, and he saw that the band was assembled, so he threw down the drink, and tried to leap over the sax section and the trombones and get in the trumpet section before the downbeat and he bowled over all the stands! Music was flying everywhere, saxophones, trombones, et cetera, and Woody was just standing there scowling.

Woody was one of my favorite people. He took me under his wing. I was with the band for two or three years. Woody was like a second father to me. We got along great. He gave me my big chance.

During the Palladium engagement, the Second Herd trumpeter Ernie Royal rejoined the band. The addition of Royal brought back a full complement of five trumpets for the Palladium and MGM recording dates. During 1953, the band worked again primarily with a four-man trumpet section.

By fall, Sonny Igoe left the band. Drummer Art Mardigan took over Sonny's chair. Art was an excellent drummer, but lacked Igoe's flash and capacity to arouse emotion and excitement.

December found the band in New York recording again for the Mars label. Dizzy Gillespie had earlier produced a tune entitled "School Days," using some choice verbiage from classic nursery rhymes, combined with his humor and bebop conceptions. Woody and Ralph Burns put together their own version of this concept on "Mother Goose Jumps."

WOODY: I don't know how many hundreds of guys went through before we wound up with what was really the beginning of the Third Herd, where you could say that this was a traveling orchestra, with some sort of a nucleus that would be there all the time. It actually took to around 1953 before it began to sound really good, and by that time we had some very interesting and good musicians in the band.

We came up with new music and Ralph did a lot of fresh, new things for this particular group of musicians. We usually try to write things that will make these guys stand out and show their true wares. I don't think *any* band can be a rehash of something that you have done before.

During that period we had to be able to play anything from an Elks' Club dance to a jazz club concert in the same week without too much time for preparation, so in that respect from 1953 on, the band started to make sense. It was probably the most versatile group I ever had. Some months it would be better than other months, because there still was the constant change.

We had some very loyal guys, like Nat Pierce, who sat there through a battle of drummers for months on end. A couple of bass players just fell by the wayside. They couldn't take it any longer, but Nat fought it out to the bitter end.

In early 1953, the Third Herd continued to grind out quality recordings for the Mars label.

HOWIE RICHMOND: It was a marvelous band, and I know after a while some
of the people said to me, "Can't you make anything a little more commercial?" I said, "I don't know, what?" But there was a little calypso vocal
coming and I said to Woody, "Maybe we could throw some calypso stuff
together and maybe get off a little bit on that." He said, "Look, first let's
put the stuff down that we have and then we'll do the other when we
come back to the studios."

On January 14, 1953, the Herd recorded a batch of calypso titles in New York
for the Mars label.

Early in the year, Chubby left the band. Red Kelly returned as the Third
Herd's bassist.

RED KELLY: As a veteran of many bands, I've always worked on the premise
that whatever band I am currently performing with has to be the greatest,
to me anyway.

With Woody it was not only easy to settle into that feeling, it was
mandatory. When you played with Woody's band, you felt a little bigger
inside. His band has always had an air of great strength and solid dignity,
due entirely to Woody.

He always played as hot as the best of them, sang as good as the best.
He had a smile that "made the lilacs wanna grow." He maintained an elegance in music that seems to be lost in most entertainment. I was honored
to call him my friend.

I think of the night that Stalin died and Woody made the announcement at the Blue Note in Chicago. We were all on the stage, ready to play,
and we weren't aware of what had taken place and Woody got on the
mike and said, "In case you haven't heard, Stalin just blew it!" [Laughter.]

When he was asked to make an announcement for a car with the
lights on, he would make it unique: "Blue Chrysler, with license number
RSF832, your trunk is leaking!"

In March the Third Herd went into the Blue Note in Chicago for approximately two weeks.

In August, tenorist Jerry Coker came on the Herd, replacing Bill Perkins.
Tenorist Bill Trujillo had joined, replacing Arno Marsh.

JERRY COKER: I joined Woody's band in August 1953 and left in June 1954.
I was 20 when I joined him, having spent the previous two years studying
music at Indiana University, to which I returned in the fall of 1954.

Having been inspired by the example of tenorist Buddy Wise, whom I
heard with the Gene Krupa band when Buddy was 20 (I was 15 at the

time), I set a personal goal of getting on Woody's band by the time I was 20. I was the youngest member of Woody's band and painfully naive. It was my first name band experience, whereas most of the members of the band had played with other well-known bands, like Stan Kenton, Harry James, and Charles Mingus. I was one of the first members of a name band to come out of university life instead of pure professionalism. Woody was especially kind to me and very protective and fatherly. Musically, he featured me heavily as an improvising soloist, encouraged me to write music, and listened to and respected my musical opinions. I would have to say that he treated me much better than I treated him.

In September and October, the band was back in New York recording. Heavyweights Ernie Royal, Bernie Glow, Kai Winding, and Vern Friley were added to bolster the trumpet and trombone sections pending the arrival of permanent replacements. With the addition of Winding, the trombone section was a quartet. On September 11, the band recorded a catchy riff by Jimmy Giuffre featuring the trombone quartet and solos from Winding, Vern Friley, Frank Rehack, and Urbie Green.

JIMMY GIUFFRE: Originally, I called it "A Quart of Bones." We rehearsed it one time, and then years went by, and I saw Woody in a club one night and he said, "We recorded your piece." He renamed it "Four Others," on his own. I had another piece called "Four Others," which I had brought in but he didn't care for it. So there are two "Four Others."

In the fall, baritonist Sam Staff's career ended when he was diagnosed as having Hodgkin's disease. He died in early 1954. His chair was filled by Jack Jerome Nimitz, nicknamed by Nat Pierce "The Admiral."

JACK NIMITZ: I was not supposed to go on the band for a steady thing. The understanding was that as soon as he got well, Sam would come back on the band. That was fine with me. Unfortunately, he died. So then I decided to stay on the band.
   Woody was always great with taking a chart and putting it together. If we got a new chart in, he might change it around. Put the middle part in front or something and make it work.
   Woody was for music! You can tell from the guys that he had on the band throughout the years and all the crap that he put up with from musicians. But they made great music. That was the thing with him. He put up with a lot to have good musicians.

In March the Third Herd embarked on a variety package tour similar to the previous year's. It was promoted as "The Big Show of '53." In addition to the Herd, the show included Ella Fitzgerald, Frankie Laine (with Carl Fischer),

Louis Jordan and His Tympani Five, comedian Frank Marlowe, dancer Bobby Ephram, and Dusty Fletcher of "Open the Door, Richard" fame.

FRANKIE LAINE: I think Denver was the third date. When we tried to fly into Denver, there was a terrible blizzard going on. We had to land in Colorado Springs and hire cars. We were with Louis Jordan and his wife, Ella Fitzgerald, Carl Fischer, the driver, Ella's pianist, and Woody. There was another limo with some other people in it. The two cars kept pace with the Highway Patrol which was giving information to the audience in Denver, and the orchestra kept playing. They got in early. The orchestra started the show at eight o'clock and we arrived about 11:30 P.M.

Out of the 7,000 people, only seventy-eight people wanted their money back and went home. We kept going until the show was over about three o'clock in the morning. So the band was on stage for almost seven hours.

ELLA FITZGERALD: We had such good times when we all worked together on the tour with Frankie Laine, which was a beautiful tour. Everybody always traveled in the bus 'cause they wanted to be close together. When we traveled on the tour, Woody insisted on riding right in the bus with everybody and I thought that was so beautiful. We had a comedian, he used to tell jokes on the bus, sing and everything. It was like a private bus and we had such a good time.

In late 1953, bass trumpeter Cy Touff joined the Herd. Prior to Herman, Cy was with Charlie Ventura, the New York City Opera Company and Shorty Sherock.

Cy sat in the trombone section. The bass trumpet resembles the valve trombone in sound. This ungainly-looking instrument has rarely been heard in the jazz field. Johnny Mandel did some experimenting with it, but he was known more as composer/arranger than as an instrumentalist.

CY TOUFF: I started out in high school on trumpet and my embouchure was just too small, so I switched to slide trombone. But I remember that I was interested in jazz and I felt handicapped. So the first year's experience on trumpet stayed with me. I got a valve trombone and I played it for a long, long time.

At the Regal Theater in Chicago, one of my fellow musicians picked up my horn and dropped it, and dented one of the valve casings, which is basically irreparable. So then I had to get another horn, and I had just heard Johnny Mandel, he came through here with Buddy Rich's band. They played at the Regal, and he was playing bass trumpet at that time and he made a terrific impression on me. I was in my early 20s. So I waltzed down to the music store and bought one and I've been playing it ever since. It had certain advantages over the valve trombone, particularly in that there's a first valve slide, or trigger. In other words, I can adjust or lower the pitch by throwing this thing out with my thumb. A valve trombone doesn't have that feature. But the trumpets usually have a slide on the first valve and the third valve.

I first joined Woody in late '53. Chubby Jackson was living in Chicago at that time and evidently Woody had mentioned to Chubby that they were going to need another trombonist and he recommended me. We knew each other socially and he had a small jazz group that I had played with.

I replaced Frank Rehack. In fact, the first night I was there was Frank's last night. So he sat next to me, helped me and pointed out things in the book that might be helpful. The main part of the jazz solos were in that book. Frank was a marvelous trombonist. I admired him tremendously.

Almost the first thing off the bat, Woody calls something like "Blues in F." And he just pointed at me and said "Stand up," and so that was my audition! It was like, you know, "Can you play the blues?" I guess I did, because I stayed on the band for three years.

Woody once described Cy Touff as "a modern-day Ziggy Elman." His style was characterized by big tone, a "down-home" straight-ahead swing, and simplicity of execution. Cy was influenced by Lester Young, Lou McGarity (the former Goodman trombonist), and trumpeter Harry "Sweets" Edison.

In early December Nat Pierce, Red Kelly, Cy Touff, and Jack Nimitz were injured when they were traveling to a one-nighter in their car near Kimball, South Dakota.

WOODY: The guys finally show up, bandaged from head to foot and ready to blow. This takes an awful lot of guts . . . the band cheered that night because the guys looked like "The Spirit of 1776" when they walked in.

JERRY COKER: The most memorable for me was the time I was very late for a gig. We were in Seattle at the time. I thought we had the night off. They didn't call me "The Fog" for nothing. I went to a late afternoon movie, alone. When I returned to the hotel, I began calling around to the others in the band. I was getting no answers. Finally, the operator asked, "Are you Jerry Coker?" When I said I was, she read a note from Abe Turchen telling me to get to a certain town, sixty miles away, as fast as I could. My stomach turned upside down, I *ran* to the bus station (I had no access to the band bus or cars), arriving at the gig one and a half hours late. When I walked in the door, I heard a peculiar cheer from the bandstand . . . they had drawn times out of a hat, gambling on the time I'd arrive. In other words *they* took it lightly. I didn't, feeling panicky, embarrassed, and very sorry. Only Woody seemed to understand the situation. He didn't go into a fit of anger or panic. . . . He simply lined up all the tunes he had needed me for, as a soloist, counting off "Early Autumn" as I was putting my horn together, followed by all the other tenor features he had delayed until my arrival.

CY TOUFF: It was a learning experience for me. It was learning about professional steadiness and coping with the music night after night.

When I first joined the band, my book was maybe like four or five inches thick. And he would call out a tune, and then I'd have to shuffle through the parts, and I didn't want to do that so I started memorizing them. So by the time I left I had it down to about half an inch, which were things that we never played. One less distraction.

Woody turned out to be a person with the same problems and stresses, pleasures and pains as we all have. The only time he would be kind of crabby, he'd call home and Charlotte would say, "Where's the money?" Then he would get on the bandstand that night and he would be a bear! But he had the capability of overlooking a lot. I can't remember him firing anybody. They sort of came and went by their own volition.

I remember he felt really good when we picked up Al Porcino. Al had dropped out. He had had some personal problems, and he was living in Dixon, Illinois, with some relatives. We played nearby and he came over and Woody hired him on the spot. We were just about ready to go to Europe, and he needed him. Al wanted to get out of Dixon and felt that he wanted to resume his career. So Woody gloated about that. He said, "I have the great Al Porcino for much less than I would have otherwise." He was right in a certain sense, but it was beneficial for both.

AL PORCINO: I rejoined Woody in February of 1954. I actually was out of the music business at that time. I had moved to Illinois and was working days. I had gotten very disenchanted with New York around the end of 1953, and was also having some domestic problems. I thought maybe a change in scenery and getting away from the music business might do me some good. Of course, what usually happens with a musician like myself is that I was back in the business before I knew it.

It was quite a lucky break for me because I needed a job and I did miss playing. I was in Chicago and I ran into Woody's band boy Jack Wamsley. He said, "Woody's in town, why don't you come down and dig the band?" By coincidence Woody was getting ready to let one of the boys go, a fellow named Jim Bonebrake. He asked me if I would be interested in joining the band. Of course, it was the third chair, and it wasn't going to pay much, I think $130 a week. But what really enticed me was getting ready to go to Europe on a tour for a month in April.

Metronome magazine called the Third Herd the "Comeback Band of the Year" and chose it the best band of 1953.

CY TOUFF: Woody was a father figure. He drank me under the table. I was just a punk, just 25, and here's a guy fifteen years my senior. Occasionally, we'd hang out together at night. I remember, he took me to Birdland in New York, and the next thing I look up and there's twelve drinks at my elbow, and I'm still workin' on the first one and he's had all twelve! I just had to laugh and say, "Forget it!"

At the beginning of 1954, the Third Herd experienced a series of personnel changes. In addition to Al Porcino, Woody added another trumpet, high-note specialist Bill Castagnino. Once again, the Herd was implementing a five-man trumpet section.

WOODY: When I hired Bill Castagnino, I was informed that he was a licensed mortician. As a matter of fact, he had quite a ball on the first trip on the road because he would get into a town, look up one or two of the boys at the local funeral parlor and have a few drinks and ask "What's new in the embalming game?" Then he would leap into the [band] job.

Bill Perkins rejoined the band in March, replacing Bill Trujillo. In late March, drummer Charles Walter (Chuck) Flores joined the band. Chuck received his musical education in the Los Angeles area, studying two years with Shelly Manne and Murray Spivack. Before Woody, Chuck briefly went with Ike Carpenter's band, Shorty Rogers's quintet, and Maynard Ferguson.

WOODY: In the case of Chuck, I got a big boot out of going along with a youngster who had never played in a big band, watching his progress, which wasn't the quickest, but he wound up to be one of the tastiest of all the young drummers that we worked with. It was a sorry day when I lost him, because to my way of thinking he had arrived at the point where he could now be a great asset to the band and to me.

The Third Herd was booked for the European tour in April. Before leaving, the band recorded four titles in New York on March 30. "Mambo the Most," a pulsating chart done in two parts, was among them. Part two was entitled "Mambo the Utmost." Solo offerings are from Nat Pierce, Jack Nimitz (who blows his heart out), Cy Touff, Reuben McFall, Woody (clarinet) and Bill Castagnino's high trumpet.

NAT PIERCE: I remember one thing that happened about two days before we went over to Europe. We were at the original Basin Street, on 53rd Street between Seventh and Broadway. Charlie Parker came down there, and I guess he was a little high or something. He said, "I want to beat the band off before you guys take off for Europe." So he put his arms out like he's flapping his wings to start the band. We didn't know what was happening, so Woody counted off "Apple Honey," and we went into that immediately! Here's Charlie Parker . . . he's got jeans on and the whole thing, and it was something else, very strange! He used to sit in with us. This is after the bootleg recording of 1951. But he sat by the baritone sax chair, because that was the only E-flat instrument we had. He would look over at the baritone parts.

WOODY: I've had a lot of favorite alto players. The only one I can be accused of really trying to get anything from was Hodges, because to me he was untouchable. However, in recent years Charlie Parker was head and shoulders above everyone else. All the ones that tried to emulate him, to me, are just kind of lost people. I hate to hear just another imitator of Charlie Parker because no one had the ability and the mind that could keep going and going and going for thoughts, silly ideas so often, and beautiful ideas on other occasions. In the middle of some intricate phrase, he played the lowest old-time blues lick you could think of. This showed his great breadth musically. He couldn't express it verbally, you know, but when he put his axe to his chops! . . .

   We did some things together at Basin Street. Charlie would come down every few nights and he loved to play with the big band. We started a little gimmick that was kind of funny. I had quite a few pretty tunes in the book where there were alto solos, and I would blow the first eight or sixteen and Charles would be standing on the side, and I would say "Go," and the contrast was so beautiful that it was fantastic, hearing me with my little nothing sound, playing the melody, and out of the blue, in came this whirlwind, and I just wish we had taped some of these things.

   Not too long before he died, we had a rehearsal at Basin Street, and it was a very hot afternoon, and the air conditioning wasn't on. We got there about three and we finally broke up about five-thirty; we just couldn't take it any longer. We were wringing wet and we were struggling up the staircase and just emerging onto the sidewalk, when up came Charlie, steaming and panting. He was perspiring like mad, and he didn't look well at all, and he says, "Wood, is the rehearsal all over?" Like it was a very important matter. "Yeah, Charlie, we got what we wanted," I said. "It's pretty hot." He said, "Man, I've been trying to get here all day," and it was five-thirty or six p.m. This man had a look on him, I can't describe it, but this tremendous perspiration and like a struggle to get there, to a stinking rehearsal, just to sit around.

On March 31 Woody was invited by producer George Avakian to participate in a recorded jam session at Columbia Studios in New York, working with musicians Buck Clayton, Al Cohn, Urbie Green, Walter Page, and Jo Jones. Woody was in top form and produced a fine example of his clarinet ability.

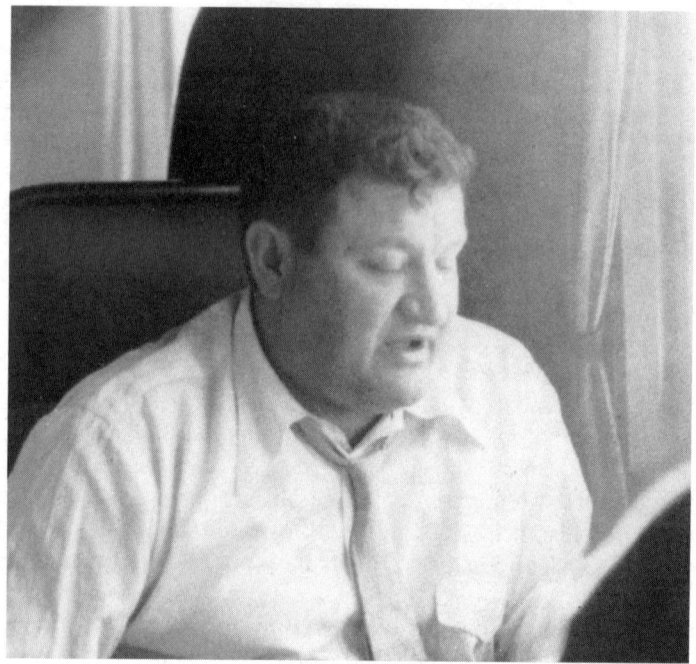

Manager Abe Turchen on a train in Europe. (Courtesy Ralph Burns)

On April 1, the Third Herd left New York for a month-long tour of Europe. The first stop was Oslo, Norway, for two concerts.

AL PORCINO: I must say, we had a swinging month in Europe. Half of it was in Scandinavia and about two weeks in Germany. Europe was everything I had imagined it would be. A slower pace of life and all, and a bigger appreciation of music and jazz.

JACK NIMITZ: Woody had his daughter Ingrid along on the tour and Herkie Stiles, the comedian. That was a great trip. Ralph Burns was on that trip too. That's when Ralph was still drinking.
    Ralph used to drink after the concerts, and we would go out to clubs at night. You know how they say, they carried the guy out of the club after he's been there a while? We used to carry Ralph *into* the club. A great player and a great composer. He doesn't do that any more. If he did, he probably wouldn't be with us right now. Ralph wrote some things expressly for the trip, for different players.

CY TOUFF: The arrangement of "Indian Summer" was done by Ralph Burns when we went to Europe and they wanted me to have some kind of a fea-

The Third Herd in Europe. Front row: Jerry Coker, Dick Hafer (partially hidden), Woody, Bill Perkins, Jack Nimitz. Second row: Red Kelly, Chuck Flores, Cy Touff, Dick Kenny, Keith Moon. Back row: Al Porcino, Dick Collins, Johnny Howell, Bill Castagnino, Reuben McFall. (Courtesy Jerry Coker)

ture number. So Ralph came to me and said, "Name a tune." So I picked that one and he did a little chart on it, and then, of course, we recorded it.

INGRID HERMAN REESE: In Europe in those days, they attached giant plastic or metal things, several inches long, to the room keys to discourage anybody from taking them. Red Kelly was determined he was going to collect these keys for souvenirs. He had a suitcase practically full of them. It was incredibly heavy. I remember, we were on a ferryboat going from Sweden to Denmark, and they called shore-to-ship. One of the hotels we had just been in was looking for him and their room key.

Ralph Burns was on that band and he often took me out for hot fudge sundaes, and I would feel like I had a little place in the sun. It was a real act of kindness because that was a difficult age, not really a little kid and certainly not a teenager.

AL PORCINO: My favorite story about Red Kelly took place on our 1954 trip to Europe with Woody. Kelly and I always roomed together. We were in Amsterdam, Holland. Kelly, being a bass player, had "knobs" on his playing fingers. They were green and thick. He never wanted to get them soft so he never took a shower. He only took baths and would leave his arms half-dangling out. Well, in Amsterdam he had been reading the Sunday paper with all of the colored comics and he fell asleep. He was in the tub and I was in the bed. The next morning the maid came in to clean up and she saw Kelly asleep in the tub with his arms dangling outside. The color from the Sunday funnies had got in the bathwater. She saw him asleep and the colored water looked like blood. She thought he was dead and ran out of the room screaming. That's my favorite Red Kelly story.

WOODY: Ingrid analyzed practically all the boys in the band from time to time, and gave them a little advice on how to live and keep straight. It was pretty funny. She was only 12 then. I remember one saxophone player in Europe, a young man who had lots of frustrations and problems, and she spent the whole tour, whenever we were in a bus or anyplace, straightening out this lad. I used to sometimes sneak in the bus seat behind them and overhear part of it, and I would get hysterical.

Our first German date was in one of the athletic buildings used by Hitler, the Sportpalast. Oh, my God, what a "garage." This was like for all diesel trucks with big trailer trucks. You could put millions of them in there. We had a very big crowd. Right after the concert, we were hustled to two or three jazz clubs.

NAT PIERCE: One time, we were in Berlin, and a whole big band escaped from East Germany to come and hear the concert. After the concert was over, they were all on the stage: "What kind of mouthpiece is this?" and "This reed?" and "Where did you get this horn?" It was "20 Questions," you know. Then they said, "We've got to get back before the guard comes. . . ."

WOODY: A big rumor started in Berlin the day after we arrived that they would try to retaliate by grabbing our band. Our guys were afraid to get out of the hotel the rest of the day and evening, until we went to work. Those things don't seem like much here, but when you're over there it seems like a hell of a lot.

CHUCK FLORES: We played a concert at Hannover, Germany. It was a two-concert deal, we had a break, and we came back and did a second concert, and during the break, we went out and got some beer. I got pretty bombed. I mean, I only had one or two beers, but there, one or two beers is like five beers here, you know. I came back and played the show and I thought I was really wailin', and just after the curtain closed, Woody looks at me with this glare, and he says, "What in the hell do you think you're doin'?" He rode me for about five or ten minutes, and just put my ass straight down, you know. I was like just crushed, just devastated. It was for my own good. It taught me a big lesson.

CY TOUFF: Particularly in Germany, the distances were not great. We would play two concerts an evening in two different towns. Plush accommodations. They had feathered quilts on the beds, it seemed like it was for royalty or something. It was all set up well in advance and they had reservations made. Each hotel seemed fancier than the other.

My wife came with me at my own expense. When the tour was over, we did some recording there with a small group in Paris [the *Herdsmen Play Paris* album]. Ralph Burns was a party to it and I was, and a couple of other guys in the band. There were some French musicians that played on it too, if I remember correctly.

WOODY: In England, we played at the U.S. Air Force base at Sculthorpe, 125 miles from London. They took us to a place about twelve to fifteen miles from Sculthorpe where we stayed. This was quite an experience. It was on the North Sea and it was a little summer resort, just beautiful in July. We were there in April. And April in Europe is still complete wintertime. Maybe they have a couple of nice days because they wouldn't write songs like "April in Paris," but most of the time it's colder than Hell. Naturally, there is no heating in these places because they are summer resorts, and most of us stayed at this one house, and the little ladies that ran it were wonderful, and made us breakfast.

After the first night at Sculthorpe we had a big bash, 'cause all the English musicians came down from London, and everybody blew and it was a pretty big, happy affair. Then when we left and drove back and got in this house, it seemed like it was forty below zero, and everybody was running around in nightshirts screaming, "You got any booze left?" (So you don't freeze to death.) They did have some beautiful hot water bottles in each bed, and this was our salvation.

The guys sat in with Ronnie Scott's group. This is where I first heard Victor Feldman. They played opposite us down there and Jack Parnell came down and many other guys. Then we played our two days there and went up to London for a holiday for a day or two, and that's when we met [Ted] Heath and got to hear his band at one of the theaters.

VICTOR FELDMAN: I first met Woody in England when I played at an American base opposite his band, with Ronnie Scott's band in 1954. Woody's band was the first American band I had heard live since Glenn Miller played in England years previously during World War II. It was a thrilling experience to actually stand in front of and listen to a real live American band. Meeting Woody was also memorable because he is such a warm human being.

WOODY: At the concert, there was Mrs. Heath, and then Ingie and Charlotte and then me sitting in a line in the second row. Ingie wouldn't keep her voice low, in a quiet baby style. She didn't know about this. A whisper to her was a giant shriek! Heath had three different singers, two boys and Lita Rosa. Now Ingie says to Mrs. Heath, "The one boy sings pretty good, but the other boy, if he could get a haircut and change his whole style," and we can't kick her because she is too far away.

We went backstage to see Ted, and it was a typical English attitude. They are so open and nice. "How did you like my band?" Now being an American, I wouldn't say that for the world, because you are liable to tell them. I never asked anybody in my life, "Well, how did you like my band?" So I said, "Gee, it was just wonderful!" Mrs. Heath, who had a nice sense of humor, said, "I don't think Miss Herman was so impressed, Ted, with our singers."

There was a great deal of enthusiasm for American jazz. We were not of the complete modernist school, and yet maybe we were more modern than Count Basie, who had been there in the same territory shortly before. The fans and critics would say that our trumpet section was the greatest. This seemed to be their nemesis. They can't seem to get it to a point where we can sometimes. I heard some very funny sessions in jazz clubs. These little night clubs, they call them all jazz clubs, because of the enthusiasm. This one in Berlin had a group blowing, a tenor and trumpet. They sounded pretty good, but then the drummer would be still marching and boy, could they march! This happened all through Germany.

NAT PIERCE: In the Reeperbahn in Hamburg, they didn't want Chuck Flores to leave. Of course, he was only 19 years old. This was like the red light district. They got him in one of those houses and captured him, believe me. We had Herkie Stiles, a comedian, with us. All these ladies are sitting in the windows, in various stages of undress or dress, and Herkie shows up and says, "Have my laundry ready by noon," you know. Finally, it got so rowdy that the gendarmes came and said, "You guys are going to get out of here, this is ridiculous!" Meanwhile, up on the third floor, a window opens and out comes Chuck Flores, and yells, "Help!" They pull him back in and they close the shutters and we never did see him any more until the next day.

WOODY: We were in Germany, and we were trying to get to some city off the Autobahn. It was on a Sunday, and this was one of the days when the bicyclists come out en masse, and there are just thousands and thousands. We had a German bus driver and a German interpreter with us, and they would get so mad because we were trying to make about 100 miles and we were taking up about six hours already and we were getting nowhere. I swear, our driver knocked over several hundred bicyclists, just brushed them, because they wouldn't move.

We did one concert in Paris. It was very interesting. From what I heard about Paris, you had to be sure you used your very best judgment, if you didn't want to get thrown out of the joint. We had a habit of closing the first half of the concert with a mambo. We were in it a minute and all of a sudden, the worst noises came out of the audience. The guys started to perspire and panic, and then I realized that we had goofed, and so we did a very quick cut. We went into "Moten Stomp," more their groove, anything of the old school in France, and we were right back in business, just as if nothing had happened. This couldn't happen anywhere else in the world. You know, where you can lose them and win them all in one minute!

Our most successful date was in Vienna. An open city. It was pretty strange. I guess there were some Russians there. I didn't ask what they were [laughter]. Nice people, and a big kick. A great experience at the Vienna date was that Radio Free Europe sent one of their real groups in, and I was very impressed with these guys. They were really doing a tremendous job and you could see that these guys had backgrounds. They just weren't young fellows who started in radio or something. They taped the show, and then spent hours with interviews and things and even got me to try to sing a couple of nursery rhymes in Polish, anything where you can reach out in one of the languages, no matter how broken it is.

Dublin was very amazing. We did two concerts there and had a terrible flight going in. We used a freight plane to get there and these guys had flown over the hump regularly and everything else, but when the crew saw the amount of equipment and people we had for this little plane, they had quite a discussion before they would try for a takeoff. They had our instruments in the aisles tied with a rope, so they wouldn't fly into the air. We finally got up and got as far as North London and we had to land at an emergency field to refuel. It was a grass field and it was pouring and muddy. We were way overweight.

We finally got to Dublin about the time the concert was supposed to go. We arrived at the airport, coming in sideways, but they were waiting with a police escort and some English visiting musicians that did a kind of impromptu session until we got there, and it worked out very nicely. After the first concert in the afternoon, the promoter took us to the local hotel, a nice hotel with caterers, wine, and wonderful food. It was just a wonderful party. We went back to the evening concert and they had buses waiting to take us out to one of the promoter's ballrooms, where they had brought Joe Lossi's band to play a dance in our honor. This man was so kind and so righteous that he wouldn't exploit us. He took us to the ballroom, let us look at the big crowd, and then took us up to a banquet room privately, where once again there were caterers with all the jazz, the wine, the booze, and we started this all over again. Well, we finally broke that party up about four, and then back to the hotel and continued on with the partying.

The April 24, 1954, issue of *Melody Maker* printed a review of the Dublin concert by Mike Nevard:

> . . . This band jumps. It retains the drive and energy of that fabulous First Herd. The only difference is the soloists. For whereas the First Herd interspersed its driving ensembles with hot, crackling solos from the Flips and Bills, its descendant contrasts the hot with the cool. . . .
>
> Perkins headed the soloists in Woody's work-out on the famous "Apple Honey"—(Everyone has his treatment of "I Got Rhythm," this is ours.) Here was proof of the Third Herd's mastery, for the '54 version has all the drive of the '45 original.
>
> Dick Collins played assured, well-thought-out trumpet in this; easy phrases, no rush, a repeat here and there on the lines of the early blues vendors.
>
> Cy Touff soloed on "Apple Honey" with a steamy cymbal backing from drummer Chuck Flores. Flores is a good drummer, unobtrusive, always there, ready to hit out when called on. Not the individualist like Lamond and the great Davey Tough, but the perfect section man; the driver.
>
> In a way, "Apple Honey" was a cameo of the Herd's performance. Woody himself soloed in this, jerking his body to the beat, shaking out notes to left and right, the sheen of his jacket twitching the light as he doubled at the knees.
>
> And then the brass crashed in, screech trumpet Bill Castagnino slid in a high one, and the whole thing finished with one of those endings that sound like a car crash. . . .

In May back in New York, the Third Herd recorded some fine jazz material for Columbia. Bill Holman's "Blame Boehme" featured Woody's clarinet, Dick Collins, Jerry Coker, and Nat Pierce, and his "Prez Conference" was renamed "Mulligan Tawny" as a salute to the then popular pianoless quartet of Gerry Mulligan. An intro and outro were added with Dick Collins and Jack Nimitz doing the line in a style that smacks of Chet Baker and Mulligan. The tenors of Coker and Perkins, Woody's clarinet, and Collins's trumpet all add to the flavor.

"Cohn's Alley," renamed "The Third Herd," has a line played by a trio out front with Woody (clarinet), Collins, and Hafer. Then Nimitz charges in, followed by Perkins, Touff, Woody on clarinet, high trumpet from Castagnino, and shouting brass, with Flores' drums and Kelly's bass signing off as band boy Wamsley is heard groaning. It's unfortunate that "These Foolish Things," a vehicle for Perkins, was never released.

On July 8, 1954, Woody teamed with the Erroll Garner Trio to record a group of love songs for an album Woody sardonically entitled *Music for Tired Lovers*.

WOODY: That was a lark. We had worked together quite often at Basin Street, New York, and a couple of other places, and during some part of the night while Erroll would be finishing up a set, I would sit down at the piano with him and sing a few old hits for kicks, and it worked out real well. We used to call it the Torch Hour or whatever, and then we had the reciprocation thing where Erroll would come up and blow the last set with the band. It was a lot of kicks and a lot of fun and the audience just loved it, because this wasn't like a two-act operation. It was one big scene, you know. I've always liked those kinds of things to happen where you can operate in a club or wherever you might play or even at a jazz concert where you can put the whole thing together and make sense out of it because it gives your audience a feeling of intimacy with the artist and vice versa.

    We went into a radio station in Detroit one afternoon and cut it, and as anyone could tell, we were pretty limited with our repertoire, and mainly this is because I only knew the words to some songs and Martha Glaser couldn't find lead sheets to hardly any songs, except ones she liked like "La Golondrina" or something. We recorded with a thought I had in mind that I felt would put it out of the category of a vocalist routine, and that was to record it so that the piano and the voice were even, so it should sound like your living room, like I was sitting on the piano bench singing without the aid of a microphone, and I think it came across that way. As far as recording technique is concerned, it's all wet. But this is what we wanted.

DOLLY HOUSTON: I left the band in 1954, when we came back from Europe. It was kind of a hectic trip, and I guess I was just tired. I had mixed emotions about leaving, but I wanted to try the New York scene.

Replacing Dolly Houston was singer Leah Matthews, a tiny, sultry brunette with vibrato and phrasing strikingly similar to Frances Wayne's. Leah's recordings with the band were never released, but her voice was captured on numerous live broadcasts, including several from Omaha, Nebraska in July 1954. The band was roaring and in top form when these broadcasts were made. Leah sang a moody "Get Out of Town," and the Frances Wayne evergreen "Happiness Is Just a Thing Called Joe."

AL PORCINO: In August we were doing a week at Jantzen Beach in Portland, Oregon. Wally Heider, the famous recording engineer, was there with all of his big equipment. At the time, it was just a hobby for him. Later, he became the most successful recording engineer in Hollywood and all over the world.

When Woody announced the chestnut "Golden Wedding" at Jantzen Beach, he pronounced, "This is 'Golden Wedding' from the film *Sal Mineo in Purgatory*." That was his Third Herd period catch phrase when announcing certain titles.

Nat Pierce's increasing influence was heard through his contributions to the Herd's book, among them "Muskrat Ramble," "Sleep," "Boo Hoo" and others. Ralph Burns continued to send in fine arrangements such as "Misty Morning," a lovely jazz ballad in the "Early Autumn" vein. There was "Strange," a Latin treatment of the pop tune of that period, featuring Woody's lush alto and Dick Kenny's trombone. It should be noted that Dick Kenny, a veteran of the Barnet and Kenton bands, was a fine, underrated player, equally effective as a lead man or a soloist with humorous and original ideas.

"Wild Apple Honey" was a fine mid-fifties example of how this score evolved from the First Herd period, featuring rousing solos from Perkins, Hafer, Touff, Collins, Walp, Woody, and Castagnino's high trumpet and climaxing in the now-famous free-for-all ending.

As "Hut" is sometimes used to start a play in football, Woody occasionally used his own language to kick off a tune. He uses his famous "Bow Bow" to kick off "Wild Apple Honey." Asked by Ralph Gleason when he started using that phrase, he said:

WOODY: Oh, I don't know, that has been going on for years and years. I have some very crummy habits, like not telling the band what the next tune is, but like by a certain gesture, or the way I yell. Will it be "Chow" or "Bow" or "How"? This may be the only introduction I'm going to make . . . and boy, this will keep them pretty lightfooted.

"Woodchopper's Mambo" was a Latin reworking of "Ball." The out chorus featured a counter-riff from the jazz classic "Jumpin' with Symphony Sid."

"Sleepy Serenade" is worthy of mention, due to Burns' lovely treatment, Woody's alto, and the sensitive, big-toned horn of Collins, who was described at the time as a "1954 version of Bunny Berigan."

CY TOUFF: The road was a hard life, even for a younger person. Long jumps and lack of sleep. The standard ploy was you'd work a gig at night and drive all night to the next gig, check in and get a day rate. Then you'd check out before the gig and then drive again. So you'd sleep going and not have to pay as much for your hotel room. The expense of your food and room was your own responsibility.

In mid-September, the band opened at the Hollywood Palladium for a two-week engagement. Tenorist Dave Madden had replaced Bill Perkins. On opening night, Stan Kenton was there to welcome Woody.

WOODY: I don't know why it is, Stan had a bear hug he gave people. I know, at least in my case, he would pick me up in the air a few times and I wouldn't be the same for a few days.

After any meeting, when he was in a jovial mood, if we had a few drinks together, he would always say, "Say something funny, Woody, oh boy, this guy's funny! Say something funny, Woody!"

AL PORCINO: The Palladium in Hollywood was a nice engagement, of course, to sit down for a week or two. I remember at the very same time, Stan Getz was with a small group at Zardi's on Hollywood Boulevard. I used to dash over there every night after our job finished about one with my tape recorder. I have some historic tapes of Stan there with his small group, and one set with Chet Baker sitting in.

During the September 1954 Palladium stint, the band went into the Hollywood studios of Capitol Records and cut a selection of fine tracks.

There was "Autobahn Blues," a medium-tempo groove by Ralph Burns that somehow stays with the listener. "Autobahn" featured solo offerings from Perkins, Woody's clarinet, Pierce, Walp, and Howell, fine-precision ensemble passages and excellent drumming by Flores.

After the Palladium stint, tenorist Richie Kamuca replaced Dave Madden. Kamuca had been with the Kenton band in 1952–53, and was a superb musician whose roots went back directly to Lester Young.

DICK HAFER: When I was in the band, we had a bad accident in Johnny Howell's car in Kentucky. John's car was wrecked. I got knocked out of my shoes. It was the weirdest thing. Some dumb truck without a taillight made a left turn in front of us without any turn signals, and we were going 80 mph at the time. I said to John, "Hey, that truck is turning and you're not going to make it to pass him." So he headed for a gas station and went through the station, between the pumps and the building. The truck kept turning in and he just caught our rear bumper and spun us through the gas station about five spins. We didn't roll over, but we spun end around and we came to a stop at the end of it.

We climbed out of the car and the car had hit part of a building, and an old Southern guy was sitting on the porch, and he said, "That was a mighty good piece of drivin', son. I've watched accidents here all year, but that was one of the better ones!" I looked down and I was in my stocking feet and my loafers were off! They were torn, and I still don't know how that happened. I didn't have any cuts or bruises.

Later that night, after we had played the job, I went into shock because of the accident. It didn't hit me right away. If we had hit the pumps, we would have blown up. I knock on wood every time I think of those road trips. Woody had no mercy with those road trips. In retrospect, if he had spent some of the money on making life more comfortable, Abe wouldn't have been able to get hold of all that money!

JACK NIMITZ: One time we had to go from Atlanta, Georgia to Bluefield, West Virginia, to play a policemen's ball. Then we had to go back to Atlanta. Woody could not get a plane to go there, so he had to ride on the bus. So we started to say, "Isn't this a great bus!" It really wasn't one of the greatest buses. Dick Collins was there and we said, "Okay, we're gonna stay up all night. Everybody's gonna stay up and drink and play cards and just show Woody what a shitty bus this is, and what it's like!" So after a few hours, he couldn't take it anymore, so he said, "Will you guys shut up and go to sleep for [expletive] sake!" So Dick went up to him and said, "Yeah, Woody, how do you like it, man? Huh? How do you like the bus? It's great huh? Do you like it?"

WOODY: We played a club in Philadelphia, a little jazz club in the Powelton Hotel. It was sort of a run-down hotel, and we were there for two nights. They had the lowest piano in the world and it was just impossible. The business was fantastic. People were waiting in line to get in, so I told the boss, "As long as we are going to be here tomorrow night . . . why don't you rent a piano? This thing is not even fit to try to play on." Nat was fighting it, hitting a note here and there, but it was bad. So the boss said, "Oh, man, that's a good piano. Erroll Garner used it last week, what are you worrying about?" Erroll probably tried to commit suicide the first night, if I know him.

So along about midnight, we were getting going pretty good, the place was just jammed, and all of a sudden, a deluge came down through the ceiling over the back part of the stand where the piano was and I noticed a few guys were scurrying and leaving. It seemed that some broad upstairs had fallen asleep in the bathtub and it overflowed. It didn't stop until the cops got there and they sent for a plumber, and we blew right through the whole mess.

So now comes the end of the gig and the two bosses were standing there, and they are the happiest. They said, "Oh what business and people we had, and we sold plenty of booze." (They cut the whiskey.) So I said, "Now look, fellows, you're going to have to do something about the piano, tonight. Now get it cleaned up, get some towels, and wipe it up. Get a guy in there and try to repair it, and if it can't be repaired, go borrow or rent one."

The next night we came to work, they said, "Oh, don't worry about a thing, man." So here is the piano full of water, some more had leaked down during the day. It was turning green with mold . . . It's the only time I've seen Nat Pierce get shook up. It finally reached his sensitivity. I sent him to a movie. I said, "Catch a double feature and come back a little later on." And that's the way we wound up.

DICK HAFER: When the Third Herd really broke up was New Year's Eve of 1954–55. Nine guys left the band for a ten dollar raise they couldn't get. It was at the Blue Note in Chicago.

I told Woody later in the month, "I can't believe that you're going to let this band disintegrate for ninety dollars a week." And he said, "Well, I don't have any money, I can't afford it." I said, "Well, if you don't have it, then there's something wrong somewhere because some money is being stolen!" It took a lot of guts for me to say that, but I said, "There's something going on that's not right." And he said, "Ah, no, it's nothing like that, I know where all the money is!" Well, he didn't!

Howell left, Porcino left. Johnny Howell, the backbone of the trumpet section, left. Bill Perkins left [to go with Stan Kenton]. There was a big hole there.

AL PORCINO: The whole month of February '55, we were at the Hotel Statler in New York. The band was swinging, but for some reason I'd had it. You could only stay on a band for so long. At least, that's the way it always was with me. I must have given them a whole month's notice, rather than just two weeks, so they had the whole month of February to find a replacement for me.

We would bring in trumpet players and have them sit next to me right on the job and I would play my lead as usual. Incidentally, by that time, I was playing 90 percent of the lead, even though I had been hired a year earlier on third. John Howell and I always got along well. He was a fine trumpet player, but knew that I had more experience as a lead player. So he was very gracious in letting me just about take over the lead book. So in essence, I was the auditioning lead player though Woody had to give his final word on it, too.

One of the trumpeters who auditioned was Jerry Kail. I remember one title we did was "Muskrat Ramble," a real long, hard thing that Nat Pierce had arranged. There was an awful lot of blowing. The last chorus was extremely strenuous and you ended up on a high G on the last chord for trumpets.

Well, we finished the set with me playing it. I didn't want to just throw it at Jerry Kail, so I played it so he could follow along. The story I got later, after we got off the stand was someone asked, "Hey, what happened to Jerry Kail?" Someone else said, "I don't know. After the set he just ran out of here in a panic!"

DICK HAFER: We re-formed again three weeks later with another band. I think Jerry Kail joined us and Art Pirie [replacing Perkins]. The band was finished. That's when I decided to leave. It never got back to that sound he had before. He still billed it as the Third Herd, but it was not the same great '54 band that went to Europe and did the Capitol album. The amazing thing about Woody was, every band he had had a distinctive style of its own.

Although the band was experiencing a gradual personnel turnover, it remained a powerhouse ensemble through the summer of 1955. Bassist Red Kelly left and was replaced by John Beal. The Herman saxophone section continued to be a habitat for a succession of talented young tenor players. Woody was asked by Ralph Gleason in 1956 if it was a letdown to hear new tenor players do the solo on "Early Autumn" after the original definitive recorded version with Stan Getz.

WOODY: On some occasions we play a much better version of the arrangement. The [tenor] solo and everything else comes off better than the original. This is not a strange coincidence, because the musicians who are playing the piece have heard it and know it a lot better than we did when we did it originally.

On June 6 and 7, 1955, the Herd cut fifteen titles for Capitol in New York. Some superb examples of big-band jazz were produced in these sessions.

Nat Pierce did an interesting arrangement of Horace Silver's "Opus de Funk," which produced five minutes of electrifying jazz with solo offerings from Pierce, Kamuca, Touff, Woody (clarinet), and Collins.

There was Woody's "I Remember Duke," with Woody on clarinet, Touff, Kamuca, Keith Moon's Ellingtonish plunger trombone, and Nimitz. The brass ensemble borrows a phrase from Rogers's "Man, Don't Be Ridiculous" and "Boar-Jibu."

Nat Pierce put together a head arrangement of "Sentimental Journey" with Collins, Keith Moon again doing plunger trombone, Touff, Pierce, and Woody playing some "dirty" alto, before the band winds up with an explosive finish.

Burns contributed "Cool Cat on a Hot Tin Roof," a lightly swinging groove piece with solos from Woody on clarinet and Nimitz's swinging baritone.

CY TOUFF: Woody thought of himself as "The Great Editor." We would get new charts and he would go to work on them. The typical example is "Early Autumn," you know, the famous record from the Second Herd. At no point on the record does the orchestra play a full chorus. It's an introduction into the tenor solo and then the band comes in. . . . It's cut up! As I understand it, the original chart was not that way. But Woody wanted it. It's very effective and he wanted to put his finger into everything that came in. . . . Generally speaking, his ideas were good. Occasionally, I did feel that he screwed up a great arrangement.

Bill Holman wrote a thing on "Where or When" that was a master-piece! It went on for four or five pages. So when we recorded it, he cut out the introduction and we skipped over to section H or whatever, and I thought that he did a hatchet job in that particular instance. I'm sure he had his reasons for wanting to cut down the time for recording purposes, but the arrangement on it was just like a work of art.

Bill Holman's elegant score of "Where or When" in its recorded version included Woody's alto playing the melody, an overbalanced piano (Nat Pierce), a beautiful saxophone section chorus, Dick Kenny's trombone, and a buoyant solo from Kamuca.

Noted composer Manny Albam sent in a chart called "Captain Ahab—The Wailer," later simply called "Captain Ahab." As author Steve Voce has stated, it's done "in the powerhouse Herman stomp tradition."[3] Solos are by Touff, Kenny (Touff and Kenny trade fours), Kamuca, Charlie Walp, and Dick Collins, taking their turn at fours, and Woody offering some tasty clarinet before the ensemble explodes. The performance concludes with a humorous pseudo-Dixieland finish.

At this point in Woody's career, he believed that his band, and the big band business in general, needed a formula that would generate some pop single record sales. At the June recording session, the band recorded four titles that he hoped would accomplish this goal. "Skinned and Skinned Again," a drum feature for Chuck Flores, was a two-sided novelty designed to reach the teenagers. Another was "The House of Bamboo," from the film of the same name. The other two titles were also from films of that period, "Love Is a Many-Splendored Thing" and "The Girl Upstairs," the latter title from the film *The Seven-Year Itch* starring Marilyn Monroe and Tom Ewell. Woody believed that when recording tunes that are connected with films, "you get natural exploitation from the showing of the film itself."

Through an idea from Capitol's Dave Dexter, Woody commissioned arranger George (The Fox) Williams to score "Skinned and Skinned Again" and "The Girl Upstairs" with an eight-voice background vocal chorus. "Love Is a Many-Splendored Thing" obviously was scored by Burns. Woody told *Down Beat,*

> I don't think that we've compromised with good taste in making these records. Sure they're more commercial, but I think it's very important to reach that other audience, that larger audience we have to reach eventually to survive. . . .
>
> Many of the other guys feel the same way. Stan Kenton, for example, is shooting for singles. After all, it's silly to leave the greatest percentage of the people excluded from what you're playing. And another thing, the guys in the band and I put in a good day's work over 300 days a year. We've got to get a payoff sometime. . . . [4]

The singles recorded at the June session enjoyed a reasonable amount of success. "Love Is a Many-Splendored Thing," particularly, had considerable air exposure from dee jays and was most likely Woody's last successful pop tune of any consequence.

In July the Herd was at George Wein's Newport Jazz Festival at Newport, Rhode Island.

Replacing Nat Pierce in the final edition of the Third Herd was pianist Norman Pockrandt (Parker). Before Woody, Norm had worked in the bands of "Toasty" Paul, Earl Gardner, Charlie Spivak, and Jerry Wald.

NORM POCKRANDT: Arno Marsh helped me get on Woody's band in the summer of 1955. Traveling from a resort gig in northwest Michigan to the Crystal Beach Ballroom at Vermilion, Ohio, where Woody was doing a one-nighter, I was a half hour late because of traffic, so when I walked into the ballroom, the band was playing. What a gas! The band was on tour for two more months before disbanding and forming the octet that was at the Riviera Hotel in Las Vegas for three months.

Keeping a big band on the road in 1955 had its share of internal stresses. It was increasingly difficult economically to keep a big band together. Woody said in 1955: "I always liked the Statler in New York and in the days when there were people around, I used to enjoy the Palladium, but now it's like going to the morgue for a weekend."[5]

Conditions being what they were in the summer of 1955, the timing couldn't have been better when Woody received a lucrative offer to take a small group into the Riviera Hotel in Las Vegas in the fall. Personnel for the Herman Octet was John Coppola (lead trumpet and arranger); Dick Collins (jazz and second trumpet); Richie Kamuca (tenor sax); Cy Touff (bass trumpet); Norm Pockrandt (piano); Monty Budwig (bass); Chuck Flores (drums); and Woody (clarinet and vocals).

WOODY: I went into it with much misgiving. When you're with a big band, you're used to a lot of horns and when you don't have them, there's a feeling of emptiness. So it was strange at first. But after the first three or four weeks, I became completely intrigued with the group. Everything fell into place just right and it was exciting. In fact, it was the first time in years I felt like playing; because of the small group, I HAD to play. In a big band it was just spots . . . eight bars here, eight bars there. Of course it was also the first time in years I could hear myself and I almost found I could be interested in what I was playing!

   Seriously, though, the group was terrifically exciting to play with. It had the old-time spirit with modern thoughts. We received lots of encouragement in Las Vegas, too. There are thousands of musicians there, you know, and we worked with the graveyard shift, so there were a lot of visi-

Woody with his Las Vegas octet at the Riviera Hotel. L to R: Norm Pockrandt (piano), Monty Budwig (bass), Woody, Chuck Flores (drums), Richie Kamuca (tenor sax), Cy Touff (bass trumpet), Dick Collins, John Coppola (trumpets). (Courtesy Norm Pockrandt)

tors. Even the Lombardos, when they were in Vegas, were in every night to hear us, en masse. I got a kick out of it, but some of the boys wondered if we were going in the right direction!

CY TOUFF: We worked seven nights a week from midnight to six o'clock in the morning. Well, after a while, your mind starts plotting. So one night, for no particular reason, I got a cocktail napkin, and I wrote, I think with a red pen, like, "You and me after the gig, Woody," and I signed it "Tootsie." I included *xxx* (kisses) at the bottom. I gave it to one of the cocktail waitresses and I said, 'When we're on the stand, bring the note up and Woody's going to say, "Who wrote this?" So just point in any direction and say, "Oh, she just left!" Just to have something to do besides playing.

So she brings the note up to him and it's perfect. He reads it and to her he says, "Who wrote it?" and she says, "She must have left, she's not there anymore." So then about twice a week, I sent a note up. It was an ongoing thing. I wrote to the effect, "If I ever get my hands on you, you'll be a changed man! Blah blah," and all kinds of erotic bullshit that I could think of. Woody started getting disturbed. . . . "Who is this Tootsie?" He started like talking to himself! We told him two years later that I was "Tootsie." His response was disgust!

Bassist Monty Budwig had worked with Red Norvo, Vido Musso, a group headed by Stan Getz and Chet Baker, and other West Coast groups.

MONTY BUDWIG: I was introduced to Woody in 1955 by Richie Kamuca who was already with the band. Woody hired me to play in Las Vegas at the Riviera Hotel with the newly formed Octet.

Woody helped the musicians in the orchestra build valuable reputations by featuring them not only at a gig, but on his albums. I was featured on a tune written for me by trumpeter John Coppola called "Bass Face." I worked with Woody from 1955 to early 1957.

NORM POCKRANDT: When the band was in Vegas, we were part of the grand opening of the Riviera Hotel. The gig was a joy for all concerned. After we finished work, the band would usually congregate around the roulette table and many times the casino boss would come to the table where we were playing, and where normally one white ball is spun, he would spin three.

Everybody had an apartment in Vegas and it was a pleasure to be in one town for three months with the band. Richie and Chuck Flores were sharing an apartment and had a rented piano, so naturally theirs was the party and session pad.

The small band was a joy because everybody got a chance to blow, as you can tell by that excellent recording of the group. We recorded at Capitol Records after we finished the gig in Las Vegas. This was after three months of playing those charts, so the band was really tight and together and the recording was excellent.

Also, we recorded with Woody's big band.* The band was so good that on the first rundown of the arrangement of Buddy Rich's solo, it was perfect. Unfortunately, they didn't record that first rundown. Buddy's solo was just sensational and inspired. They recorded two other takes of Buddy's solo chart but none as good as the first unrecorded take.

---

* Other than the Las Vegas Octet nucleus, the big band that recorded at the Capitol Studios on November 30, 1955, was made up of pick-up personnel from the Hollywood studio pool. The purpose was to record three titles for a Herman Herd contribution to the forthcoming Capitol album entitled *Dance to the Bands*. Capitol had devised the idea, knowing that the firm possessed recording contracts with the "who's who" of big name bands in 1955. Buddy Rich participated in a Herman recording session for the first time since "Your Father's Mustache" in September 1945, for his part on "Drums in Hi-Fly" (released as a single and later compiled in an album entitled *The Hits of Woody Herman*).

It's tragic that the Capitol album *Jackpot!* is out of print. The Woody Herman Octet achieved an almost full-orchestra sound. Richie Kamuca and Cy Touff were superb. Cy's feature on "Wailing Wall" was written for him and is worth the effort to find.

After a brief Christmas vacation, Woody built up a big band again. New Year's Eve 1955–1956 found a new Herd working in Philadelphia on a WCAU telecast.

In August 1956 the late Ralph J. Gleason, then a writer for *Down Beat* magazine and editor of the "Rhythm Section" jazz column in the San Francisco *Chronicle*, interviewed Woody Herman at great length. Ralph's and Woody's inspiration and motivation was to write a definitive autobiography of the legendary Herman, as stated in the preface of this volume. Unfortunately, circumstances intervened, and Ralph's and Woody's ambition was never realized.

Through special arrangements with Ralph Gleason's widow, Jean, excerpts from these edited interviews appear throughout the first five chapters of this volume. As a sidelight on Woody's frame of mind at the end of the Third Herd period, a portion of the interview material is presented below in the original format. The subject matter is eclectic, including Woody's parents, his preference in instruments, life on the road, and Woody's name.

R.G. Do you still get your shoes from him [Woody's father]?

W.H. Yes, he still makes all my shoes and he seems to improve with age. I think the last pair of alligators was the nicest pair he's ever made for me.

R.G. Some pretty wild shoes?

W.H. He's made 'em out of just about everything he could get his hands on, like pony skin. . . . And what was the last one? Seal! Without the fur. Some of them, it takes courage. It takes months sometimes before you can really wear them in public. You just wear them around the house. But they are comfortable.

R.G. Does he do them himself?

W.H. Part of the work is done right in the factory, but you know, it must be a terrible scene for the poor guy who's doing a particular operation, because of Dad's nose over his shoulder, and a boot in the can if he gets half a stitch off. Part of it he does at home, he does the hand work. He's done some beautiful things. But as I said earlier, he's a liver, and I don't think he'll ever stop. He has his personal physician, he spends a great deal of time with this man, heh, heh, and he's tried every pill in the joint. I think he's got this doctor mixed up at this point, 'cause he diagnosed his own case at all times and he tells the doctor exactly what to do about it.

R.G. Do they visit you on the Coast?

W.H.   Last Christmas they came out and visited us for the holidays. They had only about a week to spend there, but he had a pretty good time even in spite of the fact that it rained every day. And they traveled around the country down through the years quite a bit, visiting me, and I think they've been just about everywhere in the country.

R.G.   Do they have all your records?

W.H.   My dad has a collection of all of them. There's just maybe two or three that he wouldn't have out of the whole mess. He's saving them for me. They have a PA at the factory, and whenever we have a new release, the poor characters get blasted with it hour after hour.

R.G.   Is he still active in the shoe business?

W.H.   Yes, and whenever I receive a pair of shoes, he has this gold stamp . . . And you'll find it in seven different positions inside of the shoe. I get pretty good billing in my shoes and in spite of all that billing, I've lost lots of pairs of these shoes at different times, when kids would like a souvenir, and they wind up taking some of these shoes. It's heartbreaking.

R.G.   How many pairs do you carry with you?

W.H.   Oh, usually about a dozen. In Europe, we lost a whole bag of shoes. They caught up with us in a couple of countries and finally we lost 'em for good.

R.G.   Which instrument has been the most fun to play?

W.H.   It seems if I have any natural ability, it comes out on the saxophone, because I can pick up a baritone, or a tenor, or an alto or even a soprano and get a pretty decent sound out of it. And yet I've fought for years and years to get a really nice clarinet sound and it still escapes me. I have this old clarinet mouthpiece maker, a little old Italian man, in Youngstown, Ohio. Each time I break a mouthpiece or something happens, he sends me a new one, with a closer facing, hoping to get me to eventually have a legitimate embouchure, so that it will sound like a woodwind instead of a cat call, you know! This last one I got, I can hardly breathe through it. He's either going to win, or I am going to have to give up the whole thing.

R.G.   Would you rather play the clarinet, then?

W.H.   Well, it's a challenge, 'cause I can't make what I want to make on it, whereas with alto, in most instances, the only thing is that my thoughts jazzwise on alto are pretty nothing. In other words, you will find that in most cases, it will be a melodic line that I attempt and nothing more.

R.G.   What do you want to do with the clarinet?

W.H.   Break it in half, ha ha! What else?

R.G.   I can see that I am not going to get you in a serious discussion of that.

W.H.   No. In years gone by, I used to be influenced by a lot of people and I even tried to be fresh on occasion when new things would happen in music, and new guys would come along, but I finally have reached the saturation point. Not that I don't enjoy listening to other people. I do, sincerely. But I finally found that just to play whatever is in your mind without any thought about anyone else's playing and not to be influenced too strongly in any direction is much better for me. When I listen to what I've tried to do it makes more sense that way than if I really try hard . . . in other words, it would be very difficult for me to be of the modern school of playing.

R.G.   Do you have a favorite clarinet player?

W.H.   Oh, I have several of them. Naturally, Benny I've always respected in every sense of the word. I am not as happy with his playing now as I was some years ago, because he has something he wants to do and I think it takes away from his great jazz ability, and his great feeling of swinging, but nevertheless, he's done more for the instrument jazzwise than everyone put together. However, some of the newer guys I think are tremendous . . . Buddy DeFranco. Because I don't know whether people realize . . . to play some of the modern sounds and ideas on a clarinet is probably more difficult than on any other axe.

R.G.   Why is that?

W.H.   Because of the awkwardness of playing the instrument, and the fact that you have the throat tones in the lower register, the middle register and the high register, and you can get all hung between these registers. . . . There aren't too many good, technical clarinet players, except maybe in the legitimate field.

R.G.   Woody, naturally a guy who is on the road a tremendous amount of time is unable to spend much time at home. Does this give you any sort of peculiar view of family life?

W.H.   Well, everyone has problems with it. It's very difficult on the woman that you are married to and your kids sometimes, too, but mostly on that gal, you know. This is the biggest heartbreak of young musicians and their wives. This year alone, I lost five guys! It's pretty heartbreaking in a lot of ways, because lots of times, their career is ruined completely because of love for the wife and there is certainly nothing wrong with it, except it just doesn't work out. Years ago, you met some chick in a ballroom, and the next day you got married. But today it isn't that way. Most of the guys stick around their home towns or some town and go with a girl for quite a while before they get married. There is a lot of serious discussion on how they are going to be a working journeyman musician, and yet after a year or two try at this the little woman says, "Oh, no you don't!" And that's the end. In our case, we, like any two normal humans, have our ups and downs, pretty drastic ones at times. On the whole, we have been very happy and I have to give credit where it is due. I happen to be married to a woman who has the patience of Job. Besides, we try in our silly way. You know, once you get older, you realize that this is the best thing for you . . . that I must work. I must earn a living, so it has to be done this way. I only feel sorry for my wife about one thing, and that is the complete stupidity of some of our dearest friends, because their question is always the same, seven days a week . . . "How do you do it, Char?" "How can you stand it, Char?" And she says, "I'm all right, I'm happy." They won't believe you. They figure there's gotta be something wrong. We try to make up for it by spending time together. When I get to a place Charlotte likes, she'll join me. If I am in Chicago and she hasn't been in Chicago for a while, sure. New York, maybe once every two years, for a stay and then it's fun and kicks and then let me get home to my house.

R.G.   Do you always get home for Christmas?

W.H.   Not always. Sometimes we come home the day after New Year's or New Year's Day. If it looks like a profitable holiday season, then we celebrate Christmas a little late that year, and the tree is still up and everything is ready. We do things ass-backwards, a lot of times, but I think we have more fun in the long run than a lot of people I know. Sure we are gypsies and we're kind of wild. For instance, if I am in New York working a location like Basin Street and I have Monday night off, it is very possible that on my day off I'll catch a plane to L.A., get there in the afternoon, take a two-hour nap, we have a lovely dinner, go out someplace, come back, take a nap, get up, take a plane and go back to work. It costs money, but what else are you going to do? I think one of the things that helps to intrigue a gal and make her still think you're okay in her book is the fact that you do the unusual, and you never question it and you have to be a little insane.

R.G.   It's still a ball?

W.H.   Oh yes, and it's a kick to arrive in East Overshoe and know there are a couple of swinging cats there and cut up a touch! I could never completely stop. Sure, sometime I must find another way of life, but I know that there will be visits and there will be trips to New York and there will be trips here and there, because if I couldn't have these trips, I'd just have to give up. I've got mileage in my blood. That's a good title!

R.G.   Does the constant travel affect you when you lay off for a couple of months and stop traveling?

W.H.   Yes, when I go home sometimes, it takes me about a week to get accustomed to somewhat normal living, and it's still not very normal because I still sit up until about four or five in the morning, even if I'm doing nothing. Force of habit. The only difference is that now I get less sleep because I get up at ten in the morning because I don't want to miss a thing. So what should be a rest turns out to be a hell of a thing. It takes a good couple of weeks before you can even become acclimated to the whole routine.

R.G. Do the neighbors in a residential area like that regard a bandleader as a jazz musician?

W.H. Well, for the first time I think, in all the years that we've lived in different places as a family group, we have neighbors that we actually got to know and have spent time with the last couple of years and enjoyed it immensely. We just discovered the American way of life about things like this, because in New York we never knew our neighbors. We've had a lot of fun. Like with the barbecues outdoors, the whole jazz. Like briefcase-type living.

R.G. Do you have fans who travel miles to follow bands?

W.H. Oh, yeah. There have been people like this always. If it's in the same territory, they ask, "Where you gonna be for the next couple, three days?" And they try to catch up with you. It's a great kick to know there are people who enjoy something this much.

R.G. For years, I've noticed that people have been calling you Woodrow Wilson Herman. Have you been fighting this all your life?

W.H. Oh, sort of. Somebody started it because of the fact that I was born in the Wilson period, when he was in office. The reason my first name is Woodrow is because my father was evidently a pretty strong Democrat. The only story I've been able to get is that he was bagged in a bar the morning I was born and naturally, I was named Woodrow. But that Wilson shit was hung on me later. My middle name is Charles. And later, when I was confirmed, I took on Thomas. So it's Woodrow Charles Thomas Herman.

R.G. I suppose it must be a problem to keep guys from falling in love with every chick that's singing with the band, just from sheer proximity.

W.H. Well, usually I've evaded it as far as I could. I've had to fire more girl singers than musicians. Usually, sooner or later they get involved with a guy who is married. It may take a little while, or it may happen right away, but it's inevitable. As a matter of fact, I've even had girl musicians that I had to fire for the same reason. Not singers, musicians. Like, Bessie starts calling you from New York, and she says, "I hear my old man's been cutting up!" So you get rid of the broad because the guy is more important to you at the moment than the girl singer. It always was that way with us, anyway. With very few exceptions, just about every girl on the band was fired for that very reason.

If I took all the hours that I spent explaining to people in the business the reason for having a certain girl in the band, it would take half of my life to add the hours up.

We opened at the Paramount one time and we must have thrown away two or three hours of the 6:00 A.M. rehearsal to get Frances Wayne to walk out on the stage holding a bunch of roses. The microphone was disguised in the roses. The wind-up of the whole thing was that she became completely frustrated and screamed, "I won't do it," and stomped her foot. Weitman, the managing director, was in a big spin because he figured the way she walked out on the stage was bad, that this whole bit would take away from the show, that nobody would look when she was walking. These little things! They hurt you for years after. It was a thankless kind of procedure. I often wondered how other leaders could have the courage and the guts to build a band around a girl singer, which happened on numerous occasions, and really stay with the idea. 'Cause we never drew two more people, or got any more or less audience reaction because we had a great or a lousy type singer. . . .

6.

The Fourth Herd
1956–1959

The Herd that was assembled the last week of December 1955 was virtually a new band. Although the Herman band continued to be billed as the New Third Herd into 1958, it was a different band in terms of personnel and conception. By mid-1959, the band had been identified in an album title as "The Fourth Herd," and that designation is used here for the band of the late fifties.

WOODY (1956): Going from the little group to the big band this last time wasn't difficult in the least, because we had a nucleus. And we had people who knew what we were attempting and didn't need all that explanation and exploration period. As a matter of fact, we put the thing together in four days of rehearsal, hard work, and then did a three-hour TV show for our first gig. It came off and nothing collapsed! You know, that's pretty fast! Even Milton Berle wouldn't try that.

ARNO MARSH: In December 1955, I rejoined Woody in New York City. I had been in Grand Rapids, Michigan, working a small group of my own, and received a call to go back out on the road with Woody. . . .

Victor Stanley (Vic) Feldman, a former child prodigy from London, was equally proficient on piano, drums, and vibraphone.

VICTOR FELDMAN: In 1955 I emigrated to New York City. After I'd been there for a while and played a few gigs, Nat Pierce took me to one of Woody's rehearsals. So, we met again and he asked me if I'd like to join the band. My only reservation was that I had been on the road for many years in Europe, but the combination of Woody as a person and the way the band sounded

The Herd in early 1956. Front row L to R: Woody's back, Richie Kamuca, Arno Marsh, Bob Hardaway (tenor saxes), Jay Cameron (baritone sax). Hidden from camera: Vince Guaraldi (piano), Victor Feldman (vibes). Second row: Monty Budwig (bass), Will Bradley, Jr. (drums), Wayne Andre, Bill Harris, Bobby Lamb (trombones). Back row: Dick Collins, Burt Collins, John Coppola, Dud Harvey, Terry Ross (trumpets). (Courtesy Frank Driggs)

made up my mind for me. So in late 1955 I went with the band. Before going on the road, Woody asked me to come up to his hotel room. He told me that I could wear anything I wanted and suggested I get a jacket and pants different from the regular band uniform. To this day, I cannot figure out why he did this. At the time, it felt like he was giving me special treatment.

This was the new band as it went through rehearsals in late December 1955: Woody Herman (leader, clarinet, alto sax, vocals); John Coppola, Burt Collins, Dick Collins, Dud Harvey, Paul Serrano (trumpets); Wayne Andre, Bob Lamb (trombones); Cy Touff (bass trumpet); Bob Hardaway, Richie Kamuca, Arno Marsh (tenor saxes); Jay Cameron (baritone sax); Vince Guaraldi (piano); Monty Budwig (bass); Will Bradley, Jr. (drums); Victor Feldman (vibes).

A new face in the trombone section was Wayne J. Andre. He came to Woody's band via the Sauter-Finnegan Orchestra.

WAYNE ANDRE: I joined Woody's band on December 31, 1955, and left about July 1956. During that period we did many one-nighters. I was one of four drivers of Ford sedans. Woody drove to each job in his Thunderbird with his [road] manager, Dick Turchen, nephew, I believe, of Abe Turchen.

Early in the year Bill Harris rejoined the band's trombone section. Bill's contributions gave the band an explosive spirit and elicited admiration from his section mates. Cy Touff was leaving the band, but before his departure he played beside Bill for a brief period.

BOBBY LAMB: We were playing in Child's Restaurant one Sunday in 1956. . . . Bill Harris suddenly appeared to rejoin the band, and Woody asked him to sit in. . . . Suddenly there was this explosion! Bill played so strongly that Wayne and I just sat there gaping with amazement and let him get on with it. He led the whole band from the trombone section.[1]

CY TOUFF: Playing with Bill Harris was an impressive thing. Bill had a ridiculous sense of humor. . . . I was having some minor stomach troubles and would get so hungry. I would always bring a sandwich to the job. Usually a ham sandwich. So this one night the intermission came along and as I'm grabbing my sandwich . . . *uunch*! Some joker had taken the ham out of it and substituted a piece of cardboard! For some reason I suspected Jack Wamsley, the band boy. I went up to him and actually punched him in the shoulder. I said, "Jack, you took my sandwich," and *pow*! I hit him. And it was Bill Harris who did it!

VICTOR FELDMAN: We traveled in cars doing one-nighters consisting of some very long trips . . . sometimes 800 miles. When Bill Harris joined the band, I got to know him well. What a tremendous player and unusual guy he was, one of a kind! We roomed together, and at one point the band started doing concerts. One night I was awakened by Bill sitting bolt upright in his sleep shouting: "I hate concerts!" I told him about it the next morning, but he could not remember it.

In late 1955 and early 1956, the Count Basie Band experienced a comeback, primarily due to the hit single "April in Paris" and a steady stream of blues hits sung by Joe Williams. The blues had long been Woody's forte, although a controversy would rage in the sixties on the subject: "Can a white man sing the blues?" It was natural for Woody to ride the blues wave in 1956.

A recording session was scheduled in Chicago, and arrangements were written by Nat Pierce, Ralph Burns, Neal Hefti, John Coppola, and Manny Albam. The guitar of Ray Biondi was added for the recording session. The Las Vegas Octet had previously recorded "Basin Street Blues" and the Joe Williams hit "Every Day I Have the Blues." These were added to the classic blues titles "Call It Stormy Monday," "Dupree Blues," "Pinetop's Blues," and "Trouble in Mind." Woody's voice was in top form as he belted out familiar material that was part of his early repertoire.

Trumpeter Johnny Coppola wrote a hearty blues riff originally entitled "For God's Sake, Drop the Other Shoe," but changed to "Blues Groove" for the album. Later the title was changed to "Cousins." The line and the trumpet section send-off are both adapted from Lester Young's solo on the Basie recording of "Pound Cake," vintage 1939.

INGRID HERMAN REESE: I remember my parents always communicating their values to me, my father, especially. He felt that music and the arts were

The 1956 edition of the Woody Herman small group at the Riviera Hotel in Las Vegas. L to R: John Bunch (piano), Woody, Bob Hardaway (tenor sax), Monty Budwig (bass), Victor Feldman (drums/vibes), John Coppola (trumpet), Bill Harris (trombone). The band jackets worn by the group bore little shields on the breast pockets. The big band that year wore the same uniforms. (Courtesy Monty Budwig)

more important than any kind of money or status. Every time some musician he knew would go home to his family and get off the road to get a regular job, he would always talk about it like it was some kind of a terrible thing. So I absorbed the message very strongly that playing music and having an opportunity to express your art was far more important than any consideration of being home. And I never really heard my mother dispute that. Even though, I'm sure, she couldn't wholeheartedly share that opinion.

I remember that my parents both seemed to have a more lively sense of fun and humor than any of their peers. But I grew up thinking of him not as a star, or as a celebrity, but just as an artist. . . .

During June and July of 1956, the Herd was enduring the rigors of the road with the exception of location dates at the Marine Ballroom in Atlantic City and the Lagoon in Salt Lake City. At the Lagoon, Wally Heider was back recording the band privately.

VICTOR FELDMAN: I was playing vibes and one double drum feature with the band. In July 1956, Woody was booked in Lake Tahoe and Las Vegas, with a small band. He asked me to play drums and a little vibes. The band consisted of Vince Guaraldi, piano; Monty Budwig, bass, Bob Hardaway, tenor; Dick Collins and John Coppola, trumpets, Bill Harris, trombone, and myself, drums and vibes.

On September 3, 1956, while working the Riviera Hotel in Las Vegas, Woody received word that his mother, Myrtle, had passed away in Milwaukee.

RAY SHERMAN: When his mother died, Woody did not attend the funeral. He did fly in and viewed his mother's body at the funeral home, before she was in state, and flew right out again, visiting or seeing no one. I believe he was working Las Vegas and the management wouldn't give him permission to take off for a few days. Some type of Mafia directive, I believe. People talked because he wasn't here, but it was truly a personal thing and couldn't be avoided.

Joining the Las Vegas Herman Octet before the close of the engagement in the fall was pianist John L. Bunch, Jr. He had previously worked in Los Angeles with Georgie Auld. After the Riviera engagement, Woody again built up another big band with many new faces in all the sections.

JOHN BUNCH: I joined Woody in August 1956 and left in August 1957. Some of the guys in the big band when I was in it were Johnny Coppola, Bill Berry, Danny Styles, trumpets; Bill Harris, Willie Dennis, Bobby Lamb, trombones; Jay Migliori, Roger Pemberton, saxophones; and Jimmy Gannon, bass.
     One thing I learned from Woody was tempos. Any arrangement for an orchestra will fit right at just precisely the right groove. On one-night stands, sometimes he would get a head start on the next trip by leaving the bandstand a little before the last set, since at that time he drove his own car most of the time. Johnny Coppola would be the one delegated to kick off tempos for the remainder of the night. Oftentimes the tempos just weren't quite in the right groove for the particular arrangement. Nothing against Johnny; it just seemed like Woody always knew right where the right groove was for each tune. Years later, when I was conductor–pianist for Tony Bennett, I remembered what I'd learned about getting the groove right every time.

At the beginning of 1957, Woody made a decision to sign with Norman Granz's Verve record label. Granz booked him for a Hollywood recording session under the title *Woody Herman with Barney Kessel's Orchestra*. In addition to Woody and Kessel, the group included Harry "Sweets" Edison, Ben Webster, Jimmy Rowles, Joe Mondragon and Larry Bunker.
     Throughout the latter part of 1956, the "Fourth Herd" continued to experience a gradual turnover of personnel. By 1957, there were virtually new trumpet, saxophone, and rhythm sections. In the trumpet section, only Johnny Coppola was left from the band a year earlier. Victor Feldman had also departed.
     One of the new tenor players joining the band in January 1957, was Jay Migliore. During the Korean War Jay was with the 571st Air Force Band. Later he gigged opposite Erroll Garner, Oscar Peterson, Miles Davis, and Billie Holiday. He also played at Storyville with George Wein's quartet, Sonny Stitt, and Roy Eldridge.

JAY MIGLIORE: I hooked up with Woody Herman through Nat Pierce. He told me at the New York Musicians' Union Exchange Floor that Woody was looking for a saxophone player. I auditioned and got the job.

One of the most memorable times was when the band played in Chicago at the Blue Note. We had a two-week engagement there. I was very young to be traveling with the band, and I really loved it. That had to be the first part of 1957. It stands out mainly because we had done nothing but one-nighters all the time I was with the band and that was the longest time we ever played in one place.

In March, Woody recorded again for Verve in New York, under the title *Woody Herman Vocals with Orchestra Conducted by Marty Paich*. Woody's vocalizing was backed again by such excellent musicians as Charlie Shavers, Billy Bauer, Hal McKusick, Milt Hinton, and Jo Jones. Although Woody's voice was superb and the band was rich in personnel, somehow the album never quite made it.

Joining the Herd in March was trumpeter William R. (Bill) Berry. Before Woody, Bill had worked with the Herb Pomeroy Band in the Boston area in 1955–57.

BILL BERRY: My folks were musicians. So when I was about nine years old, they had lots of jazz records, among them "Who Dat Up Dere?," "Woodchopper's," and "Fur-Trapper's Ball," and I had the book of Tommy Linehan's piano solos. I learned all that stuff on the piano. I first heard the band live in 1943 in Cincinnati.

Then in March 1957, the first main band that I was a member of was Woody's! And Bill Harris, my favorite trombone player of all time, was on the band! I was just a green punk, and Woody really taught me how to live and survive on the road.

Bill Harris led the whole band from the trombone chair in that '57 band. Other than Woody, he was the bandleader. On the stand, we went his way, because you couldn't bend him. And he was right. I just adored him. He had it all, and Woody knew that. Woody always knew that about the great ones.

On July 2 and 3, 1957, the band went into the New York studios of Verve to record original material by Nat Pierce, Gene Roland, Tadd Dameron, Al Cohn, and Bill Holman. The result was a Verve album called *Woody Herman '58, Featuring the Preacher*. It was Woody's finest jazz offering during this period.

The title tune is Nat Pierce's treatment of Horace Silver's "The Preacher," a tune that suggests the atmosphere of a Southern Baptist revival meeting, thus the title. There is a loose line played by the saxes and a brass cadenza that introduces swinging solos from Jimmy Cook and Jay Migliore, tenors; Harris enjoys a typical rampage through the chart; and Woody gets his turn with lyrical clarinet, followed by some engaging brass punctuations and a brief return to the opening line as the saxes take it out.

"Why You" is a contribution from pianist Bunch, a catchy riff played by the saxes, the brass section loosely echoing with a counter-riff. It's an easy groove with solos by Bob Newman, Jay Migliore, tenors; Danny Styles, Bill Berry, trumpets; and a gradual building of the ensemble making way for the high clarinet of Woody a la Barney Bigard.

"Blue Satin" is a down-home blues score from Roland with a pungent solo from Harris, tenor contributions from Newman and Cook, some warm clarinet from Woody (his clarinet soloing was superb on these cuts), Berry (muted) and Styles on trumpets, and Harris again, before the controlled brass section nails down the score.

"Bar Fly Blues," according to Roland, its composer, "was written precisely for Woody, not the title, but for his particular type of slow blues alto playing." Woody's alto is prominent in the opening bars, with Bunch's piano, and muted trumpets provide a backdrop. Bunch sets the pace for solos by Johnny Coppola, Harris, and Migliori, and some nice ensemble work from the brass section before returning to the original blues mood.

Gene Roland's "Wailin' in the Woodshed" has a simple, persistent line played by the saxes and opening the door for Woody's clarinet, Bob Newman's tenor, and Bunch's piano before the brass ensemble builds to an exciting windup.

Roland's "Rollin'" has a Basie-ish piano intro, solos from Harris, Cook, and Woody (clarinet), and some tasty work from the polished brass ensemble before going out with a screamer finish.

"Stairway to the Blues," a Roland composition, is described in the liner notes as "a musical description of a flight of stairs in that there is an ascending character in the melody and an ascending crescendo." Solos are from Bunch; Willie Dennis, trombone; Migliori, tenor; Woody; and Bill Harris doing a talking trombone solo, demonstrating once again his unique imagination and wealth of ideas. The exquisite "brothers" saxophone voicing winds it up, assisted by the brass section.

Among these swinging performances in primarily medium tempos, the only ballad on the album is "Try to Forget," a soulful, brooding score by Al Cohn. Solos are from Coppola (playing a mournful trumpet), Berry, Woody (clarinet), Newman, and Coppola again.

"Downwind" is a typical chart of Bill Holman's reminiscent of the scores he did for the Stan Kenton band in the early to middle fifties. Solos are from Bunch, Migliori, and Berry.

Roland's "Ready, Get Set, Jump" opens with a strutting piano solo from Bunch, a muted trumpet from Berry, and an astounding, modern solo from trombonist Willie Dennis, who provided a unique contrast to Harris's bucketing style. More "brothers"-voiced saxes and some brass punctuations serve as an introduction to Cook, Woody, and Bunch.

Tadd Dameron wrote "Small Crevice," a feature for Harris. The saxes play the line and then it's all Bill, plowing his way through the score.

"Gene's Strut" opens with a repetitious figure played by the brass with the saxes responding, and then repeating in opposite manner. Solo contributions are from Bunch, Woody, Newman, and Harris.

Tenorist Jimmy Cook had joined the Army at 18 and worked with the "Jeep Show," starring Mickey Rooney. After his discharge, he joined Harry James, and in 1957, the Herman Herd.

JIMMY COOK: Being an admirer of Woody's music and of his choice of musicians, I really enjoyed the time I got to work with his band. He was a great bandleader and musician.

On the road to Savannah, Georgia, while John Bunch was driving, Jimmy Gannon and I were playing chess in the backseat with the lights on. All of a sudden, a car behind us started honking to pass us, and as we looked out the window, a guy was mooning us. We found out later that it was Bill Harris.

Another new addition to the saxophone section was the superb tenorist Joseph (Joe) Romano. After a military stint, Joe studied clarinet at Eastman School of Music, then gigged around New York and Las Vegas. Romano became another recurrent Herdsman, who would come and go for ten years. An inventive soloist, he was one of Woody's favorite tenor players.

JOE ROMANO: I was in Las Vegas and Jay Migliore and Jimmy Gannon were driving the band instrument truck. They stopped in Vegas and heard me play. I knew Jay, and he asked me if I would like to come on the Herd, somebody was leaving the band. I was very young, and there were a lot of experienced guys on the band at that time. But I felt very good about it. It had been a goal of mine.

In September 1957, the Herd traveled to the West Coast for an engagement at the Hollywood Palladium. Archie Martin and Dave Wells had replaced Willie Dennis and Bob Lamb in the trombone section. Joe Romano and Sam Firmiture had replaced tenor men Bob Newman and Jimmy Cook. There was also a new drummer, Karl Kiffe, joining the Herd after stints in the Jimmy Dorsey band.

KARL KIFFE: I played with Woody for seven months. One night I played something that Woody didn't like, and he said, "Come on Karl!" . . . And I said, "Hey, Woody! I've been on a lot of bands before yours!" And he said, "Yeah, but they were all the *wrong bands!*"

While the band was at the Palladium, Verve Records teamed Woody with Frank DeVol and His Orchestra to cut an album of superb vocals on a selection of love songs. The album was entitled *Love Is the Sweetest Thing— Sometimes*. (The title smacks of Woody, who may have suggested it.)

BILL BERRY: When I first came on the band in '57, we had a cluster of drummers. I kept pushing for Jake [Hanna], even though I was a newcomer on the band. "Oh, man, Woody, you should get Jake Hanna, he's a great drummer!" After six months or so, I finally had convinced somebody that Jake was good. We were playing someplace near Boston, and because of a misunderstanding with Dick Turchen, I got fired in the middle of the job. There were two sets of stairs, one on each end of the bandstand. As Jake was coming up to sit in with the band, I was going down the other side. So I got him on the band, but I never got to play with him on the band until years later.

Joining the Herd in early October was trombonist Roy J. Wiegand. Roy had played with Harry James and Stan Kenton. (In discographies, band reviews, and album liner notes, his name has been erroneously listed as "Wiggins.")

ROY WIEGAND: I joined Woody in the fall of 1957, replacing Bobby Lamb in the band. It was about three days after the Palladium gig. Karl [Kiffe] was the drummer when I joined the band for about two months, then Jake Hanna replaced Karl. I played a total of about four and a half months.

   I was with Bill Harris and a fellow named Archie Martin in the trombone section. Working with Bill was a tremendous and wonderful experience. He made me so aware of time, of what it is to play with time, to play independently and not depend on anybody else. As a person, I loved him like an uncle. When I knew him, he already had false teeth, but he had some great stories to tell about his time with "Jazz at the Phil" and Norman Granz.

   One time I remember a young trombone player came up to Bill on a break. Bill looked like a lawyer. I mean the bald head and meticulously dressed all the way, with the pin through the collar and the gold cuff links and everything. And this kid says, "Mr. Harris, when you play those jazz solos, do you read it?" And Bill turns the music upside down and said, "Certainly!" just like Huntz Hall or Leo Gorcey. The kid didn't know whether to believe him or not.

   He was like "The Honcho," especially timewise. He was the boss when he had a suggestion to make to anybody in the band. But if he had a suggestion to make to the trombones, he'd point to the part and he'd say: "Try some of this," instead of "Try it this way." That was one of his expressions.

   Carl Fontana replaced Bill for two weeks around Christmas, 1957. Bill Potts played piano for a few weeks during that period.

   My last job with the band was two weeks at the Peacock Lane in Hollywood. There's a live album that Wally Heider did of the band there. This was January 1958. Lenny Bruce was also there doing his comedy act.

The album referred to is an excellent representation of how this particular Herd sounded in person. West Coast pianist Pete Jolly was on the band

The Woody Herman Herd of early 1958. L to R: Kenny O'Brien (bass), Tom Montgomery (drums), Joe Romano, Jay Migliore, unidentified (behind Woody) (tenor
saxes), Roger Pemberton (baritone sax). Second row: Archie Martin, Bill Harris, Roger
DiLilo (hidden) (trombones). Back row: Willie Thomas, Danny Styles, Bobby Clark,
Hal Posey, Al Forte (hidden) (trumpets). (From the Woody Herman Collection)

replacing Bill Potts who had cut his hand severely on a broken window.
Jolly is heard playing fine piano on Horace Silver's "Opus de Funk."
By now, Gene Roland was a constant staff writer for the Herd. His
"Natchel Blues" displays Woody in a soulful mood and Harris in a typical
blustering and driving solo. "Woodchopper's Ball" is done in the mid-50s
mambo mode.

The Peacock Lane engagement was one of drummer Jake Hanna's first
stints with the Herman Herd. Jake was with the Herd briefly, only to return
in 1962, becoming the drummer most associated with the "Swingin' Herd"
of the early sixties. During the Peacock Lane engagement, pianist Oscar
Peterson dropped by and sat in with the Herd, creating a sensation.

ROY WIEGAND: At the end of the Peacock Lane engagement, five of us got
    let go when the Al Belletto Sextet came on the band. They had made their
    own recordings and all. He played baritone with Woody, and with his own
    sextet he played alto. He did a helluva job with Woody. Nobody realized
    that he was such a fine baritone player.

JAY MIGLIORE: When Al Belletto joined the band, it was right after we were
    at the Peacock Lane in Hollywood. At that time Roger Pemberton left
    and was replaced on baritone by Al. Al Belletto brought in Willie
    Thomas, trumpet, Jimmy Guinn on trombone, Fred Crane on piano,
    Kenny O'Brien on bass, and Tom Montgomery on drums.

At this juncture, apparently not satisfied with Verve, Woody signed to record a batch of titles on the Everest label. Everest was the first recording company to utilize the new 35-millimeter-wide recording tape, reproducing an exceptional sound.

Nat Pierce had been working around New York with a big band composed of heavyweight players, several of whom were Herman alumni. They included Ernie Royal, Bernie Glow, Nick Travis, Marky Markowitz (trumpets); Frank Rehak and Bob Brookmeyer (trombones); Al Cohn, Paul Quinichette, Sam Donahue (tenor saxes); Danny Bank (baritone sax); and Nat Pierce, Chubby Jackson, Don Lamond, and Billy Bauer (rhythm). Woody simply hired Nat's band to do the recording sessions at Everest's New York studios. Nat reworked many of the First Herd's old chestnuts: "Wildroot," "Northwest Passage," "Caldonia" and "The Good Earth." Bob Brookmeyer played with exquisite taste and precision on the old Harris showcase "Bijou."

Although the musicianship was unparalleled, some of the vintage titles suffer by comparison with the originals. However, the new material recorded in the Everest sessions is laudable. There's Al Cohn's "It's Coolin' Time," Johnny Mandel's "Sinbad the Sailor" (originally entitled "Sinbad The Wailer" and written for the Second Herd), Neal Hefti's "Black Orchid," and Ralph Burns' "Fire Island (The Happy Song)."

Joining the Herman trombone section at this time was James G. (Jimmy) Guinn.

JIMMY GUINN: My dad bought me a trombone at age 12. The following year, I stood outside the Silver Moon Club in Alexandria, Louisiana, and listened all night to Woody Herman's band. That night I promised myself that I would become good enough to play with Woody's band and sit next to Bill Harris. With nothing but high school band experience, I left home in 1943 to go on the road. Eighteen years later, I was sitting beside Bill Harris, we became great friends, and later I played with him in Miami.

After three months, I took over his chair as featured and lead trombonist with the band. Willie Dennis played second and Roger DiLilo played third.

The Al Belletto Sextet was an integral part of Woody's band at the time. We usually played about twenty minutes in the middle of the band's concerts.

Before the Herman Herd embarked on its historic State Department tour of South America, drummer James Lawrence (Jimmy) Campbell joined the band, replacing Tom Montgomery. Jimmy had been with the bands of Ralph Flanagan, Ralph Marterie, Sal Salvador/Don Elliott, Claude Thornhill, Tex Beneke, Maynard Ferguson, Johnny Smith, and Johnny Richards.

JIMMY CAMPBELL: Since I was 14, listening to Woody Herman 78s, I have been a fan of the band. When I joined the band in 1958, it was exactly what I wanted to do from those early days.

The Herd on tour in South America. Al Plank (piano), Major Holley (bass), Joe Romano, Jay Migliore, Marty Flax (tenor saxes), Al Belletto (baritone sax). Second row: Jimmy Campbell (drums), Willie Dennis (behind Woody), Jimmy Guinn, Roger DiLilo (trombones). Back row: Willie Thomas, Danny Stiles, Bobby Clark, Al Forte, Hal Posey (trumpets). (Courtesy The Hugh Turner Collection, Hollywood)

Woody always drove on the road in a Mercedes 190 SL, and I rode with him to help with the driving. After burning up two Mercedes, Woody got a bright red, fuel-injected Corvette convertible. One day on the Oklahoma Turnpike we pulled in for gas, and out comes a young guy about 18, and he just shakes his head in surprise. I guess that there weren't many of these cars around there yet. When he opened the hood, he just stared for a while, and said, "What are you two old guys doing with such a hot car as this?" Woody started laughing, and laughed all the way to the gig. You see, I was prematurely gray, and fifteen years his junior.

Just before the South American tour, Allan Plank took over the piano chair, replacing Fred Crane. Al had worked in New York City with Bud Freeman and Rex Stewart.

AL PLANK: I joined the Woody Herman Band in 1958, after playing a small group job with him. Abe Turchen drove me back to New York that night and told me about an upcoming tour to South America, and that Woody wanted me along.
      First we made an album on the Everest label and traveled the midwest and northeast, ending up at Birdland in New York City, then to South America for three months. The tour was a tremendous experience for me.

From July 31 to November 6, the "Fourth Herd" was on tour in South America, Central America and the Caribbean, under the auspices of the U.S. State Department.

JIMMY CAMPBELL: The trip to South America was the greatest, man! We were down there after Nixon got into trouble, if you remember. He had got stoned by the people. They threw rocks at him. So they sent the band down there to smooth things over. And we did; they loved us. Charlotte and Ingrid were on that trip. Every place we went, there were miles of people with cameramen, and all kinds of photographers.

JAY MIGLIORE: We were invited to ambassadors' houses; they had parties for us and the officials. Most of the cities were a couple days each, and there were nineteen different countries we went to. The only country we missed was Argentina, because of a labor dispute. We had one week off in Rio with pay because they wouldn't let us in Argentina.

WOODY: The State Department people were not terribly interested in having us on their shoulders as a responsibility. They were not helpful in finding places to play and audiences to play to. Some of them we had to invent ourselves, so that part was difficult. But it was very interesting. We enjoyed it. We saw a lot of hardship, because naturally, we were touring as sort of goodwill ambassadors.

JOE ROMANO: We were flying a very small airplane, and Woody had his wife with him. We were trying to take off the ground with the band, all the equipment, plus a bunch of passengers. It was a nervous situation, bouncing on the ground, and we couldn't get in the air, so Woody's wife freaked out, and finally Woody says, "*Get us off the plane!*" We had to charter a plane to get us where we were going. That South American tour was kind of a hairy trip.

After its return from the South American tour, the band went back into Everest's New York studios to record additional titles. One session was with Tito Puente and a group of his Latin percussionists to record an album entitled *Herman's Heat and Puente's Beat*, a presentation of some fine Latin jazz.

The discographies of Ernie Edwards, Jr., and Charles Garrod list this session as occurring in September. This is inaccurate, because Woody was on tour in South America until early November. It also seems unlikely that Woody would have used essentially the same Nat Pierce New York band as in the July 30 session, because Woody's South American tour band was still intact and also cut additional titles for Everest during this period. It is likely that both these sessions occurred in late November or early December and were recorded by the tour band.

Noteworthy are original and standard titles cut by the functioning Herd: Ralph Burns's lush arrangement of "Midnight Sun," Al Cohn's "Blue Station," and Gene Roland's "Lullaby of Birdland." A. K. Salim, who had been writing for Dizzy Gillespie's big band of that period, contributed "Pillar to Post" and "Balu," with its groovy and persistent line and solos from either Guinn or Willie Dennis (trombone), Al Plank, and Woody's buoyant clarinet and stirring bop figures from the brass ensemble.

When Woody disbanded the big band, he formed a sextet with Nat Adderley on trumpet and cornet; Charlie Byrd, guitar; Eddie Costa doubling on piano and vibes; Keeter Betts, bass; and Jimmy Campbell on drums. The sextet worked in the lounge of the Roundtable (a club on New York's East Side) from December until early February and recorded an album during the engagement.

Before 1958 was over Woody took a Nat Pierce-recruited studio group back into a New York recording studio and cut additional titles for the Everest label. Guitarist Charlie Byrd was now a featured soloist and is presented on a remake of Burns's *Summer Sequence*. Again, the performances do not measure up to the original 1946–47 Columbia versions. Byrd is also featured on four samba titles. The cuts from these sessions were packaged in an album entitled *Woody Herman with Guest Artists—Charlie Byrd and Tito Puente*.

In late December, leader-pianist Elliot Lawrence was brought in to conduct a recording session, a remake of *Ebony Concerto*, with essentially the same studio men but with the addition of First Herd veterans Don Lamond on drums and John La Porta on clarinet.

In early February, Woody reorganized the big Herd for a string of one-nighters beginning February 12 at Valdosta, Georgia. Second Herd veteran Don Lanphere returned, filling one of the tenor chairs. This is the Herd as it began a six-week tour of the South, Midwest, and East Coast: Danny Styles, Al Forte, Willie Thomas, John Estridge, Hal Posey (trumpets); Phil Acaro, Freddy Wood, Charlie Henry (trombones); Don Lanphere, Bo Boyd, Joe Romano (tenor saxes); Marty Flax (baritone sax); Bill Potts (piano); Jack Six (bass); and Jimmy Campbell (drums).

The short tour was not without the typical hazards of the road. At one point Lanphere and four other players had their horns and personal effects stolen, necessitating a quick trip to Elkhart, Indiana, from Chicago, to buy new horns. In Nebraska, Woody's car broke down on a 500-mile jump and he had to leave it in Omaha. The bus they were using had engine problems that caused carbon monoxide fumes to leak into the passenger compartment. On a dinner stop in a small town, Lanphere had to have stitches in both hands after he pushed on a frozen glass door that gave way.

At one point there was a dispute between the band and the bus leasing company. Woody and Abe learned that the bus company had a scheme to confiscate the band's music book for past-due payments. One step ahead of the bus company, Abe substituted a counterfeit book for the main book. However, the main book didn't arrive for the next job and the band was forced to play most of the book from memory.

In late March, Woody broke up the big band again and took a small contingent of musicians to England after a controlled exchange was worked out with the British Musicians' Union. (In the fifties, a complicated exchange system had been developed to cover appearances by American jazzmen in England.) In 1959 the British Chris Barber Band came to America, while Woody took seven musicians to England as a nucleus to build a full-strength big band using local British talent. The unit was billed as the "Anglo-American Herd."

From the United States, Woody brought trumpeters Nat Adderley and Reunald Jones (the great lead trumpeter from the Don Redman and Count Basie orchestras), Bill Harris, and a rhythm section of Vince Guaraldi (piano); Keeter Betts (bass); Jimmy Campbell (drums); and Charlie Byrd (guitar).

According to author Steve Voce, the British contingent was put together by Ronnie Ross who "chose the strongest possible sections, with the saxophones being particularly notable."[2] They were composed of trumpeters Les Condon, Kenny Wheeler, and Bert Courtley, trombonists Ken Wray and Eddie Harvey, and saxophonists Don Rendell, Art Ellefson, Johnny Scott (tenors), and Ronnie Ross (baritone).

When Woody returned to New York in early May, he reorganized the regular road band for a series of one-nighters commencing May 6 at the U.S. Armory at Vineland, New Jersey. Personnel for the reorganized Herd was Bill Chase, Larry Mosher, Paul Fontaine, Sam Scavone, Tony Phillatoni (trumpets); Freddy Wood, Joe Ciarvadone, Ray Winslow (trombones); Bo Boyd, Al Puccin, Don Lanphere (tenor saxes); Marv Holladay (baritone sax); Dolph Castellano (piano); Jack Six (bass); and Jimmy Campbell (drums).

DON LANPHERE: We played a "get out to register to vote" thing in Boston June 11, 1959, and Herb Pomeroy's band was on the same bill. They blew us right out of the park! Woody said after we got through, "You know, it might be a good idea if we got some of those kids on the band!" So I got Bill Chase, Paul Fontaine and Jimmy Mosher. I got them out of Berklee and they left Herb and came on the road with us. So that was the starting point for Bill Chase.

INGRID HERMAN REESE: I met my husband, Tom Littlefield, in college. I was going to the University of California in Riverside, and I met him through a mutual friend. We were married July 25, 1959. My dad wasn't there. My mother was there with the rest of the family. Just a very informal thing. They weren't very thrilled that I was getting married so young. I was 17. My dad was on the road and I didn't attempt to have a big family wedding because I knew that they objected to the whole thing. But I just wanted very much to get out on my own.

In mid-June, Woody broke up the big band again to work with a small group on the East Coast that consisted of Nat Adderley (trumpet/cornet); Zoot Sims (tenor sax); Eddie Costa (vibes); Nat Pierce (piano); Barry Galbraith (guitar); Milt Hinton (bass); and Don Lamond (drums).

In late July, Nat Pierce assembled a large band for Woody to record a session for the SESAC record label. The resulting album was entitled *The Fourth Herd*. The album was rich in personnel: Al Cohn, Zoot Sims, Bob Brookmeyer, Nat Pierce, Red Rodney, Ernie Royal, and Don Lamond. Nonetheless, it was a disappointment, with everyone seemingly having a simultaneous "off" day. The charts were done in excellent, straight-ahead Herman form, but the package lacked the usual Herman fire.

DON LANPHERE: We used Nat Pierce's big band to back Woody's small group. The arrangements were written so there was a lot of interplay between the band and the group. Dick Hafer took Zoot's place on some titles in the regular sax section.

JIMMY CAMPBELL: In 1959 we were working at the Metropole in New York in a room upstairs called the Top of the Pole. Once more we had a small group. Woody did this when it got hard to book the big band. At the same time Stan Kenton was at Birdland, looking for a drummer. Woody told me that he heard Stan had sent a couple of his guys up to hear us and check me out.

At this time, Woody had planned to take another long break and think about getting the big band back together again. One night after the gig he says, "Let's go down to Birdland to see Stan." When we entered the club, Woody blew his famous whistle loud enough for Stan to hear over the band. At the end of the set, Stan came over to the bar, and Woody introduced me to Stan, and told him why we were there.

Stan and I went backstage to talk business. When we came back to tell Woody that we made a deal, Woody told him, "You have to give him a bottle of Scotch a day, and also he doesn't ride in the bus, so you have to get a sports car," and that is how I joined the Kenton band.

During the summer of 1959, Woody fronted no less than five small groups, some with completely different personnel and instrumentation.

One group worked for a week in late summer at Pep's in Philadelphia. This group included Don Lanphere (tenor sax); Bob Brookmeyer (trombone); Kenny Fredrickson (piano); Major Holley (bass), who had been with Woody's big band on the South American tour; Dick Scott (drums); and Woody.

Another group Woody took to Canada included Paul Quinichette (tenor sax); Peck Morrison (bass); Al Plank (piano); and Ben Riley (drums).

In late September, Woody took a group of five into a club in Washington, D.C.—Howard McGhee (trumpet); Don Lanphere (tenor sax); Al Plank (piano); Major Holley (bass); and Ben Riley (drums).

Just before Woody reorganized a big Herd for a scheduled road tour of the South and Midwest, he went into the fledgling Monterey Jazz Festival in California with an explosive all-star big band billed as "Woody Herman's Big New Herd." An album was recorded that captured some exciting and spontaneous big-band jazz. Personnel was a collection of former Herman stars and top West Coast studio men. Among them were tenor saxophonists Zoot Sims, Bill Perkins, and Richie Kamuca, baritone saxophonist Med Flory, Don Lanphere doubling on alto and tenor, trumpeter Conte Candoli, and trombonist Urbie Green. Propelling the band was drummer Mel Lewis. The saxophonists performed compelling solos on Giuffre's classic composition, "Four Brothers."

Gene Roland's "Like Some Blues Man, Like," is a slow blues that Woody humorously counts off in Spanish, with Victor Feldman's funky vibe solo setting the mood for the rest of the performance. You can hear the annoying sound of a private plane circling overhead as Woody says, "He'll be gone in a minute." He wasn't. Additional solos are heard from Conte Candoli, trumpet; Bill Perkins, tenor; Urbie Green, trombone; and Charlie Byrd, guitar. The conclusion involves an exciting ensemble buildup with the powerhouse trumpet of Al Porcino on top.

"Skylark" was a Ralph Burns Third Herd vehicle for Urbie Green. It was dusted off and used again to showcase Urbie's lyrical ballad style.

Woody changed the title of "Apple Honey" for the festive occasion to "Monterey Apple Tree." Roland's "Skoobeedoobee" and "The Magpie," by Al Cohn, round out the album.

DON LANPHERE: Just a couple of us from the regular band came out for the Monterey Jazz Festival. The band was put together in California. Bill Chase and his wife, Nan, and my wife, Midge, and I drove cross-country for the concert. The other two that came out from the East Coast were Urbie Green and Zoot. They flew out.

Then the regular band met down in Mississippi. Bill, Nan, Midge and I, after we finished playing up in Monterey, got in the car and headed out, and drove nonstop all the way to the Deep South. The band met and re-formed there.

When the new Herd reorganized for its first date in Jackson, Mississippi, it had the following lineup: Bill Chase, Jerry Tyree, Paul Fontaine, Don Rader, John

Bennett (trumpets); Bill Hannah, Jimmy Guinn, Nat Lovelace (trombones); Bo Boyd, Jimmy Mosher, Don Lanphere (tenor saxes); Larry McKenna (baritone sax); Jim Amadeo (piano); Alex Cirin (bass); and Joe Cocuzzo (drums).

Bill Chase was a key figure in the band's resurgence to jazz prominence in the sixties. His "iron" lip gave him the capacity to be an exceptional lead trumpeter. He possessed a stunning facility for high-note work and a rich ballad style.

Bill learned at an early age to play a trumpet that his dad owned. Later, while attending Berklee School of Music, he met Herb Pomeroy, who was on the faculty. Herb was directing Berklee's top jazz ensemble and is also an excellent trumpeter in his own right. Bill joined Maynard Ferguson's band in 1955, but was back with Pomeroy when Woody first heard him in June 1959. When Woody temporarily broke up the big band in the summer of that year, Bill went with Stan Kenton briefly, returning when the Big Herd was reorganized in October.

Also joining the band was trumpeter John Hughes Bennett, Jr. Before joining the Herd, John played in various Latin and jazz bands and spent a year on the road with Johnny Long's Orchestra. With Woody, John played some split lead with Bill Chase and also served the band for a time as road manager.

JOHN BENNETT: I had my first personal contact with Woody in late fall 1959, when I, along with about fifty others, auditioned for the band in New York. His longtime friend and confidante, Nat Pierce, helped with auditions and final selection of players.

Finally, a full band was hired and we went on the road for a six-week tour. The pay was atrocious, but for many musicians this was a small sacrifice to be on this band. Through the years, jazz bands such as Woody's, Maynard Ferguson, Count Basie, and Duke Ellington were notorious for paying low wages while dance orchestras, such as the Dorseys and Glenn Miller, for example, paid very well. There's an old musicians' saying that is appropriate: "You have to save up for these kinds of gigs!"

Woody was a great organizer. He could very quickly get the most from musicians who had never played together before and whip the band into shape. He recognized talent or the potential for it, and his bands always reflected that awareness.

But despite all this, sometimes that spark of chemistry that makes a great band is not there. Woody realized this very quickly also. He would carefully assess the band and work with it over the first two weeks to determine just how good the band was. When the right chemistry was there he would extend the tour; if not, he would cut it short.

My first tour lasted only six weeks. Then some key players were added and the band really started swinging.

Trumpeter Donald Arthur (Don) Rader had studied at the U.S. Navy School of Music and Sam Houston State University. The Herman Band was his professional debut.

DON RADER: I joined the band in October 1959, in Jackson, Mississippi. I had been attending college in Huntsville, Texas. A tenor player friend of mine, Bo Boyd, who was also attending the college, and had been on a previous trip with Woody, had got called back for a seven-week trip with a new band that Nat Pierce had just formed for Woody in New York.

I had wanted to play with Woody's band ever since I first had heard it as a young kid. I mentioned to Bo that if they needed another trumpet player I would love to be that person. Three days later I got a call from New York from Abe Turchen, Woody's then manager, asking me to join the band. I quit school that same day, and a week later I was on the band.

I joined for $125 a week, out of which I had to pay my hotels and food. Woody just provided the transportation, which at that time, and for most of the time that I was on the band, was in cars or station wagons. To say that Woody was operating on a shoestring would be an understatement. However, I was the happiest cat in the world to just be there among all of those great musicians and playing those great charts every night.

Unfortunately, we didn't play many jazz gigs with that band, but mostly country clubs, officers' clubs, and small ballrooms. On most of these gigs, Woody had to keep the band under wraps because we were all young and wanted to blow. For the most part, the audience wanted background music and music for dancing. The ballrooms were the most fun because they were open to the public and the people that came were coming to hear and dance to Woody's band. At the country clubs, officers' clubs, Elks, et cetera, it didn't matter who was on the stand. During these times Woody would have the trumpet section playing down into the music stand, or using bucket mutes, to muffle the sound. Bill Chase, who was playing a Dizzy Gillespie-style horn at the time, had to practically bend over double to get the bell of his horn into the stand because he was over six feet tall. I will say that we always played the same charts on all of our gigs, whether it be a jazz concert or a country club. The only difference was the way Woody would pace each set—which tunes, in which order— and the volume.

Woody could read a crowd better than anyone that I've ever seen. He knew how to call tunes in an order to please most. We did play some college jazz concerts on this trip and those were the times when the band sounded the greatest! Almost every player in that band was a jazz musician in the sense that, with about three exceptions, everyone in the band was a soloist. Bill Chase hadn't begun to play any jazz solos yet but he did have a feature number, "I Can't Get Started." There were three other soloists in the trumpet section, Paul Fontaine, Jerry Tyree, and me. Jimmy Guinn played all of the trombone solos . . . beautifully, and all of the saxophone players got to play, except for Jimmy Mosher, because there weren't many baritone solos written. But everyone was anxious to play at all times.

There were a lot of times when we would "hit and run" a gig. That is, we would leave right after a gig and drive that night to the next town where we were working so that we could check into a hotel when the new day started for that hotel, usually 9 or 10 A.M. We would sleep all day, go to the gig that night and then return to the hotel and sleep all that night, thereby getting two "sleeps" for the price of one. Sometimes we did this two or three times a week. It was one of the few ways that we had of stretching our salary. On occasion, we would hit and run and get to the new town too early so we would have to hang around until the day sheet started. In some of those towns there were after-hours clubs, and they usually had a band, or at least a rhythm section, so a lot of us would sit in and play. It was in these places that I really got to hear how the guys played. There weren't very many stretch-out solos in Woody's book in those days, because of the nature of the gigs we were playing.

On October 29, 1959, Don Lanphere wrote to his wife, Midge:

> We're having rhythm section problems. The rest of the band has shaped up well, but it "ain't swinging." Alex Cirin put in his notice last night, because he's been getting "the ray" from all quarters of the band . . . and really what we need is an all new rhythm section. . . .

The road tour ended in December. The band broke up for a Christmas vacation, not re-forming until January in New York City.

Although 1959 was erratic in one sense, with Woody finding it difficult to book the big band consistently and forced to work with various small groups, the year ended with his fronting another big Herd. Perhaps mediocre when compared with some of his other great bands, this outfit would develop into the eminent band of the early 1960s that became known to a whole new generation of fans, disc jockeys, and the media. With the Swingin' Herd, Woody's career experienced a significant comeback as he fronted a unit of enthusiastic, straight-ahead musicians.

7.

The Swingin' Herd—
A Renaissance
1960-1967

Drummer Jimmy Campbell had gone with Stan Kenton's band the previous summer, but found himself available in time to join Woody's new outfit.

JIMMY CAMPBELL: Early in 1960 I was in Los Angeles with Stan, and he was not working too much. I was getting a little hungry, so I called the old man and said "HELP!" Woody said not to worry, Nat Pierce was putting a band together back in New York, and we should be getting plane tickets soon. We went back and had a good swinging band for another year and a half.

DON RADER: When this band started out in February 1960, the average salary was $140 to $150 per week. The lead trumpet player and the drummer got a little more. Nobody knew what anyone else was making for sure. We still paid our own room and board.

We were playing the same kinds of gigs that we had on the last trip but this time we played a lot more colleges. We also played some jazz clubs and a lot of ballrooms.

The band had its ups and downs. It just depended on who was there. Woody never had a bad band for more than two or three weeks at a time while I was there. He had a way of making any band shape up after a couple of weeks. When he thought that he should replace someone, he'd go to the section leader and tell him, "Get somebody!"

On February 9, 1960, the Hollywood Walk of Fame was initiated. The bronze stars of the Walk of Fame line both sides of Hollywood Boulevard, from

235

Gower to Sycamore Streets, and both sides of Vine Street, from Yucca to Sunset. Inside each star the name of an artist is engraved along with an emblem identifying the category of the award. Woody's star in recognition of his achievements in the recording industry was installed at the southwest corner of Hollywood and Highland Boulevards on February 9, 1960.

On March 9, 1960, Ingrid presented Woody and Charlotte with their first grandchild, Tom Littlefield, Jr.

JOHN BENNETT: The personnel of a band changes constantly on road tours as guys leave for one reason or another. What was unusual about this band was that the players were excited about it and wanted to stay. I became road manager, along with being split lead trumpet player, so I can recall the personnel very well. The trumpets were Bill Chase; John Bennett, split lead and second; Don Rader, Bill Berry, Rolf Ericson. Trombones: Jimmy Guinn; Bob Jenkins; Kent McGarity, bass trombone. Saxes: Gordon Brisker, lead tenor; Bo Boyd, Jimmy Derba, Jimmy Mosher. Rhythm: Marty Harris [piano], Alex Cirin [bass], Jimmy Campbell [drums].

The Ol' Chopper recognized mature talent, naturally, but he also encouraged budding jazz players. If you played well, he would encourage you by giving you more opportunity to play. Often when an arrangement was being played, certain sections of it were "opened up" and while the rest of the band except for the rhythm section laid out, jazz choruses were inserted. If, for instance, a trumpet player would go to the microphone and was really cooking, Woody would say, "Take another chorus," and if he kept on cooking, "Take another, and another!" If you were in a creative slump and nothing was going right for you, he'd have you sit down after one or two choruses.

Woody was such a good musician that he sometimes was very demanding of his players. We often rehearsed the horn sections without the rhythm section, a method used to good effect by some of the older-school bandleaders. By playing without the rhythm, you learned to listen more to the others, phrase better, and create good time within the horn sections.

The Chopper knew that I wasn't a jazz player and that I couldn't get up enough nerve to go down front. Yet on an album that we did, Woody insisted that I come down and do a short jazz solo with him. I think he wanted to encourage me and let me be heard on the album. The album was recorded on Crown Records in Chicago and is called *The Swingin' New Herman Herd*. There was basically the same personnel, with the addition of Don Lanphere as lead tenor and featured soloist.

Joining the band April 15, 1960, was tenor saxophonist Gordon Ira Brisker. He had studied at Cincinnati Conservatory of Music and Berklee School of Music.

GORDON BRISKER: I had mixed feelings about Woody. I respected him for what he had accomplished, but by the time I joined the band, he mistrusted jazz players. I heard that the Four Brothers band really pushed him away from the mike, and generally belittled him. One of his sayings was, "I'm not going to make any more stars."

DON RADER: Our uniform was a blue blazer and gray slacks. Later, it was changed to brown plaid jacket and black slacks. The only time that I can remember not wearing the full uniform on a gig was once in Kingsville, Texas, in July, when it was so hot that even Woody had to take his jacket off. I also remember that some guy shot his wife in the parking lot of that gig.

In the winter, we got snowed out of a lot of gigs. My VW was great in the snow, so more than once I was the only one to show up at a gig. Once, in Nebraska, I slid off the road, and an Army truck came by. The only thing the soldier had to pull me out of the ditch with was his belt, and it worked. That time, only Woody and I showed up.

Another time, we were traveling in caravan in a snowstorm in Kansas, on a hit and run. We were the lead car and we came to a railroad crossing with the train stopped. After a while, my wife checked the map to see if there was an alternate route because the train wasn't moving. We pulled a U turn, with the other four cars following, and drove for hours and ended up in a graveyard, Lord knows where. It broke everyone up, so we had a small party, then got out of there.

The 1960 band was almost the same as the 1959 band, except that Jimmy Campbell came in on drums off Stan Kenton's band. Jerry Lamy replaced Terry Tyree in the trumpet section. We had lots of piano players before the band broke up in 1961, some of whom were Tony Prentiss, Marty Harris, and John Weed. We also had a lot of tenor players: Gordon Brisker, Don Lanphere, Bo Boyd, Jimmy Derba, Gus Maas, Mickey Folus, Andy Pino, Lou Ornstien, Dave Fig, and Larry Covelli.

When Jimmy Mosher left the band in the summer of 1960, Pepper Adams came in for six months or so. Other guys that passed through the band at this time were Rolf Ericson, Willie Dennis [trombones], Burt Collins, Ziggy Harrell, Hal Espinosa, Bill Berry [trumpets]. The turnover was very high, probably because the bread was low. I can't remember all of the people that passed through during this period because some of them only lasted a week, or a day, and, in one case, one set! We were in Toronto at the Coq D'or, and we were getting a new tenor player from New York. He was so horrible that Woody wouldn't let him back on the stand for the second set.

One time in El Paso, we picked up a bass player who was always so stoned, he just stood there holding the bass. He didn't last the set. Nothing fazed Woody.

JOHN BENNETT: I don't know if Woody ever arranged music for the band, but he had an unerring sense of the formulas that make good arrangements. When new charts would come to us, he'd change titles, switch things around and change parts, usually for the better. He was also a good blues-style singer. We sometimes played some of the old First Herd charts written for five saxes and Woody would play lead alto beautifully.

Woody constantly changed arrangements to make them interesting and better musically, to help relieve the boredom of the same old charts. Nat Pierce came in with his tenth, at least, new, updated arrangement of "Woodchopper's Ball," Woody's big hit of 1939. The chart was modern and fun to play. We had no sooner finished the last note when a customer came up and asked, "When are you going to play 'Woodchopper's Ball?'" Woody got so frustrated and mad, he turned to me and said, "John, go out tomorrow and buy the stock arrangement and we'll play that from now on!"

We played the arrangement exactly as recorded for several months until Woody couldn't stand it anymore and he would say, "Let's do this here and that there," until soon it was a modern chart again.

Joining the Herd in September 1960 was trumpeter Gerald E. (Jerry) Lamy. Jerry had worked with territory bands around New Hampshire and Herb Pomeroy's band in Boston. He left the Boston Conservatory of Music to go with Woody.

JERRY LAMY: I was Woody's valet and band boy for awhile. I used to take care of Woody's clothes and he screamed at me once for getting his tuxedo cleaned in some small town. He told me, "Don't ever get my tux cleaned unless it's in New York, Chicago, or LA, because it never comes out right!" They pressed the sleeves on his tux, instead of rolling them so they wouldn't have a crease in them. He finally apologized to me in front of everybody. He'd fly off once in a while, but he was great.

DON RADER: My wife, after a few months, went home to her folks in Galveston and Jerry Lamy and I drove the equipment wagon and did the set-up gig. During this time, the most that we stayed anywhere was two or three days. The band did 90 percent one-nighters, so we had to drive, set up, work the gig, tear down, and sometimes drive again, almost every day.

JOHN BENNETT: The Chopper loved sports cars. He always had Corvettes, Porsches, or even a Mercedes 300 SL classic gull wing on the road. After every gig, it was like the Le Mans road race to the next town. At that time, we traveled in cars, and we did easily 100,000 miles a year. We didn't have a bus and sometimes it was brutal driving 400 miles after playing a hard concert.

Woody was a devoted family man, although he didn't spend too much time at home. . . . After spending maybe a month there at the end of a road trip, he would get antsy again, and call his manager to put a band together.

The Chopper could be gruff and brusque, although he appreciated humor and some clowning around. When the time came, you had to play well.

We were to play New Year's Eve at the Sunnybrook Ballroom in Pottstown, Pennsylvania. As we were traveling there, a god-awful blizzard struck about one hour before dance time. The whole band arrived late, and I was driving a station wagon with all the music and a lot of the instruments. When we got there one hour late, 3,000 people were chanting and stomping the floor, while Woody, who always carried his own clarinet, played. The drummer was playing on a pie pan with some drumsticks that he found in the back room and one trumpet player, who had somehow made it on time, was playing a few choruses.

John F. Kennedy's Inaugural Ball was the highlight of my career. We played at the Statler Hilton to a jam-packed mass of humanity. There were several sections of the Inaugural Ball spread around the city to accommodate all the party-goers. There were two top-name big bands at every ball who alternated playing for the people. We alternated with Nelson Riddle's fine recording orchestra.

On the evening of the ball, there was one of the worst snowstorms in history in Washington, D.C. We had to walk to the hotel, carrying instruments, in knee-deep snow. Elegant ladies and men in evening dress were slogging and slushing in the snow with us . . . but they had a great time!

DON RADER:　As I recall, we were in Charlie's Tavern in New York City, it must have been 1960, and I think the band had a night off. We were all in there just drinkin' and Woody got kind of "out of it," and walked out of this bar, which was a long hall with no tables. He walked straight out, and parked out front was a NYC police car and Woody got in the back seat. The cop turned around and said, "What do *you* want?" and Woody said, "Just drive, I'll tell you where to go!"

In May 1961 Woody opened with a sextet at the Waldorf-Astoria Hotel in New York City. The faithful Nat Pierce had returned to the piano bench.

NAT PIERCE:　Woody cut down to a sextet, and we had a night club act with Steve Condos dancing. We had a lady named Norma Douglas who sang. I played piano, and we had Jimmy Campbell on drums, Chuck Andrus on bass, Gordon Brisker on tenor, and Bill Chase on trumpet. We played the Waldorf-Astoria for a month. We added Willie Dennis for the dance set, when Woody would go upstairs. He didn't care about that part of it. We had a maitre d' who went to a European hotel school, you know . . . "You vil play a valse!" He jumped up on the bandstand and said, "Stop!" We were playin' like "Ain't Misbehavin'" you know, a basic tune for the people to dance to. The dance floor was packed. But he ain't used to that, he's used to Freddy Martin-type music.

He jumps up on the bandstand, and he's pounding on my shoulder. . . . "Ve don't play dot music here!" I said, "Well, look, all the tables are empty and everybody's dancing!"

We played a place called Freedomland with the small group. It was up in the Bronx, a poor man's Disneyland. It was the same group that we had at the Waldorf-Astoria. The little act still had Steve Condos, the dancer. Steve and his brother, Nick, had a dance act in the forties and had worked with Woody many times in theaters.

The only music we had at the time was for this small group. Then we added another trumpet, and then a couple more saxes, and now we're getting back into the big-band business without knowing it. They tried to sell us to Las Vegas with a night club thing, but we had no takers. So Woody says, "I guess there's only one way to go." We were all living in New York at the time, so we took a job in North Carolina for a night, then two nights a week in West Virginia, like a Friday and a Saturday. Then we would come back and spend the rest of the week at home, with no money, sitting there.

So Woody says, "Well, all these guys in New York are available to us, so put a band together, and I'll see if I can get us a trip down South or whatever." So I called this guy and that guy. Immediately, I was the road manager. It was hard work, but Woody says, "You can handle it!"

We got Gus Johnson [the drummer], and we got Joe Newman, Emmett Berry, and Clark Terry. Charlie Mariano was with us for awhile. Then we stayed around New York while Woody flew to Hollywood to do the "Tonight" show.

On September 11, 1961, Ingrid presented her husband, Tom, and Woody and Charlotte, with Alexandra, her daughter.

WOODY: I was an only child. Charlotte was an only child, and Ingrid, my daughter, is an only child, but she had two, and so she went beyond our depth.

The last half of 1961 had been unproductive musically for Woody. Gone were the days when big bands were a major entertainment attraction. Big bands were no longer booked into theaters, once a major showcase for them. Gone also were the live network radio remotes, except for an occasional New Year's Eve broadcast. Under these conditions, suddenly Woody was back in New York with a great snarling band.

The Big Herd was booked into the Metropole in New York, January 1 to 18. The band was forced to perform standing up because the "bandstand" was little more than a shelf running the length of the wall behind the bar. The orchestra would perform, strung out in a single line abreast, with the brass lined up on Woody's left and the saxes and rhythm to his right. It was next to impossible for the different sections to hear one another. Nevertheless, the band produced superb music. It is said that during its many engagements at the Metropole, the orchestra picked up the habit of playing standing.

During the Metropole engagement, Woody recorded his first album on the Phillips label. It was an album of clarinet solos with just the rhythm section of Nat Pierce, piano, Chuck Andrus, bass, and Gus Johnson, drums. The album was designed as a tribute to the great clarinetists: Artie Shaw, Benny Goodman, Pee Wee Russell, and Barney Bigard. One of the original titles recorded was "Alexandra," named after Woody's granddaughter.

In April 1962, during a lull in the Herd's bookings, Woody took a temporary job conducting the NBC Studio Orchestra on the "Tonight" show.

JIMMY ROWLES: When Jack Paar quit the "Tonight" show, they brought the show to NBC out on the Coast. They used the staff orchestra, and I was with the orchestra. They were auditioning a replacement for Jack Paar. They tried out Robert Cummings, Joey Bishop, and several guys. There were four weeks where they used the band and they got Woody to front the band. He wouldn't wear the earphones and listen to the booth. He made me wear the earphones, and I had to give him all the cues.

NAT PIERCE: Gus Johnson left the band to go with Ella Fitzgerald, so we needed a drummer. Buddy Rich went with Harry James and Jake [Hanna] called me and said, "I need a job!" Eventually we made one road trip, and one of the tenor players left in Texas and that's when we picked up Sal Nistico.

Drummer John E. (Jake) Hanna was with Woody briefly in 1957–58 and 1960 and worked with Maynard Ferguson, the Marian McPartland Trio, and Harry James before rejoining the Herd.

JAKE HANNA: It was one of the better bands to play with for the simple reason that Woody tried to incorporate into it the best of his previous bands.

We had some new stuff come in by Nat Pierce and Bill Chase. Then we had the old stuff by Neal Hefti. We went all the way back to the thirties . . . "Woodchopper's Ball." Then stuff from 1945, some of the best stuff ever written. "The Good Earth," "Sidewalks of Cuba." And we went up to the 1947–49 band, with the Four Brothers. Woody put it together as strictly a Four Brothers sound, eliminated the alto and had everything rewritten by Nat for three tenors and a baritone.

That was my favorite band to play with, because of all the good arrangements. It was very easy to play with that band. Charlie Andrus [bass] helped an awful lot, and Bill Chase laying that lead down and that was it! We got Sal Nistico down in Dallas, and that enabled Woody to play any tempo that he wanted to play!

The author asked Jake how his humorous skit of impersonations behind the drums originated.

JAKE HANNA: A guy by the name of Jack Ackerman, a tap dancer with the band, put that together for us. It was the night that Sal Nistico joined the band in Dallas. It was an afternoon job at Lou Ann's.

Woody was out in front arguing with some lady customer, and I had to play a drum solo and I was playing real quiet. I was playing the brushes, and I got down real quiet and the customers were so dumb they didn't get it [the near-silence]. . . . So I got indignant, and I started "swishing" the brushes, and the people started laughing, the band started laughing, and Woody and Jack Ackerman started watching it. Then I started playing like an "oaf," and then I started playing serious again and we took it out. And Woody said, "We've got to find a way to use that!" We tried it a couple of times and got a few laughs. So Jack said, "Look, as long as you're going to do that, let me put it together for you." He's worked with Bob Hope and Bing Crosby, and he knows how these things work. "Man," he says, "you start out like a dummy, take the dumb part as a high school drummer." Then he had me do a "Liberace." Woody would be announcing all this, and every now and then, he'd throw in something new to break the band up, because if the band wasn't laughing, the people weren't laughing.

Sal Nistico was an extremely hard-driving tenorist. His early influences were Illinois Jacquet, Coleman Hawkins, Ben Webster, Arnett Cobb, and Count Basie.

SAL NISTICO: I had already done some records before I went on Woody's band, you dig? I was with the Mangione Brothers in '59 and into '62. So I did three records with them, and I did one with Nat Adderley, Sam Jones, Barry Harris, and Walter Perkins, before I even went on Woody's band. The draft finally broke up the group, but I was 1-Y, because of my knees and my high blood pressure.

Larry Covelli, a tenor player from Buffalo, gave me a call one night and said, "Do you want to come out on the road for a couple of weeks of one-nighters, capped by a couple of weeks at the Metropole?" I said, "With Woody?" He says, "Yeah." I said, "Sure, where are you?" He says,

"I'm in Houston. You can join us in Dallas!" I said, "What happened?" He says, "Bo Boyd is gettin' off the band in Houston, his hometown."

I made it down to Houston, met the band, got on the bus, met the bus driver. He was a German cat from Berlin. He studied eight years in mechanical engineering, and if you gave him the raw materials, and the proper tools, he could probably MAKE a bus! It turned out that he needed that knowledge, because he was so reckless.

I remember on my first night, we were playing the gig, and the bus driver was dancing and drinking. I was having trouble, I was scuffling with the book. It was a huge book, with something like 400 pieces of music. I'd never played with a big band before and I was not blending at all. I didn't even talk to Woody. He just looked at me and said hello, and I said hello, and the night was a blur actually, because I couldn't read that well.

It was a "hit and run," you know, where you drive all day, play the gig, and then drive all night to the next town. The next town was Shreveport. We got back on the bus, and everybody kind of crapped out and started to sleep. This bus driver cat had been dancing and drinking all night. I hadn't learned how to sleep on a bus yet, and it was my first night. We were doing about 80 or something like that, and we hit a patch of ice and actually made a complete 360-degree turn and kept going. This cat was a tremendous driver. One time he was close to going over a cliff and Larry said, "If he had gone off the cliff, he would have been driving all the way." He had incredible technique. He needed it.

I thought everybody was asleep, but they were drinking. There were many bottles that came out of many cases, and the guys were just sitting there. Then, we came to a bridge. It was so narrow that it had a traffic light on one end. You were supposed to stop, because if another bus or large vehicle would be approaching the other way, there was no room to pass.

When we came to the bridge, the driver ignored the red light saying, "We got it dicked" (his favorite saying), which, thank God, was not a "famous last words" statement. We "threaded the needle" between the oncoming bus and the railing. We actually shot over this gorge, due to the air captured between the two buses. I tell you, man, everybody was in a crash position. Many of us thought we'd bought the farm! Like, we were up all night after that experience.

Bus drivers were very odd personalities. There was one cat whom Nat called "The Embalmer." He always dressed in full uniform, with white gloves. He was full of "speed." Another cat was "Marlon Brando," straight out of *The Wild One*. He was a hot dog who would've got us all killed if Nat hadn't busted him in the mouth. This cat jumped into the well to retrieve the wastebasket, while keeping one hand on the wheel and no feet on the pedals, doing 75 mph through North Carolina's back roads.

I think many people overlook the danger factor of riding constantly on the bus for years with tired, sometimes juiced drivers doing inhuman distances. There have been some famous wrecks.

I made it through the two weeks. Woody was going to do the Metropole, and then form his octet in May. This was March 1962, and the band was going to fold after the Metropole.

One night on the road, Woody pointed at me on "Caldonia," and I stood up and just played real fast, and he was kind of gassed, and it kept getting faster, and by the time we got to the Metropole, I was doing a twenty-minute up-tempo solo on every set. Like it would be "Northwest Passage," "Apple Honey," and "Caldonia."

Abe Turchen, the manager, came in and heard the band, saw the response and everything. We got a lot of good reviews and we took a couple of weeks off. Woody was going to let us know if he was going to keep the band going, instead of going with the octet to Vegas. Then we got the call to go back.

I wasn't sure even if I wanted to go back. I really wanted to stay in a small group because I'm a soloist. I thought it might be a trap. A lot of people told me it was. But I went back on, and they told me, "Build your name up and then leave." I ended up staying too long. I spent years and years and years with Woody, then I went with Basie. I always ended up going back because it was very hard to find work.

The first year was incredible. I remember arriving in Chicago in the middle of the summer. We worked some club on the North Side, and on "The Good Earth" the band just came together, and that's the first time Woody "growled" and grabbed the reins. The band just raised up off the floor! It was the best night the band ever had. Woody didn't expect to have another hot band. But that night, it was a hair-raising experience. The band played as one. Loose, and on all parts of the beat together.

I thought we should go on from there. A lot of the guys were satisfied with it, but you can't stay in one place. You have to keep moving, and we couldn't do it because Woody was asking too much. The up-tempos were too fast, so the rhythm section started playing safe. Once you start playing safe, you can't get back in that drawer.

But the band that night in Chicago was the peak, and I thought if Woody had used a little influence on Abe, things might have been different. There was a lot of reality involved. Woody was in debt, and it was his fiftieth year, and he just wanted to keep it going. We were really enjoying it, because he was calling tunes for us and all that, but after awhile, it ended up being the same twenty tunes every night.

NAT PIERCE: We got Phil Wilson from NORAD [North American Air Defense Command] in Colorado Springs. We also got Paul Fontaine from there.

Woody made all of these guys. Just by his reputation, people know these guys! If you think back over the history of big bands, more stars came out of Woody's bands than any other band. You never hear of any stars coming out of Harry James' Band, as an example. When they went in there, they were already stars.

The sixties band was one of the best bands ever. Woody wouldn't bother us. He only bothered you when he felt he could add something to it. We used to rehearse on our own. We would come to the job the next night and say, "Hey, Woody, we've got something we want to play for you." And we would play it and Woody would say, "Not bad, but I think you should change this over here." It was trial and error. What we were trying to do was make a combination of ALL Woody's bands, including the First Herd, the Second Herd, and the fifties band . . . with power! We rewrote a lot of the older charts like "Northwest Passage," "The Good Earth" and that kind of thing. Then we added some new things. Everybody was involved.

In May the inventive trombonist Phillips Elder (Phil) Wilson, Jr., joined the Herd. He had played with Herb Pomeroy, the Jimmy Dorsey Orchestra, and the Al Belletto Sextet and had led his own band.

PHIL WILSON: The whole experience was memorable from my point of view. I was a product of a prep school upbringing in New England. For me to be on Woody Herman's band for three-and-a-half years was like a college education for me.

There were incredibly funny incidents that would happen. One would be the contrast of playing at a ball for Governor Faubus of Arkansas, and the next night we were playing in New York, in Harlem. We played the same music for both, only for the Governor of Arkansas, we would play it in two-four until 10:30, when everybody got stoned, then it went to four-four. In Harlem, you just started right out in four-four.

WOODY: I was very proud of that sixties band. It had something of everything that had gone on before. I think that we upset the apple cart once again by having something more modern and different, and yet very swinging.

I've had the good fortune very often in my long life of being able to put the right people together. And for the sixties, I don't think there was anything more swinging than that was. . . . When you had people in your band like Bill Chase and Sal Nistico, you didn't have too much trouble building excitement. Sal had some kind of chops! He was one of the heaviest, strongest, most energetic, and greatest players I've ever worked with.

INGRID HERMAN REESE: My first marriage was brief, it only lasted about three years. I moved to San Francisco and became a bluegrass fiddle player. My dad had given me a great appreciation of music and musicians, which has been a joy to me all my life.

In 1963 I married a man named Robert Fawler with whom I had worked for years in a band. It was the first band to play bluegrass in San Francisco. It was called the Styx River Ferry Band. I made my living that way at least fifteen years. My grandfather on my mother's side had been a country fiddle player, and I guess I got a little bit of that in me.

JAKE HANNA: We had a night off when we were up in La Crosse, Wisconsin, one time, so we had a chance to get out of town and go to Chicago. All we had to do was drive.

Abe Turchen had decided to book our night off, so he booked the band in La Crosse. But we really wanted to have the night off in Chicago. Louie Bellson's band was there. But Abe sold the band to this promoter.

So we showed up at the gig and two customers showed up. One had tails and the other one had a sequin gown on! Woody just looked at this guy, then he looked at the band boy and says, "Don't set up all of the drums, just set up the bass drum, a snare and a cymbal. And you guys, don't even set up the music stands; I'll get rid of these two people right away!" So he says to me, "How fast can you play, Jake?" I said, "Well, I can go this fast right away!" He says, "Can you play any faster than that?" I said, "Yes, but I can only last about a minute and a half, otherwise I can last twenty minutes if I go the slower tempo." He said, "Make it the faster one!" So he called "Apple Honey." The band could play that very fast. We weren't even dressed in our uniforms. We were dressed like we were ready to get on the bus. And man, we start up this tempo, and these two people glide right in there on the dance floor, and it turns out, these two people are Peabody dancers, and this tempo is right up their alley. This is perfect for them. They would disappear, they would be like only an inch big down at the other end of the ballroom, and back again in front of us and giving Woody the high sign. . . . "Beautiful, baby, keep it going!" We were softening after about a minute. Fortunately, they were just two cats that heard about it, so Woody just told them to get their money back, we were going home.

We couldn't go back to Chicago because it was too early; we couldn't make check-in time. We'd get there about four in the morning if we hung around. So we went to a local bar. We had a pitcher of beer apiece, a lot of liquid. So we're all going down the road later in the band bus and right there in the crook of the road there was a big yellow house. So Joe "Silk" is drivin' the bus. We called him "Silk" because he was so smooth. So we say, "Joe, you've got to stop the bus, everybody's got to answer the call of nature!" So he just pointed the bus right at this big yellow house. So we all leap out of the bus, and we go over, and there's no toilet anywhere. So we all go against this guy's house . . . sixteen people! The guy in the house is opening up a window. "What the hell is going on down there? They're not the Ku Klux Klan, they're not burning any crosses or nothing, but they seem to be mad at us!"

Dave Yost, a drummer and friend of Woody's since 1950, told the author how Woody quit smoking about this time.

DAVE YOST: He claimed to have smoked four packs a day of Pall Malls. It was in July 1962, at Cedar Point Ballroom in Sandusky, Ohio, when he decided on a doctor's orders that he had better quit smoking because he had chronic bronchitis. He had a terrible cough. Charlotte was there and she was trying to quit also. So a few days later on a date at Chippewa Lake, Ohio, it was her birthday, and the band all signed a big long card that had the message, "So you want to get away from smoking." It had a long, plastic cigarette holder. She got a big laugh from it. Woody was very successful at it. He quit smoking cold turkey and never had another.

On October 15 and 16, the "Swingin' Herd" went into the Phillips Recording Studios in New York to cut its first records for the Phillips label.

There was Joe Newman's "Mo-Lasses," orchestrated by Nat Pierce, an easy groove, with moving solos from Sal Nistico, a fiery Bill Chase, and Woody's clarinet.

Gordon Brisker's arrangement of "Blues for J.P." is a toe tapper par excellence, with Paul Fontaine's trumpet and Gene Allen's baritone down front. Allen's solo is breathtaking, and Nat has his say before the brass takes it out.

"Don't Get Around Much Anymore" is a timeless Nat Pierce chart that remains a staple to this day in the band's library. The melody is introduced by a duet from Gene Allen's baritone and Paul Fontaine's trumpet; muted trumpet (Fontaine), Phil Wilson's trombone, and Woody's clarinet ride above the ensemble.

The period was extremely productive for Nat Pierce as he continued to turn out some of his best writing. His deft chart of "Tunin' In" features Woody on clarinet.

Nat's version of Horace Silver's "Sister Sadie" highlighted Sal Nistico's driving style, with a backdrop of shouting brass.

SAL NISTICO: Sister Sadie was ME. But in a lot of the other material, I was just playing the part. That's the thing about a big band—it's very hard to fit yourself into the arrangement sometimes, you know, solo, if you take it that seriously. It's really not that serious; it's a lighter vein.

"Sig Ep" (Sigma Epsilon) was named after the fraternity at Marquette University, to which Woody supposedly belonged. Written by Jack Gale, it features solos from Larry Covelli on tenor and Fontaine's trumpet.

Gordon Brisker's arrangement of "It's a Lonesome Old Town" was a feature for Phil Wilson that, according to Phil, "put him on the map." On it, Phil demonstrates his range and unique conception.

Bill Chase's "Camel Walk" is an eight-minute-fifteen-second blockbuster featuring Gordon Brisker's tenor, Woody, and Phil Wilson blasting his way through the chart with the ensemble effectively building up to Nat's Basie-ish piano and Woody's nutty vocal: "I rode a camel all the way to Texas . . . man, oh man, I got a hump!" The searing brass with Bill Chase on top is reminiscent of the First Herd.

After the October recording date, trombonist Henry Branch Southall joined the band, becoming an effective section mate to Phil Wilson. Before Woody, Henry worked with the bands of Dean Hudson, Larry Elliott and Stan Kenton. His style, influenced by Carl Fontana, Frank Rosolino, and Kai Winding, provided an excellent contrast to Wilson's.

Of this band, Woody said when he started again in 1962: "Don't give this one a number. Just call it 'The Swingin' Herd.'" It became one of Woody's classic bands on a par with the First and Second Herds. The magnificently integrated rhythm section comprised Nat Pierce, bassist Chuck Andrus (who could play with lightning speed), and drummer Jake Hanna, who played in the tradition of Tough and Lamond. A powerhouse trumpet section led by the iron-lipped Bill Chase, which included a more lyrical Paul Fontaine, was a distinguishing feature of this Herd. The bucketing trombone section included the agile and sometimes pyrotechnic Phil Wilson and Henry Southall, whose peppery style showed great spirit and imagination. The saxophone quartet with Nistico contributed to the overall drive, excitement, and fire.

PHIL WILSON: I can remember running out of gas one night, going towards Ashland, North Carolina. Abe hadn't been paying the bus bills, so we were reduced to a broken-down bus, one of those buses that came out of 1939, or something like that. It had cracked windows, held together with masking tape. The bus driver couldn't read signs, and we actually ran out of gas. And the bus driver or somebody got out and looked around and went over this next little hill. He could see a service station at the bottom of the next hill. So picture the whole band, lined up behind the bus, pushing it over the crest of the hill at one o'clock in the morning.

We took off for Boston one time and we went through Baltimore, and we were all getting settled down. About twenty minutes later, somebody noticed the surrounding countryside was very much like downtown Baltimore, back to the south. So we get on the bus driver who used to pop some sort of speed pill. We found a rotary and got turned around, and we went back through Baltimore. Damned if we didn't seem to be in Baltimore again about twenty minutes later. We kept coming to this rotary in the north end of town, and the driver couldn't read the signs. I don't know, maybe the "B" on the sign rang a bell with him and so he figured Boston. But we went through Baltimore five times! We finally stopped for the night in New York, and then left New York for Boston via Route 6, and Route 6 is the shoreline to Cape Cod. Ordinarily, in those days, you would take Route 20, and you would get there quicker. They would usually figure four and a half hours, New York to Boston. We were there in thirteen hours!

Another new addition was trumpeter Bill E. (Billy) Hunt, a fine soloist. He had worked with Daryl Harpa, Al Belletto, and Warren Covington. Billy joined the Herd in October 1962, replacing Ziggy Harrell.

BILLY HUNT: Woody always listened! He probably wasn't always thrilled with all that he had to hear, but he was always trying to discover something in each of us that had some musical merit. That forced us to listen to ourselves. There was never a problem of talking or loafing on the bandstand. Woody never missed or was late for a gig. He was very matter of fact about getting there.

Woody never really accepted anyone's recommendations about who could or couldn't play. He listened to each guy all the time and tried to channel each guy's type of playing in the way he thought would sound best.

On my first string of one-nighters, we played a Governor's ball for George Wallace in Montgomery, Alabama. I had a little solo to play for the first time . . . sixteen bars. Just as my time to play approached, so did the Governor to shake Woody's hand. Woody turned his back on the Governor, listened to me play, and then turned around and shook the Governor's hand.

If we got wasted, Woody would extend our soloing *forever*, it seemed. But he also was aware of our limitations. If we were scuffling, he got us out of trouble real fast, by calling up the next soloist or signaling for the shout chorus.

January 1963 found the Swingin' Herd back at the Metropole for a two-week engagement. The Metropole became this particular Herd's "headquarters." Former *Down Beat* staff writer Gene Lees had recently joined the Herman office staff as publicist. The band maintained an office with Abe Turchen directing, at 57th Street and Seventh Avenue in New York.

BILL BERRY: Now that I'm a leader of sorts, I really appreciate where Woody had to be coming from. Having also been in Duke's band, I can say that Hodges, Carney, and everybody had the greatest respect for Woody. One night, Sam Woodyard, Paul Gonsalves, Johnny Hodges, and I went into the Metropole when Woody was playing in 1963. When Woody saw Johnny Hodges, he didn't want to play alto, and Johnny came in to listen to him! But I guess that's mutual respect.

Always there were the dedicated "groupies" both male and female, who followed the band from job to job. There were the "band chicks" who made it clear that they were available to the musicians for a night, or for the duration of the band's location date. Sometimes they would be invited to travel on the bus for a couple of days; sometimes they would switch musicians and stay on for a few more days.

The big-band groupies would often live a pilgrimlike existence, following their favorite bands from state to state. Whole families would plan their vacations around a band's itinerary. They may not have been as hysterical as today's rock fans, but they were equally committed. This was particularly true of the adventurous jazz bands that offered music with substance, modern voicings and conception, in contrast with the "Mickey" hotel (society) orchestras or the middle-of-the-road dance bands.

One such fan was a middle-aged groupie dubbed "Sidewalk Stanley" by the band members.

NAT PIERCE: I don't even know his last name. He was always standing on the sidewalk. He didn't have enough money to come into the Metropole. He was always standing outside by those black doors.

    One time he was on the news. He was in a cab and somebody tried to rob the cab driver and somehow he foiled it. The media asked him, "Where were you going?" He said, "I was going to see Woody." They asked him, "What do you do?" He said, "I go see Woody every night!" So it turned out to be a big promo for Woody.

On March 6 the hazards of the road were made real once again when Woody was involved in an auto accident near Ames, Iowa. Fortunately, he survived the incident unscathed.

On May 19, 20, and 21, the Swingin' Herd went into Basin Street West, a new Los Angeles club. Bob Gefaell, the owner, was an entrepreneur with a sharp business mind and a connoisseur of fine music. The room was packed every night. Ex-Herman sidemen were present in abundance.

Woody Herman had been rediscovered. The Herd was breaking box-office records everywhere. Sal Nistico had rejoined the Herman sax section after a few months off the band. Third Herd veteran Bill Perkins had also returned for a brief period.

Recording engineer Wally Heider was present at Basin Street West to record thirty-six titles. Eight were released on a Phillips album titled *Encore*. The results were spectacular.

"That's Where It Is" was an original up-tempo blues featuring Pierce on piano and Sal Nistico's intense and driving tenor.

Nat Pierce's arrangement of Herbie Hancock's "Watermelon Man" was one of the first big-band charts flavored with the new rock influence. It features Nistico, Chase, Woody and Southall on trombone.

Nat's chart of "Body and Soul" featuring Woody's warm alto is elegant, and Phil Wilson's solo is an excellent example of his inventive imagination.

Arranger Bob Hammer interprets the "blues shouting" concepts of Charlie Mingus in the Mingus composition "Better Git It in Your Soul." Solos are by baritonist Frank Hittner, trumpeter Billy Hunt, and Nistico.

The dixieland traditional "Jazz Me Blues," updated by Pierce, effectively showcases the "Brothers"-voiced sax section and features solos from gifted tenorist Bobby Jones and Southall's trombone.

Bill Chase contributed the rousing score of "El Toro Grande," a Latin vehicle providing a solo for Nistico.

"Days of Wine and Roses" is Nat Pierce's fresh interpretation of the Mancini tune, featuring Woody's lyrical alto and the gifted trumpet of Billy Hunt.

On "Caldonia" the band takes it to nearly twice the tempo of the original 1945 recording, with steaming work by Nistico, Wilson, Southall, Fontaine, and Woody.

More updated First Herd classics, "The Good Earth," "Sidewalks of Cuba," "Apple Honey" and "Bijou," all from the Basin Street West engagement, were released later in the Phillips album *Woody's Big Band Goodies*. These performances not only are big-band jazz on a grand scale, they offer the listener a fascinating opportunity to compare them with the originals. On "Sidewalks of Cuba," trumpeter Billy Hunt begins his solo with Sonny Berman's opening quote from "Flight of the Bumblebee."

On "Bijou," the former Bill Harris showcase, Phil Wilson does an effective performance, interpreting the Burns score with his own fresh ideas. He made the following comments touching on the awkwardness of being compared to Harris.

PHIL WILSON: I loved Bill Harris, and so my remarks in Steve Voce's book weren't meant to be a scam to Bill at all. I just wanted to do more of my own stuff, rather than always having to fill Bill's shoes. So every time a big solo came around for me, Woody would always pull out "Bijou," or one of those things. I loved the solo Bill did on "Bijou"; all of his solos were magnificent. Bill was an incredible jazz player. So there was no belittling intended. I just felt that I had something to offer myself.

Every time you play some other artist's featured number, you're always subject to comparison. And so, as a soloist, you're faced with a decision. . . . "Shall I paraphrase him and pay tribute to him, or should I just go my own route?" I didn't even want to get into that position of comparison.

We've all got all sorts of influences. I was influenced by piano players more than anything else, because I was originally a piano player. Years ago, when Leonard Feather first sent those forms out to fill out for the *Encyclopedia of Jazz*, I put my three influences down, which were Louis

Armstrong, Oscar Peterson, and Duke. And it wasn't printed like that. It came out, Jack Teagarden, Bill Harris, Dickie Wells, and Tommy Dorsey.

My solo on "It's a Lonesome Old Town" did put me on the map. So I've been working off of that ever since. That was a very meaningful solo too on "Body and Soul."

Also a key figure in the resurgence to prominence of the 1960s band was Bill Chase. His warm and sensitive ballad style is demonstrated on "I Can't Get Started," from the Basin Street date.

Encore was named the best big-band record of the year by the National Academy of Recording Arts and Sciences.

NAT PIERCE: Abe Turchen had put Woody's old music in storage in the basement of the linoleum store that his father-in-law had owned on 23rd Street in New York. I went down there one day, and there were old music stands, old music, many arrangements. And like a fool, I just picked what I thought I would be able to use and left the rest.

Now, they have torn the building down and there's nothing left. It was basically the Second Herd material. The only thing I ever got of those things was like bootleg broadcasts. And you have to start from the beginning if you want to rewrite those things.

In November 1963, the Herd recorded ten additional titles for the Phillips label in New York. Nine were issued the following year in the album *Woody Herman: 1964*.

There was Nat Pierce's arrangement of Oscar Peterson's "Hallelujah Time," with shades of a "church meetin' sing-along." It features a tenor chase with Sal Nistico and newcomer Carmen Leggio.

Nat Pierce's arrangement of "Deep Purple" remains a staple in the Herd's dance library. The melody is played by the saxes, Woody on alto, with tenor offerings from Carmen Leggio and Sal Nistico, wailing Basie-like brass ensembles, and Woody's tongue-in-cheek coda concluding the piece.

Bill Holman contributed two of the charts recorded at these sessions. The first one, "Jazz Hoot," had a pseudo-rock beat, with wild ensemble work and solo contributions from Billy Hunt, Wilson, Nistico, and Woody.

Bill Chase's moody arrangement of *A Taste of Honey* has Woody on alto, Leggio on tenor, and a stratospheric solo from Bill Chase. Gene Lees writes of this performance:

On November 22, 1963, I walked into the office to be told by Abe Turchen's nephew, Dick, "The President's been shot!" I thought it was a put-on, until I saw the TV set in Abe's office.

That afternoon Woody was recording. . . . I went up to the session, numb, like the whole nation. Woody did a take on Bobby Scott's "A

Taste of Honey." But no one felt like going on, and he called the session. That take, however, is in the album, its dark mood of mourning a testament to the way jazz can almost instantaneously reflect public events, and express the emotions they engender—just as "Caldonia" and "Your Father's Mustache" were full of the euphoria of the war's last weeks. It was recorded about three hours after the assassination.[1]

Nat's interpretation of "Satin Doll" was also included at the session, with Nat, Chuck Andrus, and the powerhouse Chase.

Bill Holman's chart of "After You've Gone" begins with a sentimental introduction by celesta and Woody's low-register clarinet. The mood abruptly changes with solos from Woody on clarinet, Paul Fontaine, and Nistico, then the roaring stops and the original feeling returns.

BILL HOLMAN: One night I told him that I thought he was playing some of my charts too fast. He said, "Well, we have a line that we give to arrangers who gripe about the tempos, which is, "Why don't you start your own band?"

"The Strut" was another contribution by Bob Hammer that has an Ellingtonian trumpet-with-a-plunger intro, with Fontaine on trumpet and Wilson doing some "Tricky" Sam Nanton trombone.

"My Wish" is Nat Pierce's interpretation of a piece from Meredith Willson's *Here's Love*, with lovely alto from the Chopper, Southall on trombone, and either Billy Hunt or Paul Fontaine on trumpet.

"Cousins" is a remake of the 1956 "Blues Groove." This version features a muted Wilson and great Herman clarinet. Chase blows lead a full octave above the screaming trumpet ensemble.

Woody's talents as a clarinetist were repeatedly overlooked. He wasn't a technician on the instrument in the sense of a Shaw or Goodman, but his solos projected tremendous emotion. He often subjugated his solo contributions to provide a springboard for the more contemporary soloists, and preferred using the band as his instrument. Woody was a humble giant.

In late December, the Herd traveled west for a New Year's Eve date in Las Vegas. On January 20 they were back in New York for a week at Basin Street East; in late January, back to the Coast for an ABC telecast with Edie Adams in Hollywood, then to San Francisco for a February 14th opening at the Off Broadway club. While in the Bay Area, the Herd did a series of "Jazz Casual" telecasts with emcee Ralph J. Gleason.

In April the band guested on the "Tonight" show in New York during another engagement at the Metropole.

In June the band was on tour in the Scandinavian countries. In July it was a tour of England. In early fall, the Herd began to undergo personnel changes. The tenor sax players were all new. Replacing Sal Nistico was Andy

The "Swingin' Herd" in London, July 1964. Front row, L to R: Tom Anastas (baritone sax), Gary Klein, Joe Romano, Sal Nistico (tenor saxes), Nat Pierce (piano), Kenny Wenzel (trombone), Woody (clarinet), Phil Wilson, Henry Southall (trombone). Back row: Chuck Andrus (hidden) (bass), Billy Hunt, Danny Nolan, Bill Chase, Jerry Lamy, Paul Fontaine (trumpets). (Photo by David Redfern)

McGhee, another hard-blowing tenor from Lionel Hampton's band. The other two replacements were Gary Klein and Raoul Romero. Replacing Paul Fontaine was Yugoslavian-born trumpeter Dusan Gojkovic (Dusko Goykovich). Dusko came to the band via the International Youth Band, Berklee School of Music, and Maynard Ferguson's Band, and proved to be a brilliant asset to the Herd. Ex-Dizzy Gillespie vocalist Joe Carroll was also added for a brief tour.

In early September the Herd played at Harrah's Club, Lake Tahoe, Nevada, and another live album was recorded.

Nat's arrangement of the period tune "The Good Life" was done in the mode of his previous "Deep Purple" chart. Woody plays lead alto on top of the section as he did often in the 1960s. Gary Klein's tenor swings in an easy, Al Cohn groove and Dusko Goykovich has his Herman solo debut. Chase's lead work is magnificent.

"Bedroom Eyes" is trombonist Matthew Gee's tune, done in a Basie groove, with Woody playing lead alto and solos from Pierce, Wilson (using a bucket mute), and trumpeter Billy Hunt.

Bill Holman's score of Duke Ellington's "Just Squeeze Me" is extraordinary in approach and feeling, with Woody's alto setting the pace for Phil

Wilson's agile and humorous offering, again using a bucket mute. The performance changes character as Raoul Romero roars in on tenor and the ensemble takes over.

"Dr. Wong's Bag," a salute to jazz entrepreneur Herb Wong, is a twelve-bar blues from the pen of Nat Pierce featuring a line from the five muted trumpets, with Billy Hunt's trumpet joining the saxophone section for some rich voicing, a method used extensively in later Herds. Solos are from Andy McGhee on tenor and Billy Hunt, using a plunger mute in the tradition of Ray Nance and Clark Terry.

Dean Martin popularized "Everybody Loves Somebody" during this period. Here Woody gives the tune new elegance with earthy clarinet and a wonderful solo from Billy Hunt, an underrated trumpeter.

"Dear John C." is another score by the inventive composer/arranger Bob Hammer, patterned loosely after Miles Davis' "So What." The title is a salute to John Coltrane. Dusko Goykovich takes two choruses, followed by tenorist Gary Klein.

"Wa-Wa Blues" was written by vocalist Joe Carroll. It's in an Ellingtonian mood and features Woody on alto and Joe doing a humorous but effective imitation of solo trombone with plunger and "dueting" with Phil Wilson.

PHIL WILSON: One night in 1964, we played Goldwater's country club in Phoenix. We weren't allowed to eat there because we had Joe Carroll and Andy McGhee, two black musicians, on the band. The national election was two weeks later, and Goldwater was going for the civil rights vote and here they wouldn't even feed our mixed band in his own country club.

Woody came in behind the band and heard that we couldn't eat there. It became evident that it was because we had two black musicians. Woody told us to pack up. "We're going to split!" So we were headed out to the bus, taking the instruments and equipment, and the director of the country club came out and said "What's wrong?" and Woody told him, "They won't feed us, so we're not going to play!" And the director said, "What can I do to get you to stay?" and Woody said, "Fire the manager and feed the band at your expense!" So he fired him and we ate at their expense and played.

In October drummer Jake Hanna left the band and was replaced by Ronnie Zito.

In November the Herd returned to the Columbia label and recorded more excellent material including an album of Broadway show tunes produced by Teo Macero. Because of road commitments, it took almost four months for the Herd to record the *My Kind of Broadway* album. Charts for the sessions were done by Don Rader (who returned to the trumpet section in January), Dusko Goykovich, Nat Pierce, Bill Holman, Raoul Romero, and Bill Chase.

The studio performances were generally more relaxed than the bristling on-location recordings the band had been making. Nonetheless, the *Broadway* album contains some worthwhile material.

Bobby Shew came to the Herd via the Tommy Dorsey Band.

BOBBY SHEW: I never seemed to be able to get terribly close to the Chopper, as he and Chase were generally off on their own in Woody's Corvette, but I'll never forget the "ray" he used to emit from his eyes. Very intimidating for a young greenhorn like myself. The ONLY time he ever came to hang out with the guys was one night after a gig. Most of us had gathered in a room to listen to Lord Buckley records. He recognized Buckley's voice and knocked on the door. He sat there for a couple of hours and told us stories of how Lord Buckley had traveled with the band as a temporary replacement for a singer.

PHIL WILSON: I used to say Woody Herman does what he does better than anyone . . . if only we could figure out what he does. That set me to thinking. What did Woody do? Besides playing clarinet and sax, what quality in Woody commanded the respect of great musicians?

There are those who stated that Woody was one of those rare conductors who best ran things facing the audience. There was some truth to this. Woody was the link between the band and the audience. He sold the music. He listened to every note and, more important, reacted to what he heard. The audience saw and AGREED with Woody and at least began to understand the music.

Because of this phenomenon, Woody Herman could sell fresh music, where others failed, reverting to one formula or another.

Phil Wilson left the band in May 1965, and Sal Nistico returned.

SAL NISTICO: Woody was a master psychologist. He was in the toughest of businesses. He needed the players that he had, but Abe refused to pay the money, and so Woody would keep the guys in different ways, just by featuring them and giving them a name, which is like currency in a way, for later. He was just a very perceptive, sensitive cat. You could never fool him. He told me one time that he "hadn't been surprised since he was 45!" He loved his family, but when he would go home, he would want to come back out. He used to get very twitchy after two weeks, he told me.

When I moved to LA, we had no furniture, or anything, and Char used to come by and leave money with my family when I was out on the road. Woody didn't know about it.

DON RADER: We did *Woody's Winners* live at Basin Street West in San Francisco. Wally Heider did the recording for Columbia. He used to show up on gigs, from out of nowhere, with his trailer and all of his recording equipment hitched to the back of his Cadillac. He'd turn the band room into a control booth and record the whole gig!

The *Woody's Winners* album was a triumph for the Swingin' Herd. Herb Wong wrote the following in the liner notes: "Having Woody play for the first time in Basin Street . . . was a three-day jazz joyride. . . . Woody's stand-up firing squad nearly blew the glasses and everything else off the patrons' tables."

"23 Red" was written by Bill Chase. The title originates from Chase's experiences playing roulette in Reno, Lake Tahoe, and Las Vegas. The trumpet-centered chart features Chase, Dusko Goykovich, and Don Rader in a romping trio that initiates a dynamic series of exchanges (one chorus each of two bars, two choruses of four bars, and two choruses of two's).

Don Rader wrote the arrangement for "My Funny Valentine." Woody comes through with hearty low-register clarinet, with additional solos from Rader and Gary Klein, and Chase's lead galvanizes the ensemble into an exciting conclusion.

Nat Pierce's updated version of "Northwest Passage" begins with the line played by Woody, Nistico, and Rader, then Nistico rips through chorus after chorus, until the wind-up with Chase blowing the old Pete Candoli stratospheric finale.

"Poor Butterfly" was scored by Don Rader. It's a good dance chart with Woody's lovely alto playing the melody, followed by his warm, low-register clarinet, and nice tenor from McGhee.

Don Rader's "Greasy Sack Blues" is a funky, straight-ahead blues featuring Woody on clarinet, Nat's piano, and Rader on plunger trumpet.

"Woody's Whistle" is an original blues by Dusko Goykovich featuring down-home, funky solos from Pierce, followed by Nistico with an unusually voiced ensemble repeating a background riff and serving as an intro to Dusko's trumpet solo. There is exquisite scoring for the ensemble, and in conclusion, Woody blows his famous whistle.

"Red Roses for a Blue Lady" was scored by Dusko and has Woody playing lead alto on top of the section. Solos are by McGhee on tenor and Woody on clarinet.

Ten years after the Herd's original Capitol recording of "Opus de Funk," the band performed it again on Woody's last night at Basin Street West. This ten-minute version outswings the original by far. Nat's piano is followed by Gary Klein's swinging tenor, then an effective offering from Southall (who took most of the trombone solos after Wilson's departure). Chase reaches for the sky during the ensemble explosion. The now-famous muted trumpet solo near the close is articulated here by Dusko Goykovich. During Nat's opening piano solo, Woody jokingly called for "a nice round of applause for Mary Lou Williams," instigating a twenty-year controversy: "Was it Mary Lou or Nat?"

DON RADER: We went to Europe in the summer of 1965 and did jazz festivals at Complain La Tour, Belgium, and Antibes, in the south of France. We also did some other gigs around the Riviera and played at the Salle Pleyel in Paris. On a lot of these gigs we traveled by bus, and the other band that was along with us was John Coltrane and his quartet.

During the rest of that summer, I moved my family back to California. I knew that Woody had a week at Disneyland in August, and I decided to leave the band at that time.

But in the meantime, we were working at the Metropole, we did the Chicago Jazz Festival and the Cincinnati Jazz Festival, and we worked gigs in Lake Tahoe. During this latter tour with the band, we always traveled by bus or plane, something unheard of when I first joined the band in 1959. Woody rode on the bus as little as possible.

I paid my own expenses from Los Angeles to New York to join this band, but it was worth it to me. I guess that Woody still didn't have much money. The band's management were a real drag and, I feel, ripped us all off more than once.

As an example, when I left Woody's band for the last time in 1965, I found that I was ineligible to collect unemployment, after a year on the road, because Abe hadn't paid into it. He certainly took taxes out of our checks. Trying to get what they owed you for writing arrangements was almost impossible. I had to take Woody to the union before Abe would pay me for writing "Greasy Sack Blues."

When the Herd and John Coltrane were co-billed on the European tour during the summer of 1965, Woody became so captivated by Trane's technique on the soprano sax that on his return he purchased one and mastered its awkward character in short time.

NAT PIERCE: He played the soprano briefly in the mid-fifties, but it wasn't until the sixties that he really got serious with it, because it's kind of an out-of-tune instrument, and you have to play it a long time to really get your intonation correct, like Charlie Barnet had done years earlier.

SAL NISTICO: The thing is, Woody also played the clarinet. The fingering on the clarinet in the lower register is different notes. It's not like the saxophone, where you just push the octave key, and the note in the upper register is the same note in the lower register. The clarinet is different. The fingering for E on the clarinet is A in the bottom register. So Woody was playing the soprano like the clarinet.

He would get into a wild bag at times, and he had that very great sense of swinging time, and all the notes would really sound good. He loved it. He loved Trane. He would go down to The Half Note and listen to him.

He was a very accomplished cat. He could be difficult at times, but the thing is, man, it was a hard life. He stood up in front of that band a long time, and there were times when nobody was out there. Then he went through all that [comeback] in 1962 and 1963. We drew incredible crowds. It was good for his ego, because he'd been down so many times.

In August 1965 the band had three vacancies in the trumpet section. Filling the fifth trumpet spot was William (Bill) Byrne. Byrne attended the Cincinnati Conservatory for a year on a scholarship and played with the Cincinnati Symphony Orchestra. He then spent five years with the Navy Band at the U. S. Naval Academy, Annapolis, Maryland. When he left Annapolis in 1964, he went to New York, where he played with several groups, including Les Elgart's band and the pit orchestra for *Hello Dolly.*

Other than a six-month vacation in 1968, Byrne was a faithful Herdsman for twenty-five years. In 1967 Byrne became the band's road manager. He served Woody well as a shield from disgruntled patrons and the many adverse conditions encountered by a road band.

BILL BYRNE: I joined Woody on August 29, 1965, in Columbus, Ohio. The band had been out at Disneyland, and three of the trumpet players left. They came East the same week, and I was in New York. Bill Chase was calling around for trumpet players. He called Bill Berry, and Bill knew me from Cincinnati, and also Gary Potter, who was playing lead trombone at the time, knew me.

So Chase called me in New York, and I said, "Well, I don't play any lead, or any jazz." He said, "That's okay, man, we can't all be stars." So I went out on the road with the band. But I had already contracted to go with Fred Waring about two weeks later, and I told Bill, "I have this commitment with Fred Waring, and I also know you want jazz players." And he said, "That's okay. We want you to stay."

I think Woody asked him what the heck I was doing there in the band, because formerly, they always hired three lead [type] trumpet players and the fourth and the fifth were the jazz players. . . .

January 1966 found the Herd at the Playboy Club in Los Angeles. The unit was undergoing personnel changes, in preparation for a scheduled eleven-week State Department tour of England, Africa, and Europe, commencing March 3. During the Playboy Club engagement, trombonist Frank Rosolino came in as a temporary sub.

Herd veterans Sal Nistico and Carl Fontana rejoined for the tour. Before leaving New York for England, the band went into Columbia Recording Studios in New York and cut four titles for an album entitled *The Jazz Swinger.* The unusual concept for this album was Woody singing tunes associated with Al Jolson, supported by modern big-band charts from Ralph Burns,

The "Swingin' Herd" in concert, Rabat, Morocco, April 2, 1966. Woody soars above the band, backed by Bill Byrne, Marvin Stamm, Bill Chase, Alex Rodriguez, Dusko Goykovitch (trumpets): Henry Southall, Carl Fontana, Jerry Collins (trombones); Sal Nistico, Frank Vicari, Bob Pierson (tenor saxes); Tom Anastas (baritone sax); Nat Pierce (piano); Michael Moore (bass); and Ronnie Zito (drums). (From the Woody Herman Collection)

Nat Pierce, and other writers. Woody and the band made Jolson's dated songs a pleasure to listen to. The album was received well at the time of its release but, apparently due to poor promotion, fizzled out not long afterward. Only "Sonny Boy" remained in the band's repertoire, as Woody liked Burns' swinging treatment.

This is the Herd as it toured Europe and Africa: Bill Chase, Marvin Stamm, Alex Rodriguez, Bill Byrne, Dusko Goykovich, trumpets; Henry Southall, Jerry Collins, Carl Fontana, trombones; Sal Nistico, Frank Vicari, Bob Pierson, tenor saxes; Tom Anastas, baritone sax; Nat Pierce, piano; Michael Moore, bass; and Ronnie Zito, drums.

WOODY: We toured England, France, Morocco, then we went into Yugoslavia, Romania, and eventually we played all of Africa. The State Department had hired us to do a Russian tour, but because President Johnson
had forgotten to sign the reciprocal agreement with the Soviets, we were
sent, at the very last minute, into the darkest parts of Africa.

We were relegated to any place you could find to play. . . . Nobody in
our State Department was very interested in promoting the band.

BILL BYRNE: Dusko and Sal Nistico were both living and working in Europe when we picked them up over there. Paul Fontaine, trumpeter, and Andy McGhee, the black tenor player, didn't go. Sal took his place. Sal and Dusko stayed with us until we got through with the trip to Africa.

The author asked, "How was jazz accepted in the black countries of Africa?"

BILL BYRNE: It was just like people anywhere, who would get the feeling of it. We were in the village square in Elizabethville, The Congo. The band was playing in a gazebo-type thing, and the city officials had put these barricades up, and the audience took them down. All the people just surged to get as close as they could, and the guys' eyes [in the band] got a little wide, but it was only normal, like any crowd any place.

There was really no problem communicating at all. The guys went into some of the nightclubs in the Congo and there was a good feeling there, and the local musicians would come and take the guys to different places and show them this and that. It was a terrific trip.

It was a real easy tour because we were just thrown in there. We were originally supposed to go to Russia, and then the cultural agreement fell through, so the State Department was stuck with us for twelve weeks, and there wasn't any time to plan. They threw some concerts together at the last minute. We would play one day and would have two days off.

The guys in the band got a big kick out of that tour. They tried different cuisines, and when we were in North Africa, they all tried the hashish. When we were in Algiers, we were going through some roadblocks, and there were machine guns, and the military. We were there right after the French pulled out and the Algerians got their independence, so there was still a lot of turmoil.

When we played Elizabethville, we pulled up to the stage door and there was a line of machine gun bullet holes right up the wall. The U.N. peace-keeping force had just been there establishing order. The windows were shot out in the lobby because they had just got through fighting before we came in.

We played in concert halls, and we played out in the town squares and in little schools. In Morocco they put a Moroccan band on the stage with us. The Moroccan musicians had these long horns and Woody invited them to the stage and they were blowing with us on "Cousins" [laughter].

NAT PIERCE: Have you heard the famous African Drum Story? . . . We didn't work very hard, sometimes we were off three or four days a week. We would play one day and have another day off. So one night, it was hot. There was a porch all the way around the hotel. We decided to have a card game. Earlier, when we were in England, Ken Glancy, who was the

Columbia representative in England, had given me a portable, five-inch tape recorder, a Telefunken, yet. I had taken it to Africa to record the native drums, of all things. You know what I mean?

So we're sitting around playing cards and drinking gin and everybody is getting stoned, and I heard like, "DICKIE DONG, DICKIE DONG, DICKIE DONG." I said . . . "THE DRUMS! THE DRUMS! I GOTTA RECORD THE DRUMS!" I ran back to my room and I got the tape recorder, and went downstairs and jumped in a cab, and said, "Take me to the drums."

The next thing I know, Carl Fontana was pulling me out of this guy's cab, and I was saying . . . "THE DRUMS! It's maybe my only chance to get THE DRUMS!" He said, "Get out of this cab," and we walked across the street where they were constructing a building, and so far all they had was a hole dug in the ground. And down in the bottom of the hole was a water pump going, "DONG, DICKIE DONG, DICKIE DONG." Carl says, "There's your DRUMS, down there!" So I went down and recorded it anyway. And a guard appears at the top of the hole with a rifle and bayonet. He came charging down, saying, "No, no, no!" and Carl was saying, "He's just recording, it's not a bomb!"

BILL BYRNE: After Abidjan [Ivory Coast], we went up to Nice, France. Woody had the gout and was in a wheelchair. From there, we went on to Romania and Yugoslavia.

Dusko hadn't been home for a long time. He had been a draft evader. All during the trip, he was asking advice at different embassies, whether or not he should go back to Yugoslavia. They finally gave him the word that it was all right.

When we landed in the morning at Belgrade Airport, they met Dusko with this huge roar as the door opened. The government didn't bother him.

NAT PIERCE: They walked right on by Woody and walked over to Dusko, like it was a homecoming for Clark Gable or something! They threw flower leis around his neck and all this kind of stuff. Woody was walking in front of us and he said, "Oh, boy, the fans are great here in Yugoslavia," and they went right on by him to greet Dusko! That, I'll never forget!

In Belgrade they gave the musicians a big banquet with all the homemade sausage and *sljivovica* [plum brandy]. Woody had Dusko come down front every night to say goodnight to the people in their native language and it was touching.

Dusko's dad was in the Yugoslavian underground in WW II, on the run all the time. When Dusko became of age he escaped to Germany after the war, because otherwise, he would have been drafted, you know.

SAL NISTICO: I hated giving my notice to Woody when I wanted to leave. It was hell playing out the two weeks. He knew I was messed up about my worth, and being loyal and disloyal. He knew that I wanted to belong, and if I made more money than my buddies, I was guilt ridden.

It wasn't easy for Gordon Brisker to leave, and it was hell for Nat to break away. It happened in North Africa when we all stood together, and Nat stood with the sidemen against the embassy people. The dispute was over travel—bus or plane. There were supposed to be planes available. The hassle was all over one plane flight and was not worth the shit it caused. But when the embassy honcho in Algeria told Nat "Think of the scenery you'll miss," Nat replied, "I've had scenery, man!"

That was Nat's notice. I felt for him, because it's never easy to leave, but Nat's case was even more special. It was after four or five years for me, fifteen for Nat. I can hear the cats saying, "C'mon man, it's only a gig." But it's a band with a leader. It's not so easy to knock on the old man's door, and enter his room. Those eyes, man! The "ray," it's been called. Buddy Rich had it. Woody had it. I hear Benny Goodman had it.

Once I even changed my mind for months, which was the point of the "ray." I wasn't on the scene for Jake's departure, but Jake is a tough Irishman, man, nothing upsets him. Everybody else was not too cool when trying to stand up to Woody. He was a father figure, whether you liked it or not.

Soon after the band returned from Europe, Woody found that he couldn't swallow. He played for three days without solid food, and finally went to see Stan Levy, his physician in Detroit, who discovered he had a chicken bone lodged in the esophagus. Count Basie subbed for Woody, playing with the Herd until Woody could front the band again.

On June 10 the band recorded the remaining titles for the *Jazz Swinger* album, then headed for a one-nighter at Bridgeport, Connecticut. During this period news began to surface that Abe Turchen, Woody's manager of twenty-one years, had been investing a considerable share of the band's profits in slow-running horses and payments to loan sharks, while taxes, bus rentals, and other bills went unpaid.

BILL BYRNE: The problems with the IRS had already surfaced when I arrived. People used to chase us around with subpoenas, and take the bus and other things for lack of payments. The police would come in with a cart to take the music library away. They would say, "We're really sorry, Mr. Herman, we really like you." I would be trying to sway them with my "Irish bull," and they would say, "Okay, we won't do it this time." Nat, Jake Hanna, and Bill Chase used to say to Woody, "We're making all this money for this hot band and how come there isn't any?"

Woody plays alto as the great Bill Chase approaches for a solo. Anastas, Nistico, Pierce, Vicari, and Pierson in rear. (From the Woody Herman Collection)

WOODY: I was called to meetings in New York a couple of times, and I was called to a meeting while I was playing in Vegas, and they carefully explained to me that I owed over a million dollars, and I didn't know how we could have done this when we weren't grossing enough money to stay alive. . . . We were continuing on sheer courage.

As a matter of fact, out of my whole musical life, 1945 and 1946 were the only important grosses we ever had. Out of my entire career of fifty years! And they base everything that I did, whether it was recorded income or not, on the figures of '45 and '46, which were completely paid and never in any doubt. But while we were starving and trying to stay alive, they put all these pressures on me.

Abe was the one who upset the apple cart because he was pilfering money for his habit, which was betting, which is even more drastic than drugs. One will kill you physically and mentally, the other one will just kill you.

INGRID HERMAN REESE: My father told me that the problems with Abe's handling of the money became evident around 1966. Abe was a friend, and my father had no reason to question his honesty or competence until the damage was already done.

Abe neglected to pay taxes in 1964, 1965, and 1966. Although these were payroll taxes, for some reason they were not filed as such, but instead as personal income tax on my father. In other words, the IRS recorded the entire band's grosses for three years as my father's personal income and taxed him accordingly.

Things were pretty chaotic after that. The band's affairs were not always in the hands of an accountant, his management was uncertain, and from the late sixties on, he was personally harassed by IRS agents who came to many of his jobs and tried to collect the band's money.

BILL BYRNE: I took over as road manager in 1967 after Bill Chase left. Bill and Nat Pierce used to split the duties. Woody let me do it in my own way. He never interfered. He was glad to have it done and out of his hair.

He was a very warm person, very patient. If he could see that someone was going to develop, he would give them the time to develop.

He personally got a kick out of listening to the guys play. Just like Duke Ellington, he wanted individuals on the band to give it a different voice and a different direction all the time, to keep up with things. He could throw in something extra and different that would perk their ears up too. There was a lot of interplay on the band with fresh ideas. Sometimes the guys would force Woody into something that he'd end up liking too.

In the beginning of 1967 the Swingin' Herd was virtually a new band. Only Sal Nistico remained from the band of the early 1960s. Joining him were tenorist Al Gibbons and the inventive baritonist Joe Temperley, from Scotland. There were all new faces in the brass section with the exception of Bill Byrne. Future trombone star Bill Watrous also passed through the ranks during this period.

WOODY: We've always given a soloist every opportunity to either do himself a great deal of good or hang himself. I think in most cases it has worked out pretty well. In the last few years we've had people such as Sal Nistico, who can blow for ten minutes without suffering from a loss of ideas or continuity. I feel a guy should have a chance to stretch out and be given every opportunity to blow as long as he possibly can.[2]

In April the band went to England for its annual tour booked by English promoter Harold Davison. This is the Herd as it performed for British audiences: Lloyd Michaels, Dick Ruedebusch, John Crews, Gary Schauer, Bill Byrne, trumpets; Dominick Costanzo, Mel Wanzo, Julian Priester, trombones; Sal Nistico, Bob Pierson, Al Gibbons, tenor saxes; Joe Temperley, baritone sax; Ken Ascher, piano; Art Koenig, bass; and Jim Gall, drums.

On its return to the States, the high turnover in the touring Herd's personnel continued. Other bandleaders and fans might consider this unhealthy. Not Woody. He had the ability to turn the shifting personnel into a positive climate by tapping into an endless pool of talented players.

One of those who passed through the ranks of the 1967 Herd was the future bandleader and star tenorist Roger Lee Neumann.

ROGER NEUMANN: I joined the band June 1, 1967. I had been going to Berklee School of Music in Boston. I had told Herb Pomeroy once that the next thing I wanted to do was to go out on Woody's band. It was just good luck for me that Woody called Berklee to see if there was a tenor player there ready to go.

In August we worked Las Vegas for the whole month. Don Rader came up from Los Angeles, where he was living at that time, and brought a couple of new charts. "Big Sur Echo" was one of them. There wasn't any title on it yet. We just used to play the chart.

It was kind of a welcome change to have Don Rader come over with new charts, because while we were in Vegas we got into this habit of playing the same tunes every night. Actually, we didn't get to play too much on that show, because we also backed Renee Armand, a singer, and Jackie Gayle, a comedian. So we were just part of the show at the Blue Room at the Tropicana. We played three or four tunes every night. I guess the show was about an hour long. Then we would have an hour off, and come back, do another hour, et cetera.

In those days, Woody still liked to drive by himself from gig to gig, if he could. He would rent a car and drive, if he didn't have a car with him. If there was a long trip between gigs, he would fly, and we would ride the band bus. Of course, there were many times when the whole band had to fly, which I didn't like nearly as well as traveling by bus. It was really a pain to have to get your horns, luggage and everything off the bus and get into an airport and catch a flight somewhere, and then get back on another bus. Anyway, Woody would drive, if he could. If it was too long a drive, he would catch a flight. Sometimes it would be in-between, where he couldn't catch a flight, and he couldn't get a car, or it was too far to drive, and he would have to ride the bus.

On the nights when he would ride the bus, he would get a case of Heineken beer and set it on the floor, up by the front seat. I remember a couple of those nights were some of the most enjoyable talks that I and some of the other guys had with Woody. Once in a while, somebody would even talk him out of one of his Heinekens! Carl Pruitt, the bass player, was pretty good at that.

I remember some of those nights having the best discussions about some of the old bands, et cetera. I think sometimes Woody didn't really like to talk about the old days. But when he was relaxed like that on the bus, we had some good talks.

I don't think the band would have been able to stay together all these years if it hadn't been for Bill [Byrne]. He was such a nice guy to start with, and had such a relaxed, laid-back way of handling all the problems, the hirings, the firings, the bookings, the hotels and motels, being the buffer between the guys and Woody.

I remember one time walking into a hotel with Bill, and Woody had got to town ahead of us and wanted to know something. For some reason he either didn't know which hotel we were in, or which room Bill was in. Woody was hopping mad. We were walking into the hotel and Woody came charging up and saying something like, "Where the hell you been? I've got to know how to get in touch with you. . . . Don't do that to me!" Bill said, "Yeah, you're right, sorry." He was a saint on the road. Plus, he always knew the best restaurants in every town, and that's VERY important on the road!

One of the really great things about how Woody led a band was when he stomped off a tune, there was no doubt what the tempo was supposed to be. He made it very definite. "ONE, TWO, . . . ONE, TWO, THREE!" I hate it when bandleaders have a very "confidential" count-off, and half of the band doesn't even hear them. Woody was never like that.

Another thing he was good at was really listening to the band and the soloists. On almost any tune, he might feel it was appropriate to open up the arrangement and feature someone at a certain point. He was really in touch with what was going on with the band. He knew when it was right to have a certain guy play an extra solo, how long to let him play and when to bring the band back in, which is really like the true spirit of a jazz band.

It's no secret that through the years, there were various guys on Woody's band who were heavy drinkers, or into various drugs. Every leader probably has his own way of dealing with problems that arise if anyone is out of it on the job. I remember one particular trumpet player, who was known in the band for celebrating a lot. On this one night, he had really got out of control, and he was to have a solo. He came bursting in during the wrong part of the tune. I believe he was playing the bridge of the tune, and we were at the first eight [bars]. But he was having a good time, and he just came in loud and in the wrong place. Woody just looked back at him and yelled, "Hey, it ain't New Year's Eve, pal!" That's all he did. He didn't say, "Get off the stand," he didn't say, "You've got two weeks notice," he didn't say, "Throw the bum out!" He just let the guy know that he knew what was happening.

I felt very fortunate to have had the opportunity to play on Woody's band. It's something that I had been wanting to do since I was a teenager, and first heard the great records by the band. Joe Romano was playing lead tenor, and when he left, Woody moved me over to play lead. At that time, Sal Nistico was the other tenor, and he played most of the hot solos. But what I wanted to do was play lead tenor, and I ended up doing exactly what I wanted to do.

Some of the jazz festivals that we took part in were really exciting, because of being on the same program with other jazz stars. There was one really good night when we were the only big band on the program. Three of the other groups who were there that night were Cannonball Adderley with Nat Adderley, Dizzy Gillespie, when he had James Moody with him, and Miles Davis, while he had Wayne Shorter with him. All on the same bill!

Playing with a big band, you obviously have to limit your solo space. Whenever you DO have your solo space, you've got to be ready to jump in and make the most of it. After I left Woody's band the one important thing I had learned was to get hot instantly, when you have a solo.

On September 16, the Herd was at the Monterey Jazz Festival. Baritonist Cecil Payne, a veteran of Dizzy Gillespie's big bebop band of the late 1940s, had joined the sax section.

Wally Heider was present to record the Herd's portion of the festival for the Verve label. Unfortunately, the sound of the finished product was not up to Heider's usual standards. Still, the recording showcases a magnificently swinging Herd. One side of the Verve album is devoted to Bill Holman's three-movement composition *Concerto for Herd*.

The first movement features polyrhythms with Latin overtones, Woody on alto, Luis Gasca on trumpet; the ensemble breaks into a 4/4 swing beat with more solos from Cecil Payne, baritone, Joe Romano, tenor, Woody on clarinet; then the polyrhythmic figures return. The second movement offers bass from Carl Pruitt, a superb solo from pianist Al Dailey, Carl Fontana on trombone, and standout writing by Holman. The third movement is a provocative arrangement, with solo contributions from Gasca and Fontana. A tempo change introduces an explosive solo from Nistico and more of Dailey's piano. Tom Nygaard's lead trumpet is potent.

Ralph Gleason remarked in the liner notes that *Concerto For Herd* "ought to rank with that other Woody Herman longer performance, *Summer Sequence*, as a classic in big band jazz," but the composition was never promoted or performed enough to gain sufficient recognition. This is another long-unavailable Verve album deserving reissue.

ROGER NEUMANN: *Concerto For Herd* was rehearsed just one day in Albuquerque with Bill Holman before we got to the festival. He had been ill and he was still on crutches when he came out and conducted it.

The whole experience was really a thrill for me, because Bill Holman was my favorite arranger, from the time I was in my late teens. He made me realize how much the arranger affected the sound.

"The Horn of the Fish" features Woody playing Holman's opening line on soprano sax and improvising with surprisingly modern ideas and dashes of Coltrane. Alas, the great Carl Fontana was underrecorded. Drummer John Von Ohlen effectively propels the band, and trumpeter Neil Friel has a brief offering.

ROGER NEUMANN: "The Horn Of The Fish" had been in Woody's book for quite some time. It was my favorite chart. The performance wasn't the greatest. That part in the middle, I think it's right before the trumpet solo, sounds like the band kind of falls apart. One reason is that the lead trumpet player stopped playing. He said his glasses fogged up and he couldn't see the notes.

Don Rader's "Big Sur Echo" opens with distinctive and inventive piano playing by the late Al Dailey. Solos are by Gasca, trumpet, Neumann, tenor sax, and Woody on soprano.

Ken Ascher's "Woody's Boogaloo" offered a preview of the Herd's involvement in the coming fusion era. Characterized by a pseudo-rock beat, the piece has more brilliant solo work from Dailey and contributions from Nistico, an ebullient Herman clarinet, and Gasca's fiery trumpet.

ROGER NEUMANN: Albert Dailey came into the band during the summer, before that festival. He was such a strong player that it seemed to make it a different band.

Carl Fontana was on the band for a little while, around the time of this recording. Woody had the Monterey Jazz Festival booked, and there were a lot of changes going on in the trombone section. So I think he booked Carl in advance, to make sure he would be available for the festival. He came out and worked for two or three weeks at that time. Sal Nistico was with us for about a month, too.

By the time we came close to the festival, we had a trombone section set, but Woody had already hired Carl, so he came on and one of the extra guys took a break.

SAL NISTICO: It was quite dreary after a while for me. We did the bus and road scene, and we had some younger guys and they were pretty happy, but I felt like I was a stick in the mud. You know, one minute, you're the baby on the band, and the next minute, you're the old man.

Woody was not the most loyal of cats, either. I have to say that. He didn't stick by me when I was all alone. This was later, when the young rock musicians in the band were giving me a hard time. Woody completely forgot how hard I'd worked for him all those years.

I'm very confused about Woody and my feelings, but I loved talking to him. He was one astute cookie. . . . He could be very ignorant sometimes. A clod really, who couldn't order orange juice abroad—I'm talking about in England, man. Then, he would turn around and exhibit class and elegance to the point where I'd want to crawl in a hole.

But I think he really should have checked up on Abe. I knew it, man, at the age of 22, that something was not kosher. The band was so hot, and we didn't make shit! I was making $150, all through the first two years. I didn't go up to Abe and demand more money; I didn't know how to do that. Woody knew that. I'm still bitter about it. These days, when somebody wants me, I make sure I get my money.

JOE ROMANO: All bandleaders can get a little bitchy from time to time, but Woody was pretty cool. He was used to the idea of having guys coming and going on his band. Buddy Rich couldn't get used to that. But Woody had people coming and going all the time. He would always hire guys back that he stayed loyal to, like Sal, or me, or Paul Fontaine. Guys who could call him and say, "Hey, Woody, I want to come back," and he would drop somebody, and the player would come back on the band.

JAKE HANNA: Woody called me back in 1967. He said, "Can you help me out?" Johnny Von Ohlen had hurt his back and had to go home. We worked the Detroit Auto Show, and the second week Bobby Vinton showed up. Bobby Vinton had his own drummer, and I gave up the stand, and Woody and I went over to Jimmy Boutziarkaras' place. He had a bar called the Lindel Athletic Club. Only athletes and musicians hung out there. Alex Karas, Jimmy Boutziarkaras, and a bunch of Greeks ran it. Alex Karas was a famous old football player with the Detroit Lions. Billy Martin and Chubby Jackson actually started the bar when it was just a little place next to the Leland Hotel. Billy brought the ballplayers in and Chubby brought the musicians in, sort of a strange mixture. So Woody says, "C'mon, we'll go over to Jimmy's, get something to eat, something to drink and come back for the last show of the night."

As we were walking across the floor, Bobby Vinton was doin' his act, "Mumma Don't Want No . . ." and he plays all the instruments in the song, then he sang, then he danced. He went through about nine routines on this thing. Woody said, "Just a minute, I want to catch this guy and see what he does." So he went through the clarinet routine, and then he went through the trombone, the trumpet, then he got to the sax, the bass, then he beat the drums, then he played the piano, then he got up and beat his feet on the floor. He finally got through, and Woody looked over to me and he said, "This son of a bitch can't do ANYTHING!" Then we went over to Jimmy's and got loaded.

ROGER NEUMANN: At the end of 1967 Woody broke up his band to take a bunch of all-stars from previous bands to England. We were in Chicago working two weeks at a club called The Scotch Mist. The band was scheduled to take a vacation starting in January for a couple of weeks, then get back together, and work a week and then go to England. So some of the guys were starting to talk and were making plans about the dates that were coming up. I hadn't heard anything definite, so I finally went to Bill Byrne and said, "Bill, am I going on this trip to England, or not?" He got this sad look on his face. He said, "No, I'm sorry, man. I was going to give you your two week's notice tomorrow night." Of course, I was disappointed and hurt. But I just decided to enjoy my last two weeks on the band as much as I could. Besides myself, there were five or six other guys who got fired.

The next night after I got my notice we had off in Chicago, and Si Zentner's band came in to the club where we were working. So I decided I would spend my night off by going over to hear the Zentner Band. I walked into the club and sat down at the bar by myself, and who should come in but Woody. He came over and sat down at the bar next to me. I thought, "This is the last guy that I want to spend my night off with," but he sat down at the bar and acted as if nothing had happened. Woody said, "Let me buy you a beer." We sat there and hung out together like old buddies. It was probably the best time that I had ever had with him.

In the late 1960s and early 1970s, the Herman Herd continued to evolve. In 1968 Woody started to use an electronic rhythm section with electric piano and bass, combined with the traditional big-band instrumentation of the brass and reed sections, producing the fusion of a rock beat with the timbre of horns.

8.

"Road Father"— The Fusion Era
1968–1979

On Sunday, January 28, 1968, the Herd flew from New York to London to begin a two-week tour of England, Scotland, and Ireland. This was the personnel: Tom Nygaard, Luis Gasca, Robert Yance, Jim Bossy, Bill Byrne (trumpets); Carl Fontana, Russ Little, Mel Wanzo (trombones); Joe Alexander, Sal Nistico, Joe Romano (tenor saxes); Cecil Payne (baritone sax); Al Dailey (piano); Carl Pruitt (bass); and John Von Ohlen (drums).

WOODY: We did a lot of British television and the band received a lot of acclaim. Once again we came through and did a good job, I guess. But it certainly has kept Europe on our side, in our visits to England, because everybody saw the films.

After that [1960s] band reached its best point . . . I was hell bent again on experimentation, because I felt the jazz-rock thing was beginning with people like Miles Davis. . . . What we are playing now evolved out of that period. I'm trying to keep my ear to the ground.[1]

On February 12 the band flew home in time for a Valentine's Day opening and four weeks' engagement at Caesar's Palace in Las Vegas. From mid-March until midsummer, the Herd remained on a grueling schedule of one-nighters.

A final indignity came at George Wein's Newport Jazz Festival in July. Woody's patience with his old friend and associate Abe Turchen was exhausted when it became evident that Turchen had neglected to settle an overdue bill with a bus company, threatening the orchestra's capability to continue. The repercussions forced Woody to hire Hermie Dressel as his manager. Dressel had been a musician himself, having played drums for the late Hal McIntyre and on 52nd Street with Coleman Hawkins, Charlie Shavers, and Joe Marsala in the 1940s.

HERMIE DRESSEL: I came to work for Woody August 11, 1968. Woody and I had been friends since the thirties. The poor guy called me from his room. A sheriff and a deputy sheriff had him hostage, because Abe had not paid a bus bill, and the bus company was in Rhode Island, so they couldn't grab Woody until he played Rhode Island, and of course Newport is in Rhode Island. Both the sheriff and the deputy were going to the concert with their families. They both loved Woody dearly, but the judge had handed them the papers and this was their job. So I got the money from George Wein and I straightened the thing out, and I told Woody that he couldn't go on living like this. That's when I took over.

    The first year I took the band over, I worked for nothing, because I had to borrow $20,000 from Joe Glaser who owned ABC Booking. The reason I had to get into that situation so quickly was because Abe Turchen signed Woody's name to a bad check in Las Vegas, and you just don't do that there! Woody was going to play Vegas, so I had to extricate him from that problem.

    For some strange reason, Abe didn't file for Woody for a number of years. Not to pay is one thing, but not to file is another thing.

    But it was partly Woody's fault. Woody never questioned. I had him for seventeen years. He must have been in New York, in those years, at least seventy-five to 100 times. His accountant and I always invited him to come up and go through the books. He didn't even have to call first, that's how open I kept the operation. But he never showed up.

BILLY HUNT: I rejoined the band May 19, 1968, and stayed until the fall. There were countless scenes with Abe and bus problems. The bus company confiscated our music and Woody's alto one night at the Club Laurel, until Abe promised to pay.

    I enjoyed the times when the bus company would take our music. We just went straight ahead and played the gigs by memory.

The author asked Woody how Abe Turchen responded to the IRS charges and his termination as the band's manager.

WOODY: Well, he was horrified. I don't know why, because he knew what he had done. When I got the perspective of where I really was, I severed our relationship immediately. He wanted to still hang around because he felt he was the only one to figure out the numbers that we were involved in, but I told him I had had enough. But we were not enemies. . . .

When asked to describe his treatment by IRS agents, Woody said: "They were just too willing to take any money that I might have had something to do with. They made my life very difficult many times. They would put liens on anything I was involved with."

BILL BYRNE: Abe died in San Diego in the early seventies. We used to get reports on him every once in a while. He was still selling merchandise. He liked to sell watches.

He was a mathematical genius. He could calculate anything just like that. When the band would go to Europe, he could figure up the exchange rates fast. He had a photographic memory for cards; he got barred from Las Vegas because he would be playing 21 and consistently beat the house. He was a very smart guy. If he had put all that effort into the straight side of business, Woody would have had a lot of money.

Hermie Dressel initially served the interests of the band well by instituting a variety of shrewd promotional gimmicks to pull the band out of its financial woes. One of his marketing ideas involved displaying the band's LP album covers on the music stands.

WOODY: Jazz has always had its ups and downs. It's never been broadly popular. But it remains part of the life of a large segment of people, a big minority. You've just got to spend a great deal of effort to get them on your side, to draw them to live concerts.

In 1968 Woody signed with Cadet Records. In conjunction with this move, he tried out a combination intended to attract a broad segment of the younger generation, at the same time retaining the traditional Herman audiences. Woody introduced a more rock-oriented rhythm section, with electric piano from John Hicks (formerly with Art Blakey's Jazz Messengers), the electric bass of Arthur Harper, drummer Ed Soph, and an added percussionist, Morris Jennings. This change produced a predictable mixed reaction among the older fans.

Veteran Herd trombonist Henry Southall had returned. Other sidemen included saxophonists Frank Vicari, Steve Lederer, and Thomas Boras, alongside tenorist Sal Nistico, who by now was a veteran at age 28. New faces in the trumpet section included Gary Grant, Nat Pavone, Henry Hall, Sal Marquez, and James Bossert. (Bill Byrne had taken a six-month leave of absence.) The new lead trombonist was Bob Burgess, whose big, round sound had formerly been a part of the Donahue, Kenton, Billy May, Barnet, and Les Brown bands.

BOBBY BURGESS: I was with the band three times. Woody loved to have someone to rap with after the gigs, and I was luckily picked by him . . . to listen to his road stories, and he, mine. It was a joy.

Playing lead for Woody was demanding. You see, Bill Harris set a precedent that put a fire under your ass. For not only was Bill a great soloist, comedian, and human being, but of all the great lead players, Bill was the epitome of what lead playing is all about.

Woody gave you all the freedom you could ask for in interpretation and style, but you HAD to make it swing hard! . . . There were many solo spots for trombone, left over for the most part from Bill. But if you didn't have your shit together, you could NEVER expect him to let you play "Bijou."

I first joined the band in September 1968 at a gig in a Moose hall in Missouri. God, what a terrible gig. I was with the band about two years, and then again in 1971 for a few months, and again in 1972. Each time I left the band for one reason: tired of the road. In 1970 I left to go to NYC with Mel and Thad and the Broadway show *Promises, Promises*. . . . I got bugged with the music scene and wanted to play, REALLY play! So back to Woody. The road always offered the chance to play.

An influx of contemporary pop began to join the standard Herd charts in the band's book. Other bands, such as Basie, Kenton, and Rich, began to include samples of fusion music in their repertoires. The Herman management began to get more bookings at colleges and high schools, and the band was also cofeatured with established rock groups.

BILL BYRNE: It began with the *Light My Fire* album, recorded in the fall of 1968. Dick La Palm, who was with Chess and Cadet Records in Chicago, approached Woody. La Palm had some fresh ideas.

On October 7 and 8, 1968, the Herd went into Ter Mar Studios in Chicago to cut ten titles for the Cadet label. Most of the charts featured an electronic rhythm section and a hybrid rock beat. All were written by Richard Evans, a gifted arranger and exponent of the new sounds. A guitar and an extra percussionist were added for the date. The resulting album was nominated for a Grammy in 1969.

"Pontieo" is an exciting mood created by Evans. Solos are from tenorist Frank Vicari and high trumpet from lead man Nat Pavone.

"Here I Am Baby" could be considered the Herd's official entry into the fusion sound. Vicari is featured on tenor above the rock beat.

"MacArthur Park," the late sixties-early seventies period piece, is performed elegantly. Woody plays the melody on alto, followed by the colossal trombone sound of Bobby Burgess. Part two features Hicks's piano and tenorist Lederer, and the finale brings all five trumpeters blasting into the stratosphere.

The title piece, "Light My Fire," has Woody playing both solo and lead alto, with trumpet solos from Sal Marquez and Henry Hall. Burgess is prominently heard as is the trumpet section.

"I Say a Little Prayer" is another period piece featuring tenor from Frank Vicari and a trumpet offering from Henry Hall. Burgess plays lead trombone like a giant.

Richard Evans' "Impression of Strayhorn" features Woody's lush alto with gorgeous ensemble sounds in the background.

"Keep on Keepin' On" commences with a rock beat, then breaks loose with an up-tempo swing beat, featuring Nistico, trumpeter Hall, and scorching section work from the trumpets, with conspicuous lead from Nat Pavone.

At the end of 1968 Woody broke up the band for its annual vacation. The band reorganized in January and in March trumpeter Bill Chase rejoined for the annual tour of Europe. The April–May 1969 edition of the Herd comprised Bill Chase, John Madrid, Gary Grant, Henry Hall, Bill Byrne (trumpets); Vince Prudente, Bob Burgess, Bruce Fowler (trombones); Sal Nistico, Frank Vicari, Steve Lederer (tenor saxes); Ron Cuber (baritone sax); John Hicks (piano); Arthur Harper (bass); and Jack Ranelli (drums).

BILL BYRNE: Bill [Chase] left in August 1966, when we were in Las Vegas at the Tropicana Hotel. Then he came back in March, 1969, I believe, for six months, and went to Europe with us. He left in October 1969, about the same week that Frank Tiberi came on. He hired Frank. He was the road manager then. When I came on the band originally, Bill and Nat were splitting the duties. Bill would hire all the brass players and get all the hotel rooms. Nat would hire all the rhythm section and the saxes, and take care of the payroll.

Bill was one we all admired. He'd listen to the whole band, and he could tell you exactly what each guy could do. He would get the best out of you that way. He would work on the [sound] board, and if he thought you were overblowing, he would tell you to back off slightly. He was really listening constantly to what was going on.

BOBBY BURGESS: In 1969 Tom Malone, a student from North Texas State University, and a good friend, joined the band. I had warned him about Woody's moods, and to stay away from him this particular night. Unbeknownst to me, before the gig, Tom went up to Woody and introduced himself, and told Woody he "wrote arrangements, copied, played piano, bass, trumpet, et cetera." Woody just looked at him and said, "You're fired!" Poor Tom came to me almost in tears. I laughed and told him I would straighten it out. Woody could be a terror, from the stress of the road.

The "band boy" was a necessary fixture with touring big bands from the thirties into the sixties. Some of the better-known band boys on the Herd were "Popsie" Randolph, also a notable big-band photographer who had worked for Benny Goodman; Nat Wexler, with the First Herd; Teddy Drusdofsky and Teddy "Fats" Davis, both with the Second Herd; and Jack Wamsley, with the Third Herd.

The author asked Bill Byrne when the band boy position was finally terminated, with the musicians assuming the responsibility for care of the music library, instruments, band setup, and other duties.

BILL BYRNE: I guess we had the last band boy in the late 1960s. A friend of Steve Lederer, the tenor player with us, a drummer who had worked in a professional drum shop in New York, came out to do it. He got drunk one night in the back of the bus and he was smoking pot too, and he went berserk and was trying to beat up Frank Tiberi. Frank had to lock himself in the john, and we had to hold the band boy back. We finally got to Indianapolis and we let him off the bus. He was a real strong, adult guy, and he could pop you one.

Another guy came on, a black kid who was a guitar player and a friend of Hermie's and Dionne Warwick's. He did it for a little while, but he didn't like it, because it's frustrating for a musician. But after that, Bobby Burgess and a couple of other guys said, "We'll do the band boy job. Give us the money and we'll take care of it." So that's how that got started. First there was one guy doing it, and they said, "Why not two of us and we'll split the money and make it easier?"

On September 2 and 3, the Herd was in Chicago to record again for the Cadet label. Eleven titles were cut without any significant contributions to the Herd's jazz legacy, although Stevie Wonder's "My Cherie Amour," a pretty pop tune of the period, has some lovely Herman alto playing on Wonder's melody in a pseudo-Latin beat and a poignant trombone solo from Burgess.

Joining the band in September 1969 was pianist, composer, and arranger Alan Broadbent. Alan became a major contributor to the Herd's music in the early 1970s. Born in Auckland, New Zealand, he had his first real experience with jazz at a Dave Brubeck concert in Auckland in 1964, and only two years later won a *Down Beat* magazine scholarship to the Berklee School in Boston. He studied composition and jazz arranging with Herb Pomeroy, and at the same time worked with Lennie Tristano on jazz piano.

ALAN BROADBENT: I wasn't a Herman fan, but I remember about a year before I left New Zealand, the record "Better Git It in Your Soul" [the live recording] entered New Zealand, and it just killed us all. That was my only experience with Woody. I've always been a jazz pianist, and my direction at that time was toward the cool stuff. When I went to Berklee, I studied Gil Evans and Duke Ellington, and Woody was a "swing band" that I didn't listen to. Then I became more knowledgeable of his history.

My first album with Woody was on the Cadet label, called *Woody*. I had to adapt my writing style on my first charts for him. My second chart for him was a Blood, Sweat and Tears tune, a ballad. I decided to use the Berklee and Gil Evans style voicings, and different colorations, and it didn't work at all. So you adapt, you live and learn. I wanted to find out how to write like that anyway.

When I joined the band, it was the worst you ever heard! The drummer was hopeless; he would turn the time around. It was in a period where most of our gigs weren't that attractive. They were mostly country clubs and military bases. Bob Burgess, Sal Nistico, Frank Vicari, and Frank Tiberi were all on the band. Rigby Powell, the trumpet player from San Francisco, was also there.

The author asked Alan Broadbent if the band was striving for a "fusion" sound during this period.

ALAN BROADBENT: I never thought of it as that. At the time, Blood, Sweat and Tears was popular. So a couple of us, like Tony Klatka, Bill Stapleton, and myself, we adapted a few of those things for Woody, but that's about all. Most of the charts that I did for Woody were jazz charts.

There's nothing I really have to say, except the charts that I did for Woody stand for themselves. Some of them are "Bebop and Roses," and I like ones called "Far In" and "Blues in the Night." I have to say I also like "Children of Lima," although it could stand reorchestrating now.

Woody was separate from us most of the time, although he was very kind to me and certainly a master bandleader.

On September 20, 1969, while the band was in South Bend, Indiana, Woody received a phone call from Milwaukee that his father, Otto, had passed away. Otto was 82 at the time of his death.

RAY SHERMAN: Woody's dad had broken up housekeeping and had started living in nursing homes. I took care of him the last couple of years. I saw to it that the bills were paid. I received the checks from Abe Turchen and Woody.

Joining the band in October 1969 was tenor saxophonist Frank Tiberi, who would become leader of the Herd during Woody's illnesses and after his passing in 1987.

FRANK TIBERI: When I was eight, there was a little organization called the Mucci Post Band. They were looking for young players, and my father enrolled me. I started on the clarinet. It was all private teaching and very expensive, three times a week. Monday, Wednesday and Friday. Tuesday and Thursday were rehearsals. We would be rehearsing *Aida*, *Barber of Seville*, and *Cavalleria Rusticana*. We would perform during the evening after the processions, which were held in the Catholic Church. That would be on Saturday nights during the season, which was a ten-week period. Every week, it would be a new piece of music. It would be like a block party. We would walk around the street with the replicas of saints, and people would pin dollars on them, and the band would march and play a lot of Sousa music. Then we would do the concert. It was five nights a week, in 1936, for three dollars a month. I don't think that anyone in the world could duplicate that situation today.

That's the way it was in those days. It was very intimate. Nothing was considered too much financially. Camden [New Jersey] was a small community of mostly Italians that had come from the Old Country, and all got positions in the work that was available at RCA, Campbell Soups, and the New York shipyards.

At the age of 12 I was being prepared for the Curtiss Institute, but I didn't get to do that. My father died, and I chose to start supporting my mother and family. I got a job in a nightclub, three nights a week.

I was self-taught in jazz. I practiced on the piano, and the only formal training I had was with Sol Schoenbach on the bassoon. He was the principal soloist in the Philadelphia Symphony Orchestra.

When I got out of high school in 1946, I went with the Bob Chester Band. I traveled with some great musicians such as Frank Rosolino, Doug Mettome, and Bobby Styles.

After that, I got married and lived sort of a domesticated life. Most of my work was around Philadelphia and Camden doing jazz recording sessions with small groups. I was always interested in the jazz end of music, so I was practicing and writing during that period.

After getting into the bassoon, I started to break in some musical shows in Philadelphia, such as *Funny Girl*. I was one of the first bassoon doublers; that is, we were able to handle five instruments, and so they were able to utilize all of the instrument sounds in the musical shows.

After that, I got a call from Benny Goodman, and at the age of 29, I joined the small Benny Goodman group. It was a sextet with Kenny Burrell and Ruby Braff. This was in 1957. Then I was with Benny's big band, and we had players like Severinsen, Mel Davis, and Hank Jones, and did some concerts. Then he organized a Benny Goodman "ghost band" under the direction of Urbie Green and I went out on the road with Urbie.

The next significant thing was in 1969, when Bill Chase called me. I was referred to him by my friend Sal Nistico. That's when I joined

Woody's band. I had got a divorce in 1968, and I was just ready for something. I had substituted once for Frank Vicari, and Woody heard me.

The year 1969 ended for the Woody Herman Herd at the Washington Plaza Hotel in Seattle. The band was heard live on a radio remote broadcast on New Year's Eve, a disappearing showcase for big bands in 1969.

DICK HAFER: To be honest with you, when Woody started getting into that semirock thing, I didn't go to hear him that much. I discussed it with him one time at Charlie's, a bar in New York. A bunch of us were there who had been with the earlier band, and we said, "Where are you going with this?" Woody said, "I gotta go with what I got! The kids that I play with now are into this and I always went with the guys in the band and that's where I'm going." That's what he always did. He always let the band lead the direction. If he didn't like them, he would get rid of them. Most of his writers were working with the current band, except for Ralph Burns, who sent charts in for years and years.

In 1970 I was working the Merv Griffin Show, and I took my wife and kids down to Atlantic City. We were driving along the expressway and we saw this sign at the Steel Pier, "WOODY HERMAN." My wife said, "Oh, no, you're going to be going out with Woody all the time!"

So we went out on the pier that night to hear the band, and he was in a strange mood . . . and he was starting to get caught up in this. He really had sort of a rock band. To me it was. I hadn't been aware of it. He was playing a soprano then. There were a lot of people there who were bugging him about playing "Apple Honey," and all those tunes that they associated with him. He got salty with the audience and said, "Where were ya when I needed ya?" You know, he always told people off if they got on him about anything.

BILL BYRNE: . . . Oh, yeah. He's told off the mobsters, everybody! He's pushed around some big people. . . . He always said, "All right, pal," and gave them a big whack on the back!

FRANK TIBERI: I remember an incident that happened at the first Newport Jazz Festival in Osaka, Japan, in October 1970. Nat Pierce was also appearing there with Carmen McRae. It was just a hangout. These Japanese businessmen were really obnoxious and loud. We were playing MacArthur Park, and we had this bit at the end. The trumpet players would all perform sort of an ethereal thing. They would start shouting and playing and go to different areas of the room. Buddy Powers had just gone to one area, and there was a table there with a Japanese businessman, and his geisha girl friend. Then Buddy started playing the trumpet and shouting, and the guy threw water at Buddy. So Woody called "Woodchopper's Ball," and went off the stage, and went back to the guy and played the clarinet right in his face. He was so close that the guy backed up and fell backwards right on the floor with the chair, and Woody just kept playing in his face. Then he walked back to the stage and said, "That will show 'em!"

BILL BYRNE: That was the night that Alan Broadbent fell in the hole on the stage. The stage revolved, and Alan knocked himself cuckoo. We thought he was just being funny. Another favorite of Woody's was if somebody would start to get out of line in a country club or some big party, he would start blowing his whistle, and get on the mike and start yelling, "Security, Security, come over and get these people out of here!" He would do this if they would come up and ask for some Glenn Miller tune or something.

After the Herd's Asian tour, the band went into the Chicago studios of Cadet Records and cut six titles for the album *Woody*. Most of the material suffers from poor sound quality. Two tracks are worthy of mention. "A Time for Love," the Johnny Mandel ballad, is arranged here by Alan Broadbent and features a gorgeous and sensitive flugelhorn solo from Tom Harrell. During this period, the Herd's trumpet section began doubling on the flugelhorn. Eventually, the band played scores written for five flugelhorns.

"Blues in the Night" is a revolutionary thirteen-minute, forty-seven-second remake of the Harold Arlen–Johnny Mercer tune, a hit for Woody in 1941. Alan Broadbent's score is done as a production number in four movements. Woody vocalizes in a bluesy manner, with blistering solos from trumpeter Tom Harrell and Nistico.

FRANK TIBERI: I took care of all Woody's instruments and had them ready for him to play. I would wet his reeds for him. I had a little atomizer thing.

We were playing Frank Fontaine's club over in Pennsylvania; he was the singer that always made the appearance on the Jackie Gleason Show. It was one of those late-night places. He had about five teenage girls dancing on the stage. They were just kicking their legs up and down, and there was Woody's saxophone over there, and one of the girls slipped, and grabbed hold of the neck of the saxophone and it really bent. It was like a pretzel! Woody handed it over to me, I looked at it, and I couldn't straighten it out, but I did cover all the holes. He stuck it up to his mouth, and it really looked like it was stuck up in his nose. But some way, he sang and played through it and he performed just as well as before.

I was the sax doctor for everybody. Even now, I do all my own work in the hotels. I do soldering and welding. I carry all the equipment with me. I've been in a lot of places where I've had to fix the speakers for the band, like in Europe, where we couldn't find anybody to do it.

On November 23 the band flew to London, commencing a twenty-day annual British tour. On December 25 the Herd opened at Caesar's Palace Coliseum in Las Vegas for a three-week stand. On New Year's Eve, an enterprising promoter brought in the Duke Ellington Orchestra to share the New Year revelry with the Herd, creating a memorable occasion for jazz audiences.

A two-week vacation for the Herdsmen began on January 24, 1971. During this period, Woody signed with Fantasy Records of Berkeley, California. For the Herd's debut on the label, the album *Brand New* was recorded while the band was performing in Berkeley. Electric guitarist Mike Bloomfield, a premier instrumentalist in rock music, was brought in for the recording session and featured on four titles. Wally Heider presided over the recording responsibilities.

Broadbent's "Sidewalk Stanley" is a titular nod to the fan who achieved the undisputed record for free entrance whenever the Herd performed in the New York City area. It's a blues riff with the electronic rhythm paraphernalia featuring guitarist Bloomfield and a vocal by Woody that doesn't quite make it.

"After Hours," the earthy blues long identified with Erskine Hawkins, is wrapped in a new Nat Pierce arrangement that features Alan Broadbent's electric piano. The chart remained in the Herd's book as a staple and was later played on conventional keyboard. The score crystallizes with a gradual buildup to a brass ensemble climax. Woody would occasionally call it as the final number at dances, much to the dismay of the trumpet section, as it proved to be a lip-buster in the closing bars.

"Since I Fell for You" was arranged by Broadbent and features Woody on both solo and lead alto, with Bloomfield. The saxes achieve a lovely blend, and the brass ensemble gets a tight sound.

"Hitch Hike on the Possum Trot Line" is a Broadbent score, a "dirty blues" vehicle for Bloomfield's guitar and Woody's soprano.

"Love in Silent Amber" is a lovely tone poem, with an introduction reminiscent of Gil Evans' work. It features Bobby Burgess playing superbly and clarinet from Woody.

"I Almost Lost My Mind" is a Nat Pierce arrangement of the vintage Ivory Joe Hunter tune, with Woody vocalizing: "When I lost my baby, I almost lost my mind. . . ." Tony Klatka's trumpet adds to the mood.

Broadbent's "Adam's Apple" is an excellent blues score featuring adroit, low-register Herman clarinet, Klatka's flugelhorn, a muted offering from Burgess, and superb lead trumpet from Forrest Buchtel.

On May 17, 1971, the Woody Herman Herd conducted its first jazz clinic and concert, at Northern Illinois University. Over the years, jazz clinics not only promoted an ever-increasing crop of university student–musicians, but also helped increase the bookings of bands like Herman, Kenton, and Rich.

BILL BYRNE: Woody wanted the young people to be able to communicate with the musicians one-to-one. It's like in the years past, kids would be hanging around the bandstand, and guys in the band would talk with them. Then Stan Kenton really started this whole thing, and we kind of got in on Stan's coattails.

BOBBY BURGESS: Woody didn't know if he would like clinics at first, but he found he had a great audience, good money, and most important, he had a real message for the students by doing what he did best, leading a band.

A new face in the saxophone section in late 1971 was an exceptional black tenorist, Gregory Herbert. Herbert remained a principal soloist in the saxophone section and a key member of the Herd for nearly five and one-half years. *Down Beat* described his playing as possessing "the lyricism of Wayne Shorter, the gutsiness of Gene Ammons, the dazzling facility of John Coltrane and the rhythmic power of Sonny Rollins."[2]

Before he joined the Herd, Herbert's primary instrument was the alto. At 16, he sat in with the Miles Davis group at the Showboat in Philadelphia. Miles told him in his gravel voice, "Hey, young man, you play your ass off!" At 17, Herbert spent a summer subbing for Russell Procope on alto when Procope was filling in for Harry Carney on baritone in the Ellington band.

Herbert told *Down Beat*: "I had played tenor before, but my strong instrument was the alto. I was 'singing on the alto'; it was my 'voice.' But I had to become a tenor player because Woody was the ONLY alto player in the band. At first, low register tenor was really throwing me for a loop, because most alto players, including myself, tend to play in the middle and high registers. So it helped me as a saxophone player to get into the tenor, because you really have to play all over the horn."[3]

ALAN BROADBENT: Halfway through my tenure, Bill Stapleton came on the band. I think Tony Klatka was already on. We hit it off, because we were all writers and we wanted to change what was happening. We figured that the only way we could do this was by using some of the Blood, Sweat and Tears material. I did a chart on "Smiling Phases." It was on the *Woody* album, which unfortunately is a very bad recording, acoustically speaking.

We rehearsed the band without Woody, and about two months later, we played a high school prom somewhere, and Woody wanted to hear the charts that we did. Actually, we had to talk him into it, telling him that the kids would dig it. So we played "Smiling Phases," and the kids went crazy! It was the popular music of the time, and it was easily adaptable. So Woody said, "Wait a minute!" Suddenly the juices started to flow again, if you know what I mean. So he asked me if we could do something on "Blues in the Night." So I got to show off a little bit.

Then I did a couple other silly rock charts that I'm ashamed of, and then I did some pretty good, swinging tunes after I left the band. They're on the *Giant Steps* album. I also did the *Brand New* album with Michael Bloomfield and Woody.

I left Woody in 1972 and continued on as a pianist and a writer for my own amusement.

AL PORCINO: I rejoined the band in Las Vegas on April 19, 1972. When I came on, the trumpet personnel was Charlie Davis, John Thomas, Bill Stapleton, and Bill Byrne, the manager. The trombones were Bobby Burgess, Rick Stepton, and Harold Garrett. In the saxes, we had Frank Tiberi and the wonderful black tenor player Gregory Herbert, Steve Lederer, and Tom Anastas on baritone. In the rhythm, we had Joe La Barbera on drums. Harold Danko was on piano, and we had a young, black Fender bass player named Al Johnson.

We had fun. There were some very good charts in the book. Alan Broadbent had been writing for the band by that time. I particularly like his production on "Blues in the Night."

The next important job on our itinerary was around August, when we played at the St. Regis Roof in New York. During the engagement we went into the studio and recorded for Fantasy the album called *The Raven Speaks*, which turned out all right. Alan Broadbent had a couple of things in there. One piece that stands out was a title called "Reunion at Newport."

The Herman Herd was on location at the St. Regis Hotel, August 16–29, 1972. During this time the Herdsmen recorded *Woody Herman: The Raven Speaks*. The results were a good representation of the Herd's pattern during the fusion years. Returnees included lead trumpeter and veteran of three Herds Al Porcino, and baritonist Tom Anastas from the Herd of the early sixties.

"Alone Again (Naturally)" is an attractive treatment of the period pop piece with trombonist Burgess doing the melody, alto from Woody, and Greg Herbert demonstrating a sensitive and lyrical ballad style. The electronic rhythm section is evident throughout.

Herbie Hancock's "Watermelon Man" is performed in an updated arrangement that doesn't come off as well as Nat Pierce's 1963 version. For some reason, it's retitled "Sandia Chicano." Solos are from Greg Herbert, piccolo, Steve Lederer, tenor, Bill Stapleton, trumpet, and Woody on soprano.

"It's Too Late" is another pop tune done against the background of the electronic beat. (Guitarist Pat Martino was added for the record date.) Woody plays soprano and Harold Danko is featured on the Fender Rhodes piano.

The album's title piece, "The Raven Speaks," is a characteristic effort from the Herd's fusion phase. Solos are from Tiberi, Woody on soprano and trombonist Rick Stepton.

"The Summer of '42" is a lovely ballad arrangement showcasing the tenor artistry of Greg Herbert. According to report, Greg had been captivated by actress Jennifer O'Neill, who appeared in the film of the same title.

Alan Broadbent's "Reunion at Newport" is a rollicking flag-waver featuring a boppish line reminiscent of the late 1940s. Soloists are Woody (clarinet),

Harold Danko (piano), Tiberi (tenor), Burgess and Rick Stepton (trombones), and Bill Stapleton on flugelhorn. Drummer Joe La Barbera propels the band with well-placed fills and an effective solo.

Stapleton's "Bill's Blues" is more straight-ahead material with the exception of the electronic sounds from the rhythm section. Woody plays clarinet, Danko, piano, Herbert blows some attractive flute, while composer Stapleton does a flowing muted solo against the ensemble backdrop.

BOBBY BURGESS: In October 1972, Woody called me to come to his room. Here was Woody, like a little kid, with broken, old soprano reeds, an old, rusty ligature for the mouthpiece of a soprano sax, some old, worn-out pads, and a beautiful set of cuff links, made of silver, with Indian-head nickels in them. Laughing, he told me it was Charlie Barnet's birthday, and asked me to help him wrap all of this, and send it to Charlie.

In 1972 I got a contract in Europe. So, grudgingly, I left my first love, big band road playing. Like Nat Pierce said, "I was sick and tired of being sick and tired." He said that after a 600-mile road trip with Woody.

Joining the Herd in October 1972 was a talented trombonist with wide range, James Edward (Jim) Pugh. Jim had worked with Chuck Mangione and other groups in the Rochester, New York area.

JIM PUGH: I sort of indirectly replaced Bob Burgess, lead trombone. First, Jimmy Guinn came out [from the late fifties band] but stayed only three or four months. Then I moved over and did some things [on lead]. So it was like the two of us replacing Bob.

Before joining, I was out with the band one week subbing for Rick Stepton and played with Bob Burgess. He was an amazing lead player.

The biggest impression I had was the people who were there when I initially joined the band. But unfortunately, some of them, like Bill Stapleton and Greg Herbert, have met their demise. Greg was out with Blood, Sweat and Tears, and they were in Amsterdam, and he overdosed.

The year 1972 concluded for the Herd with a New Year's Eve engagement at the Flamingo Hotel in Las Vegas. On January 3 Woody took the band into Donte's in North Hollywood, a club with an all-jazz policy.

The Herd followed, more or less, the fusion trend for another three to four years. The electronic rhythm section and the rock beat were difficult to reconcile with the swing pulse characteristic of jazz. The overstatement from the drummers was in stark contrast to the lighter beats of the Toughs, Lamonds, Igoes, and Hannas. One characteristic that remained, however, was the intense fire and spirit, a hallmark of all Herman Herds.

BILL BYRNE: Alan Broadbent's writing was definitely significant. Andy La
   Verne was one of the first guys to introduce the synthesizers into the
   band. He got one of the earliest, crudest ones they had, and he kept coming up with a better model as they became available.

As a point of reference, this is the Herd as it appeared in concert at
Clearwater, Florida, on March 22, 1973: Larry Pyatt, Walter Blanton, Frank
Brown, Bill Stapleton, Bill Byrne (trumpets); Jim Pugh, Jeff Sharp (trom-
bones); Harold Garrett (bass trombone); Frank Tiberi, Steve Lederer,
Gregory Herbert (tenor saxes); Harry Kleintank (baritone sax); Andy La
Verne (piano); Wayne Darling (bass); and Ed Soph (drums).

   The following month, the Herd was at A&R Studios in New York, recording twelve more titles for the Fantasy label. Nine were selected for the album
Giant Steps, which won a Grammy for the band in 1974.

   Chick Corea's "La Fiesta," an exciting Latin-flavored opus in the 6/8 time
signature favored by many young musicians of the 1970s, featured solos from
Greg Herbert (piccolo), Tiberi (tenor), Andy La Verne (electric piano), and
Woody on soprano. The cut is highlighted by excellent first trumpet work
from Larry Pyatt.

   Bill Stapleton's chart of "A Song for You" is a lovely period piece utilizing
the rock beat against a lush ensemble background, with solos from La Verne,
Woody (soprano), and Stapleton (flugelhorn).

   "Meaning of the Blues" is a showcase for Jim Pugh's delicate improvisations.

   The title track, Coltrane's "Giant Steps," features superb scoring from
Stapleton and an exciting tenor chase with Tiberi and Herbert soloing in the
finest Herman tradition.

   Thad Jones's "A Child Is Born" is a rich and moody ballad featuring
Woody's clarinet and Herbert's tenor.

   Alan Broadbent's "Bebop and Roses" is a swinging, linear bop score, with
solos from Stapleton (trumpet), Pugh, and Lederer on tenor, concluding with
a trumpet-tenor duet from Stapleton and Lederer. Drummer Soph propels
the band effectively.

JIM PUGH: When I first came out, the band was doing mostly dances.
   Basically, the dance book was all that great stuff from the sixties, some
   Nat Pierce material and those things. After *Giant Steps* and the Grammys,
   we started to get more clinics and do more high schools and colleges. By
   the end of my tenure with the band, we were probably doing more concerts than dances.

      In the course of a concert, it would have probably been 30 to 40 per-
   cent of the rock-influenced things, and about 60 percent of the other.
   Maybe out of that, 20 percent was the nostalgic things like "Four

Brothers" and "Early Autumn." The rest of it would just be more recently written jazz-oriented music.

I remember one night we were at a dance, and some couple was harassing him about what we were playing. They said, "You're not playing anything that we can dance to!" So he cut the band off and made the crowd gather around and proceeded to make these people dance for him. He said, "Let me see you dance." So they danced a little bit, and he said, "We don't have anything we can play to that," and turned around and we started playing again. He was good at handling the folks.

On May 16, 1973, Woody turned 60. The forty-two years of road tours were beginning to show. He had occasional flare-ups with gout and had lost most of his teeth. Nevertheless, he continued to endure the trials of a touring band.

INGRID HERMAN REESE: After I had been in Nashville a couple of years, my husband, Bob Fawler, got involved with part ownership of a little bluegrass club. My father brought the whole band into this little, tiny club. He thought it would be fun. He squashed them all into this tiny room and played for free. He had me invite all the local musicians that I knew and idolized. People like Johnny Gimbel, a great fiddle player who had played with Bob Wills, came and sat in with the band.

In July the brilliant composer, arranger, and tenorist Gary Michael Anderson joined the Herd. Gary was born in Torrance, California, in 1947. He graduated from Berklee College of Music in Boston in 1969.

During Gary's nearly five-year association with Woody, he turned out an impressive series of contributions to the band's bulging library, most notably the striking score of Aaron Copland's "Fanfare for the Common Man."

On October 29 the band flew to Europe for a twelve-day tour. On December 12 they were back for a six-night engagement at the Half Note Club in New York City.

On January 2, 1974, the band returned to Fantasy's studios in Berkeley to record the *Thundering Herd* album. Coltrane was represented by Bill Stapleton's swinging interpretation of "Lazy Bird," with impressive solos from Tiberi and Stapleton on flugelhorn.

Tony Klatka's treatment of Coltrane's haunting "Naima" is superb, highlighting Tiberi's sensitive improvisations.

Klatka's "Blues for Poland" is a relaxed glimpse into the blues with the inventive Czech baritonist Jan Konopasek, Klatka (flugelhorn), and La Verne out front.

Alan Broadbent's lovely score of "What Are You Doing the Rest of Your Life?" is a vehicle for Bob Burgess. The chart was recorded again with soloist Stan Getz in 1979 at the Monterey Jazz Festival.

The Great American Music Hall, San Francisco, January 1974. Front row, L to R: Gary Anderson, Frank Tiberi, Gregory Herbert (hidden) (tenor saxes), John Oslawski (baritone sax). Second row: Andy LaVerne (piano), Jeff Brillinger (drums). Back row: Chip Jackson (electric bass), Bill Byrne, Nelson Hatt, John Thomas, Dennis Dotson, Buddy Powers (trumpets). Behind the band: former Herman trumpeter Forrest Buchtel. (Courtesy Fantasy Records)

"America Drinks and Goes Home" is Broadbent's interpretation of Frank Zappa's rock number, featuring Klatka's flugelhorn and La Verne's electric piano. The chart testifies to Broadbent's creative scoring for a variety of instrumentation.

"Corazon," a pop tune by Carole King, is another example of Woody's versatile approach choosing contemporary material. It was arranged by Bill Stapleton and is a feature for Woody on soprano.

"Come Saturday Morning" was arranged by Broadbent for Greg Herbert's remarkable ballad stylings and also presents Frank Tiberi's recorded debut on bassoon with the Herd.

"Bass Folk Song" by Tony Klatka features La Verne, Herbert (piccolo), and Chip Jackson, a young bassist from Connecticut, all against a rock beat.

Woody (January 1974): I think that there are only two or three necessities of life. One is eating, one is sleeping, and probably above all is being as close to your loved ones as you can be and trying to do the right kind of job in other areas. The road was never an easy way of life, but it's the only one I know, and when I'm not on the road, I'm a very unhappy old man. . . .

We've been into this high school thing for almost three years. Almost a third of our dates last year were in high schools, junior colleges, and colleges.

This is probably one of the happiest times of my life, and I feel I'm being productive in more than just being a bandleader.

The kids are learning the things being handed down as part of tradition and part of the roots of "old-time, hot American jazz music," and I think it's very important.[4]

On January 21 the band flew from Portland, Oregon, to England for its annual tour, lasting two weeks. In May they were scheduled to return to England for a one-week engagement at an Isle of Man jazz festival, canceled when the concert hall burned down.

On July 4 the Herd flew to Geneva and then boarded a train for Montreux for a July 6 appearance in the annual jazz festival. The Montreux Jazz Festival is known as the "queen" among Europe's jazz festivals. It's the longest running (sixteen nights) and, in 1974, was in its eighth year.

The concert hall at Montreux is always crowded and hot, with most fans choosing to stand for the best view. The concerts often run behind schedule, and it is not unusual for a jet-lagged band to hit the stage ninety minutes later than anticipated.

The Herd was scheduled to be the fourth and final performance of the evening, following Sonny Rollins, who did three encores. It was approaching three in the morning when Rollins completed his set. After Rollins' performance, the stage had to be set up for the Herd. At 3:30 the Herd was assembled on stage, ready to play. The Herdsmen had been struggling to stay awake, yet when Woody counted off the first piece in the presence of a full house, everyone came to life as if injected with adrenalin. The concert concluded at 5:00, then the band returned to the hotel, packed and readied themselves for a 6:00 A.M. bus departure to the airport and a flight to Ankara, Turkey.

A segment of the Herd's live performance was recorded for the Fantasy album *Herd at Montreux*.

"I Can't Get Next to You" was originally recorded for the Cadet label in 1969. According to Woody, "I wanted something to showcase the dynamic ability of Gregory Herbert on tenor." It's a potent fusion piece, displaying the brilliant brass ensemble and Herbert's distinctive technique.

"Superstar" introduces composer and tenorist Gary Michael Anderson as a staff-arranger for the Herd and features lead trumpeter Dave Stahl.

Aaron Copland's "Fanfare for the Common Man" was adapted by Gary Anderson and features Woody's soprano and Herbert's tenor. The chart remained a staple in the Herd's library for the remainder of Woody's career. He would often call it to close an evening's last set. As later Herds played the score, it came to include an added drum break and a lip-buster brass ensemble finale with great dramatic effect.

WOODY: I have had a lot of Eastman School of Music graduates who worked for me, and one of the brass requisites, as a warmup, was to play the opening theme of "Fanfare for the Common Man." It came to my attention that I had Gary Anderson, a saxophonist in the band who did a lot of writing for us. I suggested that we do a piece on this. We put a modern-day kind of rhythm feeling to it, so that we could catch a lot of young people along the way.

"Montevideo" is a chart by Broadbent, originally entitled "Broadbent's Basket." The score is a vehicle for Andy La Verne's electric piano, with Dave Stahl's stratospheric trumpet.

"Tantum Ergo" is a tribute by Alan Broadbent to Duke Ellington, and according to Woody "is based on Alan's boyhood recollections of the Catholic Church and parochial school."[5] The score features the artistry of the late tenorist Gregory Herbert.

On July 18 the band flew from Frankfurt to Toronto for a two-day performance at the Belvedere King-Size Jazz Festival. The festivals were also held in Winnipeg on July 24 and Vancouver on July 26 and 27, with the Herd participating.

On August 9, 1974, tragedy struck the jazz community when trumpeter Bill Chase was killed in a plane crash. By 1974, Bill was fronting the group he called "Chase," with the unique instrumentation of four trumpets and a rhythm section utilizing organ in lieu of piano.

BILL BYRNE: It happened about five or six o'clock at night, in Jackson, Minnesota, right out of a little airfield in the cornfields. A storm had come up and it was just pitch black when the plane tried to get in there. It was raining so heavy that the guys who were driving in the car stopped because they got scared. I guess they flew in and tried to land and they pulled up, stalled out and crashed in a cornfield. The guy at the airport thought they had passed over and gone to another airport. They didn't find them in the field until the next morning.

The band was booked for most of September and October on a tour with Frank Sinatra. On September 2 the band began rehearsals with "Old Blue Eyes" at Harrah's in Lake Tahoe, Nevada. On October 13 Frank and the Herd performed at Madison Square Garden in New York. The band backed Sinatra for a grouping of his chestnuts: "It Was a Very Good Year," "I've Got You Under My Skin," and "My Way." There is little that identifies the Herd in the music recorded that night. Entitled *Sinatra—The Main Event, Live*, the album was released on the Reprise label.

WOODY: I enjoyed working with Frank tremendously. I had known Frank at the beginning of his career when he sang with Tommy Dorsey, and even before that when he was with Harry James. He was a very nice young man then, and he's still a very nice person. He has been known to have many strange people around him sometimes, and this can be a bit shaky for me.

Asked to elaborate on this subject, Woody responded:

WOODY: Well, if anyone picks up the album we did called *The Main Event*, if they have binoculars, or some kind of seeing aid, they might be able to find the fine print where it says, "Featuring Woody Herman and the Young Thundering Herd."

BILL BYRNE: They weren't going to list the name of the band on it at all. Hermie had to go in and fight for that. I guess he finally had to ask Frank personally. There was another guy involved, a famous producer. Woody and Frank were good friends for years. But Woody wasn't much to ask people for favors.

CHUBBY JACKSON: We had a get-together in Las Vegas in the 1970s with a big band made up of members who, at one time or another, had each been a Herdsman. It was held at the Musician's Union and began at 3:20 A.M. It was extremely touching, especially when Woody took over at the mike and recounted certain musical victories of the many different Herds. Strangely enough, any group that he fronted sounded like Woody.

JOHN BENNETT: We called it the "Vegas Woody Tribute." It wasn't his birthday, nor an anniversary of the band. It was just an affectionate tribute. It was held on September 15, 1974, at the Las Vegas Union building. The place was mobbed . . . with at least 450 people including local disc jockeys, newspaper columnists, booking agents, and anyone else who knew and admired Woody. It took place early in the morning, so all the working musicians could attend after they finished their jobs at other hotels. Basically the players were Chubby Jackson, leader and M.C.; Billy Hunt, Walt Blanton, Tommy Porrello, Jerry Lamy, Dominic Barulli, John Bennett, trumpet; Jim Trimble, Jimmy Guinn, Jim Huntzinger, Morty Trautman, trombone; Bob Pierson, Murray Karman, Jimmy Cook, Arno Marsh, Gene Smookler, saxes; Russ Martino, piano; Jimmy Campbell, drums; and Chuck Andrus, bass.
    Various guest stars showed up and played a chorus or two. They included Gus Bivona, clarinet; Vido Musso, tenor; Bill Trujillo, tenor; Carl Fontana, trombone; and various others. There were assorted music arrangements played. Some of them were Herman charts, some Basie, and some various other bands' but one that stands out in my mind was one that Chubby called "God Bless You, Woody," a head arrangement. The soloists played exceptionally well, and Woody was very impressed. He had come by after his gig was over. Charlotte was with him, as was Betty Harris, Bill Harris' widow [Bill passed away in 1973].
    Many, many musicians and others dropped by Woody's table that night to wish him well.

In the midst of the concert tour with Sinatra, the Thundering Herd set aside four days to perform with the Houston Symphony Orchestra at Houston's Jesse Jones Hall, with Lawrence Foster conducting. On October 22 the combined orchestras recorded two Broadbent compositions, "Children of Lima" and "Variations on a Scene."

"Children of Lima," a brilliant work, reflects various bold and beautiful moods, featuring Woody's clarinet.

"Variations on a Scene" reconfirms Broadbent's talents as composer, arranger, and pianist. The work alternates various jazz motifs, integrated with orchestral writing. Solos are from Tiberi, La Verne, Gary Pack (flugelhorn), Woody (soprano), and drummer Jeff Brillinger, all set against the eloquent background of the Houston Symphony Orchestra's string and reed sections, with the Herd adding spice.

In November 1974, a new face appeared in the trumpet section, replacing Gary Pack. Dennis Wayne Dotson, a superb trumpeter with taste and lyricism, began his career playing in local Houston groups from 1965 to 1969, and later in Las Vegas, 1969 to 1974.

DENNIS DOTSON: Playing with Woody was an experience I will always treasure. When you joined Woody's band, you found yourself to be musically on your own. Woody didn't expect you to conform to any particular style or sound, nor did he ever try to tell you HOW or WHAT to play. Rather, you were given the time and freedom to learn, experiment, and grow as a musician. It never felt like an employer–employee kind of relationship.

The year 1974 ended for the Thundering Herd as they played a New Year's Eve party at Caesar's Palace in Las Vegas. On January 6, the band was back in Fantasy's studios at Berkeley, California, recording more original compositions by Alan Broadbent.

"Far In" is an electrifying, hard-swinging piece with solos from tenorists Tiberi, Herbert, and Anderson.

"Never Let Me Go" is a lovely ballad with rich ensemble sounds and featuring Herbert's brilliant tenor stylings.

"Where Is the Love?" is an attractive Latin treatment of the pop tune from this period, featuring Herbert on alto flute and Tiberi on bassoon.

Additional titles were cut January 7–9, comprising the Fantasy album *King Cobra*.

Gary Anderson's score of the title track, "King Cobra," features Jim Pugh and Woody playing soprano against a background of pseudo-rock rhythms and La Verne's synthesizer.

Anderson's treatment of Chick Corea's "Spain" features bassoon and flute solos from Herbert, flugelhorn from Dennis Dotson, and electric piano from La Verne.

Bill Stapleton's lovely score of "Come Rain or Come Shine" features the lyrical quality of Dotson's flugelhorn.

In March, tenorist Greg Herbert left the band and was replaced by Sal Spicola.

The Herd of the mid-seventies continued the well-worn groove of endless road tours and routine personnel changes. In mid-March 1975, the band was: Dave Stahl, Nelson Hatt, Buddy Powers, Dennis Dotson, Bill Byrne (trumpets); Jim Pugh, Dale Kirkland, Vaughn Wiester (trombones); Frank Tiberi, Gary Anderson, Sal Spicola (tenor saxes); John Oslawski (baritone sax); Alan Zavod (piano); Ron Paley (bass); and Jeff Brillinger (drums).

On April 9 Woody and the Herd were back in his hometown of Milwaukee for a Sister Fabian Benefit Concert, a tribute to his former teacher and supporter, with funds going to high school music scholarships.

FRANK TIBERI: Woody had a lot of funny expressions. I thought it was very humorous when some stout, crooked-nosed guy came up to him and started pointing a finger at Woody, and I knew that the guy was capable of handling four Woody Hermans, and Woody just started gouging him with his index finger. Apparently, the guy irritated him and maybe requested a Glenn Miller tune and Woody just gouged his index finger into his chest. . . . He would crack them first, and they would get stunned. No matter how much they thought they could probably tear into him, they would never come back. He was so effective with his first blow. He told me once, "You give them a first blow right in the kidneys, and they'll never come back at you!"

Many times, I used to cook on the road. I would see that there would be no place to eat and I would tell the band to stay in their rooms, and I would just turn every Holiday Inn room into an Italian joint. I would have chicken cacciatore, veal scallopini, and lasagna smelling all over the whole hotel. The maids would come over and ask me for the recipes. The fellows in the band would know where I was by the smell. I carried with me a twenty-five-gallon Coleman chest and a 1,000-watt burner.

On April 20 the Herd was a featured attraction at the Wichita Jazz Festival at Wichita, Kansas. One group, a trio from North Texas State University, so impressed Woody that he hired them as a unit for the rhythm section: Lyle Mays, keyboards; Kirby Stewart, bassist; and drummer Steve Houghton.

On December 13 the Herd boarded the SS Rotterdam for a seven-day jazz cruise to Nassau and Bermuda. Mr. and Mrs. Leonard Feather joined the cruise.

One night at dinner, Leonard asked Woody if he planned to do anything to celebrate the completion of his fourth decade at the helm (the following year), possibly in the form of a band-plus-alumni concert. Woody responded, "I really hadn't given it any thought; but now that you mention it, that sounds like a great idea." Woody's manager, Hermie Dressel, was brought into the conversation. Subsequently, plans began early in 1976 for a "Woody Herman 40th Anniversary Concert and Celebration."

The year 1975 ended for the band at a New Year's Eve dance at the Lincolndale Marriott Hotel in Chicago. On January 2 the Herd opened for two nights at Disneyland, a frequent venue for big bands since the early 60s.

On January 23 the Herd flew from JFK Airport, New York, to London, commencing a thirty-five-day tour of England and Europe in what by now had become an annual excursion for the band. Of special significance to Woody were the performances in Poland, February 25 through 27.

WOODY: We did two different stints in Poland, and I was doing very well there because they knew my mother's Polish background and the fact that she had been born there. We were paid by Polish television for our appearances. They had a camera crew following us everywhere, even into the men's room. We didn't have anything to worry about. We were treated very well.

To commemorate Woody's fortieth year as a bandleader, Iowa Public Television produced a ninety-minute "Woody Herman 40th Anniversary Special," during the summer of 1976. A camera crew and an interviewer traveled on the bus, capturing the Herdsmen in a typical, informal setting and providing a rare inside glimpse of life in the "Iron Lung," as touring musicians often called the band bus. The Iowa TV crew was with the band on and off for several weeks, filming school clinics and concerts from Milwaukee to Redondo Beach, California.

A number of interviews were conducted for the TV special, passages from which are included here:

WOODY (on his own playing):   I think I have fairly good judgment [of] what a solo should be in its perspective in a chart, if it's surrounded by some good plausible thinking. I should be able to come in and play a little bit on occasion. . . . If it doesn't enhance it, I'll cut myself off. I'm not that pleased with any of my playing, I never have been. Of course it gets a little harder each year, because for one thing, I'm working with store-bought teeth. And after all, having a sense of maturity about it, like, I know it will work before I attempt it, it can't collapse. It's like playing on safe ground at all times. As long as I'm able to get a reasonable sound, I'll go and play.

When the interviewer spoke to Woody about people who talk of "bringing back the big bands" but don't go out and support them when they get the opportunity:

WOODY: Well, they like to remember it like it WAS. And there's nothing like it WAS. They would like to go back and relive their youth, but it's impossible.

I like to deal with someone whose mind is open and he's aware. . . . But you show me some guy who hasn't listened to anything except his electric shaver for the last thirty years, and he comes in and says, "Well, I've got a great sound system in my house, I know all about good music! . . ." Those are the ones I can't stand the most [laughter]. I just don't like to deal with them, because if I do, I'm going to insult them. It's the only retaliation a man in my business can have, where you cleanse your soul immediately!

JIM PUGH: Woody is sort of a leader and not a leader at the same time. He's the man that calls all the tunes, and he controls what the band plays. His functions aren't like some of the other leaders', where they're always an integral part of the band's performance. He allows all these people on the band to play [their way]. And a lot of his resiliency is in the fact that he wants to hear new music too. He still plays "Woodchopper's Ball" every night, but I think he enjoys hearing new charts as much as anybody else. You can only hear the same music so many nights. . . . Some of that stuff like "Woodchopper's," he HAS to play. It's a very difficult thing to do, because there are things that audiences will like, that perhaps musicians will not cater to as much.

Woody's got a product to sell, and he's got an audience to deal with, so it has to be saleable. But it's sort of a musician's band, and musicians love to hear the band, musicians love to play on the band.

WOODY: This to me is one of the funniest things in the world. Here are these little, young kids. The only music they've really heard consistently since they were born is rock 'n' roll. In other words, the average youngster, unless he gets involved in a music program, or is around a school where it's happening, doesn't have the freedom of picking and choosing. It comes through a large funnel, and whatever the media, or the powers that be, decide is great for them to hear, and great for them to buy, that is what they get.

DENNIS DOTSON: I was kind of awed by Woody the first few months, awed by his reputation, awed by all the things that he has done. It was a long time before I was really able to talk to him. I was kind of shy around him, and he's basically a shy man. He doesn't want anybody to know this, but he is. So the two of us never seemed to communicate for a long time. But, yeah, we get along fine now. He's a good leader, because he leaves everybody alone, he knows how to stay out of the way.

WOODY: I believe that the young men who are around today . . . the right ones, are more hip and know where it's at much better than guys of twenty-five years ago. They not only play better, they think more clearly, and they're put together better as human beings. Consequently, when they're asked to do a job such as being a clinician, they really prepare themselves and have a plan of attack before they ever go in a classroom.

GARY ANDERSON: Sometimes it bothers you. He doesn't ever tell us really what to do musically. He wouldn't come up to any section in the band and say, "Do this, THIS way." He might say, "No, that's not right, try it another way." Another way that YOU might want to do it. But he won't say to do it this way.

Every once in a while, he might look unhappy, and you can't go up to him and say, "What's wrong?" because he really wouldn't want to tell you what's wrong point blank, if it meant telling you how to play.

It's pretty well known that Woody doesn't hire arrangers on the outside to write for the band. He wants the material to come from within the band. When you get in the band, then you realize why Woody makes that stipulation, because you have to really understand the direction that he wants to go with the band musically.

He's not a writer, but he knows what he wants to hear. He is very exacting in wanting to maintain a certain sound from the band. Not an idiom. I could write any idiom I want to write. I'm sure I could do a rock thing, a Latin thing, a straight-ahead blues, a jazz piece, anything from Chick Corea to Carole King, and everything in between. He's very open to any idiom. It's just a matter of sound. You have to maintain, I guess you would call it, the "Woody Herman sound." I don't really know what it is, but I think I've done it to an extent.

One of the concluding questions the TV interviewer posed to Woody was, "Why are you still on the road at 63?"

WOODY: Ellington had his standard answer, when people would say to him, "Well, Duke, when are you going to retire? What are you doing this for?" He would simply say, "Retire to what?" and basically, it's that kind of feeling with me.

I have quite a closely knit, very small family. Yet we've lived this kind of life MY entire life and career. So I guess we have all become accustomed to it. . . .

In August tenorist Joseph Salvatore (Joe) Lovano joined the Herd's reed section, replacing Pete Brewer.

In late summer Hermie Dressel started organizing the 40th Anniversary Concert and Celebration. Sixteen Herman alumni scattered across the country were brought to New York for the event. A Florida contingent of Chubby Jackson, Sam Marowitz, Don Lamond, and Flip Phillips flew in and joined Nat Pierce, Ralph Burns, the Candoli brothers, Jimmy Rowles, Jake Hanna, and Mary Ann McCall, who came in from the West Coast. Stan Getz, Zoot

Sims, Billy Bauer, Jimmy Giuffre, Al Cohn, and Phil Wilson were gathered from various points. The out-of-towners all converged at the New York Sheraton Hotel.

After a warm reunion, the alumni joined the current edition of the Herd for rehearsals. Some of the old music was retrieved from the archives at the University of Houston, where it had been donated years previously.

BILL BYRNE: It was a very hectic two days, and we rehearsed practically up to the last minute, but it was a big night, and I didn't even realize it at the time.

CHUBBY JACKSON: We rehearsed the day before at Nola Studios on West 57th Street, and everybody who was in that studio will admit the oldsters sounded as if they'd never left Woody's fold.

NAT PIERCE: Hermie Dressel got all the guys together, and unbeknownst to Woody, had to pay quite a few of them. So even though the hall was sold out, they lost money, although it was a great concert.

   That was the first time in history that two major record companies hosted a thing together. CBS Records and RCA Victor hosted the party afterwards, because Ken Glancy, Woody's old friend, had been with CBS, and he had been with Victor in Europe. In 1976 he was the president of RCA Victor.

   At the time, I was working with the Basie orchestra. So I had to take off and I sent Tommy Flanagan out with the Basie band. And then about three days after the 40th Anniversary, I was back at Carnegie Hall with the Basie orchestra and Ella Fitzgerald. So twice in one week I played Carnegie Hall with two famous orchestras. That's something else.

CONTE CANDOLI: I remember when Pete and I got there, we didn't know what we were going to play. This one trumpet player that was with the band [Tony Klatka] wrote "The Brotherhood of Man," and that's the thing we played at the concert and that was recorded. It was a great moment with Zoot and people like that on the band. Woody was in good shape then.

PETE CANDOLI: I recall that Woody's 1976 orchestra was a great band. They just sounded marvelous. He was the type of person that exploited unusual, gifted players.

FLIP PHILLIPS: That was quite a concert! I played "Sweet and Lovely," and "With Someone New," the one I wrote.

RALPH BURNS: That was a thrilling concert. Woody had another great band then. Gary Anderson did the Aaron Copland thing which I think is one of the best charts that Woody ever had, "Fanfare for the Common Man." I played "Early Autumn," and Stan Getz was there for his old solo part.

BILL BYRNE: The audience were fans who had been watching Woody for years. Many people in the audience were friends of Woody's, from New York and all over the world. Sidewalk Stanley even showed up. He got into Carnegie Hall. Stanley never had much money but he could always get in every place.

They had a big party afterwards at the Essex House. It's a famous hotel in New York City on Central Park, on the south side. The party was supposed to be for a couple hundred people, but five or six hundred ended up coming because we invited everyone [laughter].

MARY ANN MCCALL: I went with Nat Pierce and Jack Hanna. The next afternoon, we had like a reunion-rehearsal. We walked into the rehearsal, and there was Chubby, Don Lamond, Zoot, Al Cohn, Stan Getz.

The next night, we did the Carnegie Hall thing. The place was packed. Eighteen from my family were there.

We went around the corner to the Essex House for the after-concert party. Most everybody was there that was anybody in New York. All the big music publishers, Barbara Walters, and a lot of people. The Mayor was there and Woody and Charlotte, and her mother was there at our table. It was just wonderful!

After the party, we all went over to "Old Junior's," where we used to go, and then we went over to the Famous Door on 52nd Street. Roy Eldridge was working there. It was four o'clock in the morning, but it was still open.

In the first half of the November 20, 1976, concert, the augmented Herd played mostly vintage First and Second Herd material. The second half of the concert was primarily new material.

WOODY: It was a great reunion with a lot of good guys who had lots of fun down through the ages playing music. Gary Anderson came through with a couple of very interesting things—one in particular, which we are still playing, called "Fanfare for the Common Man."

JIM PUGH: I joined Woody at the end of 1972, and I left right after the 40th Anniversary Concert in late 1976. My greatest moments with the band were two things: One would be the Anniversary Concert. The other would be the first record I did with the band. It was the first time I'd done an album. It was *Giant Steps*.

JOE LOVANO: I was very excited to be a part of this celebration and have an opportunity to record at Carnegie Hall with some of my favorite musicians.

This concert featured Stan Getz, Zoot Sims, Al Cohn, Flip Phillips, Jimmy Giuffre, the Candoli Brothers, and others. I was in another world, to be playing "Early Autumn" with Stan playing lead, and the parts on "Four Brothers" with Zoot, Stan, Al, and Jimmy soloing.

    I spent two-and-a-half fantastic years playing alongside one of the greatest players I've known . . . Frank Tiberi. I learned a lot from Frank, as well as Woody.

Replacing Jim Pugh in the lead trombone chair was another brilliant player in the Herman tradition. Prior to his stint with the Herd, Martin Bircher (Birch) Johnson played for the Tommy Dorsey orchestra, under the direction of Murray McEachern.

BIRCH JOHNSON: I was the lead trombone player with Woody from November 1976 through October 1979. . . . To most, if not all, of the longer-lasting members of his band, Woody was a friend, mentor, or possibly a kind of father figure.

    I really got to know Woody in the hotel lounges late at night, after our gigs. I've always been a bit of a history buff and Woody was an encyclopedia with feet, as far as music goes. Not just jazz, as I found out. My favorite stories had to do with his relationship with Stravinsky in the 1940s.

By the end of 1976, the fusion wrinkle began to fade in the Herd's repertoire. Bill Byrne confirmed this in an interview:

BILL BYRNE: It ended sometime during the Fantasy albums era. At the Carnegie Hall concert we did one tune by Lyle Mays, which was a fusion-type thing. But after that, it went back to upright bass and everything. We performed a couple of things by Lyle Mays and some Gary Anderson material. Basically, it was jazz on pop tunes.

On December 14 the Herd was in Los Angeles playing for Carol Burnett's Christmas party. The year 1976 ended with the band playing a New Year's Eve bash at the Aladdin Hotel in Las Vegas.

    On March 27, 1977, catastrophe struck near Manhattan, Kansas, when, during a typically grueling road tour, Woody, driving alone in a rented car, fell asleep at the wheel and was involved in a head-on collision. He suffered severe facial lacerations, his left leg was mangled, and he received serious internal injuries. There was concern for his life and uncertainty whether he could lead the band again.

WOODY: For years, I normally drove Corvettes and other sports cars, and did all the miles myself. They were all high-performance cars and were exciting to drive, but too noisy to ever worry about falling asleep. When the accident occurred, I was driving a large, American, luxury-type car. I had rented it while my car was being repaired.

It was two in the afternoon when the collision occurred. Fortunately, on that particular highway, you had to go right through an old Army camp called Fort Riley. The accident happened approximately 100 yards down the road from the main gate. What saved me was the fact that in front of the main gate was parked an ambulance with full crew, and they had me out of the wrecked car within a matter of seconds. They had a base hospital there and gave me some first aid. When the doctor there saw that I had a double-fracture of my left leg and a lot of facial cuts, they sent me over to a little parochial hospital, St. Mary's, and they were very good. Otherwise, I don't think I would have made it. I'm lucky to be still walking and doing other things [1986]. I've got steel up my legs and a pin in my knee. I used a walker for a while, then crutches, and finally I used a cane when I was almost completely well.

BILL BYRNE: It was a 25-mile-an-hour zone and he just ventured off into the other lane, and the lady who was in the other car had a very heavy car and they collided. She wasn't hurt at all. Woody did have his belt on, but his leg was broken and he was thrown up against the windshield. He was all purple when I went in to see him. But whenever something happened to him, he had a good "bebop" attitude.

We were playing that day at Kansas State University, and the band director, Phil Hewitt, and his wife checked in on Woody every day and watched him and made sure everything was okay for him.

Frank fronted the band during Woody's convalescence, and then Buddy De Franco for about ten days.

Soon after Woody's accident, Frank Tiberi took the band to Honolulu for a scheduled appearance at the Kool Jazz Festival. The Herd returned to the Mainland on May 9, proceeding immediately to Redlands, California, for a performance at Redlands University with Med Flory's Supersax.

MED FLORY: Nobody expected Woody to show up, but somebody brought him. He sat on the side of the stage in a wheelchair, then they brought him out and everybody applauded. Later at intermission, somebody said, "Hey, Woody, you're getting too old for this kind of stuff," and Woody said, "I'm not old, I'm in an old body."

FRANK TIBERI: The band had a scheduled appointment to play with the Syracuse Symphony Orchestra. I was playing Alan Broadbent's "Children of Lima" on solo clarinet in front of the Symphony Orchestra with 110 great symphony musicians behind me. It was a thrill, because I didn't understand why they would have me there. I'm a jazz player.

BILL BYRNE: Woody flew down and sat there in a wheelchair while Frank played. . . .

NEAL HEFTI: Just before Frances died,* she wheeled Woody across the stage at Berklee School of Music, when he received his honorary doctorate.

Woody rejoined the band, utilizing a walker, on May 31, at Playhouse Square in Cleveland. In customary Herman form, his walker sported a bicycle horn.

The Herman Herd has a long history of brilliant drummers: Carlson, Tough, Lamond, Manne, Igoe, Mardigan, Flores, Hanna, Soph . . . Woody was always particularly careful in choosing the musician who would propel the explosive ensemble. Jeff Hamilton was no exception.

JEFF HAMILTON: I had played on the Tommy Dorsey band in 1974, under Murray McEachern. I had met Birch Johnson on the Dorsey band. He remembered that I had a lifelong dream to be on Woody's band and thought that I would be right for it and so he recommended me when Dan Dimperio was ready to leave Woody's band. Of course, I had done all my homework by listening to records of Davey Tough, Cliff Leeman, Don Lamond, and Jake in particular; and I felt like I was ready to go out and tackle the job. I was currently working with the Monty Alexander Trio.

I decided to take the job, but I wanted more money than they were starting me out with. I held out for about fifty dollars more, which ended up being a $50 pay cut from what I was making with Monty Alexander.

I joined the band in July 1977. On my opening night, Woody had just come off his car accident and approached the bandstand in a walker. He had them set up a bar stool right in front of my bass drum.

When he was announced, he came up and sat right in front of the drums, with his back to me. He didn't acknowledge my presence at all, because he was upset that "Hotshot" had held out for fifty dollars. He didn't help me with the tunes; he didn't call any directly. Birch was trying to help me as best he could with the order of the tunes but he didn't always know the order Woody would call them.

Woody threw the whole book at me. "Four Brothers," "Early Autumn," and right into "La Fiesta," "Giant Steps," "Fanfare for the Common Man," and "Caldonia," all in one set! By the time we hit "Caldonia," I was so angry. He was trying to find out if I would sink or swim, on the very first set, and also if I was worthy of getting that fifty dollars extra.

I've always loved to play fast tempos, and I knew they played "Caldonia" fast from the 1963 recording with Jake at Basin Street. I also knew that the current band had been playing it fast, so I looked over at Fred Hersh, who was playing piano, and I said, "How fast can we go?"

---

*Neal's wife, singer Frances Wayne, died of cancer in Boston, February 1978.

and he said, "Take it as fast as you want!" Woody counted off a medium tempo as he always did on "Caldonia," and let the rhythm section take over and put it where they wanted it.

And so I took it at breakneck speed. Later Bruce Johnstone, the baritone sax player, was clocking it at six seconds a chorus. We finished the song and Woody turned around and said his first words to me the whole night. . . . "Not so fast tomorrow night, Pal!" I didn't make any acknowledgment of that comment, and he turned around and introduced the band and we took a break.

I walked up to Woody on the break, against the advice of a couple of guys in the band who said, "Let Woody come to you." He was stooping over, hiding in a corner from all the people. He had his head down and was leaning on his knees, and I had my hand extended, and I said, "Woody, I'm Jeff Hamilton, I'm your new drummer." He looked up at me, not taking my hand, and looked back down and said, "I know who you are, Pal, and you sound marvelous . . . all right?"

That's all that was said for the first couple of weeks, but I could tell on the bandstand that he was appreciative of what I was trying to do. We seemed to hit it off without even talking. Just eye contact, and a little smile here and there.

Woody's loyalty and integrity was made obvious to me in sort of an uncomfortable situation for myself, on one of the bus rides. I went to the front of the bus where Woody was sitting, and sat down on the step and we talked. The conversation came around to Abe Turchen, and I made a remark about, "Gee, isn't it too bad that he's not around to take the heat for the financial problems that you're in." And Woody became very defiant, and looked me square in the face, and said, "Abe Turchen was my friend, and I trusted him. He was my selection for the person to take care of all my financial affairs, and I'm the one to blame, not Abe Turchen."

He was taking responsibility, probably up to the day he died, about his financial state. That struck me. . . . I got a warm feeling for Woody, because of his loyalty to his friends.

On September 18 the band flew to London, commencing a seven-week tour of England, Sweden, Norway, West Germany, and Poland.

The following is the Herd as it toured Europe in the fall of 1977: Allen Vizzutti, John Hoffman, Nelson Hatt, Dennis Dotson, Bill Byrne (trumpets); Birch Johnson, Larry Farrell, Jim Daniels (trombones); Frank Tiberi, Gary Anderson, Joe Lovano (tenor saxes); Bruce Johnstone (baritone sax); Pat Coil (piano); Marc Johnson (bass); and Jeff Hamilton (drums).

JEFF HAMILTON: We played the Warsaw Jazz Jamboree in the Polish Jazz Festival. There was a reception for Woody and the band before our appearance at the festival. It was sort of mandatory. There were waiters and waitresses passing around little shot glasses of vodka. We had all heard of the Polish vodka being smooth like water, and also knew that we had to play at about ten o'clock that night, and didn't want to get loaded.

So everybody was pretty careful in the intake of vodka, which, incidentally, did taste like water going down. There was a little band playing over in the corner, and before we knew it, hours had passed, and the servers had been alternating trays of Polish sausages and glasses of vodka. The vodka seemed to sneak up on all of us. By the time we were ready to go, somebody had noticed that Woody had been gone for at least an hour. I think he saw what was happening and wanted to get out of there.

So the band showed up on stage and half of the band was really loaded and the other half not far from it. They announced, "Voody Herman and the Thundering Herd," and Woody came out as we were playing "Blue Flame," and stopped and looked at the band, and he threw back his head and started laughing, and pointed at his chest, as if to say, "You're mine tonight, fellows." We were sort of helpless, and at his mercy, so he counted off a pretty rough set that night, too. Jim Daniels lost his bass trombone slide in the tenor section. Most of the trumpet section looked like they weren't going to make it. Of course, the trumpets stood up in Woody's band. There was a lot of bobbing and weaving going on.

The last laugh was had by the Polish Jazz Festival, because they recorded it that night and we didn't know it. It came out on a record and there's one session that the band fell apart on after a drum fill. I was confident that I could play this off-the-wall drum fill, and I didn't make it to the downbeat, and the band came in about five different entrances. So that was the result of the complimentary vodka and sausages served at the Warsaw Jazz Festival.

One thing I'll always remember about that concert is that people were paying a week's salary to hear one hour of music. Then the management would empty the house and bring in another audience that would pay the same cover charge. The concert hall was not in great shape, but the feeling from the audience . . . they were so hungry for any kind of music that we fed them. I remember feeling very bad during that concert because these people had saved so much money to come and hear an hour of what we did.

Afterwards, I had people coming up asking for anything that we had. So I gave out some drumsticks. I had enough for about four or five people, and a fight broke out, because I didn't have any more to give out, and I had the rest of the tour to do. There was a little scuffling between six or seven guys over the sticks, and I had to break it up and tell them, "Look, I'm sorry," and give each guy one stick. I remember leaving that town feeling very sad.

After a Christmas vacation, the Herd went into Disneyland for five nights. The year 1977 concluded with a New Year's Eve concert in Hayward, California.

JEFF HAMILTON: In Seattle in January 1978, Woody was walking without his walker and was limping a little bit. He had some more teeth knocked out from the car accident the year before, and was still not comfortable with the dental work that had been done, but he was still playing soprano, alto, and clarinet every night. We were admiring his "I'm not going to let this get the best of me" attitude.

This night in Seattle at a concert, my cousin was there and I hadn't seen him in a long time, and Roy Parnell, a jazz club owner, was also there. It was a real thrill for me to have people there that had followed my career.

Woody called "Apple Honey," so I turned around to Vizzutti, the lead trumpet player, and I said, "How fast do we take this?" and he said, "Take it up." Once again, I remembered the sixties band recording of it with Jake Hanna. They took it pretty fast as opposed to the original.

So Woody counted off a medium tempo, and I turned around and said right in the middle of the count-off, "Let's take it up there!" The trumpets went with me, because they had the introduction with the rhythm section. So we took it at Jake Hanna's tempo, and Woody just froze in his count-off pose. He was standing there, looking at the floor with his hands out, and I knew immediately that I had made a big mistake.

When I went on the band, everybody said, "Don't take Woody's count-off; he doesn't expect you to follow him, he counts four beats and then the rhythm section settles, and puts the tempo where it's supposed to be." This was true, but nobody told me that when Woody "set up," he would announce the tune, and he would turn around and look down at the floor for a moment, think about the tempo, and then he'd start tapping his foot and count off the band. When this happened, you'd BETTER take Woody's tempo!

Woody had "set up" that night, and started to count off the tempo, and of course, I went much faster than that. He stood in this frozen position through the whole first chorus and then walked slowly up to the drums. . . . He says to me, "IT'S TO-O-O-O-O F-A-A-A-S-T PA-L-L-L!" And he turned around and walked away from me at the same speed, sort of limping. So I thought, "It's too late now, we're in the middle of it, I've got to keep this thing at the same tempo all the way out." Woody picked up his clarinet for his solo, and I never felt so badly in my life for something that I had done causing someone else embarrassment. When he put the clarinet to his mouth, nothing but squeaks and squawks came out of it.

The tempo was obviously too fast. He hadn't been used to playing it at that tempo for a long time, but the band managed to scream through it, and everybody hung in there well.

After the thing was over, the audience was applauding, and he walked back over to the drums and said, "See, the band can't play it that fast." Of course I wanted to laugh, but I couldn't because he was reading me. So I said, "Yeah, you're right, we'll take it down tomorrow night." And he said, "Yeah, take MY tempo on this one."

I gave my notice at the end of 1977. I was going to stay in LA, because Ray Brown had hired me to replace Shelly Manne in the LA Four, with Laurindo Almeida, Bud Shank, and Ray. Woody asked me to stay on to record the suite that Chick Corea had written for the band. The band at that time was tight. We had just come off the European tour that fall, and we were playing well together. He had cleaned house and got some of the old regulars back, like Dennis Dotson, Gary Anderson, Pat Coil, and bassist Marc Johnson. So I stayed on for the extra month and left after the record date the end of January. We did the first two records for Century, *Together: Flip and Woody* and *Road Father*, the first week of January.

Woody was not real thrilled when I left, because it wasn't that often that he had that solid a band during the seventies. I took the job with Ray Brown and Woody said, "You'll be back."

I think that as a leader, you have to let young musicians grow. Woody let the young men in the band find their niches. He gave them enough time to find where they were supposed to be musically, how they could fit in, and knew immediately, especially in the rhythm section, if it wasn't going to work out. There were some guys who only lasted one or two nights, and he knew that there wouldn't be any hope for them fitting into the band.

I have to speak personally; he let ME find my niche within the band and let me be Jeff Hamilton. He didn't expect me to be Don Lamond or Ed Soph, and that was something that I really cherished about Woody.

Woody was a very sincere person. If you had a problem and needed to talk to him about it, he was there. He had a way of making everything so simple. It was cut and dried, and nothing was a major dilemma, because he'd been through everything. So problems that seemed pretty big at the time were absolutely minuscule compared to the things he had gone through. I learned a very simple way of thinking from Woody.

Woody signed with the new Century record label late in 1977. Producer Glen Glancy and the staff at Century, utilizing a technique of twin turntables, recorded directly from the microphones to the cutting head, thus eliminating the erosion of a pure sound and the possibility of overediting through tape splicing. Unfortunately the Century label was short-lived. Recordings made for the label by Woody, Les Brown, and other bands are in the collector's category today.

The first of three Century albums recorded in January 1978 at Capitol Studios in Hollywood was *Road Father*.

WOODY: That name was given to me by Bill Chase's father. He used to send me little notes and all, and I just became the Road Father in his eyes.

The album consisted of two vintage Herman scores and six originals submitted by Woody's current arranging staff.

Allen Vizzutti, a graduate of Eastman School of Music, wrote "Fire Dance," an exciting Spanish-influenced vehicle for his own talent as split-lead trumpeter. The piece displays startling technique from Vizzutti in the opening and closing cadenzas.

The late Charlie Mingus wrote "Duke Ellington's Sound of Love" shortly after Duke's death. It is a supremely beautiful ballad, showcasing Woody's alto, with Tiberi's elaborate harmonic form adding to the mood. Bass trombonist Vaughn Weister wrote the chart, but left the band before it was recorded.

The venerable "Woodchopper's Ball" was recorded commercially for the first time since 1954. This edition includes solos from Tiberi, trombonist Larry Farrell, and trumpeter Glenn Drewes.

Baritonist Bruce Johnstone composed and arranged "Sunrise Lady," a jazz samba. One interesting feature is the "band within the band" approach with Birch Johnson, Dennis Dotson, and Johnstone out front. Former Kenton lead trumpeter Jay Sollenberger is heard effectively on top.

Gary Anderson's treatment of Fauré's "Pavane" was a favorite of Woody's in his last eight years as leader. It features alternative instrumentation with Tiberi, bassoon; Bruce Johnstone, bass clarinet; Woody, clarinet; and Nelson Hatt's piccolo trumpet.

The classic "I've Got News for You" was revived from the Second Herd's library. Trumpeter Sollenberger blows behind Woody's tongue-in-cheek blues vocal. Wes Hensel, Les Brown's trumpet/arranger alumnus, rewrote Sam Marowitz' lead alto part for Dennis Dotson's flugelhorn. The chart is opened up to allow Johnstone a baritone solo. He also accompanies Woody on the vocal out chorus.

"Sugar Loaf Mountain" was originally written as a showcase for Jim Pugh by Alan Broadbent, and in this version features Birch Johnson.

Stevie Wonder's "Isn't She Lovely?" is a simple chart from Gary Anderson and features Bruce Johnstone, tenorist Joe Lovano, and Woody's clarinet. The rhythm section and Sollenberger's lead trumpet are outstanding.

The album *Together: Flip and Woody* is a superb collection of ballads scored by Gary Anderson and Nat Pierce, showcasing Flip Phillips with the January 1978 Thundering Herd. Phillips' Websterish, warm, full-bodied sound is scintillating against the backdrop of the ensemble and an added string section.

On January 25 and 26 the Herd was at Filmways-Heider Recording Studios in Hollywood to record six titles, including an ambitious, three-part suite submitted by Chick Corea entitled *Suite For a Hot Band*.

WOODY: Chick and I got into a thing about having him write something special for our band. Within a few days he had decided the piece would be a suite in three movements. The first movement would be a lot of fun to play and very impressive musically. In his description, it should sound like "Stravinsky meets Sousa." It was really a happy challenge for Chick because he hadn't written for a big band for many years. I think it's one of the hippest things written for a big jazz band in a long, long time.

For the record date, the standard instrumentation was augmented with guest musicians: Victor Feldman, vibes, synthesizers, and percussion; Tom Scott, tenor saxophone and lyricon; and Mitch Holder, acoustic and electric guitar.

Suite For a Hot Band features some intriguing scoring, with the first movement featuring Woody's clarinet and Lovano's tenor. The second movement displays keyboardist Pat Coil, a brief nonsensical vocal and clarinet from Woody, Tiberi, and moving trumpet work from Dotson. The third movement changes mood, with a sambalike character and solos from Coil (on electric piano), Dotson, Lovano, Birch Johnson, Woody (soprano), Nelson Hatt (piccolo trumpet), Mitch Holder (guitar), and Feldman's added percussive sounds.

On March 17, 1978, Woody and the Herd were back in Milwaukee for another Sister Fabian Scholarship Fund Concert, with Flip Phillips and Mary Lou Williams. In the morning the band conducted a clinic at the area technical college. In the afternoon, the Herdsmen judged six high school jazz bands in competitive sessions.

On October 9 the Herd flew to London from New York, commencing a month-long tour of England and Europe. This was the personnel: Tim Burke, Glenn Drewes, Dave Kennedy, Jim Powell, Bill Byrne (trumpets); Birch Johnson, Nelson Hinds, Larry Shunk (trombones); Frank Tiberi, Joe Lovano, Billy Ross (tenor saxes); Gary Smulyan (baritone sax); Dave La Lama (piano); Jay Andersen (bass); and John Riley (drums).

After a week off in December, the Herd reorganized for a six-night engagement at Knott's Berry Farm at Buena Park, California, closing on New Year's Eve.

JEFF HAMILTON: After I played with the LA Four for about a year, Bill Byrne called me to go back on Woody's band to help out for about a month. I had been playing this small group music, sort of classical jazz,

The 1978 Woody Herman Herd. Front row, L to R: Woody, Billy Ross, Frank Tiberi, Joe Lovano (tenor saxes), Bruce Johnstone (baritone sax). Second row: Bobby Leonard (behind Woody) (drums), Larry Farrell, Birch Johnson, Jim Daniels (trombones). Back row: Bill Byrne, Nelson Hatt, Jay Sollenberger, Glenn Drewes, Dennis Dotson (trumpets). (From the Woody Herman Collection)

with the LA Four. It had a lot of light bell sounds, wind chimes, triangles, and sort of tinkly effects.

On my first night back with the band, I was really working. I was through my shirt, my hair was down, I was completely drenched by the third tune. Woody walked up to the drums and he said, "This ain't no arts and crafts band, Pal!" That was sort of a welcome back to slamming in the big band.

Joining the band in January 1979 was tenorist James Robert (Bob) Belden. Bob had played at North Texas State University and backed such people as Joe Williams, Ella Fitzgerald, Zoot Sims, Bill Watrous, and Clark Terry. He also worked for the John Taylor and Warren Covington orchestras.

BOB BELDEN: I came in January of 1979, replacing Joe Lovano, and I left in May of 1980. I like to refer to it as the "Obscure Herd." We were right in that transition period between the fusion stuff and going back to more nostalgia and straight-ahead jazz.

We were in-between recording contracts. We had a wilder rhythm section than Woody had had in a long time. If you could pin him down in a conversation, he would tell you he loved the band. It was a soloist-oriented band. In England, they called us "loud and obnoxious!" I thought that was a compliment.

The group he had in the eighties was nowhere near what we were. The method to our madness was nobody could understand what we were doing. Nobody could dance to it. Some of the dances were hilarious. When people couldn't dance they would complain. I saw Woody punch a guy out because he complained.

On his first night, trumpeter Tim Burke fainted on "Early Autumn." He fell off the stand. He was nervous as hell!

One of the hippest stories that I recall: We were playing, and Woody walked out on the stage wearing this Greco-Roman outfit, with linen pants and a beautiful linen shirt. Little did I know that this was our October salary that went for this suit. He was like a boy at this one gig; it was amazing. He was just like Miles Davis!

Musically, you couldn't touch this band, with Dennis Dotson and Bill Stapleton splitting the trumpet chairs.

On June 30, 1979, the Herd flew to Frankfurt, commencing a forty-day tour of Europe.

BIRCH JOHNSON: We were Woody's family, and he sometimes would act a bit like a father. He kept an eye on any girlfriend you might have, and would sometimes hand down a verdict.

I met my wife, Amy, in Nice, France, in the summer of 1979. It was a whirlwind romance. Woody noticed that one of his boys was in love, and took the time to get to know her when she visited me in London the next weekend.

One night in the hotel bar he asked her to dance. "The moment of truth," I thought. When they came back, they were both laughing. He told us stories the rest of the evening. I left the band shortly after that, but Amy and I saw Woody several times later, and they always had a private laugh together. I wonder at what?

BOB BELDEN: On the European tour, we had just finished flying from San Sebastian, Spain, to Frankfurt, to Berlin, to Hamburg. The next night, we played an hour show opposite Ray Charles. We played a dance starting at midnight, and we finished about 1 A.M. We drove from just north of Hamburg, through East Germany into Poland, caught a plane, flew to Krakow, then drove another two hours into Krosno, and played two two-hour concerts. We got up the next day, did the same backtrack to Krakow, then flew all the way up to Gdansk, then we played that night at the Sopot Jazz Festival.

We did a video show at Sopot, and there was a fly that lit on Woody's jacket that stayed there the whole night and the whole band just kept playing to the fly. We kept trying to get the camera men to zoom in on the

Disneyland, August, 1979. Front row, L to R: Woody, Dick Mitchell, Frank Tiberi, Bob Belden (tenor saxes), Gary Smulyan (baritone sax). Second row: Ed Soph (drums), Nelson Hinds, Birch Johnson, Larry Shunk (trombones). Back row: Dave LaRocca (bass), Bill Byrne, Tim Burke, Joe Rodriguez, Dennis Dotson, Jim Powell (trumpets). (Courtesy Riley Gaynor)

fly. I think this fly wanted to defect! He found a home on Woody's cashmere jacket.

He caught me playing "God Save the Queen" in a minor key, and reamed me out for that. He said I was "disrespectful." This was in Manchester, in a concert hall in England. He said, "Don't you have any respect for these people here after what they did for my relatives?"

On September 15 Woody Herman and his young Thundering Herd were a feature attraction at the 22nd Annual Monterey Jazz Festival. By 1979 the Herd had become almost a fixture at the event. Dynamic drummer Ed Soph had returned to the band for at least the third time. Other headliners were Stan Getz, Dizzy Gillespie, Slide Hampton, and trumpeter Woody Shaw. The Herd's performance was recorded by Concord Jazz Records of Concord, California, owned by Carl Edson Jefferson, a prosperous entrepreneur who also owned an automobile business. The Herman–Concord association would continue for the remainder of Woody's career.

The album produced at the Festival was entitled *Woody and Friends*, referring to the addition of Getz, Dizzy, Hampton, and others. The record featured seven tracks of exciting big-band jazz. There was substantial evidence that the Herd's musical conceptions were shifting back to the straight-ahead, mainstream format.

"Caravan" is a Bob Belden arrangement with a distinct Ellington character. Trombonist Birch Johnson displays brilliant ideas and technique. Other offerings are from Tiberi (bassoon), Woody (soprano), and Soph.

Dave La Lama, Woody's new pianist-arranger, scored the warm "I Got It Bad," which became a staple in the book. It features a chorus from baritonist Gary Smulyan, Woody's lyrical alto and lovely piano from the arranger. Joe Rodriguez' lead trumpet is superb.

"Count Down" is Frank Tiberi's avant-garde interpretation of the Coltrane composition, derived from Miles Davis' "Tune Up." Frank transcribed Trane's solo and incorporated it into the ensemble scoring with outstanding results. The performance displays rollicking solos from tenorists Tiberi and Belden.

Charlie Mingus's "Better Git It in Your Soul" is a remake from a 1963 contribution to the Herd's book. This edition features baritonist Smulyan, trumpeter Kitt Reid, and drummer Soph.

Dizzy Gillespie wrote "Woody 'N You" as a Herman tribute in 1942, but the Herd never performed it until trombonist Slide Hampton's chart was submitted in 1979. Dizzy, Woody Shaw and Hampton combine in front of the band to make it a swinging excursion.

Alan Broadbent's score of "What Are You Doing the Rest of Your Life?" is used here as an eloquent showcase for Stan Getz's gorgeous trademark tone.

The concert concluded with Dizzy's classic "Manteca," with Dizzy, Shaw, and Hampton all out front again and some thrilling trumpet fireworks.

BOB BELDEN: We were a pivotal band, between what had gone on before and what went on after. By the time I left, we had got another piano player whom Woody loved, 'cause he knew all the old tunes. Woody was kind of getting tired, and we didn't have a record deal. But Woody paid for the Monterey Jazz Festival record out of his own pocket. He wanted to record the band, and that was an incredible two-day affair.

You can listen to the tapes when I first got on the band, and it was like half fusion, half jazz. By the time I got off the band, it was all jazz.

WOODY: I've made a lot of giant steps forward, and I've usually had to retract and go back a way to let the audience catch up with me.

I try to take in the new music, because there might be something there of quality that I should be touching. I think something of importance was happening in the early seventies. I became pretty much involved with fusion, in its earliest blossom, when I was with Fantasy Records. And I've long since decided that the great future of fusion went somewhere else.

I stayed with it for a period. We even touched on electronics and synthesizers. But I found that you hit a brick wall and a dead end when you revert back, because if you're fooling around with two chord changes too often, there's more to music than that.

The author asked Woody, "On the subject of fusion, did you consider yourself successful?"

WOODY: Well, I guess you could call it that. Once again, we weren't making money, but we were producing albums and winning Grammys. I don't think the public went for it at all, only a few jazz critics who were uninformed. They thought it was great because it was something that they hadn't heard before.

When 1979 ended, Woody Herman had eight years of life remaining. They would be bittersweet years. Bitter, in the loss of Charlotte, his wife and partner for forty-six years; the deterioration of his health; and the continuing litigation with the IRS over a staggering $1.5 million debt for back taxes. Musically sweet, in that the young Thundering Herd of the 1980s returned to the mold of the early 60s, producing a charge-on brand of swinging big band jazz.

9.

Straight Ahead
1980-1986

Woody and the band were on vacation for a month. They re-formed for a performance January 18, 1980, in Pasadena, California.

On February 19, the Herd participated in the Mardi Gras Festival and Parade in New Orleans. Contrary to certain exaggerations in the media, Woody was not actually "King of the Zulus," but served more as a grand marshal of the parade. Choosing a white band to participate was without precedent in the history of this famous black benevolent society.

BILL BYRNE: We were invited by Freddy Coleman, who was the black drummer in the Dukes of Dixieland. Freddy has traveled all over the world. He's a very well-known drummer and a very personable fellow. He was on the board of the Zulu Society and the Organization Committee.

The night before the parade, we played in the Convention Center downtown. They didn't have a piano and they didn't want to pay for one. I had to call up Werlin's, the big music company in town, and they rushed over at the last minute with a piano. The next day, the band participated in the Zulu Parade by being on a float. . . . We were all dressed in grass skirts, black leotards, black makeup, with our white eyes peering out.

WOODY: I considered it to be a great honor. Louie Armstrong was brutally criticized by [an element] of black people for accepting that honor as a bandleader, and he returned the next year and did it again. They didn't think that he should be involved with the Zulu Society. They felt that it was a putdown. I liked his attitude about the whole thing so when I was offered a chance to do it, I was extremely pleased and proud.

On March 30 the Herd performed in Carnegie Hall as a featured attraction for the Kool Super Nights Jazz Festival. Other headliners included Mel

315

Torme, the Gerry Mulligan Big Band, the Bill Evans Trio, Ruby Braff, and Zoot Sims.

On April 14 the Herd flew to South America for a two-week tour. After a brief hiatus, the band re-formed to tour the British Isles, May 12 to 24. Commencing June 14, the band was booked at Disneyland for two weeks. At this time, Frank Tiberi took a leave of absence.

On July 6 four replacements joined: pianist-arranger-composer John Oddo, trumpeter Steve Harrow, trombonist-arranger-composer John Fedchock and baritone saxophonist Mike Brignola (not related to baritonist Nick Brignola).

John Fedchock attended Ohio State University and earned a master's degree in jazz studies at the Eastman School of Music.

JOHN FEDCHOCK: I've always wanted to play with Woody ever since I was in the eleventh grade. I had majored in music at Ohio State and I had heard that Woody was getting a lot of his trombone players like Jim Pugh, Birch Johnson and Jim Daniels, people like that, from Eastman School of Music. I applied at Eastman for grad work just knowing that all those great players had come out of there.

I was sort of like Mark Lewis, in that he had grown up with Woody Herman's band. I had pretty much been collecting all the records since I first saw the band. So even before I came on the band I had actually got some of my parts memorized.

Woody was very cool on my first night on the band. At that time there were a lot of solos in the second trombone book. We were playing in a three-hour outdoor jazz concert. I had six solos and I was a little uptight. Previously, in my experience playing with big bands, the PA system was set so you could stand back a little bit [from the mike]. But with our PA system, you had to kind of get up on it, especially with the round sound of a trombone, because the sound doesn't want to cut. So I got back a little bit, and at the end of the concert, Woody came up to me and said, "You gotta be funkier, you're not going to make it, and I'll have to do something about it!" But luckily, I had been following the band a long time and I really knew that I could do it. Instead of being intimidated, I got mad.

So the next night, I buried the mike with my horn, and played every blues lick I had ever heard in my life. After the gig, Woody said, "That was fine, it's going to work out fine!"

After that night he was real responsive to my playing, and he let me play a lot, which I was real happy about. John Oddo was on the band. Mike Brignola and Steve Harrow also came in on the same day. So things were kind of loose, because there was a new guy in every section.

Mike Brignola received his music education at the Eastman School of Music.

MIKE BRIGNOLA: I joined the band in July 1980. At the time, Frank Tiberi had left the band. He was going to quit, it wasn't just a vacation. It had something to do with building his house, and he had a relationship with a chick. Paul McGinley had returned to the band for the third tenor chair, and in an unusual move, Woody just promoted McGinley to lead tenor. Frank had been doing it for so long, they wouldn't hire someone from the outside.

In my last two years at Rochester, Paul was getting his master's degree at Eastman. He was the lead alto player in the Eastman Jazz Ensemble when I was the baritone player. So he knew about me. Paul didn't like the guy that Woody had on baritone at the time. So Paul called me to see if I could do it and so I got the gig.

I've played the baritone chair much longer than anyone else on the band. I've got the record for baritone players. I'm not the best and I'm not the worst, but I'm the most stubborn. I won't quit.

On Friday and Saturday, September 12 and 13, the Herd played at Knott's Berry Farm, Buena Park, California, along with the Count Basie, Maynard Ferguson, and Harry James bands. A portion of the performance is available on the Forum Home Video label.

On October 17, 1980, Woody hired Mark Lewis, the son of trumpeter Cappy Lewis, to take over the third chair from Matt Cornish. Mark's father was noted for his Bunny Beriganish artistry during the "Band That Plays the Blues" period.

A superb soloist, Mark has the ability to develop delicate and intricate lines at a rapid pace and to interpret ballads with warmth and emotion. The Herd's third and fourth trumpet parts are liberally laced with solo space. Consequently, Mark was an often-featured soloist in the Herd's five-man trumpet section of the early to mid-1980s.

Prior to joining the Herd, Mark worked with Los Angeles-based rehearsal bands and with Nelson Riddle, Ralph Carmichael, and Abe Most.

MARK LEWIS: My father was a major influence in my life. After hearing him play, I started studying trumpet. I think Louis Armstrong is the one that made the greatest lasting impression on me. There were a lot of other players that influenced me. I listened to so many players. There were two guys that really made an impression on me—Clifford Brown and Frank Rosolino, the trombone player.

I joined the band at Bloomfield Hills, Michigan. I felt confident that I could play, and the people would like my playing. But I wasn't sure how I would physically last playing that hard, night after night. That kind of scared me. I shared the cab with Woody, from the hotel to the job. I expressed to him just a little bit of doubt about how I could play, because I had been real sick with bronchitis, and I still had it. Woody said, "Ah, don't worry, we won't listen to you for the first two weeks."

On that first night, Woody called up "I Can't Get Started," and I had to go out front to play it. I didn't want to cover up any of the sax players' music, and I was wondering how I could do it. I had hoped that he wouldn't call it on that first night, so I could go over it with somebody. I said to the fourth trumpet player, "Can you play this tonight? Then I can see how you do it and then I'll play it the next time." He said, "Well, Woody wants you to do it, but I'll play it for you," and he took the music down front. I could see that Woody was really mad. I went up to him later, and I said, "I'm sorry I didn't play that tonight, Woody, I wanted to figure out the routine and see how it's done." He said to me, "YOU SHOULD HAVE PLAYED IT!" After that, I understood where Woody was coming from.

To play a solo trumpet chair on Woody's band, your style should be swinging and melodic to an extent. He definitely wouldn't just take anything you could dish out. One night on "Woodchopper's Ball," I decided to play a very quick beboppish solo with lots of sixteenth notes. Woody gave me a dirty look and said, "PLAY THE BEBOP LATER."

On November 3, the Herd went into Blues Alley in Washington, D.C., for a performance broadcast live on WMAL radio and hosted by jazz deejay Felix Grant. Woody met Third Herd band boy Jack Wamsley for dinner before the gig.

JACK WAMSLEY: Woody had three martinis at dinner. We had dinner at Mel Krupin's Restaurant. It was directly across the street from the entrance to the Mayflower Hotel where Woody was staying. The old man could walk over there.

BILL BYRNE: It was Woody's favorite place, across from the Mayflower Hotel. The politicians and all the famous people would go there. It had excellent crab cakes.

When Woody got too much to drink he rambled a lot. He could have told the stories in five minutes, but he got to rambling. Actually, the guys in the band were getting embarrassed because he was stoned enough that some of his conversation wasn't making sense. . . .

WOODY: I would like to, if I may, take the liberty to dedicate this next tune to Felix Grant, because he was around . . . well, he's a much younger man than me, but he was around in some of the earlier periods of our careers together, and he heard us trying things back in those years when it was fashionable to be very far out, you know. It was the first time that three of these [pointing to the tenor saxes and asking the three tenor men to place their horns together], in other words, it's three like this, and one like this [the baritone], with the "grabber" on the end there. It was like a weird sound back in those days. They thought, "Oh my God, are they kidding?"

During the performance of "Four Brothers," Woody was heard growling with pleasure.

WOODY: I would like once again to take time to get these messages out because if I don't get them across, I might forget them. . . . This is a message to Felix. I've been retired now for two years, you know that, don't you? I've been goofing around doing one-nighters. It's a better way of retiring than playing golf. Believe me, I've watched them other mothers, and I don't want nothing to do with that! You know, they follow that little ball around and they ride in the cart. I ride in the bus and it's really groovier! Particularly if Ray [Preuss] is sober. He's our bus driver. He's a lovely man. He knows if the bus is going forwards or backwards, which is a pretty good step ahead.

But this is what I really would like to tell you, my very dear friends, is that I have now, for the first time in maybe 10 years, a steady job. [Audience laughter.] It's the truth. The guys and me, we're going to open in my club in New Orleans on January 16. That's at least the target date, unless they run us out of town before that. But I think it will work out. We're having a jazz room put together for us, and it's in the Hyatt Regency Hotel, which gives us kind of a respectable address. I would hope, Felix, that you and a lot of your friends would make it down. . . .

VOICE FROM THE AUDIENCE: What town is it in?

WOODY: What town is it in? Are you serious? Where else could it be but New Orleans? Right? That's where it all began, and that's where it's going down. I'm taking it right to the depths of despair!

But anyway, I would like for you now to meet some more of my people, because I'm very proud of these cats. I'm not sure why. . . . I would like now to do a tune that we did some years ago, and it shows their prowess.

After the band performed "Reunion at Newport" and "You Are So Beautiful," Woody continued his monologue.

WOODY: I have never been in Washington so close to election day, but in the past, I have been here for inaugural balls and things of that nature. There was once a Truman dinner, a little get-together, you know, the "boys from Kansas City." It was very lovely, and we played a gig at the Kavakos Club. . . . SOMETIMES, THEY PAID US! [Laughter.] We always showed up on time. You didn't want to have any ill feelings, you might go out feet first! We used to play the game for what it was. But the night of this Truman party there was a little after-the-party get-together, and it took place at a place called the Turf and Grid. . . .

I was standing at the bar trying to get to the front [of the line], trying to muscle my way in to get a drink. I had a baritone saxophone player, the late Serge Chaloff, who was not only a great musician, but probably one of the greatest exponents of the drugs of America! [Laughter.] He knew what to turn you down, up, and sideways.

Serge had been on the gig all night, staring out into space. He was fine, he was just dandy. But the point was, sometime during the night, we had to get together. The problem was that I could not really reach Serge. . . .

So I went to the Turf and Grid with the rest of the guys. And I'm fighting my way to get to the bar, because the place was crowded. It was quite a heavy night, everybody was in black tie. I finally pushed my way up to the bar and I said, "Scotch! Any kind, just lay some on me!" The bartender laid one right in my hand, and then I got this nudge right in my gut feeling, and naturally, it was Serge. He said, "H-E-Y-Y-Y, M-A-A-N-N-N, why did you give me all that tonight, I was C-C-O-O-L-L-L!" I said, "You were cool?" Well, one word led to another, and it wasn't really very heavy, but the point was, he kept noodging me. In the expression of an old time New York musician . . . "To be noodged, is really a bad riff!" Have you ever been noodged?

VOICE FROM THE AUDIENCE: Yes.

WOODY: Okay, then you know what I'm speaking about. And you're pretty young to know about that [laughter].

Anyway, he got up to me, and he's now bugging me, because he's screaming in my ear, how groovy he is and how much he loves me and "Why are we into this, man? . . . You're putting me down!" I said, "I'M NOT PUTTING YOU DOWN, JUST GET AWAY FROM ME, BABY, STAY AWAY. GO OVER THERE!" Of course, that didn't work at all.

The rest of the story, I can't really tell you. [Laughter.]

Later Woody made the following comments:

WOODY: Thank you very much. I enjoy being here with you ladies and gentlemen. . . . I would like to start this set with something unusual, but I can't think of a damned thing. Do you have any thoughts in mind?

VOICE FROM THE AUDIENCE: "Make Someone Happy."

WOODY [in a guttural voice]:   That's not very unusual!

AUDIENCE: [Laughter.] "Blues in the Night." "Jazz Man." "Woodchopper's Ball."

WOODY: I want the whole back row back there to get out!

AUDIENCE: [screaming en masse] "Woodchopper's Ball" [plus other unintelligible and boisterous comments and requests].

WOODY: If you'll please hold it down, otherwise, you ain't gonna get shit! Let's put it down where it really is! You know me, and I know you!

At this point, Woody addresses an unidentified colleague in the audience.

WOODY: . . . and "Captain." I meant to tell you this all night. REPLACE YOUR TEETH! [More laughter.] Get some like mine. They're much groovier, you just put a little powder on and you hold them in that way. You can hit some of the wildest high notes you've ever heard . . . if the powder is working right. What would YOU like us to play?

After more raucous requests from the audience, Woody called the Second Herd classic "I've Got News for You."

Before the broadcast concluded, the Herd performed "Caldonia," at the noted express tempo. As drummer Dave Ratajczak completed his solo, Woody announced: "Captain Ratajczak, of the Polish marines!"

Leonard Feather wrote in the November 16 *Los Angeles Times* on Woody's plans to make New Orleans his home base:

> "Starting in January," the maestro said last week, "we'll be spending 36 weeks a year at the same place: a room that's now being built for us adjacent to the Hyatt Regency Hotel in New Orleans. It's my own enterprise; the room will be called Woody Herman's. . . ."[1]

At this time, Woody signed with Concord Jazz Records to produce a series of recordings called "Woody Herman Presents," featuring all-star musicians in small group settings.

On New Year's Eve, December 31, 1980, the Herd played the Hyatt Regency Hotel in New Orleans. Unfortunately, the "Woody Herman's Room" project was plagued with adversity almost from its inception. The opening of the club was delayed for almost a year.

HERMIE DRESSEL: For me to build this room for him and to be an absentee wasn't the best situation. There were many things that I had to contend with, contractors who didn't keep their word, getting the proper financing, getting the proper management to run the room, getting Woody in there to put the time into the room. . . .

MARK LEWIS: They planned to open the room much earlier, and I was really hoping they wouldn't because I was dying to do some traveling, like in a real road band. They didn't open it right away. So, fortunately, I got a whole year on the road before it opened.

After a two-week vacation, the Herd recommenced the grind of one-nighters. Lead trumpeter Brian O'Flaherty had replaced Howie Shear.

On January 20, 1981, the band played at President Reagan's inaugural ball at the Washington Hilton Hotel.

WOODY: It was a typical inaugural. I had played one earlier at Kennedy's presidential inaugural party. However, it was nice in the fact that President Reagan and his wife greeted me very warmly, because he had earlier been an associate of mine in television. We had done some television shows together in the fifties. We did a jazz show with Stan Kenton's band, our band, Peggy Lee and her husband Dave Barbour, and some other people. Reagan was the emcee.

During January and February, the band played one-nighters throughout New England and the East Coast.

JOHN FEDCHOCK: We were playing a dance outside Boston. It was a policemen's ball. It was one of those kind of dances where no one was really listening to the band and they were doing their thank-yous and their little speeches. One of the guys happened to have one of those whoopee cushions on the bandstand. When a soloist would come down to the mike, they would put it on his seat. So Woody started to get into it and he would designate who would get the whoopee cushion on his seat. It helped boost the morale a lot for that one-nighter. So then Woody asked trumpeter Steve Harrow to come down and play a Harmon mute solo on a blues, and he had one of the guys go to the other mike with the whoopee cushion and "trade fours" with him. No one in the audience even noticed and the band was in stitches.

MARK LEWIS: I had recently purchased the whoopee cushion. One of the guys put it on someone's chair, and when Woody heard it, he laughed. It was during the blues called "Cousins." Woody had him bring it down front to the mike and blow a solo, so to speak. I don't know if I ever saw Woody laugh any harder.

On April 23, 1981, George Rabbai joined the Herd, replacing Steve Harrow on fourth trumpet. A fluent soloist and singer possessing a sense of humor reminiscent of the First Herd, George remained with the Herd until November 1982.

GEORGE RABBAI: When I was in high school I played with my dad's dance band. Every Saturday night we played in a small group in a little town called Millville. What was so hip about it was the fact that my dad and I both played trumpets on it. The piano player, Bob Carter, had been with the Dorsey and James bands. I also played a couple of gigs with Tex Beneke.

When I first got on Woody's band, I hadn't played with many people in a big band who were that good on their instruments and practiced a lot. I was living in Atlantic City then, working there with some farmed-out cats. The guys didn't practice much and just played shows. I never had a chance to really play anything that good. When I got on Woody's band, everybody had good pitch. The trumpet section was great. Brian O'Flaherty, Mark Lewis, Scott Wagstaff, and Bill Byrne. I remember playing the stock arrangement of "Woodchopper's Ball" in all kinds of bands, and just honking it. But Woody's band played it real easy and precise. "Four Brothers" was great to play, too. We would tongue those notes like "bop, bop" real light, and it just exploded! The section was that much in tune. . . .

You had to be some kind of player to play with Woody, I thought. More than if you went with Maynard or Buddy's band. They had different kinds of flag wavers. But with Woody, there was a lot of music going on. A lot of sensitive things, nice little flugelhorn arrangements and muted things, and you could swing! With Woody's band you could play like you would play on Basie's band or the Ellington band, because to me, that was Woody. Woody always loved Duke and Johnny Hodges.

So for me, playing with Woody was incredible. As a boss, he was always real fair. I saw him with people who would come on that band and he would give them their two weeks. . . . He even gave one guy almost a month before we had to send him home. He just wasn't quite making the book. He hated to let people go. I would talk to John Fedchock once in a while and he always told me that when they had to let someone go, Woody always rebelled a bit, because he always wanted to give someone his fair chance. Maybe he thought some people took longer. But he was an old pro . . . I loved him like a grandpop or like an uncle. He really took care of me. He let me play all the time. I played a lot of solos in that fourth trumpet chair. He'd always call me up. He'd open a chart up . . . he'd yell "George, put a mute in it." "Come up with the flugelhorn." That was the best thing that happened to me. I never experienced anything like that. So playing with Woody was the greatest. I miss him real bad.

In July 1981, Woody recorded Volume Two of his "Woody Herman Presents" series in New York. The band included four tenor saxophonists from four previous Herds: Flip Phillips, Al Cohn, Bill Perkins, and Sal Nistico. The four-tenor idea, voiced minus the baritone, goes back to the original Gene Roland conception. The rhythm section consisted of John Bunch, piano, Don Lamond, drums, and bassist George Duvivier. (Bunch and Lamond were alumni.)

On August 15, 1981, the Herd was recorded live at the Concord Jazz Festival with guest artists Stan Getz and Al Cohn. The album received a Grammy nomination.

"Things Ain't What They Used to Be" is a rousing arrangement of the Ellington classic by Woody's former pianist Dave La Lama, with pianist John Oddo opening. Guest soloist Al Cohn breaks loose in a stirring contribution. The band's biting ensemble introduces the Chopper's clarinet. Then the ensemble detonates again to cap the performance.

"Theme in Search of a Movie" was composed and arranged by pianist Oddo. The performance features Oddo, George Rabbai (flugelhorn), and Woody's warm alto.

WOODY:　In the last few years I've had some very good writers, people like John Oddo. They all kind of set the pattern for what our bands have tried to do down the years. And as long as I have any energy left, I'll still try to produce something that I think has musical merit.

Bill Holman's "Midnight Run" is an up-tempo score with a repetitive line, featuring solos from George Rabbai (trumpet), Bill Stapleton (flugelhorn), who had returned briefly, Bill Ross (tenor), and Woody (clarinet).

"You Are So Beautiful" is a lovely jazz ballad arranged by John Oddo, featuring lead trombonist Gene Smith.

"John Brown's Other Body" is John Oddo's update of the "Battle Hymn of the Republic," performed with a pseudo-rock beat. There are moving solos from Bill Ross (piccolo) and Randy Russell (tenor). It was a highlight to observe Woody's dance antics during this piece.

"Especially for You" is a light score by Oddo, featuring tenorist Paul McGinley. "North Beach Breakdown," another contribution by pianist Oddo, is slightly reminiscent of the seventies fusion period, replete with rock rhythms and showcasing Fedchock and Paul McGinley's tenor. Bill Holman arranged "The Dolphin," which features guest artist Stan Getz in this performance.

John Oddo transcribed the almost forgotten Second Herd Shorty Rogers score of George Wallington's "Lemon Drop." A welcome surprise in 1981, this version features Rabbai, Woody and Brignola doing the bebop vocal. Exciting solo contributions are from Brignola, Cohn, Smith, and Fedchock in a trombone chase, and Mark Lewis and Rabbai in a trumpet-flugelhorn chase. Woody's clarinet comes in before the vocal out-chorus, with an added low voice from trumpeter O'Flaherty. Woody remarks at the conclusion: "That's the way bebop was!"

After an absence of a year and a half, Frank Tiberi returned to the lead tenor chair on August 18, 1981.

GEORGE RABBAI:　Frank Tiberi taught me a lot. I tried to pick his brain about how he approached reading chord changes and improvising. He's a very, very individual type of guy. He tried to explain some of the ways he did it and I really couldn't pick up on how he approached it.

　　I remember a lot of neat things with Woody. He'd be funny on the bus or on a gig. One night, we were at a gig in a gymnasium. I used to do some fireworks impressions. I'd get on the microphone and do those sounds . . . SHOOOO . . . BOOM! Over the mike it sounded pretty neat. I was doing it this night on our break. I can't believe I did this. Normally, I was pretty straight, but I was in this kind of mood. You know, you travel a lot and you get punchy and I would like to break the guys up.

So this one night I did the sounds of rifle shots and bullets whizzing. It was going all over the gymnasium like "BOOM, BOOM, PHU-U-U-U!" It was break time and Woody was out in the lobby. So he came back for the next set and he says, "Any survivors?" I thought he was going to get upset and say, "What the hell are you pulling?" But actually, he didn't care.

On August 29 Woody flew alone from New York to Tokyo for the Aurex Jazz Festival at Osaka, Japan. He was featured with an all-star big band, including Chubby Jackson and fronted by Lionel Hampton. The Herd took a two-week vacation during this period.

On September 12 the Herd convened at Oral Roberts University in Tulsa for a concert and commenced a new road tour. Jim Carroll had replaced Randy Russell on third tenor.

On December 27, 1981, the long-delayed "Woody Herman's Room" opened.

MARK LEWIS:　The management was very positive that they wanted the opening then. Everybody in the band was bugged about it. Most of the guys drove their cars to get there. They had to leave either a few days before Christmas or on Christmas Day to make it.

The club was only half finished. It was really ridiculous, but they were in such a hurry to open this club that they opened too soon. They had all this nice, plush furniture and there were no backs on the chairs. You could see the wood frames on the backs.

It took them so long to complete it. They were fixing things all the way. They didn't even have a bathroom in there. People who wanted to go to the bathroom had to walk down the plaza into another building. It was done really terribly. It was too bad, but none of this was Woody's fault.

"Woody Herman's" was spacious and comfortable and decorated in apricot and blue. It had seating capacity for 550. The dance floor was located in a rear corner, so the dancers had a degree of privacy and the view of the stage was not obstructed. The band was competing with two other long-standing New Orleans attractions, Pete Fountain and Al Hirt. Woody's was the only big band and the only one in the country with its own club.

On January 25 drummer Jim Rupp replaced Dave Ratajczak.

JOHN FEDCHOCK:　We were taping TV shows in New Orleans, along with featuring guest stars with the band. The sort of co-host of the shows, along with Woody, was Pete Barbutti. He did a lot of bits with the band and Woody. Pete had a bit where he played "jazz cigar" on the breaks of Neal Hefti's "Cute." He was bragging to Woody about how he was the world's ONLY jazz cigar player, and Woody responded by telling him the band was called the Cigar-Puffing Herd. We did a chart where the entire band smoked cigars. The trombones would play a figure, and then the trumpets would puff it. The trombone section puffed cigars through plunger mutes! ...

I would say the highlight of the TV shows was Ray Charles. He came out and did "I've Got News for You" with Woody, and played piano on "After Hours."

This is the personnel of the Herd in the initial week's performances at "Woody Herman's": Brian O'Flaherty, Scott Wagstaff, Mark Lewis, George Rabbai, Bill Byrne (trumpets); Gene Smith, John Fedchock, Larry Shunk (trombones); Frank Tiberi, Paul McGinley, Jim Carroll (tenor saxes); Mike Brignola (baritone sax); John Oddo (piano); John Arbo (bass, later replaced by Dave Shapiro); Jim Rupp (drums); and Woody (leader, clarinet, alto sax, soprano sax, vocals).

GEORGE RABBAI: When we went to New Orleans we had a lot of fun. . . . We had two shows every night and in-between we'd have the Heritage Hall Dixieland Band. It was an excellent, traditional Dixie band. Six musicians, three up front and three in the back. They had an "umbrella man," one of the grand marshals. He had an umbrella with all these ribbons and decor. He was an old black cat named Mr. Dudley. He had known Kid Ory and he also knew Louis Armstrong.

New Orleans was a neat experience for all of us; for Woody, it was kind of a drag, because he liked to be on the road. He had friends everywhere.

WOODY: I'm not in this for the money. There isn't any. Let me tell you why I keep playing dates on the road. I've given this a great deal of thought. The real reason for the road is very basic. If you want musical independence, which I have needed my whole life, you better keep moving. Then you won't become a target.

If you want to settle in any one area of the country to make a living at music, you are now confronted by the fact that you will play the music that someone else wants you to play, and you've now made a big concession. . . .

MARK LEWIS: We were drawing only about fifty people a night. But worst of all, the people didn't come to hear the players in the band. They came only to see Woody. . . .

One night he got angry because my solo was coming out of the speakers very loud. The sound man was barely getting paid and did a horrible job. So Woody came over and slapped the mike straight up in the middle of my solo. I didn't like it and we exchanged stares.

On the next tune, I had a Harmon mute solo. This time I didn't raise the mike and my solo was inaudible. Woody came over and raised the mike. I immediately moved my horn away to the side. Woody followed me. I moved to the other side. Woody followed. He was determined to get the last word in!

But later, on "Caldonia," I played my solo with a bucket mute, which looks funny and muffles the sound quite a bit. By this time, Woody was actually laughing. That was one of the great things about Woody. He would let you blow your stack and not fire you.

The Herd played at the first annual St. Augustine Florida Festival of Jazz on April 4. Other headliners were Doc Severinsen and his new group "Nebron," Maynard Ferguson's band, and pianist and Herd alumnus Jimmy Rowles and his Quartet.

During Dave Shapiro's bass solo on "Greasy Sack Blues," Woody addressed the sound booth: "Light up the bass player . . . make him somebody!"

After the buildup from the brass ensemble, Shapiro did the gliss that Woody relished and requested from all his bassists. To Woody's mind, the sound suggested an upset stomach, sparking him to spell out "R-O-L-A-I-D-S!"

WOODY (continued): "This is an old tune written by Hoagy Carmichael, whom we lost recently. You know, everybody remembers Stardust, but I think they forget about a lot of other great tunes that he wrote. I'll be aided and abetted by my very athletic trumpet player. . . . He's president of the New Orleans Weight Watchers, he's just here under duress. . . . "

VOICE FROM THE AUDIENCE: He's cute!

WOODY: Of course, he's cute! Are you kidding? He's my very own favorite. And here's "Old Rockin' Chair's Got Me." This is George Rabbai. . . .

After the Herman/Rabbai vocal duet of "Rockin' Chair," where George Rabbai does an excellent impression of Satchmo's trumpet and gravel voice, Woody detains him down front for a straight vocal on "Sunny Side of the Street."

GEORGE RABBAI: We used to do that "Old Rockin' Chair" number, the old one that Jack Teagarden and Louis used to do. Woody talked to John

Woody and George Rabbai doing their routine on "Rockin' Chair" in 1985. (Courtesy Mark Vinci)

Oddo, our pianist-arranger at the time. He said, "Why don't you write a nice arrangement of that and George and I'll sing it?"

We had to play this jazz festival up in Connecticut, and we were traveling all day on the bus to get to this gig. . . . So on this tour, everybody was getting pretty much drugged with this "Rockin' Chair" number we were doing, and even I got tired of it. Woody and I had been doing it at every single concert. It was about the seventh tune on the agenda, and you would just go through them like clockwork, so I went up to the front center stage with Woody. They had a lot of microphones up there and they had a good sound tech and each of us had his own mike.

We started the tune and I looked at these microphones that we each had, and the sound techs had wrapped yellow sheets of foam around the mikes, to filter out the wind. It was windy outside. These mikes looked like ice cream cones. I just couldn't take it. We started to sing and I was looking at my mike and Woody was holding his, and it looked like two kids up there with ice cream cones.

Anyway, we started the tune and I started breaking up. I was just falling apart. Woody was looking at me, kinda scowling. I don't think that he caught the humor at that point.

I kept singing, ". . . cane by my side," and I'd start laughing again and just fall apart. Then the crowd started really getting into it. I had to play the old Satchmo thing, "RAH BAP BAAA BAP BE BA BAAA" and was having a hard time even getting it out. I was just laughing, and I looked back at Frank Tiberi, and he was in tears, and I looked at the rest of the band and they were all in tears. The rhythm section was still going along playing and Woody started laughing. I held up my mike and he caught the joke. There was so much foam on those microphones. . . .

On July 2, 1982, drummer Dave Ratajczak returned temporarily. During the next several months numerous drummers came in and out, including Jeff Hamilton, Ed Soph, Jeff Boudreaux, Bobby Breaux, and Don Lamond as a sub.

On August 29 the band flew to Japan for a one-week tour, including the Aurex Jazz Festival at Osaka. Traveling with the band were four Herman alumni tenorists Woody called the "Four Others": Flip Phillips, Al Cohn, Med Flory, and Sal Nistico.

SAL NISTICO:　Woody approached me about doing the Japan thing in '82. I said, "Yes, and this is what I want. . . ." It was steep, and he winced and said, "Okay, kid." He understood that. He didn't begrudge me that. I've done a lot of thinking about Woody. When we were in Japan, we did a lot of talking. Actually, we did another tour over in Switzerland [July 1983], with Zoot, Bill Perkins and Billy Mitchell with the big band. We did some more talking, and we kind of squared things away. It was nice. . . .

GEORGE RABBAI:　The Japan tour was real hip. When we got off the plane, we walked into the airport, and there were guys with microphones, cameras, and flash bulbs. We were like stars . . . I'm serious! That was a strange feeling for me. It was a real neat experience. We stayed in a real classy, modern, state-of-the-art hotel. We went over with an all-star "jam" that included Clark Terry, Tommy Flanagan, Dexter Gordon, Kenny Burrell, J. J. Johnson, and Kai Winding.

We were all getting the royal treatment, eating great food. We recorded over there and we hung out with Clark Terry on the breaks. I talked to Clark a lot, picking his brain. Toots Thielemans was there, too.

We went to Yokohama, we went to Osaka. The audiences were incredible, they loved us. They loved the music. They KNEW the music! The places were packed and they were screaming for us. That doesn't happen in this country anymore. That only happens for people like David Lee Roth or whoever the hell is hot right now, Dire Straits or Bruce Springsteen. The people were just screaming!

By special arrangement with Toshiba, Concord recorded the band with the four guest tenors. The album was released by East World Jazz (Toshiba) as *The Woody Herman Big Band—Aurex Jazz Festival '82*. Concord later released an almost identical album, *The Woody Herman Big Band—World Class*.

The Second Herd standard "Four Brothers" was included, taken at a faster clip than the original Columbia recording, with solos by McGinley,

Brignola, Carroll, and Tiberi. The rhythm section is excellent, particularly drummer Ratajczak.

GEORGE RABBAI: When we recorded "Rockin' Chair" over there, I was in my best voice at that concert. I remember, I tried to sound like Louie Armstrong as much as I could. I didn't really have any identity of myself in the tune. I heard Roy Eldridge play it and I heard Louis and Jack Teagarden, "The Big T," do it. I really didn't feel comfortable doing it. Woody first wanted me to do it in my regular voice and I did it, but I felt that I didn't sing it well. So I started emulating Louie, trying to get Louie's thing going, and I've naturally got a high voice. I've heard people comment who heard me do it . . . "What the hell are you doing?" Anyway, I did my best.

There was a lot of magic in the Yokohama Stadium when we recorded that thing. I mean that. I nailed that high F in the air . . . wham! People were waiting for it and then when I played it, the place went nuts! It was probably the neatest experience I've had playing, because I am not a high-note player. I never was. But on that tune, I would always go for the F because Louis did it. It was the way Louis did those things. That was all I heard in my head and it came out.

I think very few times I missed it. One time I missed it in a mall somewhere in Chicago. But I didn't really care. When it counted I could do it. That was a feat for me, because I played fourth trumpet on the band. . . .

"The Claw" (on the Concord album only) features the four guest tenorists. Solos are, in order, by Phillips, Cohn, Flory, and Nistico. The score demonstrates a little-known talent of Flip Phillips as composer and arranger. On "Tiny's Blues" solos are by guest stars Nistico, Cohn, Phillips, and Flory.

"Peanut Vendor," long associated with Stan Kenton, is redressed by arranger Oddo in a more contemporary mode. The score is highlighted by a pulsating harmonic pattern with plenty of room for the soloists to stretch out. Paul McGinley states the melody on flute and Rabbai on trumpet. Additional contributions are from Gene Smith, trombone, McGinley and Tiberi, and Ratajczak.

"Crystal Silence," Chick Corea and Neville Potter's poignant jazz ballad, is interpreted here by John Oddo and features a warm solo by Gene Smith.

Don Rader's 1965 vintage Herd classic "Greasy Sack Blues" sounds as fresh as it did in the 1960s. Woody's gorgeous, low-register clarinet swings and demonstrates once again his often overlooked skill. Rabbai deftly performs the plunger-trumpet solo and bassist Shapiro and trumpeter Scott Wagstaff contribute to a consuming performance.

Juan Tizol's jazz classic "Perdido" was arranged for the 1980s Herd by John Oddo. Here it's a feature for Flip Phillips' smoky tenor. The band effectively performs in background riffs behind Flip's flowing solo.

JOHN FEDCHOCK: It's always a kick to play the jazz festivals and in places where there's an intelligent jazz crowd present. You know that they're actually listening to the solos and trying to understand what you're doing.

After returning from Japan on September 7, the band went back on the road for a string of one-nighters in the West, beginning on the 10th in Eugene, Oregon. On September 21, the band came to Anaheim, California, to play a ballroom called the Phoenix Club. Woody appeared sullen and preoccupied and almost got into a scuffle with a patron who requested a waltz.

After the brief tour ended, the band returned to its home base at "Woody Herman's." These were dark days for Woody and the Herd. The club was not taking in the expected revenues. Woody was keeping the negative reports from Charlotte, who by this time had received a diagnosis of terminal cancer. However, one of the musicians in the band wrote a letter to a musician friend, also a friend of Woody's, disclosing the inauspicious news, and so the word reached Charlotte. Meanwhile the IRS was still nagging Woody and placing a choke hold on his personal finances.

HERMIE DRESSEL: No one knew that the recession was coming in 1982, when the South American, European, and Japanese tourist business fell through the bottom, and the oil business fell. . . . In later years Woody wanted some place to sit down. But Woody's music was not New Orleans kind of music. . . . New Orleans is much more traditional. Woody's band never was that style, except way back in the early days of "The Band That Plays the Blues."

WOODY: We lasted the better part of a year, with part of the year out on the road because we had planned to always be out on the road for a few months a year. . . . But the people that supposedly invested the money had used up whatever monies they had when the club opened, just building the club and putting it in order to open. When they opened, there were no funds whatsoever to exploit or properly publicize the club, so it was destined to be a bad one.

They weren't getting enough money to even pay the taxes. Once again, taxes I'd be responsible for. It was withholding tax, because Hermie never received any monies while we were in the club. They were just paying the band and that's all. But he should have never allowed the band to get into that kind of situation.

At this point the author commented: "You've had some bad luck with managers, haven't you?"

WOODY: Well . . . I'm thoroughly concerned about music, and that keeps me more than busy, and I just felt that if you had competent people that they should be able to handle your affairs, but evidently, I missed badly in several cases.

There were private individuals, not a corporation, who would finance the room. Hermie was deeply involved with them. They were selling him a lot of "shellac," so it was destined to be a bust before we ever began. But I didn't realize it and a lot of us didn't. We thought that if we came up with something that was very good, it would have a market, but you have to have money to exploit it and sell it.

The author asked Bill Byrne what caused the "Woody Herman's Room" failure.

BILL BYRNE: Complete mismanagement. No concept at all as to what the club could do, which was really up to Hermie. . . .

Basically, it was just one man who financed the thing. He ran an optical business and they created this limited partnership. When the smoke cleared one person had put all the money in it. Then the investor reorganized it and got some very competent people, but then he couldn't get any more backing.

Hermie didn't pay our income tax. So the IRS decreed that all three of us were responsible for it [Dressel, Herman and Byrne]. Woody and I didn't even know that they hadn't paid it until three years later when the IRS. sent the notice.

On October 22 the band broke away to participate in the "Big Bands at Epcot" extravaganza near Orlando, Florida. Second Herd drummer Don Lamond sat in.

MARK LEWIS: We flew to Florida to play a job at the Epcot Center, which also featured Count Basie, Harry James, Lionel Hampton, and a few other bands.

Our drummer couldn't make that job, so Woody thought of using Don Lamond, who lives down there. Of course, the guys wanted the band to burn, since all the guys from the other bands would be checking us out. We were a bit uneasy having to play the concert without a rehearsal. But it was an honor to play with one of Woody's greatest drummers. . . .

The Herd then returned to New Orleans.

MARK LEWIS: It was kind of sad and depressing for everybody because the German fellow who was financing the whole thing had left town. We didn't get paid one week and we just wondered what was going on. Then another week went by and then we found out from Bill that he didn't have the money to pay us our salary.

Bill had told us that Woody wanted to go on and play and what we would do is work for the "door" [receipts], a small amount of money. It came out to like fifteen bucks a night per guy. We all went into the back room where we dressed and started debating. Some guys didn't want to continue right off the bat. Some guys needed the money more than others. Some guys wanted to continue because they wanted the fifteen bucks. Some guys had taken draws on their salary from Bill, so some guys were already ahead of other guys.

We finally decided to go ahead and play. I don't even remember how many nights it was, I think it was only two nights. Then Charlotte's condition got bad and Woody flew home, and that ended it.

He had the old-time attitude that "the show must go on . . . until the end!" But it was tough.

WOODY: I just left New Orleans in the middle of the night. I had never signed a piece of paper with anybody. I had become cagey enough about that because of previous legal battles. . . . After that I was with Charlotte every moment I could be. . . .

She had been sick over ten years, but she lived pretty well with the treatment she was receiving. She had cancer throughout her body.

In a published interview with Woody, Gene Lees gives a brief and touching glimpse of a moment in Charlotte Herman's final days:

"I think the reason Charlotte and I were survivors," he said, "is humor. We could always laugh at each other." He paused, looking inward. . . . "She was lying in there," he said, his hand indicating a bedroom off the living room "a few days before she died, and I was sitting on the bed. And what can you say to anyone in those circumstances? And I put my face in my hands and I started to cry. And she raised her hand . . ." He imitated the gesture, a slow and hesitant lift of the arm ". . . and who knows how much it cost her, and she put it on my shoulder, and she said, 'Straighten up, Boy!' "[2]

Charlotte Herman died on Saturday, November 20, 1982.

WOODY: So she had a lot of good years, and even after she had cancer and had numerous operations, she would feel that the Lord was looking upon her, because she could handle the drugs they gave her and the cobalt treatments.

She had ten good years of reasonably good health, and she traveled with me again for our fortieth anniversary. We were in England, and we were everywhere. She was able to get something out of life. She was a lovely lady, very bright. But the day we got married was the day she quit show business and never looked back, never wanted any part of it.

That's why, when she passed away, we were married forty-six years, and for a musician that's pretty good. And that's totally due to her efforts.

NAT PIERCE: She was a wonderful lady. She had a pacemaker put in a couple of years before she died. I happened to call one day while the doctor was monitoring the pacemaker and she said to me, "I can't talk now . . . I'm recording!"

INGRID HERMAN REESE: I gave up my music career when my mother got sick and I came out to Los Angeles from Nashville in 1982. I had been pretty much functioning at the same level monetarily and every other way for about the last fifteen years, and I didn't see it getting much better.

I had been editing articles for quite a while for George Gruhn. He's an authority on stringed instruments and I worked part-time for him for years. He has regular columns in *Guitar Player* and *Pickin'* magazines I worked with him on. So when I came out to Los Angeles in 1982, I decided to get more involved with writing and editing.

Ingrid's marriage to Robert Fawler ended in 1976. In 1981 she married Jim Reese.

On December 8 the band reorganized for a two-week tour booked by the Jim Halsey Company of Tulsa, Oklahoma.

JOHN FEDCHOCK: John [Oddo] was writing a lot of the charts. A great writer. I always wanted to write a chart for Woody but was kind of intimidated. I didn't write one for Woody until after two years.

Woody was very cool about it. He gave me a couple of suggestions, then I started doing a little writing. "Fried Buzzard," the Lou Donaldson thing, was the first chart that I did for the band in 1982. Then after John left, I kind of picked up the slack because nobody was writing for the band.

Actually, the only writing that I had done previously was in a school situation, so I learned a lot just writing for the band. Plus, when you're sitting in the band playing these great charts night after night, things are bound to sink in sooner or later. Like how to make things swing, and how to make things build.

I learned a lot in the time I played in the band. My playing improved tenfold just from doing it night after night and having to produce. One of the hard things on the band is having to produce, night after night. Even if you're sick or don't feel like playing, you still have to go up there and put out 100 percent. It's really a challenge if you're sick.

After a three-week vacation, the Herd was back on the one-nighter circuit, beginning January 10, 1983.

Between February and August 1983, the band's drum chair was occupied by Jim Rupp, Jay Cummings (Kenton alumnus), Jim Rupp (again), Dave Ratajczak, John Riley, Paul Johnson, Jeff Hamilton, and Steve Houghton, finally settling with Dave Miller on August 23. After serving on and off as a sub for several months, John Adams became the bassist for a season.

In April, Woody continued the "Woody Herman Presents" series on the Concord Jazz label, supervising and participating in recording sessions that included alumni Nat Pierce, Jeff Hamilton, Jake Hanna, and Monty Budwig.

MARK LEWIS:　Bill Byrne was such a great manager and trumpeter. To do both is a twenty-four-hour job.

　　We were all on an airline once, and preparing to taxi to the runway, when Bill got out in front of the plane and started waving to the pilots to wait! Bill hadn't boarded because he was waiting to make sure all the band equipment had been loaded onto the plane, which it hadn't. . . .

On July 7 the Herd departed for the annual European tour. While at the jazz festival at Nice, Woody met an attractive redhead with whom he became quite enamored. Her name in full was Haji Catton, but she preferred to be known simply as Haji. She would become one of two female companions Woody sometimes referred to as "my nurses."

HAJI:　I had an apartment in Paris at the time I met Woody. I was in the South of France in Nice with Herbie Hancock and his wife, Gigi. Herbie's wife and I are very good friends. We were staying at the same hotel where Woody was.

　　Gigi and I were swimming at the pool on top of the hotel and Woody was there. I think Woody always had an eye for redheads. I wasn't aware that he had his eye on me that day.

　　That evening Gigi and I came back from the jazz festival that was going on at the time in Nice. We were listening to Fats Domino at the downstairs bar. Woody was there but I wasn't aware of it. After a few minutes we left to go upstairs to the pool bar.

　　We went up the elevator to the pool lounge and we were there about ten minutes talking to a friend of Gigi's when Woody came upstairs. He was very nonchalant. He just came over and sat down next to us and joined in our conversation.

　　He said, "I saw you walk out, and I had a hunch that you were going upstairs to the pool bar, so when I saw you walk out, I followed you!" That's how we met.

　　I gave him my Paris number, then I went to Italy. About a month or two later, I went back to Paris and he called me from England and I flew over and joined him there. I traveled with him quite a bit after that.

MIKE BRIGNOLA: Woody would do some funny stuff during the performance of the tunes. He wore full upper and lower dentures. Sometimes, he would be looking at the band with his back to the audience and he would open his mouth and literally pop out the whole lower teeth, and it would be disgusting and hilarious at the same time.

One time at the Nice Jazz Festival he got real pissed off. There were these people who were really into taking pictures of the guys in the band. They had taken pictures of us from every angle and Woody, as always before the gig, had to find someplace to put in his teeth. He had to take them out and put on extra powder to make them stick in better. He was just trying to do it backstage and these people caught him with the camera.

Sometimes he was in the dressing room and he would have something he wanted to say to you. He would be in the middle of putting in his teeth and he would start to talk without his dentures. It was hard to understand him. I'm not sure if there's any humor in this, it's just a fact of old age. It was like dealing with your grandfather.

On August 6 the band opened at Disneyland for its annual stint. The following week, the Herd teamed with Rosemary Clooney to record the *My Buddy* album. Pianist John Oddo penned most of the arrangements. He would leave the band shortly afterward to become Clooney's music director.

WOODY: I liked doing the album with Clooney and, for the record, she sings better today than she did as a young gal. She was successful then, and I think the reason that she's very strong in the history of show biz today is that she still sings very well and people have good ears.

JEFF HAMILTON: I want to mention Woody's wisdom in the recording studio. . . . They had called me back to do the Rosemary Clooney album. The band was pretty well stretched out all over the studio, and I think Dan Fornero, the lead trumpet player, was having trouble hearing the rhythm section and the time with the rest of the band because we were pretty far away. They were having trouble getting the headphone mix right and Woody was up to his neck in waiting for this thing to get right. So finally, he said, "That's it! No headphones, we're not recording with headphones. We'll record like we did in the old days!" He was pretty mad at this point, and the band was looking at each other like, "We've got to use headphones, because we've got to hear the rhythm section!"

So I took it upon myself to be the spokesman. I walked up to Woody on a break and I said, "I know the effect you're trying to get and I think it's a good idea, but I think that some of the guys need to hear the rhythm section, and I need to hear them, so can we try just a few of the headphones?" He said, "Well, if you really think we need them, we'll try them later, but let's take one first and see how it sounds."

I was sure that it was going to sound like we weren't in the same room together. So we did one of the tunes that John Oddo had arranged, and they played it back and it sounded perfect.

So Woody walked up to me during the playback and he said, "How's it sound to you?" and I said, "I've got to hand it to you, it sounds great!" But I added, "It just makes my job a little harder without the headphones because I'm so far from the band and I feel like I'm pulling the band through the whole date." He just threw his head back and laughed, and said, "I'm paying you enough money, pal."

On August 23 the Herd had a new drummer, Dave Miller. Dave was educated at Indiana University and North Texas State University.

DAVE MILLER: A funny, but embarrassing thing happened to me on my first night with the band. We played "Caldonia." On the end of it, Woody always did a thing like "Vegas show-biz." He would do some funny movements with his arms, like he was hitting a ball, and he would put one arm under the other arm and bring his elbow into it and then do a rowing motion. The drummer was supposed to catch all these little motions and make a rumble sound to coincide with them. Well, nobody filled me in on that. When the last chord was finished, he started making all those motions and without the drum sounds behind him he looked like a fool. So he turned around and said to me, "CATCH ME . . . CATCH ME!" I didn't know what the hell he was talking about. So I just jumped up from my drums and went around behind him thinking he was going to fall and I was supposed to catch him. I was waiting for Woody to collapse in my arms, and Woody said, "No, I don't mean to catch me literally, I mean to catch me on the drums!"

On August 29, 1983, pianist Phil DeGreg joined the band, replacing John Oddo. On September 22, Byron Stripling replaced Dan Fornero on lead trumpet. Stripling was featured on a superb chart entitled "Dog Day Blues," unfortunately never recorded.

On October 19 lead trombonist Gene Smith, recently married, left the band, and John Fedchock moved over to the lead chair. On November 16 the band left from New York for an eighteen-day tour of Europe.

DAVE MILLER: The first British tour that we did in 1983 was probably my most memorable experience with the band. At that time there was the "First Camera" television show, who were doing a special on the band. They were traveling around with us on tour. It was going to be about their last show. I think it was on NBC. It was competing against "20/20" and "60 Minutes," kind of stiff competition. They were with us both in the States and then over in Europe. They were taping live shows and they interviewed John Fedchock, Byron Stripling, and myself, so it was fun. It was a combination of being out with Woody's band, being over in Europe and playing places like the Royal Albert Hall, doing jazz festivals, and touring around with people like Sarah Vaughn and any number of different groups.

The year 1983 ended with the Herd in the main ballroom of the Las Vegas Hilton Hotel. In the early 1980s, a resurgence of interest in big bands was seen. This was partially a result of the "disco culture" and the public's desire to dance. In the case of the Herd, the renewed interest was due in part to the base of fans attracted by Herman and other jazz bands performing in the schools.

After a week's vacation, the Herd opened January 7, 1984, at the Westin Peach Tree Plaza Hotel in Atlanta, Georgia. Dave Riekenberg had joined on second tenor, replacing Mark Vinci, and Paul McKee had joined on second trombone.

Paul McKee received his bachelor's degree from the University of Northern Iowa. Later, he attended the University of Texas in Austin, where he received the invitation to join the Herd.

PAUL McKEE: Woody was great to work for. He was a real encouraging person. He didn't try to tell guys in the band how to play, other than encouraging them to play in the way that fit the band's style. He did expect a player to put forth 100 percent.

One time Woody had his daughter send out some tapes he had of the Second Herd band with Bill Harris. They featured a bunch of Bill Harris solos, and Woody told me to check them out. He said, "I don't want you to copy anything but I just want you to notice what an aggressive player he was and he believed in what he was playing, and that quality can be transferred to any style of musician."

Bill was an extremely confident player and a very original and gifted player. The way that he fit into the band is something unparalleled by anyone. He was probably the most famous trombonist to come out of Woody's band, and also had the most singular style ever developed within the band.

We do a lot of clinics and a lot of young players don't think the history of jazz goes back much beyond 1960. We always tell them, in learning how to develop as a jazz player and an improviser, you need to have an idea of the lineage of your particular instrument, as well as jazz in general, which involves digging back and listening to Louis Armstrong, Bill Harris, Jack Teagarden and some of the other early stylists.

In late January, Woody temporarily broke up the big band to front a small group at the Rainbow Room in New York City. The Willard Alexander

Agency was having difficulty keeping the big Herd booked. Besides, Woody enjoyed the occasional freedom of working with a small group.

GEORGE RABBAI: I went back in 1984 and worked with Woody in New York at the Rainbow Room with George Duvivier [bass], Jake Hanna [drums], John Bunch [piano], Scott Hamilton [tenor], and Warren Vaché [cornet]. It was a real great little band. We worked there about a month. On the final night, we recorded for Concord. I've heard that they have it in the can, and that it's not going to be released for a while.

Making her debut with Woody at the Rainbow Room was singer Polly Podewell. One of the better jazz singers to emerge on the scene in decades, Polly subsequently joined the big band in late 1986 and also became Woody's other "nurse" and companion.

A friend of Third Herd bass trumpeter Cy Touff, Polly was first widely heard when she toured with the Benny Goodman band in 1979.

POLLY PODEWELL: A friend of mine recorded me and he was a friend of Benny's too. His name is John McDonough. He writes for *Down Beat*. He's a very good jazz writer and did a lot of liner notes. John heard me sing at a club in Chicago called Andy's. So he sent Benny a tape, and he hired me sight unseen from listening to the tape.

The first time I met Woody, I was with Cy Touff. He's a jewel of a friend. Cy and I were walking into the Jazz Showcase, which used to be the Happy Medium, in Chicago. At that time, Woody was in a wheelchair. This was after his car accident.

Before going out on the big band tour, I worked with Woody at the Rainbow Room, with a small group. Many celebrities came in. It was the fiftieth anniversary of the Rainbow Room. Zoot Sims, Lionel Hampton, and Tony Bennett all came in occasionally.

We all shared this little, tiny dressing room. The band and I would take turns. They would go out and I would get dressed. Woody was wearing his dentures and he would use this powdered adhesive. It would just fly all over the place when he "powdered" his teeth. He would get it all over my gowns. It was a crazy time.

There was a night when Buddy [Rich] came in, and that was kind of fun, because Woody knew that I was seeing Buddy. He was by himself, and he went and sat down in the back. He was trying to be inconspicuous. So Woody took me by the hand and led me over to him and said something like, "I think you want to dance with him."

It was a great band. The management doesn't always know when they have a good thing. They couldn't understand why we didn't have music stands and music. Everything was improvised and it was wonderful.

Woody and I would go out every night after the job to Eddie Condon's and get totally wiped out. One night on our night off, we had just been to a party at Jim Hill's [the guitar player]. It was a Monday night and Mel Lewis was playing at the Vanguard. Woody and I thought we would go over and hear his big band. So we were feeling no pain, and walked in and sat down. There was a new manager. He didn't know Woody. Woody took his whistle out and blew it real loud. The band all knew who it was, but the manager didn't. So he came over and asked us to leave. Woody was so upset. He didn't say anything about his identity. He always demonstrated class. He just said, "Okay."

He did love his martinis. We both did. We would have some good times. Those are some of my fondest memories of us going out drinking after the shows we did, or sometimes before them. He had such good taste in restaurants and we'd always have such a nice meal. . . . So I knew Woody for a while before I toured with the big band.

BILL BYRNE: Woody put up with an awful lot from his players if he liked the way they played. He put up with lots because he could be such a character himself. He could come up with some pretty funny stuff . . . OUT STUFF, you know. That's why when people would call me and apologize for a musician's behavior in the band, and say, "Such and such is really a nice guy," I would say, "Don't worry about him, because the worst guy in the band could be Woody. If you could top some of his shenanigans, then you accomplished something." Woody had a way that could control any situation if it was getting out of hand. Or, he could MAKE things happen if things were really tame and he wanted to liven them up. Frank and I watched this for years, and I imagine all the guys who worked for him can say the same thing. He could really start raising hell. . . .

WOODY (1984):   The majority of the young men that I have in the band now have been with me for three to four years. Then I have what I call ringers. One of the trumpet players, Bill Byrne, is also my road manager. He's been with me nineteen years.

It's nice to have somebody that I can have a normal conversation with, because when I'm with most of the younger guys, the only thing that we can really discuss is music. The age difference is just too much. . . .

On April 26 just before the Herd left for the International Jazz Festival in Berne, Switzerland, Woody received the news of Count Basie's death. Woody and Nat Pierce attended the funeral with numerous other jazz luminaries.

May 16, 1984, marked Woody's 71st birthday. The band was playing at the Radisson Hotel in Wilmington, Delaware. Included among many plaudits was a city proclamation declaring "WOODY HERMAN BIG BAND DAY." Coincidentally, on the same day, Woody was inducted into the Big Band Hall

Nat Pierce and Woody arrive at Count Basie's funeral held at the Abyssinian Baptist Church in New York on April 30, 1984. (Courtesy Nancy Miller Elliott)

of Fame by the Big Band Society, the first living big-name bandleader to be so honored.

During the festivities at the Radisson, Woody received numerous congratulatory telegrams. Among them were these:

> "Happy Birthday Woody, from Artie Shaw, Dick Johnson, and the Gang. Love ya."

> " . . . It is an honor that you have chosen to celebrate your birthday in Delaware today, and all the Delawareans wish you a very happy birthday. Pete DuPont, Governor."

> " . . . I wanted to extend my personal congratulations. Your contributions to the entertainment industry have made you a legend and have earned you the admiration of all of us. . . . Sincerely, Ronald Reagan."

During May several personnel changes took place in each section. On May 15 pianist Brad Williams replaced DeGreg. Jerry Pinter joined the band in the third tenor chair, replacing Jim Carroll. Ron Stout joined on fourth trumpet, replacing Steve Fulton.

Ronald Lee Stout, son of a tenor saxophonist father and a pianist mother, was initiated into jazz at an early age. His early gigs included stints with The

Righteous Brothers, Lou Rawls, Jose Feliciano, Bill Watrous, and Ralph Blaze. His musical influences were Louis Armstrong, Charlie Parker, John Coltrane, Chet Baker, Art Farmer, and "my mom and dad." Ron proved to be an ideal complement to Mark Lewis.

RON STOUT: My first night was May 22, 1984, my 26th birthday. Before I left town to go on the band, I was driving a flower delivery truck trying to make a living.

About the week before I was supposed to leave town, Roger Ingram arrived in town from Vegas where they had a big [musicians'] strike. Roger called me in LA, and he said, "Do you have any work? I'm hurting." I just laughed because I was starving and driving a truck to make it. I told Roger that I was about to go out on the road with Woody Herman because there was no other work available in town for me.

He was hurting so bad, he said, "Who's going to be taking over your gig with the flowers?" As a matter of fact, I was supposed to train somebody right away. He said, "Okay," and took the job.

My first year on the band was pretty hard, because there were times once or twice a week when I didn't get to blow. Many nights, I would have only my one solo on "Greasy Sack Blues." It was really hard when the only solo I would have was a B-flat plunger blues. B-flat blues and a plunger were the only things I could count on all night long. But I'll tell you, I was thankful for that one solo!

Woody was beautiful. Very rarely was he in a bad mood. All of us have our moods at one time or another, and Woody was pretty damn consistent about things when he got on the stand. He was usually right on. Although he did a lot of funny stuff. He used to always mouth words on the intro of "Common Man." He would maybe sing the part with the trombones, using some obscene words. That was usually good for a laugh.

Everybody in the band was so protective of Woody. It was more than just wanting to keep our jobs.

Woody's patience sometimes really blew our minds. Like when customers made requests and didn't understand that he had to deal with the same shit night after night. If he was real nice about it, he would say, "No, I won't play any Glenn Miller. I was a contemporary of Glenn Miller. He didn't play any of my music and I don't play any of his!"

One night, a guy had been annoying him and Woody started talking to him with a mike in his hand, and he was emphasizing his point by waving it, and when he finished talking, he bopped him on the head with the mike and it went "BOOM." You could hear it over the whole sound system. . . .

In July, the band was back at Disneyland. On July 3 the band taped a live television performance for the Disney Channel.

Full band at Disneyland, June 1984. Front row, L to R: Brad Williams (piano), Woody, Dave Riekenberg (behind Woody), Frank Tiberi, Jerry Pinter (tenor saxes), Mike Brignola (baritone sax). Second row: John Adams (bass), Dave Miller (drums), Paul McKee, John Fedchock, Mark Lusk (trombones). Back row: Bill Byrne, Scott Wagstaff, Don Downs, Mark Lewis, Ron Stout (trumpets). (Courtesy Riley Gaynor)

From August 6 through 18, 1984, the Herd was booked at North Shore Music Theater in Beverly, Massachusetts. On September 1–5, the Herd appeared with singers Tony Bennett and Nancy Wilson at Harrah's Headliner Room in Reno, Nevada. Contributions from each performer were filmed for cable television. Later the special was shown on PBS.

BILL BYRNE: Mark Lewis is a great player. He's a terrific musician. A natural. Everything he hears, he hears it naturally and can detect what's wrong. He likes to fix it and make sure it's right. He plays everything correctly, I mean, in the first reading, he's got it.

We were playing the Tony Bennett show in Reno, and I happened to look over and Mark had his book closed. He had memorized it the first or second time through, which is really something. He's got the ears. He hears how and he puts it to work. He's got a great memory.

On September 6, bassist Lynn Seaton joined the band, replacing Dave Finck. Seaton, an exceptionally agile bassist, could be termed a modern-day Slam Stewart, as one of his fortes is singing in unison with his arco bass.

On October 12–13, the Herd participated in the jazz festival at Metro Park in Jacksonville, Florida.

RON STOUT: The jazz clubs and jazz festivals are always the most exciting experiences for the band. We've done some gigs that would be considered heavy gigs. We did a thing with Quincy Jones and another with Roberta Flack. But I think the most exciting is when we do a jazz festival and there's about 100,000 people there. Jacksonville, Florida, was the first one I did with the band. All kinds of headliners appeared with us, including Phil Woods and Freddie Hubbard. It was very exciting and I ended up getting bugged about the whole evening because I didn't get to blow at all. I sat in the section all night and didn't do a thing. Of course, we only played an hour and in those days, I was still trying to earn my stripes. . . .

In 1984 Woody did a television commercial for Rigident, a dental adhesive. He appeared holding his clarinet and stating: "Hi, I'm Woody Herman, and blowin' this baby sure puts pressure on my dentures. I need the strongest hold, and that's why I use Rigident."

October 20 saw the band departing Miami for the first of three annual "Floating Jazz Cruises," aboard the S.S. Norway. Other performers on the junket were Joe Williams, Dizzy Gillespie, and Benny Carter. One night on the cruise Woody's wit was in evidence:

WOODY: Here's a little original tune that we hope to be able to record in the future, along with some other things written by the same gentleman. He's our lead trombonist, and his name is John Fedchock. He's been writing for our band and this is one of his earlier ones. I think it's a good, swinging little tune. It's called "Fried Buzzard." I'm sure you folks aren't really aware of it, but in Mississippi, it's considered a very wonderful dish . . . fried buzzard. I haven't really tried it, and if you're wise, you won't either! Here is some "Fried Buzzard."

RON STOUT: In October of 1984 on one of the jazz cruises, the band was before a heavy jazz crowd and Woody forgot my name. It was embarrassing to me what he said after that. He got into a cheap fat joke about me and [Paul] McKee. It was the first time that Woody had ever talked about me without mentioning my name in introduction. I realized that he had forgotten my name and was embarrassed in trying to get his footing. In the process, he had remembered my name but only so that he could mention this joke, that "Paul and I were the heads of the local Weight Watchers' chapter." Before he could even get it out, I whispered to Mark Lewis, "Fat joke!" I smelled it coming.

I went to Bill [Byrne] and said, "That can't happen again . . . I don't dig it. That's one strike as far as I'm concerned!" Bill said, "Hey, everybody on that fourth trumpet chair has been fat and they all got jokes." I said, "Well, nevertheless, I'm proud of what I am. I've been dieting all my life and if I didn't I'd be 5000 pounds right now! I'll make a deal. If

Woody can remember my name, he can make all the fat jokes he wants."
So Bill said, "Okay, I'll talk to him."

It turned out that Bill didn't talk to him, he was just protecting
Woody from my wrath. So it happened again a week later after we had
got off the ship. We were playing in Florida somewhere, and I was in a
rage. The first time it happened, I very politely smiled and laughed for the
sake of show business. The second time, we were both stone-faced. We
played the first half and on the break I went to Bill and was in tears. I told
Bill, "You lied to me. That's two strikes, I'm almost gone!" Bill said, "You
can't let what has happened affect your attitude on the band." I told him,
"One of the reasons that I play the way I do is because I respect Woody
Herman and the tradition. I'm fast losing respect for that. Consequently,
when I solo, it'll be just me, and I'll just play what I want to. I'll just go out
and learn and make it a practice session for me."

So on the next set, I had my solo on "Greasy Sack," and I went out
front with a flugelhorn instead of a trumpet with plunger mute. I played
the most incredibly aggressive, atonal, bizarre, wild solo, and my eyes
were looking right into Woody's face. If I hadn't been so mad I could
have pulled it off a little better, but I was able to pull most of it off and I
think that more than anything, I earned respect from the guys in the band.
I'm sure that I earned respect from Woody at the same time. It kind of
backfired on me, because my solo was so aggressive that I pulled off most
of what I wanted. The audience loved it. I got a big round of applause. As
soon as the applause started getting big, Woody rushed over to the mike
and said, "Ron Stout!" and he caught a little bit of the limelight.

That's not the end of the story. This is the good part. We had two
days to drive from Florida to Texas. I was sure that Bill was going to tell
Woody now. The gig was a drag. It was a country club. On the first break,
I got off the stand and was going to the mens' room, and I was walking
fast down the hall and Woody was walking as fast as he could behind me,
a good twenty-five yards from me, trying to catch up. "Ron, Ron!"
screaming at me. So I stopped and he came up and gave me the most
right on, complete and humble apology. He said, "I had no idea. . . . What
I said was tasteless and I had no idea that you were sensitive about it."

I told him that it meant a lot to me that HE came to me personally
about it and said all that. All of the respect that I had lost for him suddenly came back. I realized that a lot of what he had said was from an "under
fire" situation. He was under those lights and everybody's looking at him,
he forgets my name, he's embarrassed. . . . After that, more often, he
remembered my name.

After that incident, we had a lot of fun. Woody was nicer and nicer to
me. He got me playing solos where I didn't have them. Woody was the
one that got me playing on the beginning of "Watermelon Man." He
thought that the chart was a little rough without it, so he gave me a couple

of choruses on the front of it. I was getting "filthy" on it, growling the horn, the horn would be just dripping. It was one of the things that I could just sink my teeth into.

On December 10 Woody broke up the band for Christmas vacation. However, a crew of alumni and current sidemen assembled for a New Year's Eve dance at Caesar's in Atlantic City: Brian O'Flaherty, Marvin Stamm, Jeff Beal, Jim Powell, and Bill Byrne (trumpets); John Fedchock, Dave Panichi, and Jim Daniels (trombones); Frank Tiberi, Paul McGinley, and Joe Lovano (tenor saxes); Mike Brignola (baritone sax); Brad Williams (piano); Bill Moring (bass); and Andy Watson (drums).

The year ended with the classic Giuffre chart of "Four Brothers" being inducted into the Grammy Hall of Fame. Later Woody had the following to say:

> I want to do a tune that I first introduced on record in 1947, and just last year it was finally inducted into the Jazz Hall of Fame, and then later last year it was announced on the Grammy Awards television show. They discovered it after almost 40 years! . . . I'll never know why it was announced on THAT show, I didn't understand any of the music on the show. . . .

On January 28, 1985, Woody opened in the St. Regis Hotel in New York City, fronting an all-star group consisting of George Rabbai (trumpet, vocals); Frank Wess (tenor sax/flute); Nat Pierce (piano); George Duvivier (bass); and Jake Hanna (drums).

GEORGE RABBAI: Woody and I were in the front line. It was sort of a dixieland band, actually. The St. Regis is a big, beautiful, old hotel. We played in the King Cole Room.

During the engagement, many of Woody's old friends came by, among them Charlie Barnet and guitarist Billy Bauer.

BILLY BAUER: I met Woody at the St. Regis Hotel in New York. I told him my wife and I were in New York. He said, "Call me, and I'll get you a good table." He sat with us and congratulated us for being married for forty years. When I went to pay the check, the waiter told us Woody had paid the tab. I called Woody the next day and told him he embarrassed me.

On March 5 the IRS seized Woody's Hollywood Hills home and sold it at auction for $100,000, approximately one fourth of its appraised value. At that time, Woody owed the Federal government $1,499,860.10.

BILL BYRNE: When they announced that his house had been taken, it didn't bother him for a couple of weeks, then he started thinking about it and he became very, very depressed. I thought he was going to die. One day I found him curled up in bed. I asked him about his condition and he said, "Well, whenever I had problems when I was a kid I would go to bed and curl up and relax and get my head straight." So I figured that he knew how to handle himself. I didn't worry about him too much. Other people told me, "Why don't you tell Woody to do this or that," and I didn't because he always knew how to handle himself. . . .

Woody's tax problems now began to surface through the national media. *Jazz Podium* magazine initiated a worldwide campaign to raise funds for Woody and Ingrid to buy back their home. With additional help from Fred Turco of OLB Jazz Books in Rhode Island and Ray Avery of Rare Records in California, relief funds began to filter in.

The pressure was alleviated when Woody and Ingrid were able to rent their house back from the new owner. Under the terms of the IRS seizure, they had until September 5, 1985, to redeem the home for the purchase price of $100,000.

TOM CASSIDY: I had worked for the Willard Alexander Agency and was the manager and vice-president in charge of the Midwest and West Coast Division for thirteen years, and that's how I got to know Woody. Woody left the Willard Alexander Agency and changed to the Jim Halsey Company. When he left the Alexander agency, they opened the club in New Orleans. When they were in New Orleans, they weren't really doing any booking. Jim Halsey became an investor in the club and when the club went under, Jim Halsey said, "Well, I'll book the Herman Band." The Jim Halsey Company is basically a Country-and-Western agency and they really weren't capable of booking the band.

Willard Alexander died in August 1984. The Herman Band wasn't doing very well at that point. They were on the verge of taking it off the road. In fact, they did. They booked a small group for three months into the St. Regis Hotel.

When Willard died, I immediately started to make plans to open my own company. Hermie Dressel came to me and asked what I was going to do. I told him that I wasn't exactly sure. He said, "Whatever you do, we would like to have you consider representing Woody." So on January 1, 1985, we contacted Hermie and said that we would like to represent the band, and he said, "Great!"

I basically started booking the band in the western part of the United States and Richie Barz handled the eastern part. He had also been with the Willard Alexander Agency and the Jim Halsey Company. After a few months, we took over, booking the whole country and booking Woody on an exclusive basis entirely.

While the all-star group was working at the St. Regis, Woody received word that Zoot Sims, the internationally acclaimed tenorist and Second Herd veteran, had passed away. It was estimated that over 2,500 people attended the funeral. Among the speakers were Ira Gitler, Roger Kellaway, George Shearing, and Woody.

On April 15 the big Herd convened at Columbus, Indiana. Jeff Hamilton and John Oddo were back on the band temporarily.

PAUL MCKEE: The most humorous incidents mostly happened when we played dances. A lot of times people came up to Woody and wanted to hear "In the Mood" or "String of Pearls," or even some of Woody's old hits. Mostly, they would ask for music by other bandleaders. This was kind of a pet peeve of Woody's. He would go off about that and say something like, "As long as I'm alive, we'll play MY music!"

He wasn't afraid of anything. On one hand you could say, "Well, he was an entertainer, and it was his responsibility to satisfy the needs of the audience." But on the other hand, playing his own music all of those years is why the band is still in existence, and why it still has an original sound, and why it's still popular.

It has always been hard for married musicians to exist on the road. Tenorist Jerry Pinter and his wife, Vonda, learned how to adapt.

JERRY PINTER: They called my wife "Vondry." She did the guys' laundry. It just kind of came about one time when everybody needed clean clothes and we were so busy, and she got to doing it. Then every week, everybody would pay her by the load to do their clothes. It helped us a lot financially, because of the added expense for an extra person on the road. When we had to fly a couple of times, the band chipped in and helped pay for her flight. She traveled with the band for two and a half years. She gave up a lot to travel with me.

AL PORCINO: I've often said that trumpet players are slaves to the mouthpiece, meaning that we have to play the horn almost every day of our lives in order to keep the muscles strong which support the lips. This applies to all brass players, but is especially important to lead players because their notes are usually in the upper register, and this puts a lot of pressure on them to be consistent in avoiding wrong notes. The first trumpet is the one that everybody actually hears. While it is fun and satisfying to be the lead voice in a band, it is also a very demanding responsibility.

Joining the Herd on first trumpet May 21 was Roger Ingram, a superb trumpeter. Roger had been on the road briefly at age 16 with the Louie Bellson Orchestra. His other experience included time with the Quincy Jones/ Brothers Johnson U.S. Tour, the Connie Stevens back-up orchestra, and Tom Jones world tours.

RON STOUT: Coincidentally, I not only got Roger the flower delivery gig when I left to come on Woody's band, a year almost to the day later, I got Roger on Woody's band. I love Roger, he swings his butt off!

In the Woody Herman Band, that's the first and foremost consideration. You have to be as strong as a bull and never get tired. The strength is primary, but you have to swing, and Roger has both. I got him on the band because of his strength. I was a little disappointed with where the trumpets were prior to Roger's arrival. The section didn't have that powerful thing that really makes you blow in a session, the motivation that really makes you want to put some air through the horn. That to me, is what makes it fun.

ROGER INGRAM: In September of 1984, I started doing cruise ship gigs. In fact from September to December, I took a cruise ship gig in the Caribbean and it was really nice. I knew the ship contractor and he used to let me go out for a couple weeks at a time starting in early 1985, so I could go on the ship for a couple of weeks and then come back into town with enough money to get by on.

In May 1985, I got off one of those little two-week junkets. The first thing I would always do when I got home would be to call my message service to find out if I got any calls for work. I had received a message from Ron Stout's mom saying that Ron had been desperately looking for me for about a week because they needed a lead trumpet player for Woody's band.

On the first night I was on the band, I got to look at the lead trumpet book for about five minutes on the bus drive over to the gig. There's no rehearsal when you get on Woody's band. You just start on the gig. It was a concert and I was so nervous, my legs were literally shaking because the experience meant so much to me. . . .

After my first night, I took the book home and I started getting into it. I'd pull out a chart and it would say, "Gozzo," et cetera. Everyone's name would be written on the upper left hand corner. Some sheets would say, "Chase," others would say "Al," and I knew it was Al Porcino, because of how old the paper was. I would remember what year that chart was written in. It was like all those great lead trumpet players had actually touched and opened up these charts, put them on their music stand and emptied their spit valves. There was spit stains from some of the greatest lead trumpet players that ever lived! The lead trumpet book was a piece of history. I mean, if the band ever folds, that book should be put in a museum with every page showing, with everyone's spit marks and names displayed. In fact, there was some great little notes on a lot of the music that Dave Stahl and others played. The notes would include their personal opinions of what they would think of a chart, or if they were in a bad mood some night they would write something. The writing was preserved and on through the years every lead trumpet player that went through the band wouldn't tamper or erase anything.

Anyone who sits in that lead trumpet chair should feel very honored to do so. I did. I think that's one of the things that helped me get through some nights when I didn't feel good. I'd start saying, "Well, shit, man, I'm sure Gozzo sat here when he didn't feel good and Bill Chase and Dave Stahl, when they didn't feel good, and THEY got through it."

The reasons why I feel so much about that book is I've played a lot of lead trumpet books in a lot of big bands and shows and they're all hard work. They're really physically demanding. The lead trumpet player has a lot of responsibility, so there's a lot of mental energy that goes into playing the lead book. If the lead trumpet player doesn't come in or if he comes in wrong, it can start a train wreck in the band.

I've played all these different lead books and the majority of them don't give you anything back. It's just like you're sitting there for an hour, two hours, or however long it is, for whoever it is that you're playing for and you just bust your ass playing extreme high notes and playing all the time. Woody's lead trumpet book makes you sound good.

When John Fedchock started writing for the band, he knew WHO was in the band. He knew who could do what, and it was like that book was tailor-made for me. In the last two years I was on the band, the book became even more suited for me as newer charts kept getting added to the book for the records that we were doing. I could go on that band and play lead trumpet on a bad night and I'd still sound good because of the way it was written.

In a lot of bands, the lead trumpet book will be full of charts by arrangers that aren't very good, but they got the job anyway. Woody's book was better than say, Buddy Rich's. Buddy's lead trumpet book is just like playing in a marching band, up an octave. But Woody's book is musical.

After I was with the band a few weeks, we started getting the bugs out. I had to adapt to the different phrasings, different intonation, different feel, the dynamics, everything. I didn't have a problem about listening to other people's comments or suggestions. Most of the time I was pretty open-minded. Ron helped me out a lot, although we got into a big fight one time about intonation. We worked everything out though. . . .

At the end of June 1985, Woody disbanded the big band again, and on July 4 flew from New York to Paris with an all-star unit: Harry "Sweets" Edison on trumpet, Buddy Tate and Al Cohn on tenors, John Bunch on piano, Steve Wallace on bass, Jake Hanna on drums.

On July 24 Woody flew to Japan, continuing the small-group tour there. Nat Pierce had come in for John Bunch. From Japan, the group flew to Australia to continue the tour without Buddy Tate, who had other commitments. Haji accompanied Woody for the Australian leg of the tour.

WOODY: I like Australia. I think that it's one of the most refreshing countries left in the world because it's new. There's still something that can be obtained from Australia. I'd like to go back, but it doesn't seem very logical because they can't afford us. They have a union problem like America and England used to have. To take a big band over there, you have to hire a local big band every night. . . .

HAJI: Woody was such a great man. When we were on the plane together coming back from Australia, there was a man in front of us who had heard Woody's band. He didn't know that I was with Woody. I sat down before Woody did. Woody was in the back doing something, and I heard the man: "I was at the Woody Herman concert and he isn't what he used to be." Hearing that comment upset me a little bit. People can be very critical. They can't see beyond certain things. Here was a man up there in years, and all you had to do was hear his group. They put out some wonderful music. Most of his band were very young boys. They didn't see that. They're always so ready to pick you apart, to look for things to downgrade, the ugly and negative things.

The Herd was reorganized in late August sans Woody, who was still in Australia completing the tour. The band started a new road tour on August 21 in Kansas City, Missouri. Les Lovitt had replaced Jay Sollenberger on second trumpet, and bassist Bill Moring had replaced Lynn Seaton.

The band opened at Disneyland on August 25. A very exhausted Woody Herman was on the bandstand feeling the effects of jet lag.

In the fall of 1985 Woody began to announce to audiences a contemplated 50th Anniversary Concert and celebration to be held the following summer. The band was already wearing blue T-shirts proclaiming the event, although Woody's actual fiftieth anniversary date would not be until November 1986.

On September 19, 1985, the Herd was booked for the Hemet, California, Fairgrounds. The concert was sponsored by Jim Hamza, a local car dealer and friend of singer Herb Jeffries, Maynard Ferguson and other jazz notables. Jeffries emceed the event.

During the pregig dinner, Woody and the author conversed on the subject of his troubles with the IRS and the recent seizure of his home. Woody said that his primary concern was the reclamation of his home for Ingrid's financial benefit, and that he had little or no personal interest in the property.

Band at Hemet, California, fairgrounds, September 19, 1985. Woody holds mike for Dave Riekenberg, with Frank Tiberi, Jerry Pinter also visible in the sax section. Paul McKee, John Fedchock, John Wasson (trombones). Bill Byrne, Les Lovitt, Roger Ingram, Mark Lewis, Ron Stout (trumpets). (Courtesy the *Hemet News*)

The crowd at the Hemet ranged from high school students to senior citizens. Both young and old found they couldn't stop bobbing their heads and tapping their feet on the concrete floor.

Woody's wit came through as he introduced John Fedchock's new arrangement of "What's New?"

WOODY: I'd like now to do a lovely old tune that was popular in the thirties, and last year it became popular once again because of a new recording . . . by a very talented young lady. What's her name? . . . Linda Ronstadt. However, she was accompanied by an old fella, a guy about my age, by the name of Nelson Riddle. The only reason that I bring this up is that I want to assure you, there's nothing really happening between this young lady and Nelson. [Laughter.] No way. It would be fruitless. You know what I mean?

Though he usually resisted older audience members' predilection for hits from the early days, that night Woody was kind to them and voluntarily called "Woodchopper's Ball."

WOODY: I'd like to reminisce just for a moment and do one that I first introduced on record in [Woody covers his mouth] "BLUB," and I thought I'd repeat it tonight [laughter.] . . . and if we have any former jitterbugs here tonight, jump right into your swingin' boots and come down here and dance. That's my best invitation.

Woody introduced "Sonny Boy" as follows.

WOODY: I would like to tell you that years ago, I did a lot of vocals on record with our band. But it wasn't because I thought I sang well, I didn't sing well at all. But I found that every time I sang on a record, we sold more records. So I had a motive, you see. I never thought that I was a singer in any sense of the word. But I'm going to do one of these things for you. This is from a group of songs that were all done originally by the late Al Jolson, a great showman. If you can't place him, really, he was THE singer BEFORE Bing Crosby. . . .

During Woody's introduction of "Four Brothers," the four saxophonists were standing at Woody's left getting set up. Mike Brignola was twisting his mouthpiece to achieve better intonation and inadvertently blew into his horn resulting in a loud honk midway through Woody's introduction.

WOODY: One that I had done a bit earlier in 1947, as a matter of fact, was the beginning of this kind of saxophone section, three tenors and a baritone. That tune was just put into the Hall of Fame . . . [HONK!] . . . this past season. Thanks a lot! Is that an opinion? . . . It's leaking, you know!

Woody concluded the performance with Nat Pierce's bristling chart of "After Hours," the tune long associated with Erskine Hawkins. He had the following comments to make during the bluesy piano introduction by Brad Williams:

WOODY: Here's an old blues tune, a very good one. It's called "After Hours." This is the tempo where you can get to know your partner MUCH better!

During the buildup portion of the performance, Woody made his way over to one of two huge floral spray arrangements placed at each end of the bandstand. It was as tall as he was. While the audience watched intently, Woody with some effort carried and dragged the potted arrangement to the front of the band and voiced a characteristic one-liner: "I just got this bouquet from my nurse. . . . " Then the trumpet section went into the finale.

RON STOUT: That's a tough chart! When Woody would call that one at the end of the night, the trumpet players would all groan. It was fun, but it hurt. . . .

ROGER INGRAM: Yes, "After Hours" was a chop-buster, although I made it
    nine times out of ten. Woody used to like to do it for the last tune at the
    end of a three or four hour dance night, mainly because it was a slow
    blues and the stragglers on the dance floor could really groove for the last
    time and get into the mood for whatever might come about later. Hence
    the title.

        Also I think Woody got a kick out of seeing the trumpets sweat a lit-
    tle . . . or a lot! The first lead trumpeter who played that chart was Forrest
    Buchtel [1971]. He wrote on the manuscript, "Before playing this chart,
    contact the nearest office of the Red Cross and give your blood type."

In October 1985, Woody decided to let go Hermie Dressel, his personal manager for seventeen years. Ingrid began to assume personal management
duties for Woody.

    From October 5 through 18, 1985, the Herd was on its second annual
Floating Jazz Cruise. Also performing were Mel Torme, Gary Burton, Major
Holley (bassist and Herd alumnus), Buddy Tate, Al Cohn, Jake Hanna, Dizzy
Gillespie, and his old boss Cab Calloway.

ROGER INGRAM: When I was in high school, my dad, who was a sax player,
    brought home the first big band record I ever heard. It was Woody's *Big
    Band Goodies*. My dad wanted to hear Sal Nistico on it. It had Bill Chase
    playing lead trumpet, Jake Hanna, Nat Pierce, and Phil Wilson in the
    trombone section. It was really a great band.

        That was the first time that I had ever heard Bill Chase playing lead
    trumpet. When I heard him playing, something clicked in my mind and I
    decided, "That's the way to play lead trumpet!" Just the way Bill was
    phrasing and how he was working with Jake, the drummer. An old saying
    of Woody's used to be, "Give me a lead trumpet player and a drummer,
    and I'll give you a band!" Because that's all it takes. It takes those two
    guys doing their job and everyone else just throwing their anchors into
    them and let them take it away.

        That's what I started to learn just by listening to the way Jake
    Hanna and Bill Chase played together on that record. I said, That's it.
    That's the way to do it!" I'd already been playing in jazz bands and so I
    immediately went to the school and I got together with the drummer
    and brought him over to the house and I said to him, "Listen to this
    record. Listen to how these guys are working together. That's what you
    and I have got to do." We started doing it and our band started winning
    awards and honors.

        One tune in particular that I really loved from that album was "The
    Good Earth." It's a great Neal Hefti chart, and it's still in the book. In
    fact, it still has Bill Chase's name written on the chart.

Anyway, we were on the jazz cruise, and I was hanging at the bar with Woody and Jake Hanna. Jake is a really nice cat, and I told Jake the same story about how much I enjoyed hearing that record when I was a kid and the inspiration it gave me.

I didn't know about this, but the next night at the concert, Woody had told Jake to sit in on drums and said, "I'll pull out "The Good Earth," because I know Roger likes that chart." It was a big surprise for me, man. All of a sudden, Jake Hanna walked up on the bandstand and Jim Rupp got off and Woody called "The Good Earth." I was in heaven, man, because I never dreamed I'd get to do that! It was the chart and performance of it that opened my mind up as a kid and helped me to understand the inner workings of a big band. Here I was in Woody's trumpet section, playing lead on the same chart with the same drummer! I never dreamed I'd be on Woody's band anyway when I was a kid.

From what I understand about Bill Chase, he recorded his first record as a lead trumpet player with Maynard Ferguson's late fifties or early sixties band. He had a weak high F, and he didn't really have the tremendous range that he developed in the later years. He later attributed his skill to watching Maynard every night, watching him breathe, and seeing what he went through with his chops.

On October 21 the band inaugurated a one-week tour with legitimate clarinetist Richard Stoltzman. Stoltzman had successfully bridged the gap between classical and jazz music, being himself an ardent admirer of Benny Goodman. Woody was one of Stoltzman's greatest fans.

WOODY: We recently did a tour of concerts with a young, great, legitimate clarinetist playing my solo on *Ebony Concerto*. His name is Richard Stoltzman. I was so pleased to hear it played correctly for the first time.

To play the classical material for the Herman-Stoltzman tour, Alex Brodsky (French horn), Alice Giles (harp), and Kieth Karabell (alto and clarinet) were added.

On November 28, 1985, the band appeared in the annual New York City Macy's Thanksgiving Day Parade. The musicians were huddled together on a mock-antique steam train float furnished by Parker Brothers Game Company, commemorating the fiftieth anniversary of Monopoly.

The day was dark, drizzly, and cold. The band was wearing special rain gear and simulating playing to the First Herd recording of "Apple Honey." Paradoxically, pianist Brad Williams was standing next to Woody, mouthing a trumpet. Woody was clearly cold and uncomfortable, but endured the observance with his characteristic grit. His clarinet was wrapped in cellophane to protect it from the elements. Some band members declined to participate because of the weather. The parade committee was generous, however, and paid all the musicians whether they participated or not.

The year 1985 ended for the band at Greenfield, Massachusetts High School on December 10. While the big band was on vacation, Woody opened on January 7, 1986, at the Vine Street Bar and Grill, a jazz club in Hollywood. Woody fronted an all-star sextet with Jack Sheldon (trumpet) and Bob Cooper (tenor) in the front line. The rhythm section was made up of Ross Tompkins, piano (from the NBC Tonight Show band), John Heard (bass), and Jake Hanna (drums), the only Herman veteran in the lineup.

The sextet effectively emulated some of Woody's big band classics such as "Woodchopper's Ball," "Lemon Drop" and "I've Got the World on a String." The latter was particularly amusing with Woody and Jack Sheldon teamed together vocally. Bob Cooper never sounded better.

BOB COOPER: We had a great time at the Vine Street Bar and Grill. Woody still knew how to get the band to swing and make the crowd happy.

One night after "Caldonia," he said to me, "Next time don't stop blowing until I tell you to." Woody loved to get the most from a soloist, whereas I don't believe I ever heard Stan Kenton say, "Take another one" to anyone in the band.

WOODY: I like working in a smaller setting every so often; it gets me out of my doldrums. When my band sounds good, I'm up there having a marvelous time, but I do much less playing and a lot of listening. With a small combo I really have to get down to business and play. It gives me a workout. It's better than practicing, believe me.

JACK SHELDON: The Vine Street gig was the only time that I ever worked with Woody. . . . It was a real thrill for me working for him at Vine Street. He's had every great musician working for him. He was a great bandleader because he always got the best out of everybody. He didn't act like a leader, that's what I liked about him. He just wanted the music to be good. He didn't try to be a level above you. Woody was very generous to me at Vine Street. He let me do anything I wanted to and really let me shine.

He was very gracious and a very good showman. He was just one of the guys, even though he was a world-famous bandleader. He was in town and his band was off for a little while. We were going to do Vine Street, but I had this other job lined up first at the Alley Cat. I called him up and asked him, "Will you work with me?" And he said, "Okay, great," and you know he was there on time as a sideman. He worked as a sideman for seventy-five bucks. He was a real jazz musician himself. A lot of guys wouldn't have done that. . . .

On January 17 the full Herd had reorganized and played in Atlanta. Bill Byrne and Frank Tiberi were back; newcomers were John Riley, drummer, and Don Gladstone, bassist.

RON STOUT: When the band is on the road, there's always funny stuff going on, like little inside jokes. Every night you are basically on the same set. . . . It becomes necessary to find ways of making it interesting. The most fun we've had are at the dances. Woody was pretty disciplined. He didn't like a lot of warming up on the stand before the gig.

One real funny thing occurred when Roger Ingram was on the band for only nine or ten months. It was just one of those typical dances and the people were very discourteous to us. It was one of those gigs that you just wanted to get over with. There were a lot of balloons floating around the room. Some of the balloons started falling off the ceiling and the trombone section took their slides and began hitting them. There were all these balloons flying around and it was just chaos.

We had just finished a whole new flurry of balloons and Woody turned around and Roger had chosen just that moment to stand up and readjust his pants. He was the only guy standing in the back of the band, and all the balloons were floating down and he got caught standing up at the wrong time. Woody looked at him with a ray, like, "You're out of here!"

The other night someone was talking on the stand in the trumpet section and Woody looked up, and he looked right at Roger and gave him a look like, "Shut up!" Roger looked back at Woody and mouthed, "I didn't say anything." We all laughed and Woody even laughed because he realized that Roger hadn't said anything. But the fear in Roger's eyes was really funny.

In mid-February, drummer Jim Rupp and bassist Lynn Seaton returned, bolstering the rhythm section in preparation for the 50th Anniversary album.

MARK LEWIS: Woody seemed to be able to front the band no matter how sick he was. Knowing that, it made it very tough for us to stay off the bandstand when we were very sick.

JOHN FEDCHOCK: He'd always be there for the gig. He might have been backstage slumped over in a chair looking like he couldn't even move, but in the next minute, when the spotlight came on him, he was dancing around and smiling. It seemed like he would save all his energy for that two hours.

ROGER INGRAM: After I was with the band a while I started to develop a relationship with Woody. Now here was a guy who was about 73 years old, and the average age of the guys in the band was about 28. Most of the people were a little spooked at Woody. They were kind of scared of him. When I got on the band, Woody's health had started to deteriorate and he could become kind of a crusty old bastard sometimes. He could be quite a cantankerous old guy. Nevertheless, he always maintained his great sense of humor.

Sometimes the young guys in the band would underestimate him. They just thought he was an old man. I knew better. You see, my father was ten years older than Woody was. I had a lot of experience dealing with older folks. In fact, I had always hung out with guys 45 or 50 years old.

Whenever I'd see Woody in a bar after the gig, I'd just go sit down right next to him and we'd buy each other drinks. He was the "old man of the big bands" that I was sitting next to. He was like a history book. I was talking to somebody who had been around and had seen everything. If I needed to know anything or receive any advice, I guarantee I could get it from Woody because he had seen it all. I would talk to him about Stravinsky, Charlie Parker . . . what it was like making that record called *Bird with the Herd*. Bird just walked in there, listened to the charts and just blew. He didn't read anything, just opened up his ears and blew. Woody hung out with Glenn Miller, he hung out with Tommy Dorsey. He used to hang out with Jimmy Dorsey. He told me all about those guys.

I had a great rapport with Woody, but still he was never biased. Just because I used to hang out with him at the bar, he'd still go off on me if I was doing something on the bandstand that he didn't like. Woody didn't play any favorites. Anybody in that band could have hung out with Woody and he could still go off on them if it was warranted. That was a beautiful thing about him. I couldn't get away with shit. Woody would keep me in line, man. He would give you that stare from the front if you were acting up. . . .

On March 20 the band was recorded live at the Great American Music Hall in San Francisco. Flawless acoustics and a brilliant performance produced a magnificent album entitled *50th Anniversary Tour*.

"It Don't Mean a Thing (If It Ain't Got That Swing)" is an up-tempo Fedchock interpretation of the Ellington classic. The band is tight and swings (they had been performing the chart for six months). Solo contributions are from Brignola; McKee and Fedchock each taking a chorus; then the two trombonists. Trumpeters Mark Lewis and Ron Stout follow the same formula. Woody makes a statement on clarinet before the ensemble finish.

"What's New" is Fedchock's scoring of the 1930s Bob Haggart-Johnny Burke standard revived by Linda Ronstadt. The performance is a shimmering vehicle for the arranger's trombone.

"Pools" was composed by Don Grolnick of the group Steps Ahead. Fedchock's score is both inventive and cogitative. Bassist Lynn Seaton's part creates an ethereal mood, first as a solo, then combining with Tiberi's tenor. Woody commences his soprano solo with a quote from "Sweet and Lovely," followed by Seaton in a solo. Tiberi plays with intensity and the ensemble takes it out.

"Blues for Red" is a salute to Third Herd bassist Red Kelly. The Fedchock chart is a wonderful straight-ahead blues in the tradition of "Greasy Sack." A brief piano introduction by Brad Williams sets the stage for Lynn Seaton's arco bass solo performed in the unison voice mode of the late Slam Stewart. The brass emerges with biting punctuations led by the superb lead trumpet of Roger Ingram. Additional solos are from Woody (clarinet) and Mark Lewis. The ensemble takes it out with Ingram's trumpet on top.

ROGER INGRAM: Lynn Seaton was playing bass on Woody's band when I first joined in May 1985, and he stayed until August of that year, then he went with Basie. He stayed with Basie until March 1986. He took a leave from Basie's band just to come back with us long enough to record the *50th Anniversary* album.

Lynn and Woody were real tight. Woody just loved the way Lynn played. He was really disappointed when Lynn finally left the band. But Woody was glad that he was going with Basie. If someone would leave the band and go with somebody like Maynard, who has a rock band now [1986], Woody would disapprove. As an example, Dave Miller left Woody's band to go with Maynard and on Dave's last night, Woody walked up to him and said, "You'll never swing again!"

But if Woody knew you were going with somebody that is still in jazz, like Basie, then he would give you his blessing. The bottom line with Woody was MUSIC, not the fact that you were leaving HIM. He didn't take that as a personal offense. There were so many thousands of musicians who came through that band.

"The Conga" is a brisk adaptation of a pop tune made known by the Miami Sound Machine group in 1986. Frank Tiberi had heard them perform it and took Woody to hear them in Florida. Later, Tiberi collaborated with pianist Brad Williams on the Herman chart. Woody's vocal adds to the festive mood.

ROGER INGRAM: When we did the *50th Anniversary* album, there's a tune on there called "The Conga," where Woody made me and the second trumpet player trade fours back and forth on this Latin thing. It wasn't a tremendous jazz performance, it was more for effect than anything. It was supposed to be kind of an exciting peak to the tune with added high notes. But the point I want to make is that I HAD to blow it. I had to create something in there. Woody made me do it. I had never had to do that type of thing before. That's one of the good things that man did, and that's where his talents were. He used to take things out of people they didn't know they were capable of doing and nurture it and make it even better. He made me a much better lead trumpet player than I was when I went on the band.

I had an inconsistent double C when I went on that band, and when I got off I had a consistent one. I had more chops. It's still with me to this day. I can play a double C in my sleep if I had to now because I had to play so many damn double C's in that band. . . .

"Central Park West" is John Fedchock's moving interpretation of Coltrane's jazz ballad. Tiberi's tenor solo evokes a warm and sensitive mood. This gorgeous chart reflects shades of other Herds, with added Kenton and Thornhill moods.

Lou Donaldson's "Fried Buzzard" was trombonist-composer-arranger Fedchock's first contribution to the Herman book. The line is played by the duo of Fedchock and Brignola. Solo contributions are from Brignola (one of the most consistently inventive soloists in the band), Fedchock and Woody on clarinet. The chart has a provocative sax chorus with voicing incorporating Ron Stout's flugelhorn lead.

Thelonious Monk's "Epistrophy" was arranged by John Fedchock. An avant-garde composition that remains faithful to Monk's original concept, it features brilliant and unusual scoring from Fedchock. Solo honors go to Ron Stout, tenorist Jerry Pinter, and Woody on soprano. Woody often alleged that pronouncing "Epistrophy" was hard for him and would hand the mike to tenorist Dave Riekenberg to articulate the title.

RON STOUT: Woody was a breeze to work for. I think that everybody in the band at one time or another went through a little thing with Woody. You usually went through a testing period with him, and it reflected on the stand. It didn't mean that Woody was always rude. He could be very agreeable and very easy to talk to. During your initial period, you usually didn't get a whole lot of solo space and what you did get was Woody's decision.

During a performance early in May, near Gettysburg, Pennsylvania, an actor made up as Abraham Lincoln walked out on stage and delivered the following address: "Two score and ten years ago, Woody Herman brought forth on this continent a new orchestra, conceived in harmony and dedicated to the proposition that all music is not created equal. . . ."

BILL BYRNE: Tom Phillips, who is a disc jockey and a friend of the band and Woody's, set the thing up. There is an actor in Gettysburg that does Lincoln impersonations for a living, and he did this as a favor for Tom. . . .

In May pianist Joel Weiskopf replaced Brad Williams (May 1); drummer Joe Pulice replaced Jim Rupp (May 15); and bassist Dave Carpenter joined the band (May 27), after a series of substitutes. In June the band was on vacation for sixteen days.

On June 16, the American Society of Music Arrangers and Composers (ASMAC) convened for its forty-eighth anniversary banquet at the Castaway Restaurant in Burbank, California. A small group fronted by trumpeter Jack Sheldon provided the evening's music and included Bob Cooper on tenor; Jimmy Rowles on piano; John Heard, bass; and Jake Hanna on drums. The highlight of the evening was the honoring of two distinguished guests: Woody Herman and film music composer Alex North.

During the evening it was announced that on July 16, 1986, the Herd would be at the Hollywood Bowl for a pre-Fiftieth Anniversary Concert, and that *Ebony Concerto* would be performed with classical clarinetist Richard Stoltzman as the soloist.

Neal Hefti made some laudatory comments about Woody. Woody was then presented with the President's Award by former bandleader and ASMAC president Van Alexander. Woody graciously accepted the award, thanking the officers and the distinguished audience that included Les Brown, Billy May, Ralph Burns, Stumpy Brown, and Butch Stone, then retrieved his disassembled clarinet from a Safeway shopping bag and sat in with Sheldon's little group. At 73, Woody had long ago ceased trying to impress anyone.

On June 20 and 21, an all-star "Famous Alumni" Herman band performed at Wild Animal Park in San Diego County. Dubbed by jazz impresario Jimmy Lyons the "Seldom Heard," the crew was hastily assembled by Nat Pierce and included such Herd veterans as Dick Collins, Dick Hafer, Jack Nimitz, Chuck Flores, and Mark Lewis of the current Herman band, as well as Bob Cooper, Med Flory and Ellington trombonist Buster Cooper. The concert was videotaped by Rendezvous Productions of San Clemente, California, with narration by Pete Smith, jazz aficionado and deejay at Los Angeles radio station KMPC.

On June 30 the Herd played for a private party at Troy, Michigan, hosted by Woody's personal physician, Dr. Stan Levy.

A few days later, the Herd was part of a "Summer Fest" at the lakefront in Woody's hometown of Milwaukee. During the concert Woody began coughing up phlegm on stage. His lungs had started to fill with fluid. The next day (July 2) he checked into a local hospital, but was back that night fronting the band.

The many years of grueling road tours had taken their toll on his small frame. In addition, Woody was never particularly diligent in matters of health and physical fitness. It became necessary to hire a factotum who could drive Woody to the various jobs, travel with him on airline flights, and deal with countless demands and obligations. The position was filled by Ed Dye, a friend of Ingrid's.

ED DYE: Ingrid and I had played music together. We had both been in our first band venture in San Francisco in the sixties. Then she came to Nashville and I was there also. We worked in some bands together down there. We had been very close for years and had been on the road together in various country band and bluegrass capacities. As a consequence, I had known Woody for over a twenty-year period. So Ingrid asked me to do the job.

NAT PIERCE (1986):   Woody used to be sharper, of course. Now he gets a little forgetful. When I work with him now he may forget some of the player's names, and he starts spewing for a few seconds about people like Billie Holiday, Teddy Wilson, and a story about the Famous Door, and all that. So I have to prompt him in the back like a stage prompter.

Woody is something else. He has slowed down over the years, but anyone would with all those miles on them. About his reversals, he's built a shelter around him. It's very hard to penetrate, unless you really know him well. Otherwise, he couldn't get out of bed in the morning. . . .

Lee Hildebrand reported on Woody's July 13 appearance in San Francisco:

Woody Herman, the last of the old-time big bandleaders, had just finished playing a free outdoor concert in a plaza next to the Hyatt Regency Hotel. The 15-piece orchestra, all of its members except two under the age of 30, had performed a cooking potpourri of arrangements from the thick Herman book, including 1939's "Woodchopper's Ball," and a flag-waving treatment of the Miami Sound Machine's recent hit, "Conga," before an appreciative audience of several thousand.

"There ought to be a law against playing a gig in the daytime," the feisty 73-year-old musician complained as he ambled slowly through downtown San Francisco streets. Searching for a men's shop open on a Sunday afternoon, he recalled his 1930 stint in San Francisco with Tom Gerun's dance band. It was during that engagement, Herman said, that he met his wife, Charlotte, who died four years ago after a long illness.

"Sir, you look very familiar," said the clerk in an exclusive store on Union Square as Herman tried on a $1,050 off-white formal jacket for his 50th Anniversary Concert three nights later at the Hollywood Bowl.

"All old men look the same," the bandleader responded.

After trying on a similarly priced coat, Herman left without making a purchase. "You can get the same coats for around $750 in New York," he said, flagging down a cab for a short ride up Nob Hill to the Fairmont Hotel.[3]

Woody Herman 50th Anniversary Concert, Hollywood Bowl, July 16, 1986. Left is the Young Thundering Herd, right is the All-Star Alumni Band. Trumpeter Arturo Sandoval is performing in front with Woody. (Photo by Mal Levin)

DON RADER: The funniest—sad, but true—thing that I ever heard Woody say was at the rehearsal for his 50th Anniversary Concert at the Hollywood Bowl in the summer of 1986. A friend of mine, Jack Redmond, who is the lead trombone player with Les Brown, came to the rehearsal with me. I was playing with the alumni band. Jack asked me to introduce him to Woody, and when I did Jack told him that of all of the bands that he'd ever played on, the one that he most wanted to play with, but never got the chance to, was Woody's. Woody looked at him, and without batting an eye said, "Think of the money that you've saved!"

There were two bands on stage at the Hollywood Bowl for Woody Herman's fiftieth anniversary celebration on Wednesday, July 16. Seated on the audience's left was the current Young Thundering Herd. To the right was the "All Star" Alumni Band, organized and rehearsed by Nat Pierce. It was a beautiful California sunset when Woody, with some effort, walked out onto the stage for the opening bars of "Blue Flame."

The December 1986 issue of *Jazz Times* carried an extensive review of the 50th Anniversary Concert by renowned jazz critic Leonard Feather:

The evening was marked by visits to the distant and not-quite-so-distant past, by presentation of the present and indications of the future. . . .

For those who didn't hear "The Good Earth" or "Opus de Funk" in its pristine form, the revivals probably sounded fine; yet a number like "Blowin' Up A Storm," originally a head arrangement, inevitably lost some spontaneity when these men had to read their parts.

Oddly, the band included Herman Riley on tenor and Buster Cooper with his long, played-for-laughs cadenzas on trombone. Neither is a

Herman alumnus. Surely such genuine ex-Hermanites as Jimmy Giuffre (whose "Four Brothers" wasn't played) or Phil Wilson or Nat Adderley or Milt Jackson would have more logically belonged. (Woody's track record of hiring great vibes players certainly should have been acknowledged. In addition to Bags (Milt Jackson), at one time or another he had Red Norvo, Margie Hyams, Terry Gibbs, the late Eddie Costa, and Victor Feldman.)

Stacy Rowles is not an alumna, but her presence with her father, Jimmy, who played in an early Herman band, provided some of the most exquisitely lyrical moments of the evening. Stacy's muted trumpet on the Larry Gales tune "Loco Motif" and her gorgeous flugelhorn on Strayhorn's "Lotus Blossom" were among the concert's few moments of subtle understatement.

After a rousing "Things Ain't" by the alumni, emcee Jimmy Lyons introduced a surprise guest: Rosemary Clooney singing "My Buddy." She was never a band member, yet Mary Ann McCall, who was with Woody for several years and sat in the audience, was not invited.

The inclusion of Richard Stoltzman was a brainstorm on Woody's part. After warming up with De Bussey's [sic] "Maid With the Flaxen Hair," he took over what was originally Woody's role in the Stravinsky *Ebony Concerto*, written for the band in 1946. This strange work in three movements is neither typical Stravinsky nor jazz by any stretch of the imagination, but The Young Thundering Herd played it expertly. Stoltzman stayed on stage to take part in Gary Anderson's emotionally charged arrangement of Copland's "Fanfare for the Common Man," which Herman played at his 40th Anniversary Concert in 1976 at Carnegie Hall. Stoltzman, the renowned classical virtuoso, then revealed his able jazz chops, trading fours with Woody on a blues ("Greasy Sack"). . . .

After intermission, it was the current band's time to shine on its own. Most of the arrangements were the work of John Fedchock, whose writing is as skillful as his trombone. He and Paul McKee traded bone passages on "It Don't Mean a Thing," as did the trumpeters Ron Stout and Mark Lewis. . . . Mike Brignola's baritone was exemplary. The entire reed section, and Frank Tiberi's tenor especially, brought out the beautiful essence of John Coltrane's "Central Park West." "Battle Royal," though not one of the most distinguished of Ellington pieces, was an adequate vehicle for some "I Got Rhythm" blowing.

Next on stage was Stan Getz, by now probably the most famous and successful of all the Herman graduates. Opening with an unidentified samba ["Ti-Land"], he eased into a superbly relaxed "Easy Living," then picked up the pace for a cheerful, loping original by Frank Tiberi.

Elegant though Getz's pieces were with the orchestra, he brought the evening to an emotional climax when he and Jimmy Rowles teamed for a Rowles original they recorded together some years ago, "The Peacocks." . . .

Arturo Sandoval, the Cuban trumpeter whom Woody said he had heard last year [1985] at Ronnie Scott's in London, opened with a surprising vehicle — Ralph Burns' "Bijou," originally a showcase for the trombone of Bill Harris. Sandoval came on like a combination of Harry James, Cat Anderson and Rafael Mendez — predictably, a great crowd-pleaser. He stayed on to take part in "The Godmother," a new work written especially for this occasion by Ralph Burns and dedicated to the memory of Woody's wife, Charlotte. This was a strange piece, not at all typical of the early Burns originals for the old Herd, with Dave Carpenter switching from upright to electric bass. . . .

Ironically, in a number called "Conga," from Woody's current 50th Anniversary Tour album, the members of The Young Thundering Herd's trumpet section began screaming and screeching, as if trying to outdo Sandoval's pyrotechnics. Sandoval played timbales during part of this number, then picked up his horn again to return to the stratosphere while members of the audience formed a conga line to dance through the aisles and around the boxes.

For a finale, the young band and the alumni group joined forces for yet another variation of the blues. (In the light of Woody's original reputation as leader of "The Band That Plays the Blues" it was interesting to note how many of the tunes played in the course of this evening were based on the 12-bar format.) . . .

The concert was an extraordinary tribute to the indomitable spirit and energy of Herman.

This is The Young Thundering Herd as it appeared at the 50th Anniversary Concert: Roger Ingram, Scott Wagstaff, Mark Lewis, Ron Stout, Bill Byrne (trumpets); John Fedchock, Paul McKee, Ken Kugler (trombones); Frank Tiberi, Dave Riekenberg, Jerry Pinter (tenor saxes); Mike Brignola (baritone sax); Joel Weiskopf (piano); Dave Carpenter (bass); and Joe Pulice (drums). Added for *Ebony Concerto*: JoAnn Turofsky (harp); Rick Todd (French horn); and Larry Honda (alto clarinet).

The "All-Star Alumni Band": Pete Candoli, John Audino, Conte Candoli, Don Rader, Bill Berry (trumpets); Carl Fontana, Dick Hyde, Buster Cooper (trombone); Med Flory (alto sax); Dick Hafer, Bob Cooper, Herman Riley (tenor saxes); Jack Nimitz (baritone sax); Nat Pierce (piano); Monty Budwig (bass); and Chuck Flores (drums).

MED FLORY: Herman Riley was taking a solo, so I had a chance to sit there, listen, look around, and dig. It was just getting dark and a big, beautiful full moon was hanging over the scene. Woody was holding the mike in front of Herman and staring off in a dead-pan concentration. He looked over and saw me watching him and gave me a wink and a sly smile. And it flashed on me, "Hey, this is one of those moments."

It was a funny thing about that old cat. A guy could be Phi Beta Kappa, Olympic champ, chairman of the board, he could be President of the United States, but you were on even ground when you could look him in the eye and say, "Yeah, I played with Woody."

Many musicians and critics believed that the 50th Anniversary Concert did not measure up to the 40th, in terms of planning, projection, and the arrangements made for Herman alumni to participate.

CONTE CANDOLI: The 50th Anniversary Concert was kind of a drag. I didn't enjoy it at all. I didn't get to play once. They had that Cuban trumpet player there [Arturo Sandoval], who had previously played "The Hot Canary." He was all chops, no feeling. He did two or three numbers with the band. I was kind of disappointed in Woody in a way, 'cause both Buster Cooper and Carl Fontana were on the [Alumni] band, and he let Buster Cooper play all of the solos. I don't know, I guess it was Woody's old age. He wasn't together as much. You can't compare Buster Cooper to Carl Fontana! You can't compare hardly anyone to Carl. That surprised me. Then there was a trumpet thing and I thought Woody would nod to me and say, "Why don't you blow something, Count?" and nothing happened. So it was kind of disappointing, but that's history.

The important, bottom line is that I've always respected Woody for giving me a break with the band. Every time I saw him, I always thanked him for it.

MIKE BRIGNOLA: That Hollywood Bowl 50th Anniversary Concert, I felt, was musically on the disastrous side. First of all, to try and play a piece like *Ebony Concerto*, which is basically chamber music, in a huge outdoor festival situation was difficult.

We played one opening tune and then we had to sit there with woodwind instruments in the Los Angeles summer night air which gets cool, for about five tunes while the Alumni Band played music. We had to sit there and let ourselves get unwarmed up and then play *Ebony* cold after that. . . . The Bowl is geared only for the audience. It's a great atmosphere for the audience. But as far as the performers, I don't know, although I have played there on numerous occasions.

You would think that the concerts would be the most outstanding performances but they don't always end up that way. I mean, we played in front of 200,000 people once at the Jacksonville Jazz Festival and once for an insurance company in Connecticut that had a free outdoor thing in the summer and the whole state showed up! Then, we played in Japan at the Aurex Jazz Festival and thousands of people were there in a big stadium. But in those kinds of situations, there's usually all those problems to contend with, like the sound system, and they're always trying to mike everybody in the band to get a good sound. Even in places like Monterey, or even at the Hollywood Bowl, so those places become harder to play in.

After the concert, Woody and Ingrid gave a party for their many friends. Woody's home was standing room only. Celebrities from the music and entertainment community in attendance included Rosemary Clooney, Benny Carter, Ray Anthony, members of both The Young Thundering Herd and the Alumni Bands, songwriters, and the press. Woody was standing in the midst of it all with Haji on his left and Polly on his right. The party continued well past 4 A.M.; however, Woody retired at the conservative hour of 1:30 A.M.

WOODY: [The 50th Anniversary Concert] was very exciting, and we certainly received a lot of good press. . . . This whole 50th Anniversary tour has been very good all year. In most instances, we had phenomenal business! I don't think that the IRS can do anything further to me, so that's the reason I can make this statement.

By the end of this year [1986], we will have grossed as much as we did in my two best years, 1945 and 1946 . . . !

On the evening following the 50th Anniversary Concert, the Herd was booked for an outdoor concert on the campus of the University of California at Irvine. Shortly after the bus arrived, Woody and Bill Byrne were standing alone behind a group of buildings adjacent to the stage area. Woody appeared colorless, somewhat disoriented and furious all at the same time. It seems that the management had neglected to have a greeter escort Woody to a designated dressing room. Less than an hour later, Woody walked out on stage in the presence of 3,000 cheering people, his countenance transformed.

ED DYE: Before I went out with Woody, I had quit flying for ten years 'cause I wasn't real thrilled with it. The first two weeks I was with Woody, I was on more planes than I had been on for fifteen years! But this time I never had any fear of flying because I knew nothing was going to happen to Woody that way.

I don't know how many planes we were on in nine months' time, but it was a lot. There were several times we'd be on at least two flights a day. Sometimes three. Because of the logistics of making it around some resort areas by plane, the whole experience could get pretty complicated. It was always reassuring to me that when things got real scary in flight, all Woody would do was raise an eyebrow or say something funny.

On one flight, this little commuter job hit an air pocket and turned absolutely sideways. Talk about white knuckles. Everybody else was screaming, and I looked at him and he just cocked his head at me and started laughing.

On August 17 drummer Dave Miller returned to the Herd's rhythm section. On September 20 bass trombonist Joe Barati joined the Herd, replacing Ken Kugler.

On September 21 the Young Thundering Herd returned to Hemet, California, for an afternoon jazz festival. The event was sponsored again by Jim Hamza, with Herb Jeffries again present as master of ceremonies. As the band bus rolled to a stop, the first two musicians who leaped out were Mike Brignola and a recent addition, trumpeter Larry Gillespie. The two sidemen immediately engaged in sailing a Frisbee back and forth.

MIKE BRIGNOLA: We play Frisbees a lot every time the bus stops. It's a long time sometimes between stops. . . .

WOODY: In the latter forties, drugs entered the scene and there was a prevalence of that. However, I'm very pleased to state that I think that the young musicians today live a cleaner life than ever before in the history of jazz music and dance bands. This is a period where they're all very serious about their music and about everything else. They all exercise, they run, they jog. It's a whole different ball game. . . .

HERB JEFFRIES: Woody was very sick the last time I saw him. When I walked into the motor home there in Hemet that Jim had for him to dress in, I said hello to him and spent a few minutes with him. He was just sitting there. It seemed that he was even breathing hard and I thought . . . "I don't know how this guy's going to even make it out there on the stage." Yet, the moment he walked out there, it seemed like energy had come into his body from I don't know where. Not only was he vibrant and could play his instruments with great elegance, but he became very humorous. Just the fact that he was playing sort of brought him an energy from a source that is everything in the whole world where we come from.

The author arrived at Woody's home for the first of a series of interviews late in the afternoon of September 26, 1986. Woody arrived a little late. His calendar that day was filled.

B.C.   What does it cost to keep your band on the road these days?

W.H.   Just to break even, we need to take in $22,500 a week. That covers salaries, transportation, and commissions, but not hotel rooms.

B.C.   Have you made any arrangements to have a "ghost band" after you have departed from the earthly scene?

W.H.   I offered it to my grandson [rock musician Tom Littlefield, Jr.] a few years ago. I would like for him to front it because he would be a direct contact with the blood line. He's musician enough, and he's traveled with me enough to know what the possibilities are. He said, "Granddad, if you want to help me and if you really care about me, if you have any old copyrights you can let me have, I would sure love that."

I don't think he's interested, and without him, I don't think I would want a ghost band. . . . I think fifty years is long enough to devote to any business, especially when it's a hobby!

B.C.   Do you look for any revival of big band music that might challenge rock and roll?

W.H.   I don't have a crystal ball, but there's so much money spent on marketing and advertising in general by the major record companies that it's very difficult to oppose them. And, of course, the major record companies today are controlled by lawyers and accountants. I don't know of a major record label today that's doing anything really progressive in jazz. . . .

B.C.   Not even Concord?

W.H.   Well, he's doing what's been done before by many people, and he's done it well. Except he's weak in the distribution vein. . . .

B.C.   Would you say that the most significant change in the sound of a big jazz band from the forties would be in the rhythm section?

W.H.   Well, I think it's a combination of everything, but that would be one.

B.C.   As an example, the rhythm section in your band today plays "Woodchopper's Ball" distinctly differently from the way the First Herd did.

W.H.   The First Herd had a plodding kind of rhythm and that seemed to be the style of the music of the early forties.

B.C.   Do you have any comments about the change of tone and conception in tenor players? We used to hear the soft, flowing Lester Young school. But the coarser sound and advanced harmonics of the Coltrane school have been prevalent from the early sixties on.

W.H.   Well, actually it came out of the fifties and the sixties. It was the "forward movement," blowing into stretched-out music. . . . It's where the melodic line is never very well stated.

B.C.   Are you describing Coltrane's musical concepts?

W.H.   Well, he was one of the innovators of that style. There are more people today who play that way, but now it's dictated to these players by the record industry. If they're willing to put any jazz on record, it has to be that form, which is no form. I experimented with it in the early seventies and we won two Grammys back-to-back. So it proves that something was happening in the early seventies. . . .

B.C.   Does the use of synthesizers and computerized gadgetry in music bother you?

W.H.   No, it doesn't strike me in any way, except for the fact that I still feel that music has to be played the very best with the best kind of instruments and the clarinet happens to be one of them. To be unamplified is a great feeling and a great source of sound.

B.C.   Who were some of your most original players?

W.H.   Bill Harris was one of my very favorite musicians of all time. He came to me via Benny Goodman. Benny used to warm up some very good players for me. Unfortunately, Bill passed away a few years ago [1973]. Before he became ill, he had been fired from one of the leading hotels in Las Vegas because the management had said to the bandleader, "You don't need that many brass players. Get rid of a couple of them." So they got rid of Bill Harris, who was a giant musically. It's just beyond all imagination!

B.C.   Did you ever have a "gentleman's agreement" with other leaders, for example, Stan Kenton, that your bands had musicians who went back and forth?

W.H.   Oh, I wouldn't say that we had an agreement or not. We would advise each other if someone was leaving and you thought he could be helpful to another leader. But Stan and I were friends socially.

B.C.   Why does American jazz and big band music seem to be more popular and respected overseas?

W.H.   I think it's because they recognize that it is probably the only true art form that belongs to us as Americans. Everything else we have has been borrowed.

B.C.   Does living out of a suitcase ever get tiring?

W.H.   It does to some people but I thrive on it. I like the room service, if that adds up to anything. I LOVE the room service! At home, I have to raid my own refrigerator and I'm not very good at it.

B.C.   Where does Woody Herman go from here? What are your plans?

W.H.   As long as I have reasonable health, I'll be doing what I'm doing.

B.C.   Is there any one thing that you have not done, that you would like to do musically?

W.H.   I've had one for a long time that I would like to do before I "blow it." It's the concept of having someone like Ralph Burns and a couple other of my favorite composers write material for a brass choir with a huge church organ underneath as a quality of sound, and record it in a cathedral in Europe or over here. A place where there is a great natural sound without amplification.

After the interview Woody spoke eagerly of some new clothes he had purchased the day before at Gucci's in Beverly Hills and asked permission to "model" them. An abrasive sound could be heard from the metal pins in his left leg as he made his way to the bedroom to change. He emerged a few moments later wearing a luxurious, imported navy blue sweater with a pair of Black Watch plaid slacks, and tennis shoes without socks, "Miami Vice" style. Woody was style conscious.

Early in September dissension had erupted in the trumpet section, ending in a stalemate. Woody refused to take sides.

RON STOUT: Woody would leave it up to the section leader about who goes or who stays, with his final approval. Woody was never the kind of leader who believed in controversy. He got the talent and he let them play, and just the fact that he did that was his way of complimenting them. Woody was always the biggest flag waver for his guys.

After six years as third trumpeter, Mark Lewis resigned effective September 27. He was replaced by Paul Mazzio and later Jim Powell.

Dave Yost spoke of Woody's tender side in an incident that took place on October 4.

DAVE YOST: The setting was in the band bus in front of the Campus Inn at Ann Arbor, Michigan. As my two sons and I escorted Woody onto the bus he said, "Wait, I almost forgot something," and reached into his pocket for his money clip. The boys started yelling, "No, Woody. No, we can't!" He said to Jay, "Come here, you little twerp." Jay and Sonny continued to protest as I added my humble "No," too. Woody insisted and the bus was not about to move onward to East Lansing until the boys received their gift. The boys yelled, "What should we do, Dad?" I said, "You better receive it." Woody gave them a $100 bill.

They jumped onto the bus and I witnessed the warm embraces and saw the love in Woody's eyes as the boys hugged him and told him of their love. I jumped on the bus and did the same as the band watched and cheered and clapped for us. Then the bus pulled off into a rainy, dark day for a sixty-five-mile jaunt to the next gig in East Lansing. Woodrow was a dear, generous, and loving man.

On October 11 the band departed from Miami for its third annual jazz cruise. Immediately after the cruise, Polly Podewell joined for a two-month tour commencing October 19.

POLLY PODEWELL: My first gig with the big band was in Toronto. It was a scary thing because I didn't rehearse at all before I sang with them. Of that two-month tour, I think that first night was the biggest crowd we played for.

Right before this date, the band had been on a jazz cruise. They came straight from the jazz cruise to Toronto. I couldn't meet them beforehand because they were on the cruise. Woody didn't even have the old vocal charts anymore. They contacted Berklee School of Music to look up some of the old music. Somebody at Berklee pulled the music and they sent the charts directly to me. They sent "Happiness," and "Wrap Your Troubles in Dreams," and "Romance in the Dark." I never did that last one. Bill Byrne said, "Oh, please don't remind Woody of that one!"

I started to learn those tunes. Luckily, I had recordings of Mary Ann McCall and Frances doing them.

We literally went on stage with no rehearsal at all. I never did have an opportunity to run over the charts in advance with the band. We did it cold and it worked out. That's a scary thing to do. But I lived through it.

November 3, 1986, was Woody's real fiftieth anniversary as a bandleader. The band played at a high school in Dyersburg, Tennessee, without fanfare.

At 3:30 P.M. on November 13, Woody collapsed in his room at the Sheraton-Russell Hotel in New York City. He called Bill Byrne and Ed Dye and complained of breathing problems. His lungs were rapidly filling with fluid.

ED DYE: His heart had stopped. We hadn't known just how sick he was. He had been getting sick on the road and still working. In New York, the band would stay in another hotel on the other side of town. So the communications weren't good. When he was talking to Bill and me, we knew he was sick, but we didn't know how sick.

As a matter of fact, Dr. Levy had trouble reaching a pharmacist that Woody's hotel had recommended. I just beat it straight over to Woody's hotel and then when I got there, I decided that I better beat it down to the pharmacist and get the antibiotics stuff for colds. I had no cause to be alarmed. I had cause only to expedite.

When I arrived at Woody's room he was in the throes of trouble. The paramedics were there. There were two batches of them up there in his room. His heart actually stopped for a time.

Woody was rushed to Bellevue Hospital and doctors stabilized his vital signs.

POLLY PODEWELL: It was a terrible hospital. I visited him every day. In fact, I just stayed in New York because I have friends there.

Instead of giving him a private room, they put him in this huge room. It was like a four-patient ward with other people. The other patients were all doing okay. A couple of the guys . . . had their girlfriends visit at night and they would have parties. Poor Woody. I mean, the whole situation was totally ridiculous. That was a terrible time. I'll never forget it.

Finally, they got him a room by himself. He was in that room for about a week or whatever. It seemed like forever. But there was no privacy there at all. He was very ill at that time.

On November 24 Woody was released and convalesced for a few more days at Jack Siefert's home outside Philadelphia. Frank Tiberi was fronting the Herd.

On December 7 an obviously frail Woody reappeared, sporting a freshly grown beard, to front the band at the Kennedy Center in Washington, D.C. This was a crucial performance that the promoters would have canceled if Woody had been unable to appear.

ED DYE: It was an awards banquet for Hume Cronyn, Jessica Tandy, Lucille Ball, and Ray Charles. There were a million people there! You know, the President [Reagan] and [Vice President] Bush, and all those cats, were there briefly. After the awards thing was over, they all came out into the lobby. Then the band played for the ball and they served dinner.

Stevie Wonder was there. Joe Williams was actually working with the band at that gig, and Stevie Wonder sat in. He, Joe and Woody were all singing a blues tune together.

JOE WILLIAMS: I'm on the Advisory Committee at the Kennedy Center in Washington. They had said to me, "Basie's band can't make it, what are we gonna do?" I said, "Easy, get Woody Herman, he's the greatest dance band I know," and they did.

I was pleased that he could make it physically. When the band left the stage on a break, he stayed up there and blew! Then, he and I did some things with the rhythm section and his clarinet. That's what he wanted to do, man. He was another breed of person altogether!

QUINCY JONES: The last time I saw Woody was the night that Ray Charles got his Kennedy Center award. We sat together on the "royal steps" right in front of the band. I could see that he wasn't feeling too well. He and Joe Williams sang the blues all night, man, and the band was playing its ass off. It was so beautiful!

The following night, the band played at Blues Alley in Washington, D.C. After a high school gig at Hudson, New York, Woody led the Herd on December 10 at the Waldorf Astoria Hotel in New York.

DAVE YOST: Woody was flown home to Los Angeles on the night of December 12, 1986. I joined him and Jake Hanna at Donte's in North Hollywood during that weekend. He looked terrible, but was determined to play on the Queen Mary on New Year's Eve, and afterwards hit the road again for a winter tour in California, Washington, Oregon, Utah, Colorado, Nebraska, and Minnesota. . . .

The December 31, 1986, edition of the Herd, assembled in the ballroom of the Queen Mary in Long Beach Harbor, was a mixed contingent of veterans, current members, and newcomers: John Madrid, Larry Gillespie, Mark Lewis, Ron Stout, Bill Byrne (trumpets); John Fedchock, Kim Scharnberg, Ken Kugler (trombones); Dick Hafer, Dick Mitchell, Jerry Pinter (tenor saxes); Mike Brignola (baritone sax); Alan Broadbent (piano); John Clayton (bass); Jake Hanna (drums); and Woody Herman (leader, clarinet, alto sax, soprano sax, vocals).

DICK HAFER: He was pretty good, except when he had to get up on the bandstand. I helped him by walking ahead of him so people wouldn't bump him. He was brittle. . . . Once he got on the bandstand, he was great.

Charlie Barnet and Artie Shaw had long since retired. Duke Ellington, Stan Kenton, Harry James, the Dorseys, Count Basie, Benny Goodman, and Glenn Miller were deceased. Only two other working leaders remained from the big band era: Lionel Hampton and Les Brown. Woody had outlived one trauma after another. Providence had permitted him to stand in front of fifty years of Thundering Herds with polish, drive, and enthusiasm.

10.

Final Bars
1987

On January 15 the band assembled at Statesville, North Carolina, to start a series of one-nighters throughout the South and Central United States. John Fedchock was temporarily absent, preparing new material for a recording date in March.

This was the January 15, 1987, edition of the Herd: Roger Ingram, George Baker, Jim Powell, Ron Stout, Bill Byrne (trumpets); Paul McKee, John Allred, Joe Barati (trombones); Frank Tiberi, Dave Riekenberg, Jerry Pinter (tenor saxes); Mike Brignola (baritone sax); Joel Weiskopf (piano); Dave Carpenter (bass); and Jim Rupp (drums).

CHUBBY JACKSON: When I was living in Vero Beach, Florida, as president of the Treasure Coast Jazz Society, I was responsible for bringing Woody into town for a double performance with his present Herd [January 31, 1987]. An afternoon concert clinic was performed free of charge for all the high school musicians in the area as well as a night concert for all the adults.

I sat in on bass, played some blues and then Woody and I scatted "Lemon Drop." We dined together and I asked him how he managed to work seven nights a week on the road after all these years. He told me that he was the last of the big bandleaders still going and that he felt devoted and dedicated to his millions of fans.

It was the truth because I, for one, know that Woody never had any need to lie about anything.

ED DYE: Woody was so brazen. He hardly ever complained. A lot of times he was grumpy as hell, but he would rarely tell you how he felt. If he said he "didn't feel good," that meant that he REALLY didn't feel good. He had those pins in his legs and we would be in snow and ice and he was like 200 years old, and still going, just like a young rock and roller. I mean sometimes, we went like the wind, in limos, large airplanes, and small commuter planes and all the wear and tear of trying to get to the gig.

Sometimes, it was harder the way we went. He hated the bus from all those early years and he just liked goin' his own way. We would be in 200-mile taxi cab rides.

In mid-February, the band traveled through the Southwest. After arriving in Flagstaff, Arizona, to meet the band, the author and his wife learned that Woody had taken ill in Santa Fe the previous night and flown home to Los Angeles.

ED DYE: He got really ill in Santa Fe. When you're up at that altitude, even the young musicians have problems blowing their horns.

I had got some oxygen for him. It was the first time that Woody had ever really needed any assistance from me. He was in the bathtub and was really messed up. I was trying to get a doctor to come up to the room. I had earlier met some cab guys while running around and getting airline tickets and doing my errands, and the doctor never came, so I called one of the cab guys and we beat it down to Albuquerque which was about 1000 feet lower. He started feeling better almost immediately.

While in Flagstaff, the author interviewed Frank Tiberi, Bill Byrne, and drummer Dave Miller, who had replaced Jim Rupp on February 3.

B.C.   Who influenced you the most as far as your tenor playing? . . . Did you dig Hawk [Coleman Hawkins]?

F.T.   Oh, certainly. I could play his solos. I could transcribe them like everyone else. I would have liked to have heard more of Frankie Trumbauer. After him, there was Herschel Evans, there was Coleman, and right on down the line.

B.C.   What about Prez [Lester Young]?

F.T.   Well, of course. There was also that fellow who went to Europe . . . Don Byas. The other big tenor player was Ben Webster. Charlie Ventura was also a great executionist. I liked him and also played with him. But then, Prez, Brew Moore, Allen Eager, all those guys I listened to and also [Charlie] Parker, of course. I used to hear Parker and Prez at the Famous Door on 52nd Street. I was 14 years old. I grew a long moustache. I looked about 70!

I played like all of them at one time or another. I guess I settled on Trane [John Coltrane]. I've never played just like him, but he's the one that I've most accepted and got my harmonics from. He had a lot to offer. He was an exponent. You can read between the lines.

I asked Bill Byrne: "Do you think that the IRS litigations have shortened Woody's life?"

B.B.   I don't know. Woody doesn't really worry about stuff like that too much. As long as it doesn't really get too close to him, he can put it off completely. Woody always liked to play, and so long as we gave him a draw he was happy. If he had money enough for Charlotte to operate on he was okay. So I don't really think he looked at it too realistically.

D.M.   The thing that I really got the most out of from my time with Woody's band was learning to appreciate the roots of jazz. When I say the roots of jazz, I mean going even further back than even the bebop that some people consider the roots. I mean going way back to the earlier swing era, checking out Jo Jones, and even earlier than that, people like Davey Tough and Sid Catlett, really checking out where swing came from. It adds so much more when you get that kind of foundation. As a drummer, or a rhythm player, it adds to your swing feel. If you really get those roots together it helps all of your playing. It gives you more authenticity when you're playing jazz.

Woody often told me, "Check out Gus Johnson, Sam Woodyard [Ellington's old drummer], check out some of those earlier guys." You know, man, it really helped me a lot. It helped me get a real traditional feel together. I received an invaluable experience, especially playing some of the older Woody charts. Many of the younger musicians want to check out the more recent, modern guys, but they don't really take the time to check out where it all really originated.

On February 21, Woody fronted the Herd for a one-nighter at Thermal, California.

FLIP PHILLIPS: Woody Herman is one tough guy. His doctor said it and I said it. Paul Anka may have had him in mind when he wrote the song "My Way." He has had many things happen to him, many mishaps, but he always comes back swinging.

Woody has put many musicians into the limelight. Up until today, he is still doing the one-nighters. God bless him. I don't know how he does it.

On March 3 the band went into the Willows Theater, Concord, California, to record the *Woody's Gold Star* album. It would be Woody's last commercial recording. John Fedchock coordinated the music and contributed most of the charts.

"Battle Royal" is the opening number. A Duke Ellington title based on the chords of "I Got Rhythm," it's a flag-waver scored by Fedchock, featuring a series of hard-driving solos and exchanges from saxophonists Dave Riekenberg, Mike Brignola, Jerry Pinter, and Tiberi.

The title track of "Woody's Gold Star" is a reference to the star in the Hollywood "Walk of Fame" commemorating Woody's achievements. The chart is performed in an easy groove with unusual voicings created by composer Fedchock. The performance features tasty muted trumpet from Jim Powell and a contribution from baritonist Brignola. The chart concludes with fine precision ensemble work showing off the brilliant lead of trumpeter Ingram.

"Mambo Rockland" is a fine Latin/jazz score written for the Herd by Tito Puente, with whom Woody had collaborated on an album in 1958. The performance is ignited by guest Latin percussionists Pete Escovedo, Poncho Sanchez, and Ramon Banda. The music features solos by pianist Joel Weiskopf, Tiberi, and the guest percussionists.

Thelonious Monk's classic ballad "'Round Midnight" is another arrangement by the brilliant Fedchock. The tune enjoyed somewhat of a revival during this period because of the film of the same name featuring Dexter Gordon. This version features the arranger's resonant trombone and Roger Ingram's lead trumpet.

Fedchock penned "The Great Escape," a term Woody often used. At high school and college clinics, he would tell the students that "anything that is good jazz to me is a great escape." It's another up-tempo chart, with the theme initially stated by the saxes, followed by the trombone trio and solos from Tiberi and trombonist McKee.

Fedchock scored Miles Davis's "Dig," a reworking of "Sweet Georgia Brown." The rhythm section has the intro; trumpeter Ron Stout and tenorist Jerry Pinter play the boppish line. It's taken at a clipped tempo with solo statements from Pinter and Woody on clarinet. The failing lungs of the Old Chopper still had sufficient vigor to create solos of emotion and substance.

"Rose Room/In a Mellow Tone" is a medley scored by Maria Schneider (who married John Fedchock in 1988). Woody creates superb deep-toned sounds on "Room." The "Mellow Tone" portion features excellent scoring with solo contributions by Fedchock and pianist Weiskopf. The out-chorus has Woody's clarinet on top, followed by Ingram's skybound lead.

The album includes the third arrangement of Herbie Hancock's "Watermelon Man" submitted to the Herd's book since Nat Pierce's chart for the sixties band. In the author's opinion, the score is anticlimactic after Pierce's version. According to Fedchock, he did the chart reluctantly after Woody gave him the assignment. Nonetheless, this Latin/rock version has some bright moments with the added Latin percussion contingent and Ron Stout's "dirty" solo. Additional solos are from Riekenberg, Weiskopf, and Woody's soprano.

Fedchock's chart of "Samba Song" is a thrilling closer, an aggressive Latin opus with pulsating solos from Weiskopf on piano and Riekenberg's flute.

MIKE BRIGNOLA (March 1987):   I've been getting Woody's horns and his mouthpieces together for him before each gig for about seven years. I know when he wants to play and sometimes when he doesn't feel like playing.

His main decline has been with his muscle control, his dexterity, and his wind power. But it's amazing even in the condition that he's in now, he can still take a simple jazz melody and phrase it. His ability to phrase and play a melody musically is just a God-given talent that he has.

PAUL MCKEE: Jazz has always been known as underground, a less than popular art form with the masses. I always have hopes that perhaps someday it will become better accepted. It went through a period where the big bands made it extremely popular, and I think that as people become better educated, they will become enlightened. Jazz is a listener's art. You really have to have a degree of sophistication to appreciate an improvised solo and sounds like that.

The rate of music education has been increasing over the years and musicians are extremely well-schooled. A lot of them aren't working, but the sophistication level of listening and the amount of critical quality that the audience has now is hopefully going to keep the art alive.

A lot of people who appreciate it don't necessarily understand it, but they appreciate what's going on. And even though the music theoretically, harmonically, or rhythmically, may be going over their heads, at least they get some excitement from it. There's some heart and soul to it. It's not just a machine. Especially with big bands, you've got fifteen guys up there on the stand and these days, you could just as easily get a synthesizer, a sampler, and have all the parts played perfectly, with no mistakes, but there would be no heart, no emotion, no excitement to it. It's the idea of the guys up there coordinating their efforts into a band sound. That's one of the best things about this band. . . . When we're gathered together on the stage, and when there's been the same personnel for awhile, the music develops a definite character. When it's tight and everything's popping, it's really an exciting thing. There are the dance bands and the musicians in them sort of go through the motions and play the music. But as far as jazz concert bands, this is about the only thing left and I hope that when Woody's gone, the people remember that he never sold out.

After the recording date, the Herd played one-nighters through the Pacific Northwest. Red Kelly, the Third Herd bassist, then owner of Kelly's restaurant

in Tacoma and head of his own political party, the "Owl Party," recalls the last
visit with Woody.

RED KELLY: My wife, Donna, and I went down and spent the day with him
in Portland. We were his guests at the job that night and we took him to
dinner. I finally had a chance to take HIM out for a change.

My wife and Woody hadn't known each other a long time, but they
became "lovers," fast pals, immediately. He really liked her. The last picture I have of him was when we were in the hotel room after closing the
hotel bar. It was about two o'clock in the morning, and he had an early
day and so did we. We were leaving and Woody was embracing my wife
and saying, "Take care of my boy." I cry when I think about it.

ED DYE: Woody knew that the Colorado Rockies were going to be hard
because of what happened in Santa Fe. We had maybe eight dates and
one of them was Aspen.

We had traveled on the bus a little bit of that time and we were also
doing some flying around the mountains. We were on the last leg of
the Colorado trip and we were getting down to a lower altitude, but he
kept saying, "I don't feel any better, it's weird, I've got to see Stan [Dr.
Stan Levy]."

I said, "Well, let's go now, man." He said, "No, I want to do this deal
for Nathan [Davidson] in Grand Meadow, Minnesota."

MIKE BRIGNOLA (March 14):   Woody's fine today. But I didn't think he'd
make it through the gig in Aspen, because that's 8,000 feet. In Santa Fe,
he was taking his medication, but you can't take the same dosage when
you're in the mountains, or it will screw you up. They hadn't told him that.

He was feeling bad for a couple of the gigs. We've been up here at
this altitude for about a week now. Aspen was the highest gig we had to
do and he got through that okay. Now we're in Denver, which is 5,200
feet. He was okay last night.

I've been with Woody for the past eight years, and it's definitely been
a long, gradual decline for him. He just stands in front of the band, and
when he's not announcing a tune, he just stands in a daze.

In March, Woody hired Diane White on second trumpet, again demonstrating his nondiscriminatory ideals. Diane stayed with the Herd until July.

Woody's last gig was at Grand Meadow High School, in Grand Meadow,
Minnesota, population 1,000. Grand Meadow High School band director
Nathan Davidson had been a zealous Herman fan since a friend first took
him to hear the Herman Band perform in La Crosse, Wisconsin, in 1970.
Davidson is the epitome of a big band jazz aficionado. A special room in his

Woody's "Last Hurrah," as he conducts the Young Thundering Herd on the final blasting chord of "Fanfare for the Common Man" at Grand Meadow High School, March 23, 1987. (Courtesy Judy McDermott, Austin [Minnesota] *Daily Herald*)

house is well stocked with records, books, magazines, and photos of the famous bands, dominated by pictures of Woody and the Herd.

It had always been Davidson's dream to have Woody and the band play at the school in Grand Meadow. Davidson felt that it was important for his students to be exposed in person to the excitement of a smoking big jazz band. He was also in awe that Woody would consider traveling to this little town in rural Minnesota.

NATHAN DAVIDSON: One of the goals was simply to raise money for our band mothers group. I also wanted it to be an educational experience for our students as well as area students, and to raise the musical consciousness of the community. Not only did we succeed at these goals, it was also good overall PR for the town and school.

For the senior citizens, it was a trip down memory lane. Many of those folks hadn't seen Woody for thirty years, back when they used to dance to the band during the Swing Era. For the young folks, it was perhaps their first exposure to a live performance of a professional big band jazz group with the original leader still fronting the band. Others came simply out of curiosity.

Woody's performance that evening was nothing but professional. Even though appearing frail and showing the rigors of travel, he gave his all. During the concert, Woody played, sang, and even danced during the Conga. During the intermission, he also found time for interviews and photos, and gave autographs after the concert.

ED DYE: Woody was going to go for some more of the road, and I met with Bill and I said, Hey, man, we've got to get the old man off the road!"

I called Stan [Levy], but before we flew to Detroit to see Levy, we went to Chicago for a couple of days. I think Woody wanted a last party. It may have been a premonition, but who knows? He was thinking that when he got with Stan, Stan would lock him in for a long duration of tests and things.

POLLY PODEWELL: He came to Chicago and we went out to the Jazz Showcase at the Blackstone Hotel. He was looking awful. The next day he went to Detroit and was hospitalized.

ED DYE: We rented a car and drove to Stan's office in Detroit. He spent an hour examining Woody and I went out and grabbed something to eat. When I came back, Stan told me, "We're going to the hospital!" Woody's heart was still out of sync.

While undergoing treatment at Sinai Hospital in Detroit, Woody learned that Buddy Rich had had surgery to remove a brain tumor. Woody asked the nurses if he could put in a call to Buddy at UCLA Medical Center. The ailing Rich was barely able to hum "Blue Flame" for Woody. Buddy died a few days later.

ED DYE: They were still trying to stabilize Woody's heart when he had a cardiac arrest. Fortunately, he had a very competent young male nurse with him when it happened, and Woody never lost consciousness or any oxygen. During the resuscitation procedure a hospital intern inadvertently cracked one of his ribs. Then the series of things happened to him that he never recovered from.

He went into intensive care and that was the start of many things. He was hallucinating for about a week.

BILL BYRNE: Polly was staying at the hospital looking after him. So was Midge Ellis. She's a lady in Detroit who has sponsored all the big jazz bands like Stan Kenton, Maynard Ferguson, and Duke Ellington at Clarenceville High School. Every year she would promote a series of concerts. She's quite a jazz promoter and knew Woody real well. She was able to get things done to help Woody in the hospital.

POLLY PODEWELL: I don't know if it was the medication they were giving him or what, but he really went out of his gourd. He hallucinated. That was a horrendous experience. He would talk about becoming the President of the United States and he was talking crazy.

ED DYE: I remember a couple of times he was not aware. He thought that he was in a hotel for a little bit. He was talking to me about getting in touch with people from a dozen years back.

The author spoke to Jack Siefert, Woody's old friend, on April 6.

JACK SIEFERT: My kids are so broken up you wouldn't believe it. When they were born, Woody and Charlotte flew in just to present my wife with roses, then flew back again. That's why I don't mind flying to Detroit to see Woody or flying any other place, if necessary. I flew out for the 50th Anniversary Concert. That man . . . he's part of our family!

I knew Charlotte very well. She stayed here sometimes when Woody was on the road. My wife and she were very friendly. They used to do a lot of things together. She was lovely company and we loved her dearly.

Early in April the Herd, fronted by Frank Tiberi, was touring Illinois. Time out was taken for a trip to Detroit.

BILL BYRNE: The whole band was there to visit him before the European tour. We went into the room in shifts, four or five guys at a time.

Ultimately, Woody's condition improved. On April 17, the author telephoned him. Woody was rational but could not talk above a whisper. We prayed together. A spiritual rebirth took place as Woody made peace with his Maker.

DAVE YOST: On April 20 my boys and I drove to Detroit, found the hospital and saw Woody. Oh, my God, he was skin and bones. The sad look in his eyes turned to a twinkle when he saw us. We kissed him on the forehead and the three of us joined hands in prayer for his peace and recovery. It was a touching hour we spent with him. He wanted us to see the jacket the band had brought him. It was white satin and bore the inscription "Coach."

ED DYE: One of the first times he was really able to get out of bed after weeks of intensive care, they were taking him down to the X-ray room and he said to the nurse—motioning to me—"Make sure he gets the 8 x 10 glossies." . . .

Earlier, when he was in the throes of intensive care, his grandson, Tommy Littlefield, Jr., was there visiting him, and he still was coming forth with the one-liners. He was an amazing man.

ED DYE (May 12):   Woody's strength is coming back in leaps and bounds!
Going back two weeks ago, he was still in the straw stage of taking his nour-
ishment. Then, he went to being able to sip out of a cup. Then, the next day,
he could hold the cup. About three days later, he was sitting up in a chair.
Then, the following day, he fed himself three meals like a lumberjack!

As far as when he's coming home, there's been another delay—not a
setback. They were trying to shoot for his birthday. He was going to get
out that day and we were going to get a limo and get him home.

They still have the monitor on him, but at least they've got all the
tubes out. He can get to the bathroom and back to bed. Those are major
victories now. He's lost an enormous amount of weight from being laid up
all this time. He's going to need somebody to work with him.

On May 11 and 12, 1987, the Herd and Richard Stoltzman, minus Woody,
went into RCA Recording Studios in New York City to record a group
of titles for the album *Ebony*. Since meeting Stoltzman, it had been Woody's
aspiration to record the *Ebony Concerto* with him "the way it should
be played."

"American Medley" was arranged by John Oddo. It features Stoltzman's
clarinet, accompanied by Joel Weiskopf's piano on "Amazing Grace," followed by "America, the Beautiful," as the ensemble gently enters. Then the
mood changes with a rousing version of "Battle Hymn of the Republic."

John Fedchock arranged Ellington's tone poem "Come Sunday" for the
album, because, as Stoltzman said, "Woody idolized Duke and I couldn't see
doing an album without one of his works." The ensemble weaves elegant patterns as Stoltzman's legit chops spark the performance.

The ageless "Apple Honey" is performed again, with bristling work from
tenor saxophonists Tiberi and Pinter, Brignola's baritone, McKee, and trumpeters Greg Gisbert and Ron Stout. Stoltzman assists with the famous free-
for-all finish with Ingram's trumpet solo on top.

Stoltzman and the Herd, bolstered by the added instrumentation of
French horn, guitar, and harp, turn in a stellar performance of Stravinsky's
Ebony Concerto. Woody was proud of the results as he assiduously listened to
the tape from his sickbed.

The 1946 Rogers-Norvo Woodchoppers score of "Igor" is appropriately
revived for the album. Despite its title, it's strictly a bebop line. According to
Stoltzman, "I play exactly what Woody played on the original version. . . .
There's also a little passage at the end where I just decided to toss in a brief
quote from the *Ebony Concerto*." Other solo contributions are from Joel
Weiskopf, Fedchock, Riekenberg, Stout, and Howard Alden, added on guitar.

"Stories from the West Side" is an elegant sequence of themes from *West
Side Story*, scored by Frank Bennett. Stoltzman is primarily featured, with a
solo from bassist Dave Carpenter.

"Waltz for Woody" was written by Bill Douglas, a Yale classmate of Stoltzman's. The chart features a trio of clarinets, Stoltzman, Tiberi, and Riekenberg, in a light, frothy performance.

John Coppola and Vince Guaraldi's vintage 1956 score of "Cousins" is performed again by the 1987 Herd. According to Stoltzman: "I wanted to include this because the brass section plays a quote from Stravinsky's *Petrushka* at the end." Again, Stoltzman displays his skill, and Tiberi contributes a solo.

JOHN FEDCHOCK: We recorded a version of "Cousins" with some open choruses in case Woody got well enough to come back and overdub a solo, but it never happened.

On May 13 the author spoke to Woody on the phone. Woody could speak more clearly than in April but was very weak.

WOODY: How are you? I understand from Ingrid and everybody the book is [shaping up] great. . . .

I am a lot better. I hope within the next week or a little more to come home. I'm anxious to get together with you. Let's try to spend as much time as possible at the house. . . .

The band finished the classical record at Victor. I had a message from Stoltzman saying he felt it was great, and so did everybody else. That's good. The band leaves Saturday for Europe. Buddy De Franco will front the band some. Frank will do the emcee-ing. . . .

I got a thought the other day, which I gave to Tom Cassidy in Chicago. It was just an idea. Tom was worried about what it would be called. I explained to him, "We don't get involved with titles, we just sell." It would involve three clarinets: Stoltzman, and a new, very wonderful player . . . what's his name? [Eddie Daniels.] He's new, and very hot and very big. He's great! I've got a digital recording over here of him. He's not a classical bird, he's a jazz bird, but a great, great technician. So I figured we would sell it. Stoltzman, Daniels, and myself, and try to get as much money as possible for the tour. It would be like "the last of the clarinet summits." I think we could do some world-wide business. Anyway, it's an idea. . . .

We'll get together when I get home. . . . Here's my doctor, I better leave you.

ED DYE: I was in Detroit with him for thirteen weeks. Then I got sort of stir crazy. I had to get out of there. . . . So I went away for a few weeks and then I came back out to LA when Woody came home from the hospital that first time. Then, I stayed through the end. . . .

May 16 was Woody's 74th birthday.

TOM CASSIDY: He was in a great mood that day and was looking forward to going back to work. We went over the details of the upcoming tour, and it made him very excited. He was also very excited about Eddie Daniels and about the possibility of working with him.

Concord Jazz Records, assisted by Nat Pierce, assembled two cassettes of Happy Birthday and get-well wishes from Herd alumni and friends and sent them to Woody. Nat Pierce's voice was full of emotion as he introduced what he termed "Woody Herman-style music," featuring Woody's favorites: Ellington and Basie.

On May 15 the Herd, fronted by Frank Tiberi and special guest stars Buddy De Franco and Anita O'Day, left New York to begin a two-week tour of six European countries. Returning from the tour, the band took a two-week vacation beginning June 1. Meanwhile, Woody was still at Sinai Hospital in serious condition. By now the press was terming his condition a "heart ailment and congested lungs."

In June, Ingrid asked the author to look into the possibilities of Woody teaching at Orange Coast College in Costa Mesa, as an artist-in-residence after he recovered sufficiently. It would be a while before he could cope with the rigors of the road again, and with the IRS at his heels, he still required an income.

We put out some feelers in the Orange County community. There was some interest. But Woody's lot was destined otherwise.

DAVE YOST: It became obvious that he was getting weaker and suffering some setbacks. On Sunday, June 14, we drove over to Detroit to Sinai Hospital. When we entered Woody's room, Dr. Levy was there. Woody was so frail looking, but he perked up when he saw us and said, "Here comes the hugging and the kissing!" He told Dr. Levy, "This is Mr. Yost, my dear friend, and one of my greatest fans."

We spent the afternoon with him. He was so talkative and silly at times. He made a big issue that he was going to run for President and be in the White House, Frank [Tiberi] was going to be Vice President. He was nonstop talk. He wanted us to hold his hands. We each prayed for him and he cried. Then the hugging and the kissing started.

It was a long but pleasant afternoon with our dear, dying friend. As we left, he stretched his arms wide, head way back, a big smile, "band-leader pose," that I had witnessed so often down through the years. As we waved to him from the hall, he was blowing kisses to us. It was difficult to leave as I knew this would be my last sight of him, although I called him on the phone several times after that.

On Thursday, June 18, Woody flew to Los Angeles in an air ambulance chartered by Concord Jazz president Carl Jefferson and entered Century City Hospital.

INGRID HERMAN REESE (June 20):   If Carl Jefferson had not donated the air ambulance, I would have never got him out of Detroit. I was in Detroit last week and he had had a relapse even before I got there. He was as sick as I'd ever seen him.

At Century City Hospital, it was a real ritzy, special care pavilion that he was in. It's all decorated and doesn't even look like a hospital. They have a "chef" instead of a cook. It's just splendid and very expensive.

He's been so sick. I really got a better picture of his condition when I saw the list of medicines on which about eight are for circulation alone, and the doctor says, "We are going to start easing him up on them," but he added that they are not duplicating each other. He really does need all of them. This is how bad it's been.

He's got a registered nurse. Medicare doesn't take care of anything at home. Actually, it took care of only one day at the hospital. My bill for one day at the hospital was $1,500, and I don't own a credit card. I had to give them cash on the barrelhead. We've got a registered nurse right now for twelve hours a day.

Woody suffered additional cardiac seizures on June 24.

INGRID HERMAN REESE: He's back in the hospital and was in intensive care. We almost lost him. It was a scene, but things are better now [July 4]. He's in Cedars-Sinai Medical Center in West Los Angeles. We came through a big one. He wasn't swallowing right. Food was going down into his lungs and he had a couple of respiratory arrests that were real scary. But now he's well back on the road to recovery.

The author and his wife Pauline visited Woody at Cedars-Sinai on the afternoon of July 6. Upon walking in, he was in a chair reading a newspaper, wearing grandpa-style reading glasses and a baseball cap (a gift from Jimmy Rowles). When we were going to leave, he insisted that we extend our stay. He said that he had "sworn off booze."

He was alternately in a joking mood with us and then rather caustic with the hospital staff over why they wouldn't get him a walker. Virtually every name that came up in the conversation, Woody would say, "Call them . . . get them on the phone." Between visits of nurses and interns, Woody had us listen to the birthday greetings and "get well" message tapes sent to him by his musician friends and Concord Records.

There was a stack of 8 by 10 glossies of a Herman publicity photo on the windowsill, available for nurses and fans who might happen to hear that Woody was there. Woody asked me to hand him one of the photos. With a shaky hand, he inscribed: "To Bill and Pauline, my very best company, Love, Sincerely, Woody. . . . Bill: Spiritual advisor. W.H. (W.C.T. Herman). The Herd, Love."

INGRID HERMAN REESE (July 13):   They were trying to improve his swallow-ing today and they couldn't do it. He got all congested again and they fig-ured that something had got down into his lungs again. They have pretty well decided that they are going to put a tube into his stomach. When he comes home, he's going to have to tolerate that. He won't be able to eat food or drink liquids for an indefinite period, which is kind of depressing. He's not nearly as well as he was. He's been real weak and congested this evening. I don't know, I'm kind of discouraged about the whole thing. Lee [his nurse] is taking good care of him when she's on duty.

Roger Ingram and Ron Stout came in to see him. It does him good to see somebody. It perks him up.

On July 20, the author called Woody's room at Cedars-Sinai Medical Center. Woody had undergone stomach surgery on July 14 to install a pump and tube, replacing the tube in his nose. He still couldn't swallow; consequently, his nour-ishment was channeled directly to his stomach as was all his medication.

When Woody picked up the phone, his voice was surprisingly clear.

WOODY: Hello, Bill. I'm [feeling] pretty good. Glad to hear from you. Yes, Sir, my man. I want to be out with the band again. I'm going to play at Disneyland with the band. It will be a family act. My friends will open the show, my daughter will be in the show and I will wind up the show. It should be great for Disneyland. They're very anxious about it. I'm also taking on the management of the Harry James Band. . . .

It was apparent that his faculties had been impaired by the medication, oxy-gen loss to the brain, or both, although most of the time, when conversing on the subject of music, he was lucid.

By early August, Woody was back home. The author visited him August 6. Howie Richmond had visited him earlier, and a barber had come in to cut his hair.

It was apparent that he had suffered significant physical deterioration since our last visit with him a month earlier. He kept turning his body in a vain attempt to alleviate his discomfort. In addition, he was enduring the oxy-gen tube in his nose. He called for his private nurse to elevate his head. He was both watching television and listening to a music cassette on a headset. He wasn't too talkative but asked if I wanted to hear the new album, *Woody's*

Gold Star. We listened between visits from the nurse. Woody was pleased with the band's performance.

On leaving, I told him to keep looking up. He nodded and uttered the name "Jesus."

After a series of cardiac arrests, Woody returned to Cedars-Sinai on August 12.

INGRID HERMAN REESE (August 24):   "He was real, real bad for a couple of days. We all thought he was going to pass away. I took one day to call some people who are out of town that I thought he should see. By the second day, when I would have called you and other local people, he had got better again.

He's still real, real weak, and he couldn't talk at all for a few days, but now he's saying a few things. It's obvious he understands. But all this has taken a lot out of him. They're talking about bringing him home again this week.

He's real weak, but he doesn't want to die of boredom either. We put a VCR in his room and we're showing him tapes. He enjoys that. They have more attraction than just audio tapes.

The medical bills were adding to the already staggering debt owed to the IRS. Woody hadn't worked in five months. The author, who was pastor of a Christian church in Newport Beach, California, consulted with the church leaders on Woody's dilemma. A fund was started to help defray Woody's medical expenses.

Woody came home from the hospital on August 26. On August 27, four days before going into surgery himself for a tumor behind his heart, Stan Getz visited. A few days later, Nat Pierce also went to see Woody.

NAT PIERCE: I brought him my copy of the Wild Animal Park [band performance] video. The nurse said, "Okay, I'll play it for him later on, but you can't stay too long." I COULD have stayed, but what was the use? After ten minutes I got so depressed. I was shaking when I got back to my car.

The Herd, fronted by Frank Tiberi, moved into Disneyland for a week on August 29. During the week, several sidemen came to see Woody. Bill Byrne was there virtually every day.

MIKE BRIGNOLA: He couldn't talk. I was looking at him, I didn't expect him to say anything, and he grabbed my hand, and looked at me in the eye and said, "Mike." That's the only word he said the whole time we were there.

One day Bill Byrne, Frank Tiberi, and Joe Conte, the Herd's bus driver, walked into Woody's bedroom. Woody gazed at Joe for a moment. Suddenly he rose up to a seated position and said to the 350-pound bus driver, "I see you lost weight!"

FRANK TIBERI: That was the clearest that he ever talked during the visit. He hadn't been able to even mumble. He had been trying to say something about a trombone player to me and I kept saying, "I can't think of him." But when he spoke to Joe, he said it so clear. He loved to crack jokes. This was the vaudevillian that he was. He could die for humor. That was a funny incident.

INGRID HERMAN REESE (September 1): He's so absolutely feeble, just hanging by a thread.

BILL BYRNE: I asked him point-blank, "Do you want us to keep the band going?" He grabbed my arm, and he looked me right in the eye and said really strong, "YEAH-H-H!"

FRANK TIBERI: He told me that he wanted the band to go on after his first serious siege of being sick [November 1986]. We drank at the bar and he told me, "Frank, I want this to happen and I want YOU to do it."

He had said previously, "No ghost band, everything goes down with me!" He could be a pretty stern guy. We had been still performing while he was in the hospital and he received letters from some of his childhood friends, such as the Shermans and people who had been following the band. They told him how great the band was doing under my direction. That certainly was an encouragement to him.

Then later, we confirmed it when he was on his sick bed. He had been really out of it and he really couldn't say anything at all. It was pathetic to see him. He really suffered a lot. We just asked him . . . "Do you really want it to go on?" He grabbed my hand and held it tightly without even saying a word.

While Woody lay dying, the Herd was thundering at Disneyland. There were new faces in every section. This is the Herd as it appeared in late summer 1987: Eric Miyashiro, Kevin Lawson, Greg Gisbert, Ron Stout, Bill Byrne (trumpets); Alex Iles, John Allred, Joe Barati (trombones); Charlie Pillows, Jerry Pinter (tenor saxes); Mike Brignola (baritone sax); Mark Lebrun (piano); Tony Scherr (bass); Dave Miller (drums); and Frank Tiberi (leader, tenor sax, clarinet).

It was a swinging unit. As with all personnel changes, there were pluses and minuses. Ingram's potent lead trumpet was missed. However, lead trombonist Alex Iles was a distinct asset. The addition of Tony Scherr, a brilliant bassist, bolstered the rhythm section.

Meanwhile, a deputy from the Los Angeles Sheriff's Office hand-delivered an eviction notice to Ingrid on Thursday morning, September 3. The court order carried with it a mandate that the family must vacate the property in five days. Woody was oblivious to the threat. Most of the time he was sleeping.

Ingrid immediately contacted her attorneys, Kirk Pasich in Los Angeles and Leonard Garment in Washington, D.C. Upon conferring, the two attorneys hoped to negotiate a settlement with William Little, owner of the house; if that failed, they planned to seek a court order blocking the eviction. The timing wasn't in Ingrid's favor, with the Labor Day weekend at hand. On Friday, Pasich went to the Superior Court to request a restraining order. Judge Ricardo Torres scheduled a hearing for Tuesday, September 8.

On Monday and Tuesday, the Herman home was inundated with reporters and cameramen.

POLLY PODEWELL: Woody found out about it by watching the TV news. Isn't that awful? But he had a smile on his face. He came out to the living room in his wheelchair and the media was taking pictures and he was smiling and waving. We didn't want him to do too much. The excitement could have killed him.

INGRID HERMAN REESE (September 8):   I was on TV today! The wildest thing has happened. He found out about it last night by accident. I didn't want him to know anything and he found out anyway. He was thrilled that we were in there fighting and that the thing had come down to the nitty gritty. He had always said, "If they come to throw us out, we'll do a sit-in, the likes they never saw during the hippie era!" So when he heard about this on TV, he wouldn't let us turn it down. I said, "Daddy, I didn't want you to feel bad and lose your strength over it." He said in his gravel voice, "I don't feel bad!"

So this morning, I was trying to get ready to go to court, my makeup wasn't on, I wasn't upstairs yet, and the media is here. My dad told his nurse to get him in the wheelchair. He hasn't had the strength to get in the chair since he got back from the hospital two weeks ago. He was put in the chair, came out and greeted the media, then got back in his bed and they took more pictures. All this has brought him back to life. This is great. Frank Sinatra called and Daddy talked to him.

Ed Flynn, who is an old family friend and a professional PR fellow, is the one who has got all this going. He did it single-handedly. Len Garment just called me. He is ecstatic!

With the news out, Woody's many fans and friends responded swiftly with donations. Ingrid had mentioned the church's fund for her father to a Los Angeles TV anchorwoman. Within two days we were flooded with mail. A secretary had to be hired to process the mail and set up a bookkeeping system. Within a month over $34,000 came in.

Typical of the letters the church received was the following: "Money? Woody, you're priceless! Hang in there. When I get some more, I'll send some more. There isn't anyone like you. . . . " The letter included a check for twenty-five dollars.

Within a few days, Kirk Pasich established a fund for Woody at Gilmore Commercial Bank in Los Angeles. Representative John Conyers, Jr., of Michigan introduced a bill in Congress that would wipe out Woody's $1.6 million tax debt. Senator Daniel Patrick Moynihan of New York also offered his assistance.

Meanwhile donations continued to pour in. Some even offered their homes for Woody and Ingrid. Benefits were scheduled all over the nation. Actor Clint Eastwood sent financial assistance.

SAL NISTICO: Woody was a wise cat. I think he suffered a lot in the end, though. I don't know why the government had to harass him about the taxes, and why they just didn't drop it. Consider all the money and entertainment he gave them over the years. The tax problems must have been torturing to the guy.

I remember him telling me they weren't going to get the platinum piece in his leg and the implant lenses in his eyes. They were worth a lot of money. He said, "When I die, I want to make sure those MOTHER-GRABBERS don't get those!" I said, "Are you serious, Woody?" He said, "I'm serious!"

On September 22 the author and his wife drove to Woody's house on Hollywood Boulevard. When we entered the bedroom and looked at the gaunt figure, it was apparent that he was dying. His weight was less than 100 pounds. He made an effort to rise up and acknowledge us but was unsuccessful. He tried to talk but no sounds came out. We attempted to encourage him, but seeing him in that wasted condition was unnerving. I kissed him on the forehead and we left.

On September 28 and 29 Al Cohn, Urbie Green and other jazz greats joined forces to pay tribute to the Chopper at the Blue Note in New York City. On September 30, Annette Mosher, widow of the saxophonist Jimmy Mosher and proprietress of Sonesta Hotels, joined forces with Whale Productions of Revere Beach, Massachusetts, to coproduce "A Tribute to Woody Herman" at the Royal Sonesta Hotel in Cambridge with proceeds going to the Woody Herman Fund.

At approximately 7 A.M. on the morning of October 1, after a particularly distressing night, an emergency call was placed for paramedics. Apparently Woody had experienced a dangerous buildup of fluid in his ravaged lungs. Woody returned to Cedars-Sinai Medical Center, where he remained for his last days in various stages of semiconsciousness.

On Friday, October 2, a tribute-benefit concert was staged by KLON, an FM jazz station on the campus of California State University in Long Beach. Appearing with the Young Thundering Herd were Herd alumni Shorty Rogers, Terry Gibbs, and four of the former "Brothers," Al Cohn, Jimmy Giuffre, Bill Perkins, and Med Flory.

The Herd was electrifying as it played a combination of charts from the past and present. Mike Brignola joined veterans Terry Gibbs and Shorty Rogers on the scat line of "Lemon Drop." Terry and Shorty were also featured on the Second Herd standard "Keen and Peachy." Polly Podewell was present to add her vocal stylings to "Happiness Is Just a Thing Called Joe" and "Wrap Your Troubles in Dreams." Ingrid made some brief comments of appreciation. All proceeds from the sold-out event were forwarded to the Woody Herman Fund.

On October 11 bandleader Bill Saks held a "Woody Herman Benefit" concert, utilizing several groups of local musicians, at the Flamingo Resort Hotel in Santa Rosa, California, just north of San Francisco. Throughout October, numerous other fund-raiser programs were held across the nation to help Woody.

Perhaps the most impressive was organized by deejay Chuck Niles of Los Angeles jazz station KKGO-FM and was held October 23, at the Wadsworth Theater in West Los Angeles. Preceding the event was a lavish reception and buffet dinner held under an enormous tent. The roster included Tony Bennett, Rosemary Clooney, Dudley Moore, Doc Severinsen and the Tonight Show Orchestra, comedian John Byner, Nat Pierce and Shorty Rogers leading a Herman alumni band, Chubby Jackson, singer Mary Ann McCall and a surprise appearance from actor Robert Wagner. Actor James Coburn was also present in the audience. The segment with Chubby Jackson was the most stimulating, as he performed in true Jackson form, dancing, shuffling, twisting, and shouting all over the stage.

CHUBBY JACKSON: I'm not going to stand there on the stage with that dropped eyelid look and try to sell you. I want to make you enjoy what you're listening to. I've always been an exponent of the "grin on the face" of music. I've always loved that little happy grin and that's where I'm at. The happy grin will get across to the public and help them understand and love what you're playing, because there's a lot of musicians that take for granted the public should know all of the intricacies that the musicians employ, and that's a lot of crap. That doesn't happen.

On Thursday afternoon, October 29, 1987, at 2:45 P.M., Woodrow Charles Thomas Herman quietly breathed his last. According to a spokesman at Cedars-Sinai, the immediate cause of death was cardiopulmonary arrest. No relatives were with Woody when he died, although Ingrid had visited him that day.

Pallbearers carry Woody's casket to the hearse. Back row: Woody's grandson Tom Littlefield, Jr., Bill Byrne, Jack Siefert, funeral director, Ingrid (wearing dark glasses), Polly Podewell. Front row: unidentified woman, Nat Pierce, Bill Clancy, photographer, Ed Dye at far right. (Courtesy *The Los Angeles Times*)

HAJI: He started fading pretty fast. It was his lungs that really gave out. The doctor claimed that it was from the years of heavy smoking.

I give anyone credit that's in [show] business like he was and can continue until the end. They had to almost carry him to the hospital with his clarinet in his hand. He was so devoted to music.

He wanted us to get married. I don't know what would have happened if he would have hung around for awhile. He always introduced me as his fiancee. He told his daughter Ingrid to get my wedding ring and pick out the wedding dress. I just went along with it. I told him, "As soon as you get well, we'll start making plans." I figured that my positive attitude might get him going a little bit. I stayed with him up until the end.

Woody's funeral was held November 2 at St. Victor's Roman Catholic Church in Hollywood, where Woody and Charlotte had reaffirmed their wedding vows in 1947, and where the funeral mass was performed for Charlotte in 1982.

The funeral service was subdued and traditionally Catholic. Ingrid was there with her children, Tom Littlefield, Jr., and Alexandra Nichols. Charlotte's mother, 92-year-old Inga Neste, was also present. Many luminaries, former sidemen and friends were there, among them Les Brown, Ray Anthony, Henry Mancini, Bill Holman, Nat Pierce, Mark and Cappy Lewis, Don Menza, John Fedchock, Diane White, Pete Candoli, Don Rader, Mary Ann McCall, Chuck Flores, Bill Perkins, Jimmy Rowles, Terry Gibbs, Jack

Siefert, Polly Podewell, Ross Tompkins, Ralph Burns, Dave Riekenberg, Tom Cassidy, and Stan Kenton's widow Audree.

Bill Byrne flew in to represent the current Herd, which was performing a one-nighter at Oklahoma State University. Bill stood out in the throng wearing the distinctive black band jacket with "Woody Herman and His Young Thundering Herd" inscribed in bright orange on the back.

Near her father's carnation-and-rose-covered casket sat Ingrid, the faithful Ed Dye at her side. The mass was delivered by Monsignor George Parnassus. He alluded to Woody's financial burdens by reminding the mourners, "There wasn't a bit of bitterness on Woody's part. He had faith that tomorrow would be better. Woody had many blessings, and I would say that you" (he motioned to Ingrid and the mourners who nearly filled the church) "were among those blessings."

Jack Siefert, Woody's close friend for over fifty years, delivered a moving eulogy:

> And so it is with Woody. Woodrow Charles Herman is fine. We all know where Woody is, for Woody knew what was important; he had the proper sense of values, and he knew what was right and what was wrong. With a spirit like Woody had, he will live in our memories forever. And if we do happen to forget for a moment, we will soon be able to receive a potent and powerful reminder when we hear a strain of the legacy of music he left behind played by one of the proteges he coached. . . .
>
> Woody always felt that Johnny Mercer was one of America's greatest poets, and what could be more appropriate on this occasion and at this time of the year than the lyrics of one of Woody's greatest hits ["Early Autumn," in Woody's recorded vocal version of 1952]. . . .
>
> > "There's a dance pavilion in the rain
> > All shuttered down . . ."
>
> America's Ambassador of Good Will and Good Music will no longer be doing those endless strings of one-nighters to every hamlet in the world that brought so much happiness to so many.
>
> We have just lost the GREATEST PIED PIPER THAT AMERICAN MUSIC HAS EVER PRODUCED . . . and I have just lost the greatest friend any man ever had.
>
> May his soul rest in peace.

Woody was buried in his white silk Italian suit, wearing a Gucci scarf and blue deck shoes. Polly Podewell placed in the casket a lead sheet to "Happiness Is Just a Thing Called Joe," arranged by Ralph Burns, and a photo of Woody and Charlotte. Ed Dye contributed a half-pint of vodka. About fifty of

Frank Tiberi fronts the Young Thundering Herd in 1990. (Courtesy Riley Gaynor)

Woody's family members and close friends drove in motorcade to Hollywood Memorial Park, where Charlotte Herman was also laid to rest.

On Sunday, November 15, 1,000 enthusiastic Herman fans attended the only benefit concert for Woody Herman outside the United States. The event was organized by Boyd and Joy Denman of Poole, Dorset, England, with proceeds donated to the Woody Herman Trust Fund. Performing the Herd's music was the National Youth Jazz Orchestra directed by Bill Ashton, Herman alumnus Bobby Lamb, and Paul Eshelby. Boyd Denman, a retired lawyer, and his wife were fans and friends of Woody for more than twenty years.

In an interview with Frank Tiberi, I asked, "What would you like to see included in this book from the standpoint of sentiments from your heart?"

FRANK TIBERI: Woody was always one that you were able to really hang with. He was just a very loyal leader and musician friend. I like to refer to what Nat Pierce said, "You always play with him, you don't play for him." I felt that way. He was always appreciative of all of my suggestions. He was just a great guy to be with.

He always had an old-fashioned kind of loyalty which you don't always find in people of his stature. I felt that intimacy that we had. He was also a damn good player. He was the best lead alto player, and he could really "slurp" on the alto. Of course, Johnny Hodges was his mentor. He played that way, but Woody "slurped" even more. He was also a great singer. My association with him, needless to say, has been the best part of my life.

He gave so many guys an opportunity, even if they were not capable at the beginning. He would see their talents and wait. He was always very understanding and just desired to be considered a coach, and was patient and watched the musicians' talents grow. But he wasn't weak, he wasn't a Milquetoast. He was certainly a strong-headed man.

The author asked Tiberi what his thoughts were when he realized that he was going to be leader of the Herd.

FRANK TIBERI: At the beginning, when I would see my name on the marquee it was a little frightening. Now, I'm proud to present the band and it's not going to be any less than what I witnessed in the past twenty years with Woody. I'm not going to give any less effort than Woody did. Woody never played a polka in his life. I still wouldn't play a polka, and I wouldn't play anyone else's arrangements. They're all nice to hear, I like to hear them, too, but certainly we're not going to be a territorial band and play everyone else's music. We're going to remain with what he was doing.

DIZZY GILLESPIE: There is one word I was looking for to describe Woody Herman. Here's a guy that went through all of the eras of jazz almost from the beginning and stayed fresh. Woody stuck with it. He had LONGEVITY, that's the word!

From the March 1988 issue of the Hilton Head, South Carolina, *Sun*:

"WOODCHOPPER'S BALL STILL SLAYS 'EM AS THE HERD GOES THUNDERING ONWARD."

Notes

Chapter 1. Genesis: 1913–1936

1. George T. Simon, *The Big Bands*, fourth edition (New York, Schirmer Books, 1981), 247.

Chapter 2. "The Band That Plays the Blues": 1936–1943

1. Frederick C. Othman, *Chicago Sun*, January 18, 1942.
2. Gene Lees, *Gene Lees Jazzletter*, June 1984, 4.

Chapter 3. The First Herd: 1944–1946

1. George T. Simon, *Metronome*, September 1944.
2. George T. Simon, liner notes for *Woody Herman: The Thundering Herds* (boxed set of LPs), CBS 66378, 8.
3. George T. Simon, liner notes for *Woody Herman: The Thundering Herds* (boxed set of LPs), CBS 66378, 9.
4. George T. Simon, *The Big Bands*, fourth edition (New York: Schirmer Books, 1981), 255.

Chapter 4. The Second Herd: 1947–1949

1. Ira Gitler, quoted in "Closing Chord," *International Musician*, May 1985.
2. James A. Treichel, *Woody Herman and His Second Herd* (Zephyrhills, Fla.: Joyce Record Club Publications, 1978), 11.
3. George T. Simon and Woody Herman, liner notes for *Woody Herman: The Thundering Herds* (boxed set of LPs), CBS 66378.
4. Ibid.
5. James A. Treichel, *Woody Herman and His Second Herd* (Zephyrhills, Fla.: Joyce Record Club Publications, 1978), 44.
6. Quoted in *Metronome*, June 1952, 12.

Chapter 5. The Third Herd: 1950–1955

1. Michael Levin, "Woody Hits Road after N.Y.C. Bow," *Down Beat*, June 2, 1950, 16.
2. "Woody, Gastel Split Up," *Down Beat*, June 16, 1950, 1.
3. Steve Voce, *Woody Herman* (London: Apollo Press, 1986), 70.
4. Quoted in Nat Hentoff, "Pop Record Hit for Woody Could Help Whole Band Biz," *Down Beat*, July 27, 1955, 11.
5. Quoted in Nat Hentoff, "Pop Record Hit for Woody Could Help Whole Band Biz," *Down Beat*, July 27, 1955, 11.

Chapter 6. The Fourth Herd: 1956–1959

1. Steve Voce, liner notes for *Woody Herman's Anglo-American Herd,* Jazz Groove 004.
2. Ibid.

Chapter 7. The Swingin' Herd—A Renaissance: 1960–1967

1. Gene Lees, *Gene Lees Jazzletter*, June 1984, 7.
2. Tape-recorded interview with Dave Yost, Seattle, January 1974.

Chapter 8. "Road Father"—The Fusion Era: 1968–1979

1. Quoted in Herb Nolan, "Woody Herman: 40 Years of His Nomadic Herd," *Down Beat*, November 4, 1976, 38.
2. Bill Kirchner, "Profile: Gregory Herbert," *Down Beat*, June 2, 1977, 34.
3. Bill Kirchner, "Profile: Gregory Herbert," *Down Beat*, June 2, 1977, 34.
4. Tape-recorded interview with Dave Yost, Seattle, January 1974.
5. Herb Wong, liner notes for *Herd at Montreux*, Fantasy.

Chapter 9. Straight Ahead: 1980–1986

1. Leonard Feather, "Herman Dropping Anchor in Dixie," *Los Angeles Times*, November 16, 1980.
2. Gene Lees, "A Portrait of Woody," *Gene Lees Jazzletter*, June 1984, 8.
3. Lee Hildebrand, "Woody Herman: Still on the Road with His Thundering Herd," *Pulse*, October 1986, 33.

Bibliography

Albert, Dick: "Then and Again—Woody Herman." *Different Drummer*, 8/74.

Anderson, Ed: "King Zulu, Herman Parade to Soul Beat." *New Orleans Times-Picayune*, 2/20/80.

Balliet, Whitney: "Big Band." *New Yorker*, 9/9/72.

Caen, Herb: "So Long, Woody Herman." *San Francisco Chronicle*, 11/1/87.

Coss, Bill: Woody Herman's 25th Anniversary." *Metronome*, 1/61.

Courtwright, Debbie: "Happy Birthday, Woody." Elyria, Ohio, *Chronicle-Telegram*, 5/16/85.

Davidson, Keith: "Woody Herman Swings for His Supper." *Globe*, 9/23/86.

Dexter, Dave: "And So the Hermans Chose a Laundry." *Capitol News*

Edwards, Ernest, Jr.: *Discography of Woody Herman*. Volumes I & II, Debut Records.

Elwood, Phillip: Liner notes from *The Woody Herman Band—World Class.* Concord CJ-240.

Feather, Leonard: *The Encyclopedia of Jazz in the Sixties*. DaCapo Press, New York, 1986.

———: Liner notes from *Woody Herman at Carnegie Hall/40th Anniv.* RCA BGL2-2203.

———: "Woody Herman on His NTH Herd." *L.A. Times Calendar*, 1/29/84.

———: "Woody Herman and Co. All Together Again." *L.A. Times Calendar*, 5/6/85.

———: "Woody Herman Still Thundering After 50 Years." *L.A. Times Calendar*, 7/13/86.

———: "Celebrating Woody Herman." *Jazz Times*, 12/86.

———: "Richard Stoltzman—Herd Instincts." *L.A. Times Calendar*, 2/14/88.

———: Herman Dropping Anchor in Dixie. *L.A. Times*, 11/16/80.

Fumar, Vincent: "Herman Roars into Town with His Forceful Swing." *New Orleans Times-Picayune*, 12/30/81.

Garrod, Charles: *Woody Herman Orchestra*. 3 volume discography, Joyce Record Club.

Gehman, Richard: "Woody." *Saturday Review*, 5/11/68.

Giddins, Gary: "Woody Herman: Winding Down a 46-Year Road Tour." *Esquire*, 9/82.

Gieske, Tony: "Pied Piper of Jazz Laid to Rest." *L.A. Herald Examiner*, 11/3/87.

Gleason, Ralph: Liner notes from *Woody Herman's Big New Herd at the Monterey Jazz Festival.* Atlantic 1328.

———: Liner notes from *Jackpot.* Capitol T748.

———: "Woody Reorganizes to Go After Dance Crowd."*Down Beat*, 5/5/50.

"Godfather Of Jazz." *Newsweek*, 1/18/82.

Gold, Don: "Heard in Person—The Woody Herman Band." *Down Beat*, 11/14/57.

Hall, George: "Woody Herman and His Orchestra." Liner notes from Hindsight Records HSR-116. Hindsight Records.

———: "Woody Herman and His First Herd" Vol. II. Liner notes from Hindsight Records HSR-134.

Hentoff, Nat: "Urbie's Playing It All." *Down Beat*, 4/6/55.

———: Liner notes from *Woody Herman '58.* Verve MGV 8255.

Herman, Woody: "My 3 Herds? It Seems Like 80!" *Down Beat*, 6/30/54.

Hildebrand, Lee: "Woody Herman, Still on the Road with His Thundering Herd." *Pulse*, 10/86.

Jensen, Dean: "Woody Keeps Vow to Sister Fabian." *Milwaukee Sentinel*, 4/10/75.

Kart, Larry: "Leading Survivors." *Chicago Tribune*, 3/29/87.

Kendall, John: "Friends Orchestrate a Reprise for Herman." *L.A. Times*, 9/9/87.

Kirchner, Bill: "Profile: Gregory Herbert." *Down Beat*, 6/2/77.

Kloss, Jerry: "A New Twist to the Old Story about a Star and His Friend." *Milwaukee Journal*, 4/4/81.

Korall, Burt: "Woody Herman." *International Musician*, 4/76.

———: "Closing Chord." *International Musician*, 5/85.

Lee, Dr. William F.: "Stan Kenton: Artistry in Rhythm." *Creative Press of Los Angeles*, 1980.

Lees, Gene: "Herman's Swinging New Herd." *Down Beat*, 4/25/63.

———: "The Herman Band at Forty—A Time for Cheering." *Saturday Review*, 10/30/76.

———: "A Portrait of Woody." *Gene Lees Jazzletter*, 6/84.

Levin, Michael: "Woody Hits Road after N.Y.C. Bow." *Down Beat*, 6/2/50.

Lind, Angus: "Woody Comes Thundering to Town." *New Orleans Times-Picayune*, 1/4/82.

Liska, A. James: "Woody Herman Fronts Sextet." *L.A. Times*, 1/9/86.

Lorando, Mark: "W.H. on TV—Hurry Up and Wait." *New Orleans Times-Picayune*, 3/82.

Lucraft, Howard: "Putting on a Show for Woody." Crescendo International.

Long, Doug: "Interview with Red Rodney." *Cadence*, 12/86.

Martin, John: "Woody Herman, Past and Present." *International Jazz Journal*, 4/59.

McDonough, John: "Woody Herman: 50 Years in the Big Band Business." *Down Beat*, 11/86.

McFarland, Myra Mae: "Woody So Cool, He's on Ice." Ft. Wayne, Indiana, *Journal Gazette*, 1/19/83.

McKinney, Jack: "Woody Herman and the First Herd." *Metronome*, 3/59, 4/59.

Morgenstern, Dan: "Woody Herman: Forty in Front." *Radio Free Jazz*, 1/77.

News Release: "Woody, Gastel Split Up; Still on Friendly Terms." *Down Beat*, 6/16/50.

Nolan, Herb: "Forty Years of the Nomadic Herd." *Down Beat*, 11/4/76.

Raddue, Gordon: Liner notes from *Woody's Gold Star*. Concord CJ-330.

Rozek, Michael: "On the Road Again." *American Way*, 5/82.

Santosuosso, Ernie: "Woody Herman to Be Feted." *Boston Globe*, 8/10/84.

————: "The Return of the Herds." *Boston Globe*, 8/14/84.

Scott, Allen: "Keeping a Big Band on the Road." *Jazz Times*, 7/80.

————: "Woody: Quick with the Answers." *Jazz Times*, 7/80.

————: "Jazz Educated Man." *American International Publishers*, 1973.

————: *The Big Bands*. Schirmer Books, Macmillan, 1978.

————: Liner notes to *The Thundering Herds*. CBS 66378.

Smith, Alan Braham: "Bandleader Woody Herman, 72, Struggling to Pay $1.5 Million Tax Bill . . ." *National Enquirer*, 4/29/86.

Szantor, Jim: "Woody Herman's Seminar Scene." *Down Beat*, 10/14/71.

Tracy, Jack: "Jazz Being Plagued by a Cult." *Down Beat*, 10/20/50.

————: "Versatility Is Keynote of Woody's Fine Dance Ork." *Down Beat*, 5/4/51.

————: "Meet Cy Touff." *Down Beat*, 12/14/55.

————: Liner notes from *Children of Lima*. Fantasy F-9477.

Treichel, James A.: "Woody Herman and His Second Herd." Joyce Record Club Publications.

Voce, Steve: *Woody Herman*. Apollo Press Ltd., London, 1986.

————: "It Don't Mean a Thing" column. *International Jazz Journal*, 8/87.

Weiser, Norman: "Pop Record Hit for Woody Could Help Whole Band Biz." *Down Beat*, 7/27/55.

Wong, Herb: Liner notes from *Woody's Winners*. Columbia CL 2436.

————: Liner notes from *Light My Fire*. Cadet 819.

————: Liner notes from *Herd at Montreux*. Fantasy F9470.

Wyatt, Fred: "Herman Herd Is Smash with Dallas Symphony." *Down Beat*, 11/23/72.

Index